THE ENDURING MONUMENT

The Enduring Monument

A Study of the Idea of Praise in Renaissance Literary Theory and Practice

By

O. B. HARDISON, JR.

GREENWOOD PRESS, PUBLISHERS
WESTPORT, CONNECTICUT

The Library of Congress has catalogued this publication as follows:

Library of Congress Cataloging in Publication Data

Hardison, O B
The enduring monument.

Reprint of the ed. published by University of North Carolina Press, Chapel Hill.
1. Criticism--History. 2. Renaissance. 3. Literature, Modern--15th and 16th centuries--History and criticism. I. Title.
[PN88.H34 1973] 801'.951 73-3023
ISBN 0-8371-6821-X

Originally published in 1962
by The University of North Carolina Press, Chapel Hill

Reprinted with the permission
of The University of North Carolina Press

First Greenwood Reprinting 1973

Library of Congress Catalogue Card Number 73-3023

ISBN 0-8371-6821-X

Printed in the United States of America

In memoriam

RUTH C. WALLERSTEIN

1893-1958

Preface

Of the many debts of gratitude incurred in the course of the present study the greatest is that which I owe to Professor Ruth Wallerstein, formerly of the University of Wisconsin. Before her tragic death in 1958 in an automobile accident in England, Professor Wallerstein gave freely of her friendship, advice, and learning, and it is from a sense of deep obligation and affection that I have dedicated this book to her.

Second only to the debt which I owe to Professor Wallerstein is that which I gratefully acknowledge to Professor Bernard Weinberg of the University of Chicago. During the year 1956-57, while I was revising my manuscript with the object of eventual publication, I had the privilege of many discussions with Professor Weinberg on the subject of Italian literary criticism. I am particularly grateful for his suggestions concerning the importance of Averroes to the tradition that I have examined. His *History of Literary Criticism in the Italian Renaissance* (Chicago, 1961) brilliantly fills the need, mentioned in my first chapter, for a full-scale history of the subject and should be consulted by readers who wish to place the tradition examined here against the historical context of sixteenth-century Italian criticism. Although Professor Weinberg's *History* was published too late for references to it to be incorporated elsewhere than in the footnotes of the present study, Professor Weinberg generously allowed me to read parts of his work in manuscript. Thus, my own study has benefited from a knowledge of the general direction and, in some cases, the specific conclusions of Professor Weinberg's *History*. Inevitably, our differing approaches have led to differences of subject matter, scope, emphasis, and conclusion. Where these occur I hope that I have presented sufficient evidence to justify my position and would add that had I been writing a history of criticism, rather than the study of a single tradition with emphasis on its effect on literary practice, the divergences would have been fewer and my claim to offering an original and, I hope, useful approach to Renaissance literature correspondingly less.

Among many others who have offered valuable suggestions, I wish particularly to thank Professor J. P. Hieronymus of the University of Wisconsin, Professor John Lievsay of the University of Tennessee, Professor Alfred Engstrom of the University of North Carolina, and Mr. William Boggess also of the University of North Carolina.

The basic research for the present study was done during a year in Rome in 1953-54 made possible by a Fulbright Fellowship and facilitated by the advice and assistance of the members of the Fulbright Commission in Rome. Two grants, one from the Humanities Council of Princeton University and the other from the Research Council of the Graduate School of Arts and Sciences of the University of North Carolina, greatly simplified the preparation of the manuscript for the press. I wish also to acknowledge my indebtedness to the Alumni Annual Giving funds of the University of North Carolina administered by the University Research Council and to the Ford Foundation for a grant under its program for assisting American university presses in the publication of works in the humanities and the social sciences. Finally, the debt which I owe my wife is one which can be acknowledged but never measured.

Chapel Hill, N.C.
August 24, 1962

Introduction

The character of Swift's Gulliver is a compound of simplicity and sophistication that becomes more intriguing the more it is studied. In this it resembles other consummate works of art, the Parthenon, Michelangelo's David, or—on a miniature scale—one of Ben Jonson's lyrics, in which the artist has come close to the ideal of *ars celare artem*. In such art the craftsmanship is there but resists discovery because the illusion of inevitability is so strong.

To a lesser degree Renaissance literary criticism presents a similar problem. Superficial examination leaves one with the impression of intellectual naïveté. A few texts—the *Ars poetica,* Cicero's *Pro Archia poeta,* fragments from writers as various as Strabo, Plutarch, and Donatus; and, later, Aristotle's *Poetics* read through the rhetorician's spectacles—these and the basic works of Roman rhetoric comprise the essential critical equipment of an age that produced Politian, Ariosto, Tasso, Ronsard, Montaigne, Spenser, and Shakespeare.

The paradox is so curious as to suggest the desirability of a re-examination of the relationship between Renaissance critical theory and literary practice. Such an examination might usefully begin with the premise that the critics of the sixteenth century have something significant to say, even today, about the nature of poetry. Or, to put the matter differently, that their ideas, when translated into twentieth-century idiom, may prove to deserve the respect of the modern critic. To do this is by no means easy, and there can be no hope of so far translating sixteenth-century criticism as to show that Minturno or Scaliger, to cite two typical critics of the period, are the intellectual peers of writers like T. S. Eliot or I. A. Richards. However, it might be possible to show that the critical systems within which Minturno and Scaliger worked were subtle enough to be of genuine service to the sixteenth-century poet in search of guidance.

Past studies of Renaissance criticism such as those by Spingarn, Trabalza, Baldwin, and Atkins have done much to open the field.[1] However, the earlier of these studies have been somewhat vitiated by prejudice. Anyone working in criticism before the nineteenth century is faced with the problem of coming to terms with didactic theories of art. To numerous critics of Spingarn's generation, influenced by the aestheticism of Pater and the expressionism of Croce, didacticism was heresy. Art existed for art's sake. It was autonomous. The idea that the artist should teach moral or political lessons was part of an insidious plot to make him the lackey of church and state. The followers of Arnold in England and the new humanists in America claimed otherwise, but it is apparent from the perspective of 1962 that their support was a liability rather than an asset to the cause of moral criticism.[2]

No one would deny the value of the aesthetic movement, particularly as a liberating force upon the artist. But it had at least one unfortunate effect. It created an atmosphere in which it was next to impossible to evaluate didactic theories of art objectively. Since these theories dominated criticism from hellenistic times through the eighteenth century, it seriously distorted ideas about the relationship between criticism and literature before 1800. Thus it is that *The Faerie Queene* was often valued more for its sensuous verse than for the serious moral insights which were of such deep concern to Spenser; that Shakespeare's interest in religion was thought negligible by such an acute critic as A. C. Bradley; that "Lycidas" has been described as a personal lyric only disguised as a formal pastoral elegy; and that Satan was proposed as the real hero of *Paradise Lost.*

It seems inevitable in the history of criticism that whenever a theory of poetry becomes widespread, a commentary on the *Poetics* appears that makes Aristotle a proponent of the theory and, in turn, helps to transform it from speculation into dogma. The aesthetic Aristotle appeared in 1894 in S. H. Butcher's *Aristotle's Theory of Poetry and Fine Art.* Since then Butcher has been the standard English authority on Aristotle. The merits of his commentary are more than sufficient to justify his continued popularity. His thesis—that Aristotle's theory of poetry is uncompromisingly aesthetic—is doubtless correct, although several scholars including Ingram Bywater and Hamilton Fyfe have suggested the need for qualification.[3] At any rate, after 1894 the immense authority of Aristotle could be cited to prove that non-moral theories of literature are "right" and didactic theories, "wrong."

The consequence is apparent in numerous books and articles on Renaissance criticism. Joel Spingarn's *History of Literary Criticism in the Renaissance,* first published in 1899 and strongly influenced by Butcher, was the pioneer work in its field and is still invaluable. To Spingarn the history of Renaissance criticism was largely the history of the supplanting of moral theories inherited from the Middle Ages by classic-aesthetic ones stimulated by the rediscovery of Aristotle in the second half of the sixteenth century. The basic issue was given in Horace's phrase, "aut prodesse volunt aut delectare poetae" (*Ars poetica,* l. 333), which conservatives interpreted "poets should *both* profit *and* delight" but which the *avant garde* preferred to translate "*either* profit *or* delight," with emphasis on delight. Spingarn believed that the publication in 1570 of Lodovico Castelvetro's *Poetica d'Aristotele vulgarizzata* was an event of particular significance. Along with a formalism that encouraged such dogmas as the theory of the three unities, Castelvetro taught that delight was the chief end of poetry and that instruction was secondary, perhaps even irrelevant. Subsequent writers, while giving lip service to the venerable didactic formulae, tended to follow the lead of Castelvetro.

Spingarn's approach influenced several later studies. In 1913 H. B. Charlton published a monograph on Castelvetro largely confirming Spingarn.[4] Gregory Smith applied Spingarn's thesis to English critics in the introduction to his *Elizabethan Critical Essays,* which appeared in 1904. An example of the direction in which Spingarn's views led is Smith's claim that Sidney is a moralist by profession but an aesthete "by natural sympathy."[5] And as recently as 1951 J. W. H. Atkins remarked concerning Renaissance criticism, "while fresh light was being thrown on the nature and function of poetry from various angles, some of the medieval doctrines still held their ground, thus hindering a clearer and fuller apprehension of the truth concerning poetry."[6] It is doubtless reassuring to be in possession of "the truth" concerning poetry, but it can be dangerous if it implies, as Atkins' statement seems to, that Dante, Petrarch, Spenser, and Shakespeare wrote under the influence of false theories.

Certain recent studies have moved away from Spingarn's assumptions. Vernon Hall's *Renaissance Literary Criticism*[7] investigates the influence of social thought on sixteenth-century theory and practice. Numerous scholars including J. V. Cunningham, Madeline Doran, and Marvin Herrick have examined Renaissance dramatic theory without feeling compelled to explain away its didactic elements.[8] These studies, however, being restricted to a single genre, cast only fitful light on the larger problems of criticism.

The extremely large bulk of Renaissance criticism, most of it in Latin or Italian,[9] makes it certain that much further study will be necessary before we have recovered an adequate understanding of its chief features. One particularly large gap—now solidly filled by Bernard Weinberg's *History of Literary Criticism in the Italian Renaissance*[10]—has been the lack of a truly comprehensive history of the complex currents and counter-currents of the criticism of the *Cinquecento.*

Another need—a need which the present essay attempts to fill in part—

is for studies of specific critical traditions, both in the abstract and in terms of their practical application in representative sixteenth-century poems, dramas, and prose works. In the following pages I have examined what seems to me to be the dominant sixteenth-century theory of poetry, the didactic theory. First, I have considered it in relation to other theories of poetry which were common in the period but which I believe to be of less relevance to the interpretation of Renaissance literature. In Chapter II, I have traced the didactic theory from its somewhat amorphous formulation by classical critics, through its codification as what I have called "the theory of praise" by writers of the Roman decadence, and then into the Renaissance. In Chapters III and IV, I have examined several characteristics of this theory as elaborated by critics and practicing authors; and in the later chapters I have examined special topics suggested by the earlier discussion. Throughout, I have attempted to emphasize the interrelationship of theory and practice. Generally speaking, "theory" predominates in the first half of the book and "practice" in the second half.

One point needs emphasis at the beginning. I wish to distinguish between a vague critical bias—such as the idea that literature "ought to improve our minds"—and a critical system. A system is a set of statements that attempt to be comprehensive and internally consistent. Historically, the didactic theory began as a bias. As is evolved it became more systematic, and the means whereby it achieved this were ideas borrowed from rhetoric. A large number of recent scholarly studies testify to the fusion of Renaissance rhetoric and poetic,[11] but they tend to concentrate on schemes and tropes—that is, on diction—rather than on the principles that justified and explained the fusion. I wish to call attention to principles and especially those principles borrowed from the branch of rhetoric called *epideictic* by Aristotle, dealing with praise and blame. Didactic criticism drew upon these principles constantly. They were useful both for harmonizing the various parts of literary theory and for defending literature against its enemies. I hope to show that they form a key to the *system* of didactic criticism most common during the Renaissance. I also hope to show that they are clearly incorporated into several important Renaissance poems.

A work of literary history must in some measure be a compromise between the need for rigor and the need for a lively, entertaining presentation. Rigor demands emphatic statement of important points, logical progression, and adequate citation of evidence. The more technical the subject, the more imperative these demands. On the other hand, it is fatally easy to become so obsessed with the demands of rigor as to produce a work that is almost unreadable. Recognizing this fact, I have tried to achieve a compromise that would satisfy the non-specialist as well as the professional scholar. Foreign-language quotations are translated in the text, and the originals are decently interred in the footnotes. Occasionally the translation is an abbreviated version of the fuller quotation given in the notes. Renaissance texts have been lightly normalized: modern practice has been followed in respect to *v*'s, *u*'s and long *s*'s; regular principles of accenting have been followed; and Latin ligatures have been expanded where abbreviations are not immediately obvious. Quotations are introduced where necessary as evidence, but I have tried to avoid unnecessary repetition. Finally, I have tried throughout to place the discussion in the widest possible context by relating Renaissance ideas to general issues of literary theory—issues that are still debated, although in terms much different from those used by sixteenth-century authors.

Contents

THE ENDURING MONUMENT

CHAPTER I

The Classification of Systems of Criticism

The poetics of poetics can probably never be written. There are too many ways of interpreting a poem for one system to accommodate them all. Therefore, all systems are inadequate. Every system-maker must be prepared to whittle edges off numerous square pegs for which he has only round holes; and one might even guess that no matter what system is used, one ends up with the same number of misshapen pegs.

Yet to discuss the criticism of a period intelligently, one must attempt to classify its typical systems. Fortunately, this presents less of a problem for Renaissance criticism than for the post-romantic period. The romantics drew on innumerable sources—with emphasis on personal experience—for their theories. Often their criticism seems as subjective as their lyric poems. Since the critics did not even agree on the proper subjects for disagreement, there are no intrinsic standards for relating diverse systems. The most successful attempt to classify romantic critics, that made by M. H. Abrams in *The Mirror and the Lamp,*[1] is extrinsic and would doubtless surprise many of the authors to whom it is so successfully applied.

Renaissance—and even medieval—critics were individualistic, a fact to which the many furious debates of the *Cinquecento* eloquently testify. But they were more fortunate than the romantics in being able to refer their arguments to a traditionally accepted set of categories through which individual positions could be defined. These categories were of immense antiquity and authority. They were first suggested by Aristotle. In the *Metaphysics,* VI (1025[b] 26) the human sciences are classified as "theoretical" (*theoretikai*), "practical" (*praktikai*), and "productive" (*poietikai*), and the first category is further subdivided into physics, mathematics, and "first philosophy" (*prote philosophia*), which is also called "theology" (1026[a] 19). Beginning with Andronicus of Rhodes, Aristotle's first editor (c. 70 B.C.), the categories were elaborated into what can be seen as either a convenient cataloguing system, or an ambitious attempt to classify types of human knowledge, or both. Andronicus separated the logical writings from the corpus of Aristotle's work, and these eventually became known as the *Organon,* or instrumental disciplines, the "rational philosophy" of the schoolmen. Eudemus, a later scholiast, clarified the nature of "practical philosophy" by declaring that it was composed of politics, economics, and ethics.[2] These distinctions were repeated and elaborated by such later commentators as Alexander of Aphrodesias (200 A.D.), Porphyry (d. 301 A.D.), Boethius (d. 524)—whose Latin commentary on Porphyry's *Isagoge* formed part of the *logica vetus* of medieval education—Cassiodorus (d. 575), and Isidore of Seville (d. 636).[3]

The following diagram from A. E. Taylor's *Aristotle,*[4] illustrates the Aristotelian system schematically:

Science

Theoretical
- "First Philosophy"
- Mathematics
- Physics

Practical

The continuity of this system and the more highly codified forms worked out by the commentators is shown by the scheme offered in the treatise *On the Division of Philosophy* by Dominicus Gundissalinus, a German monk, around 1150.[5] Gundissalinus begins with grammar, a propaedeutic subject and a necessary prelude to all other studies. He then proceeds to logic which, being the study of method, must precede philosophy proper. Along with the six parts comprising the modern *Organon,* Gundissalinus includes rhetoric and poetics on the authority of Al-farabi.[6] Then he advances to the familiar areas of theoretical and practical philosophy. Reduced to their simplest form, his categories are as follows:

Knowledge:

1. Grammar
2. Logic
3. Philosophy Proper

Theoretical	Practical
Metaphysics	Politics
Mathematics	Economics
Physics	Ethics[7]

To study in detail the vicissitudes of this system would carry us far beyond limits appropriate to the historian of criticism. At times it was accepted in the form employed by Gundissalinus. At other times it was modified, and almost always its modifications reflected important changes in philosophical outlook.[8] Several of its many variants were summarized by

Vincent of Beauvais in the *Speculum doctrinale* (I, xii-xviii). From the schoolmen it was transmitted to Renaissance authors and can be traced from Savonarola's *On the Division, Order, and Use of Each Science* (1496) through the *Nature of Logic* by Iacomo Zabarella (1578).[9]

The traditional division of the sciences is important in the history of criticism because it served as a standard reference point, a kind of North Star, from which the critic could take his bearings. Time and again Renaissance critical essays begin with discussions of the place of poetry among the sciences. These discussions are most explicit among the Aristotelians, who are conscious of the need to make their initial assumptions perfectly clear. The treatises of Robortello, Maggi and Lombardi, and Varchi, for example, all begin in this way. Critics of the first half of the *Cinquecento* also discuss the "placing" of literature, but their discussions are usually less elaborate—probably because most of them felt that the subordination of literature to moral philosophy was self-evident and hardly debatable.

Whether debatable or not, the placing of poetry among the sciences is central to systematic criticism. Many characteristic features of critical theory are corollary to the position taken, and the more systematic the critic, the more true this is. The Aristotelian scheme, therefore, provides not only a classification of the sciences but also a ready-made and intrinsic set of categories for Renaissance criticism.

The simplest theories of poetry assumed that it was a part of grammar. A more sophisticated group began with an attempt to prove that the *Poetics* should be included among the works comprising the *Organon,* thus making poetry a branch of logic. Still another group, heavily influenced by Platonism, included poetry among the practical sciences and insisted that its function was to teach virtue.

I.

MINOR THEORIES: POETRY AS PHILOSOPHY, POETRY AS THEOLOGY

Very few critics of the sixteenth or any other century have claimed that poetry is a part of theoretical philosophy. However, the idea was not entirely without classical precedent. In the first book of the *Geography* (I, 2, 3ff). Strabo commended Homer for the immense amount of factual information that he included in the *Odyssey,* and Macrobius later praised Virgil for the same reason. Although Ciceronian rhetoric stressed the importance of "civil philosophy," in the *De oratore* (I, 34, 158; III, 14, 54; 20, 76; etc.) and elsewhere, it is emphasized that the orator has need of a great deal of miscellaneous learning (*doctrina*). Neoplatonic critics went considerably further. Maximus Tyrius and Proclus, both of whom were frequently quoted during the sixteenth century, believed that the highest forms of poetry are esoteric theoretical philosophy.

During the Renaissance these ideas were occasionally revived. Girolamo Fracastoro, for example, was a philosopher before he was a critic. Although he would not have accepted the classification of poetry among the theoretical sciences, the following quotation will suggest how far he tended in this direction: "[Poets] narrate histories, descriptions of places, regions, and the conventions of life. They write much concerning emperor, soldier, father, and the state; concerning agriculture, sailing, the arts . . . the stars above and the things of nature—plants, and animals; concerning God, hell, . . . and, to sum up, they seem to offer doctrine (*doctrinam*) concerning all those things. . . ."[10] Without wishing to labor a point, I suggest that the poets described by Fracastoro must be especially well-versed in the natural sciences and the various technical studies (astronomy, botany, geography, etc.) which derive from them.

Another factor that supported the idea of a close connection between poetry and philosophy was the existence of a good deal of frankly philosophical poetry. Aristotle (*Poetics,* 1447^b 18) had specifically exempted Empedocles from the ranks of the poets, but he was often challenged. Francesco Patrizi, for example, devoted the seventh book of his *Deca disputata* to the proposition that "if Aristotle . . . denied that Empedocles was a poet, he himself fell into error in that statement."[11] In the course of his discussion, Patrizi indicated how large a category "philosophical poetry" could be. His examples include Hesiod, Empedocles, Virgil (in the *Georgics*), Aratus, Manilius, Pontanus (*Urania*), Fracastoro (*Syphilis*), and the "law-giving" verses of Solon and Moses.

The tendency to relate poetry to theology was of considerably greater historical importance. It was encouraged by the tradition of theological allegory and by at least three others: the poet as *vates* or prophet; the poet as divinely inspired culture-hero on the model of Orpheus or Moses; and the poem as truth too sacred for the vulgar rabble. Plato's *Ion* was a standard precedent for this idea, especially after the enthusiastic introduction composed by Marsilio Ficino for his edition of Plato's *Opera omnia* (1482). Aristotle (*Metaphysics,* 1000^a 5-10) called the early poets "theologians." Both the *Ars poetica* (ll. 391-407) and Cicero's *Pro Archia poeta* (VIII, 18-19) contributed something to the tradition, which found early expression in the self-consciously "divine" poetry of Christian writers like Prudentius and Juvencus. By the age of Dante the idea of poetry as theology had become a definite, if not quite respectable, literary theory. Albertino Mussato (1261-1329) wrote in his seventh epistle that "the divine poets of early ages . . . were . . . called by the name *vates;* whoever was a vates was a vessel (*vas*) of God. Therefore, that poetry which we must now consider was once a second theology."[12]

Later critics continued to insist on the close relationship of poetry and theology, though most commonly in eclectic defenses or encomia of poetry. Petrarch informed his brother Gherardo that "poetry is in no sense opposed to theology. I might almost say that theology is a poetry which proceeds from God."[13] And Boccaccio, who refers to the notion *passim* in books XIV and XV of the *Genealogy of the Gods,* devoted a whole chapter (XV, viii) to the proposition that "The Pagan Poets of Mythology are Theologians."[14]

Not unnaturally, the same men who waxed eloquent over the Eleusinian Mysteries, the Orphic hymns, and the works ascribed to Hermes Trismegistus were enthusiastic supporters of the idea that poetry is (or can at times be) a form of theology. Pico della Mirandola speaks of poetry in this way, and the idea is a recurrent *motif* in the first two poems of Politian's *Sylvae.* Later in the century its influence can be traced in Minturno's *De poeta,* Tasso's *Discorsi,* and Sidney's *Defense.* In these works it is a minor, not a major, element. Not until the very end of the century, in Campanella's *La poetica* (wr. c. 1596), is there a return to a critical system in which theology could be called central.

There were practical reasons for the abandonment of the theory of poetry as theology. The most important one is that theologians bitterly opposed it. If poets were allowed genuine divine inspiration, and if mythological poems contained profound theological truths, the authority of scripture as unique revelation would be undermined. Savonarola directed his most withering invective against those humanists who claimed that "since Sacred Scripture and poetry both use metaphors, poetry is nothing else than Theology."[15] As proof of the chasm separating poetry and scripture, Savonarola pointed out that holy writ is forced to use figurative language because its sense is "spiritual" and ineffable; whereas poetry uses ornament to prop itself up: "It is one thing to use metaphors because of necessity and the magnitude of the subject; another to use them for pleasure and weakness of truth."[16] The debate did not, of course, end with Savonarola, but we may leave it here and turn to three theories of poetry which, historically speaking, were of greater importance.

II. POETRY AS GRAMMAR

Perhaps the simplest of all methods of classifying poetry is to include it in the study of grammar. Originally, this was probably a matter of convenience, which was evidently as great a virtue to the *magistri* of antiquity as to the modern disciples of John Dewey. Grammar was the first of the seven liberal arts. For the present we will consider it apart from rhetoric, although the rhetorical tropes and schemes were first introduced to the student in textbooks of grammar.

Part of grammar was devoted to orthography and rules of syntax, but the reading of poetry formed an important adjunct to more advanced studies.

Dionysius of Thrace (b. 166 B.C.) was one of the earliest grammarians to make poetry a part of formal grammar.[17] Through him and his Greek contemporaries the tradition was transmitted to Rome. Quintilian (*Institutio oratoria,* I, iv, 2) divided grammar into "knowledge of speaking correctly and interpretation of the poets."[18] His purpose was chiefly to inculcate the principles of good style, but his program also would have satisfied moralists, since he firmly believed in the elevating effect of great literature on the young.

Grammatical definitions have one factor in common. Since quantity and accent were standard parts of grammar, the grammatical theory of poetry made meter the *differentia* between poetry and prose. This stimulated many detailed and often arid studies of prosody. Works like Servius' *De centum metris* and *De metris Horatii* are a direct result. They fill most of the sixth volume of Keil's *Grammatici Latini,* which is titled simply *Scriptores artis metricae* and includes such full-scale grammars as the *Ars grammatica* of Marius Victorinus as well as explicitly prosodic essays by Rufinus, Atilius Fortunantianus, and Terentianus.[19]

Several definitions of poetry reflecting the grammatical tradition have been preserved. According to the grammarian Diomedes, ". . . poetry is a composition in metre narrating either feigned or true events in appropriate rhythm and foot."[20] And a fragment ascribed to Donatus preserved in Keil's *Grammatici Latini* says simply that "a poem is a narration composed in metrical feet."[21] Similar definitions can be found scattered widely through the grammar texts collected in Keil's eight volumes and in such medieval writers as Isidore (*Etymologiarum libri XX,* I, xxxix); Cassiodorus (*Institutiones divinarum et saecularium litterarum,* II, i, 1); and John of Salisbury, who wrote, ". . . either grammar will contain poetics, or poetics will be excluded from the liberal arts."[22]

It would be unjust to claim that all late classical grammarians thought of poetry simply as "speech in meter." Several authors, particularly the earlier ones like Diomedes and Priscian, move from discussion of meter to discussion of tropes and figures. This, however, goes beyond the limits of the strict grammatical definition of poetry. Moreover, whatever else they consider, all late grammarians who discuss poetry stress the prosodic element. This had two results, one bad and the other, perhaps, valuable.

The bad result is an emphasis on meter so strong that other aspects of poetry are all but forgotten. The more detailed the analysis, the more obvious the tendency. Diomedes codified the study of prosody. After praising the dactylic hexameter as the noblest and most beautiful of forms, he treated the other forms in rigidly systematic fashion: first the "nine meters," from iamb through paeonic; then the five "kinds of verse" beginning with dimeter and ending with hexameter; then the special forms such as comic pentameter, scazon, choriamb, and Anacreontic; then a final section "On the Meters of Horace."[23] Here—and to an increasing degree in later writers like Marius Victorinus (Keil, VI, 50-173)—what would normally be considered the appropriate order of precedence has been inverted. Instead of theme dictating form (in this case, meter), it is form that dictates theme. Dactylic hexameter is *only* adaptable to heroic subjects; the elegiac distich is *intrinsically* sad or amorous; iambic verse is *necessarily* conversational and comic or satiric. And so forth.

The good feature of the *ars metrica* was its emphasis on an aspect of poetry often slighted by critics preoccupied with the mysteries of allegory or divine inspiration. Even in an age of free verse and prose poems, it is possible to maintain that control of rhythm, of which meter is a special case, is an essential feature of poetry. If poetry and prose are both considered forms of communication, control of rhythm is the most important technique available to the poet and not to the prose writer. It can thus be a true *differentia* between prose and poetry. It does not permit a sharp line of distinction because of such intermediate forms as rhythmic prose (what Norden has called *Kunstprosa*[24]) and free verse; but it avoids the pitfalls of defining poetry as fiction, history, or philosophy, all of which were at times suggested. The grammarian Mallus Theodorus seems to have thought of meter as a functional part of the poet's technique: "I do not think any doubts can arise . . . that the regular rhythm (*modulatio*) of a poem renders sweeter to the ear those things which are expressed with excellent sense and words. Therefore [poets] consulted their hearing as to what in poems would be soft and sweet, what sharp and harsh; and they followed these so that in writing their poems they joined art with pleasure."[25] Interpreted with a certain amount of charity this comment does not seem inferior to the explanation of meter given by Wordsworth in the "Preface" to *Lyrical Ballads*.

Despite its limitations the *ars metrica* persisted throughout the Renaissance. It often figured in the battles fought in Italy, France, and England between advocates of Latin and advocates of the vernacular. Drawing upon the tradition that meter determines genre, the Latinists could (and did) claim that great poetry was impossible in the vernacular because it could not be adapted to the rules of classical prosody. In some cases the moderns were duped into trying to prove that Latin forms, such as dactylic hexameter, could be reproduced in the modern tongues. Claudio Tolomei's *Versi et regole della nuova poesia toscana* (1539) is a notorious Italian example, while the correspondence between Edmund Spenser and Gabriel Harvey preserves the melancholy record of an attempt to make English conform to classical rules. Richard Stanyhurst's experimental translation of the *Aeneid* is another example; and the elaborate and anachronistic *Art of English Poesie*

(1602) by Thomas Campion is a third. Indeed, Campion's idea of poetry, for all his consummate skill as a musician and poet, is hardly more sophisticated than that of Bede.

A far more practical position was taken by those critics who recognized the importance of the *ars metrica* but maintained, to quote Samuel Daniel, that "Custome . . . is before all Law, Nature . . . is above all Arte. Every language hath her proper number or measure fitted to use and delight. . . ."[26] In Italy this argument was as old as Dante's praise of the *canzone* in the *De vulgari eloquentia.* The first four books of G. G. Trissino's *Poetica* (1529) contain a large body of material on vernacular prosody, and his *Italia liberata dai goti* (1547) was a conscious attempt to find in "versi sciolti" an Italian equivalent to classical dactylic hexameter—an experiment occasionally said to have influenced the development of English blank verse *via* Surrey.[27]

As the century progressed and non-grammatical theories of poetry gained ground, the *ars metrica* diminished in importance. The second book of Scaliger's *Poetics* (1561) contains some forty-two chapters on meter and is one of the most encyclopaedic treatments of the subject during the century. However, Scaliger was sufficiently emancipated from the *ars metrica* to find an epic poem in Heliodorus' prose *Aethiopian History* (*Poet.,* III, xcv). Although he repeats the grammatical definitions of poetry he is in no way limited to them.

In the 1580's the question of the relationship between meter and poetry became the topic of a heated debate. Francesco Patrizi devoted one chapter of his *Della poetica, la deca disputata* (1586) to the question, "Was Empedocles a Greater or Lesser Poet than Homer?" and another to "Whether a Poem can be Composed from History." In the latter chapter he listed no less than sixty-four "kinds" of poems that lack "fable"; while in the former he argued that, irrespective of content, a composition had to be in verse to have true poetic elevation.[28] He was soon answered by Agostino Michele, who argued violently against an undue stress on verse in his *Discourse . . . in which it is Clearly Demonstrated that One Can Write Comedies and Tragedies in Prose with much Acclaim* (1592).[29] Unfortunately, Michele's retort convinced no one but those who already agreed with him. The *ars metrica* continued sporadically to influence criticism until the end of the century. It is evidently a dominant influence in the crtical thought of Gabriello Chiabrera.[30] And although Sidney and Ben Jonson both believed the poet to be a maker rather than a versifier, there is extant a manuscript reply to Sidney's *Defense* in which Sidney is attacked for failing to make meter his central criterion.[31] Since this reply is manifestly the work of a Ramist—William Temple—it may be that Ramus' famous reforms encouraged prosody as well as plainness.[32]

III. POETRY AS A PART OF LOGIC

That poetry should have been widely regarded during the Middle Ages and Renaissance as a branch of logic is one of the anomalies of literary history. Poetry uses the devices of logic, as does any other form of discourse. Aristotle recognized this when he made thought (*dianoia*) one of the components of drama. A perhaps more general view of the interdependence of poetry and logic is reflected in the use of the word *argument* as a synonym for *plot.*

Still, it is surprising to find medieval philosophers, whose experience with poetry must have been almost nil, arguing with considerable subtlety that poetics is a special form (or perversion) of logic. Moreover, this approach to poetry did not die out in the sixteenth century although it was strongly opposed. It was common procedure for ambitious works on poetics—and particularly on the *Poetics*—to begin with a review of the *Organon* in order to relate poetry to demonstrative logic, dialectic, and rhetoric.

The original stimulus toward including poetics in logic was the fact that Aristotle left its position ambiguous. This was an open invitation to his commentators to fit it into his system of the sciences wherever an opening could be found. The status of the *Rhetoric* was similar to that of the *Poetics,* and this fact eventually determined the category of both works. The first sentence of the *Rhetoric* (1354^a 1-3) asserts, "Rhetoric is the counterpart of Dialectic. Both alike are concerned with such things as come, more or less, within the general view of all men and belong to no definite science." Since dialectic was a recognized part of the *Organon,* it was natural to include the *Rhetoric* in this category. And since poetics is an obvious cousin to rhetoric, it, too, could be assimilated. The idea is found in the late Greek commentaries and was passed along by Boethius and other intermediary writers to the Latin West.[33]

Before the thirteenth century the placing of poetry among the logical sciences had no effect whatsoever on criticism. In the thirteenth century a dramatic change occurred.

During the early Middle Ages the Latin West was dominated by a Platonic Christianity. Aristotle was known only imperfectly and several of the standard expositors (like Boethius) were themselves Platonically inclined. On the other hand, a vital Aristotelianism had been inherited by the Arabs, who acted as midwives to the rebirth of Aristotelianism at Paris during the thirteenth century. The story of the preservation of Aristotle's works at Alexandria, their translation into Syriac and then into Arabic, and the numerous Arabic commentaries culminating in those of Al-farabi and Averroes has often been told. Etienne Gilson presents a graceful summary in his *History of Christian Philosophy in the Middle Ages* (1955), and there are numerous more specialized studies available to the interested reader.[34]

For our purposes only one phase of this history is important, and that is the Arab treatment of the *Poetics*. The work was translated from Syriac into Arabic around 930 by Abu-Bishr (d. 940). It stimulated comment by the three major figures in Arabic philosophy of the period, Al-farabi, Avicenna, and Averroes. Two features of the comment are important. First, beginning at least with Al-farabi (d. 950), the Arabs followed the late Greek commentators in placing the *Poetics* in the *Organon*. Second, the commentary of Averroes (1126-1198) is in the form of a paraphrase of the *Poetics*. This paraphrase has been charitably described by its most dedicated student as "a medley of monstrous misunderstandings and wild fantasies,"[35] but it was translated into Latin by a German monk, Hermannus Alemannus, in 1256, and thereafter gained rather wide circulation in Europe.[36]

Al-farabi's version of Aristotle's division of the sciences was translated into Latin by Gerard of Cremona (1114-87). Here the *Organon* is divided into five parts: demonstrative logic, which has as its object demonstration (that is, absolute proof); topics, with its object probable proof; sophistic, with its object "error made to seem like truth"; rhetoric, with its object persuasion; and poetic, with its object "imaginative discourse."[37] Averroes followed this lead in his commentaries on the *Rhetoric* and *Poetics*. In the introduction to the translation of Averroes, Hermannus Alemannus carefully distinguishes between the new theory of poetry as logic and the older grammatical and didactic theories, which he attributes to Horace and Cicero respectively: "That these two books [i.e., *Rhetoric, Poetics*] are part of logic no one will doubt who has read the books of Al-farabi, Avicenna, and Averroes, and various others. Indeed, this is quite obvious from this text itself. Nor can one be excused (as some may think) because of the rhetoric of Marcus Tullius Cicero and the poetics of Horace. Tully made rhetoric part of civil philosophy [i.e., "practical philosophy"] and thoroughly dealt with it from this point of view. Horace, however, treated poetry rather as it pertains to grammar."[38]

The assimilation of Arab theories of poetry in the West followed the larger pattern of the assimilation of Arab philosophy. In his treatise *On the Division of Philosophy* (c. 1150), Dominicus Gundissalinus shows himself equally attracted to a traditional understanding of poetry, derived from such standard authorities as Bede, Donatus and Isidore of Seville, and the radical new system which he derived from Al-farabi. Thus his treatise has two unrelated, apparently contradictory discussions of poetry. In the first, which is the traditional one, we learn (a) that "Poetics is the science of composing metrical lyrics" (the grammatical definition);[39] and (b) that

"The *genus* of this art is . . . part of civil philosophy . . . because it delights or edifies in knowledge or morals" (the didactic definition).[40]

The second discussion of poetry is part of a consideration of the *Organon*, the substance of which Gundissalinus attributes to Al-farabi.[41] Logic is divided into eight parts. The first six are the ones normally considered part of the *Organon*—the *Categories, Peri hermenias, Prior* and *Posterior Analytics, Topics,* and *Sophistic*. The next two are *Rhetoric* and *Poetics*.

To be intelligible the eight parts of logic must be clearly distinguished from each other. This leads to an extremely important set of distinctions that are taken over by Gundissalinus from Al-farabi's *Catalogue of the Sciences*.[42] Each part of logic is classified according to the criteria of purpose and characteristic device, and the "parts" are listed in order of the decreasing certainty of their results:

(a) "Parts" of *Organon*	(b) Purpose	(c) Device
[Categories Peri Hermenias] Prior Analytics Posterior Analytics	"Demonstration" (i.e., absolute proof)	Demonstrative Syllogism
Topics	"Probable Demonstration" (i.e., Dialectic)	Probable (*putativa*) Syllogism
Sophistic	Error Given Appearance of Truth	False (*errativa*) Syllogism
Rhetoric	Persuasion	"Sufficient" (*sufficiens*) Syllogism (or enthymeme)
Poetics	Imaginative Representation	"Imaginative" (*ymaginativa*) Syllogism[43]

It will be seen that a rather sophisticated and even radical poetic theory is adumbrated by Gundissalinus. In the first place, both *ars metrica* and didactic purpose have been dispensed with. The object of poetry is no longer to teach but simply to create illusion. In the second place, attention is focused on a technical device whereby the illusion is created, and this device is treated as the distinguishing feature—the *differentia*—of poetics. Unfortunately, "imaginative syllogism" is rather vague. Gundissalinus shows no sign of being seriously concerned with poetry, and his discussion is doubtless the result of nothing more than a desire to follow his source faithfully. The closest approach to a definition of "imaginative syllogism" is the suggestion by Gundissalinus that "the property of poetic speeches is to make an object be imagined ugly or beautiful which is not so; so that the listener is moved to belief and is repelled by it or attracted; even though we are certain that it is not so in reality."[44] Here, at least, "imaginative syllogism" would seem to be a form of exaggeration or heightening, and the illusion one of beauty or ugliness.

The association of poetry and logic has a long and honorable history. St. Thomas was aware of it and, in his commentary on the *Posterior Analytics,* gave it a twist that recombined it with traditional didactic theories.[45] According to St. Thomas, *Poetics* is a part of the "inventive" phase of logic, which also includes *Dialectic, Sophistic* and *Rhetoric.* Its purpose is "representation" and its characteristic device is "resemblance" (*similitudo*). St. Thomas believed that the poetic representation creates the illusion of beauty or ugliness, with a corresponding psychological reaction in the reader of desire or repulsion. This leads to the moral function of art, which is to "induce to virtue" through favorable representation, and to warn from vice by making it seem abhorrent.[46] Thus, while poetry considered as technique is a part of "rational philosophy" (logic), considered in terms of function, it is a part of civil or moral philosophy.

Generally speaking, St. Thomas' version was the one that prevailed during the later Middle Ages. Roger Bacon, St. Thomas' contemporary, simply divided poetics into two phases, a theoretical (*docens*) according to which it is a part of logic, and a practical (*utens*) according to which it is a part of civil philosophy.[47] Vincent of Beauvais, whose *Speculum doctrinale* was an important channel through which medieval ideas entered the Renaissance, contented himself with quoting Gundissalinus.[48] The Paduan Averroists, in whose work the Arab theory of poetry was naturally quite emphatic, usually gave it a Thomistic interpretation.[49]

Although taught at Padua, the theory associating poetry with logic received one of its fullest and most able expositions where we would least expect it—in Florence, the very bastion of humanism. Needless to say the expositor was not a humanist. He was Fra Girolamo Savonarola, archenemy of the humanists.

We have already seen that Savonarola opposed the theological pretensions of the humanist poets. He also rejected the metrical definition of poetry: "Meter and harmony are not essential to it. The poet can pursue his argument and discourse through proper images without verse."[50] On the other hand, logic is essential—he asserts, "without logic no one can be called a poet."[51]

Despite his modern reputation, Savonarola was not hostile to poetry *per se*. His wrath was chiefly directed against what he felt were the false pretensions and indecencies of the humanists of his age. His insistence that poetry is a part of logic strips it of many of the fanciful trappings in which it was clothed by men like Pico della Mirandola and Politian, but the result is not wholly negative. Among other things, Savonarola offered a well-considered and useful interpretation of the "imaginative syllogism": "Clearly, the syllogism which the Philosopher calls Example is the object of the poetic art, just as the enthymeme is the object of rhetoric, induction and the probable syllogism of dialectic, demonstration, of the *Posterior Analytics,* the 'syllogism proper' of the *Prior Analytics. . . .*"[52] By "example" Savonarola did not mean Sidney's "lively images of the virtues and vices" (or even the *exemplum* of the medieval sermon), but the technical device explained in the *Prior Analytics* (68^b-69^a), which is "a syllogism in which the middle is shown to be in the final term because it is similar to the third."[53] Having set up these co-ordinates, Savonarola proceeds to a triumphal reconciliation of poetry—albeit a chastened, unpretentious poetry—and morality. Quite fittingly, he begins by quoting St. Thomas' remark about representation: "The end of the poet is to lead men to virtue through some fitting representation. . . . But it is characteristic of the poet to proceed from particulars . . . example does not exist in terms of part to whole, or whole to part, but as part to part. But since single things are uncertain, it is necessary, on account of the debility of their logic, to introduce some fitting images and in diverse ways, with allurements and ornaments of words, to attract men's spirits to them and delight them."[54]

Although it generated little enthusiasm in Florence during the early years of the *Cinquecento,* the tradition associating poetry and logic was not forgotten. It was revived by the early commentators on Aristotle and forms an important element in Italian criticism from the 1540's until well into the seventeenth century. Robortello, the first critic to publish a full-scale commentary on the *Poetics* (1548), repeated the standard scholastic summary of the parts of logic (under the heading of *oratio*), assigning to poetry the domain of "the false" or "the fabulous."[55] Following the earlier discussion, Robortello avoided an interpretation of the poetic category which would make it synonymous with the modern categories fiction or illusion. Rather, he explained the "falseness" of poetry with the doctrine of idealization—the poet shows the object "as it ought to be" rather than "as it is."

A somewhat more elaborate reinterpretation of the tradition is presented at the beginning of the commentary on the *Poetics* by Maggi (Pius Madius) and Lombardi (1550). Lombardi and Maggi had lectured on the *Poetics* at Padua during the 1540's, and they, rather than Robortello, deserve credit for being the first of the many commentators of the century. Lombardi's "Preface" consciously draws on the Arab tradition—particularly on Averroes[56]—while making creative variations where these seem desirable. It begins with an eulogy of poetry which would delight the heart of any humanist. Poetry includes grammar, oratory, logic, natural philosophy; and poets are the best geographers, astronomers, and philosophers, not to mention being the first theologians. This is a characteristic bit of Renaissance exaggeration and may be taken somewhat skeptically. Its chief function is to lead to a more technical section. Here poetry is classified as part of "rational philosophy," which is sub-divided into the arts of dispute (demonstration, dialectic, sophistic) and two "faculties" (rhetoric and poetic).[57]

Poetry is considered a faculty by Lombardi because it has no specific subject matter except "words and speech," a point based on Aristotle's similar description of rhetoric (*Rhetoric,* 1355^b 32-36). Poetic is different from dialectic in that it does not proceed by syllogistic arguments and formal proof. Instead it uses enthymeme and example, described by Lombardi as forms of "popular reasoning." The difference between rhetoric and poetic is that rhetoric has a strong admixture of dialectic and deals with prose. Thus rhetoric is "the faculty of finding whatever can be used for persuasion in a given case," while poetry offers fictitious examples that create the illusion of reality and thereby instruct the audience in the ways of virtue.[58] Lombardi follows Al-farabi and Averroes in his belief that meter is an ornament that increases the pleasure of poetry rather than an essential. The same applies to spectacle in dramatic poetry.[59]

All of these assumptions appear to lead toward a poetic theory which, like that of Savonarola, would make poetry pleasant but trivial. However, Lombardi's feeling for literature was too strong for such a theory to content him. Perhaps because he lacked Savonarola's religious fervor, Lombardi felt that the moral instruction of mankind by a secular instrument such as poetry was a noble objective. His final definition of poetry represents a fusion of the logical with didactic tradition. It is all the more significant for the fact that it paraphrases Cicero's definition of rhetoric: "The object of poetics is to see whatever can be used for imitation of a man's action, passion and mores, in delightful speech, for the correcting of life and good and pious living."[60]

Today, Lombardi's fusion of the logical and moral tradition may appear somewhat disappointing. Often he seems on the verge of a theory of poetry that may be no deeper or more true than the prevailing theories of the age, but at least has the merit of originality. To understand his unwillingness to exploit fully the ideas that he presents we need to recall that in the 1540's the battle for poetry was far from won. In a sense, the esoteric questions of literary criticism were luxuries which were not possible until later in the century. In fact, even the mild speculations that Lombardi permitted himself were apparently too much for Maggi. In a separate introduction, written after Lombardi's death, Maggi carefully emphasized the fact that the real essence of poetry is morality. Its end is instruction ("to improve the mind"; "to induce good habits by imitation"); and its true *genus* is not logic but "moral philosophy." Only if considered from the limited standpoint of grammar, figures of speech, and rules is it part of "rational philosophy, as Averroes, Avicenna and others thought."[61]

Numerous variations on this approach can be found in the critical work of Varchi, Gelli, Mazzoni, Campanella, and others. Varchi, whose *Lezzioni* were delivered in Florence during the 1550's and later published by the Florentine Academy, asserted that "poetics is part or a variety of logic, deriving from logic all of its rational philosophy . . . the better a logician anyone is, the more excellent a poet he will be."[62] For him, as for Savonarola, example is the characteristic tool of the poet, and this theory enables him to reconcile logic and morality. Since in example "one restricts himself for the most part to civil matters . . . who doubts . . . that [the poet] has need of ethics and politics?"[63] Giovan Batista Gelli, author of the famous *Circe,* also believed that "poetry is an instrument and art, and not a science . . . and is contained in Logic."[64]

Later in the century it was not uncommon for writers to emphasize the fictional aspect of poetry. Stress on poetry as fiction naturally led to a re-examination of poetry's place among the logical arts. Jacopo Mazzoni followed this tack in his *Defense of the Comedy of Dante* (1587), where it is asserted that "poetry, because of paying more attention to the credible than the true, ought to be classed as a subdivision of the rational faculty, called by the ancients sophistic."[65] And Niccolò Rossi, replying to Jason Denores, wrote that "poetry does not depend on politics [i.e., practical philosophy], but on sophistic and rhetoric. . . ."[66] This shift of poetry from its unique category to the category of sophistic may seem trivial, but, actually, it signals a minor revolution in thinking about poetry and in some measure foreshadows the concern with technique at the expense of content characteristic of so much second-rate baroque art.

At any rate, the shift in emphasis did not go unchallenged by traditionalists. Both Scaliger and Tasso vigorously denied that poetry was a branch of sophistic. Tasso is particularly interesting because he accepted the inclusion of poetry among the "rational sciences" but argued that it is related to dialectic (the study of "the probable") rather than sophistic: "Poetry is included in order under dialectic along with rhetoric, which, as Aristotle says, is the other branch of the dialectic faculty, to which applies the consideration not of the false but the probable."[67]

At the end of the century Paolo Beni, Chiodino da Montemilone, and Rinaldini continued to insist on the connection between poetry and logic.[68] Their work was not particularly significant, since the great days of Italian criticism had already passed. However, it shows the trend of the times. In general, the later developments of the theory relating poetry and logic tended to emphasize illusion rather than truth, delight rather than edification, and the exploitation of poetic devices such as metaphor, comparison, and "concetto" rather than larger aspects of structure. These tendencies had been encouraged at various times during the sixteenth century, but they reached a kind of culmination in Emmanuele Tesauro's *Il Cannocchiale Aristotelico* (*The Aristotelian Telescope*). This work, which is typical of *concettismo,* is based on a peculiar theory of imitation that may have roots as far back as Averroes' commentary on the *Poetics.*[69] According to Tesauro all speech is imitative. The difference between prose and poetic speech (*orazione poetiche*) is that the latter is carried out by means of ingenious deviations from the simple (hence un-delightful) names of everyday language: "The whole force of a word is in imitating (*rappresentare*) the thing signified to the human mind. But this representation can be made either with the nude and appropriate word . . . or with some ingenious expression which simultaneously imitates and delights."[70]

Predictably, poetry is the most "ingenious" form of expression. Just as Gundissalinus had made "imaginative syllogism" the *differentia* between poetry and other forms of expression, Tesauro makes metaphor his *differentia.* Metaphor is "the great mother" of clever sayings, and imitation is "a wisdom (*sagacità*) with which, having proposed a metaphor or some other flower of human wit, you carefully consider its bases, and transplanting them in different categories . . . propagate the flowers of the same species but not the same individuals."[71] This leads to a curious discussion of divine and natural "arguzie" and finally to an elaborate treatise on metaphor and *concetto* as the highest forms of wit.[72] In sum, Tesauro's *concettismo* is a variant of the method of defining poetry by a device which distinguishes it from other branches of "rational science." Its obsession with technique is a corollary of this method. In both respects it is the end-product of a tradition stretching back through critics like Mazzoni and Savonarola to St. Thomas, Averroes, and Al-farabi.

IV. POETRY AS A BRANCH OF MORAL PHILOSOPHY

The idea that poetry should teach is the most universal of critical theories. It is so universal that it is amorphous. The formula of "delight mingled with instruction" was popular in antiquity and remained so in the Renaissance. Often the formula was expressed symbolically in the image of the sugar-coated pill or the medicine cup with the honeyed rim.

Behind both the formula and the images lay the ideal of *paideia* formulated by the Greeks and given its most lasting expression in the dialogues of Plato.[73] This tradition held that all human activities should be directed toward the harmonious development of the individual within the community. Literature could contribute to this program by instruction and indoctrination. From one point of view *paideia* assigns literature a noble mission and thereby elevates it. From another point of view, it degrades literature to the level of propaganda. Only by exercising charity can one think of the literature admitted by Plato to the ideal state as anything other than propaganda—although it might be said in mitigation that since the state is defined as ideal, the propaganda is justified. Fortunately, Plato's successors were less austere. The authors who transmitted the tradition of *paideia* to the Middle Ages and Renaissance were men like Isocrates, Plutarch, St. Basil, Cicero, Horace, and Quintilian. They were not fanatics. They enjoyed their Homer as well as the next reader, and they agreed that he should be treated as a classic, not banished. Despite many vicissitudes, their liberalized version of *paideia* prevailed. It became a standard article of faith for the fifteenth- and sixteenth-century humanist.

Paideia is a comforting tradition. It is sympathetic to literature and useful in refuting the attacks of fanatics on the sweetness and light of art. On the other hand, it is not precise enough to be of much use in formal criticism. In so far as it aspires to the status of critical doctrine it must be modified so as to offer a definition of poetry designating its *genus* and *differentia*. In other words, it must locate poetry in the Aristotelian scheme of the sciences.

Here, as in so many other problems debated by Renaissance critics, the solution was achieved by adapting to poetics ideas originally developed in connection with rhetoric. These ideas were a reaction to Aristotle's treatment of rhetoric. Aristotle had insisted that rhetoric was a "faculty" rather than an art with a particular subject-matter like medicine or geometry (*Rhetoric,* 1355^b 26ff). The assertion was revolutionary in itself. Aristotle compounded his sin against tradition by explicitly denying that any close relationship existed between rhetoric and ethics or politics: "It . . . appears that rhetoric is an offshoot of dialectic and also of ethical studies. Ethical studies may fairly be called political; and for this reason rhetoric masquerades as political science, and the professors of it as political experts—sometimes from want of education, sometimes from ostentation, sometimes owing to other human failings. As a matter of fact, it is a branch of dialectic" (*Rhetoric,* 1356^a 25-30).

Aristotle's comments amount to an insult to the whole school of Attic oratory. The great orators of Greece had been statesmen rather than lawyers or rhetoricians. Through their efforts oratory achieved nobility and splendor. Oratory was considered not the result of skill with the tricks of rhetoric, but a by-product of deep understanding of political affairs combined with intense patriotism. The orator clarified great issues of policy, stimulated heroic courage in times of crisis, cowed the enemies of the state when on foreign embassies, and encouraged virtue in times of peace. It should be emphasized that this was an empirical estimate of the power of oratory, based on the accomplishments of men like Demosthenes, Lysias, Isocrates, and Isaeus. Yet Aristotle coldly rejected it in favor of a theory which appears to make the orator into a dilettante who wins his points by clever manipulation of language.

The major spokesman for the anti-Aristotelian position in antiquity was Cicero. As a practicing orator who liked to think of himself as a Roman Demosthenes, Cicero felt that knowledge of rhetorical devices was far less important than a broad, philosophical understanding of the issues being debated. Therefore, from the early *De inventione* to the mature *De oratore* he insisted that rhetoric *did* include subject matter as well as techniques, that the public speaker must have a well-rounded education, and that rhetoric was most properly included in the category of civil science.[74]

Before examining a few typical expressions of Cicero's thought we will do well to attempt a precise definition of the point at issue between Aristotle and Cicero. Although Aristotle does not commit himself fully, his discussion clearly points in the direction taken by his commentators and later by the Arabs—that is, rhetoric is a "rational science" and belongs with the conventionally accepted parts of the *Organon*. Aristotle is quite definite about the opinion that he rejects. This is the opinion that rhetoric is a sub-category of ethics and/or politics, or, in other words, of Aristotle's "practical philosophy." Practical philosophy, it will be recalled, consists of politics, economics, and ethics. It was given several labels by Aristotle's successors. Because politics was its most inclusive subject, it was often simply labeled "politics." A synonym, emphasizing the social orientation of the practical sciences, was "civil philosophy," the term frequently used by Cicero. Another label, perhaps the most indicative of the real concern of practical philosophy, was "moral philosophy," occasionally shortened simply to "philosophy." Thus, the argument between Aristotle and Cicero and their various followers in the sixteenth century can be understood as a debate over whether rhetoric should be placed among the logical disciplines and to some extent abandon its moral pretensions, or whether it should be made a part of practical philosophy and hence a "moral" or "civil" science.

The *De oratore* is Cicero's most mature examination of the great questions of rhetoric. The first of its three books is wholly devoted to the question of whether oratory is a skill or depends on philosophy. The theory that oratory is a skill is correctly traced to Aristotle and Theophrastus and treated as the dominant Greek theory of Cicero's day. It is defended tenaciously by Antonius in the second half of the book. However, Cicero's sympathies are wholly with Crassus, his spokesman in *De oratore,* who maintains that the orator must be a philosopher. Crassus supports his contention with many ringing tributes to the great orators of Greece and to the benefits conferred by oratory on both Greek and Roman civilization.

The classification of rhetoric under "practical philosophy" is clearly implied throughout. It is made definite in the following passage:

> Nevertheless, if he will listen to me, since philosophy is divided into three branches, which respectively deal with the mysteries of nature, with the subleties of dialectic, and with human life and conduct, let us quit claim to the first two, by way of concession to our indolence, but unless we keep our hold on the third, which has ever been the orator's province, we shall leave the orator no sphere wherein to attain greatness. For which reason the division of philosophy, concerned with human life and manners, must all of it be mastered by the orator; as for the other matters, even though he has not studied them, he will still be able, whenever the necessity arises, to beautify them by his eloquence, if only they are brought to his notice and described to him (*De oratore,* I, xv).[75]

In the sixteenth century, the issues were the same as those which concerned Cicero, and they were usually formulated by writers who were thoroughly familiar with the *De oratore.* Bernardino Tomitano, for example, began his *Considerations of the Tuscan Language* (1545) with an argument "in which it is proved that philosophy is necessary to the acquisition of rhetoric and poetic."[76] Here he rebukes the "misguided men who believe that eloquence is only common and vulgar speech without knowledge of philosophy and capable of being acquired by itself. . . ." As might be expected, the type of philosophy that is stressed is civil philosophy.[77] More or less the same position is taken by Nizolius in his *Concerning the True Principles and Method of Philosophy* (1553), and M. A. Majoragius (a pseudonym for Antonio de'Conti) in his commentary on Aristotle's *Rhetoric* (1572), in which the Greek work is interpreted according to Ciceronian principles.[78] A more sophisticated work than any of these, Sperone Speroni's *Dialogue on Rhetoric* (wr. 1542), begins with the speakers discussing not rhetoric but "civil philosophy." In the course of the argument it is revealed that this category includes not only morality (*costumi*) but also eloquence (*il parlar bene*).[79] A final case in point is Ieronimo Zoppio's essay on *The Divine Comedy,* where it is asserted, "to the idea that poetics is not a part of moral philosophy is opposed rhetoric, which resembles poetic, and gives precepts in the same fashion. And the rhetoric is called by Aristotle in Rhetoric, chapter ii, . . . part of civil philosophy; and this is confirmed by Cicero in de Inventione, I, the chapter 'On Civil Law.' "[80]

Although Zoppio misconstrued his Aristotle, his remarks provide what I believe to be a key to the position of poetry as understood by critics in the didactic tradition. The position of poetry was determined by analogy from the position of rhetoric. Since rhetoric had, on the authority of Cicero, been placed in the category of practical philosophy, poetics could also be placed in this category. Technically speaking, this means that the orator and poet joined their eloquence to the knowledge of the politician and moralist in one grand and noble effort to lead mankind to virtue. In fact, since the orator and poet were skilled in the art of translating dry theory into practical social action, it could be claimed that they were the leaders of the enterprise. This at least is the idea that was commonly expressed during the age of "rhetorica regina" when, as Ciro Trabalza has put it, rhetoric was "the central spirit of the whole humanistic system of criticism."[81] From the age of Petrarch to the age of Milton, European humanists vied to express their contempt for the sterile chop-logic of formal—especially scholastic—philosophy, and their admiration for the eloquence and poetry that would make social realities out of the dreams of the philosophers.

It hardly seems necessary to point to the numerous definitions of poetry as part of practical philosophy. Dante was perfectly clear on the point when he wrote to Can Grande della Scala that "the genus of philosophy under which the work proceeds . . . is moral activity or ethics, for the whole and the part are devised not for the sake of speculation but of possible action."[82] In 1536 Bernardino Daniello consciously based his *Poetics* on Cicero's *De oratore,* and the philosopher-poet who emerges from his pages is a sixteenth-century version of Cicero's philosopher-orator Crassus. To cite only two more examples, Giraldi Cinthio wrote in 1554 that "poetry and philosophy . . . were in substance the same thing."[83] Mazzoni, writing in 1587, sampled a variety of poetic theories. After considering poetic as a part of sophistic, he turned to its moral aspects, and, drawing on Plato and Proclus, insisted on its subordination to "the civil faculty, or moral philosophy."[84] Mazzoni was so convinced of the rightness of this classification, that he attributed it to Aristotle, suggesting that "the *Poetics* is the ninth book of the *Politics*."[85]

It would be tedious to continue citing authorities to prove a point which is, after all, commonplace. What is often overlooked by students of criticism, and what needs to be stressed here, is that there are two modes of the relationship of poetry to practical philosophy. The first is a general one in which poetics is simply added to the list of disciplines in that category. The second is more specific. It tends to divide practical philosophy into two large categories of (a) action, and (b) eloquence. The first category includes the standard subjects of politics, economics, and ethics. The second is dominated by rhetoric, to which the specific disciplines of oratory and poetry are subordinate.

Consideration of the grammatical, logical, and moral categories helps to bring sixteenth-century criticism into focus. On the other hand, the categories do not offer simple, final answers that eliminate the need for close examination of individual critics. Any illusion that they do will be quickly dispelled by reference to the texts themselves. Two critics may use the same classification but differ widely in method, topics considered, and observations. A single critic may employ different classifications in different sections of the same work—sometimes self-consciously, but sometimes, one feels, from an uncritical desire to repeat everything that he has read about poetry.

With due regard, then, to the need for humility, it may be said that the placing of poetry among the other branches of human learning helped to shape critical theory throughout the Renaissance. The dominant theories were those relating poetry to grammar, logic, and moral philosophy. The theory relating poetry to logic was associated with Aristotle and the scholastics. Conversely, the grammatical and moral theories were associated with such classical authors as Plato, Isocrates, Cicero, Quintilian, and Horace. Sixteenth-century humanists were hostile to scholasticism and idolized Plato. They stressed the moral utility of literature, and they powerfully influenced both the interpretation of classical authors and the new literature of their own age. The principles which they formulated remained influential until the end of the eighteenth century, and, at least in the area of education, command respect even today.

CHAPTER II

Rhetoric, Poetics, and the Theory of Praise

Unlike technology, literature is unprogressive. The naïve poet is different from the sentimental one, but he is certainly not inferior. Virgil is not better than Homer, despite the sophistication of Augustan civilization; and there are few facts about love discovered by a post-Freudian generation that Catullus did not know as well or better. Ironically, it often seems that civilization is a curse rather than a blessing to the poet, and Macaulay predicted that art would inevitably decay as science advanced.

In the *Ion,* Socrates half-ironically suggests that poetry is a divinely inspired madness; and Horace, one of the most deliberate craftsmen who ever lived, maintained that the poet was born, not made. Even Ovid confessed that "there is a god in us; when he moves us we become inspired."

These sentiments have more than a grain of truth. Primitive poetry and the poetry of direct inspiration touch the deepest roots of experience, whereas in more self-conscious poetry, rules and conventions are interposed between reader and author. This unfortunate fact has often been blamed on criticism. Critics are accused of fostering Alexandrianism in antiquity, flowery ornament in medieval literature, mannerism in the seventeenth century, frigidity in the eighteenth, and dry-as-dust formalism in the twentieth. If the case were proven, the study of criticism would be a melancholy occupation, the tracing of an endlessly repeated tragedy in which freshness and life are blighted by rules, authorities, schools, and fine points.

However, criticism is more the scapegoat than the villain. A civilization exists in time. As time passes experience accumulates. The spontaneous responses of early poetry become ever less satisfactory until copying them becomes not simplicity or spontaneity but primitivism, a sign of decadence. Pindar's enthusiasm for the victors in the Olympic games commands assent even now; but that a modern poet could describe baseball in Pindaric terms is ridiculous. Sappho has captured a universal aspect of love, but most readers would agree, I believe, that Marvell's "To his Coy Mistress" comes closer to the emotion as experienced—or endured—after age eighteen. Certainly the heroes of the *Iliad* would be out of place in the age of push-button warfare, but sad-wise Aeneas is a man like ourselves, condemned to plod ahead with the burden of the past on his shoulders. For better or worse the increasing complexity of criticism is a symptom of cultural growth, not a cause of the decay of art.

These observations lead us back to the problem of the moral tradition in literary criticism. In primitive times it was probably the result of observation rather than theory. In almost all cultures—Hindu, near-Eastern, Greek, Saxon, Japanese—the earliest literature is religious and patriotic. It consists of a mélange of hymns, charms, cosmological and legendary poems, and poems celebrating dimly remembered tribal heroes. In this mélange two "kinds" stand out fairly clearly—the hymns and the "celebrations." In Greece such poetry lay behind and partly inspired the *Iliad,* Hesiod's *Theogony,* and the lyrics of Pindar and Callimachus.

Plato was the first Greek to formulate a reasonably coherent theory of poetry. Being chiefly concerned with practical ethical problems, he demanded that poetry contribute to the welfare of society. Since Homer's poems presented the gods in an unflattering light, thereby undermining the authority of religion, he banned them from the ideal state. Although Plato introduced a topic of immense importance to criticism in his discussion of imitation, he himself used the topic to attack rather than defend poetry. The recurrent effort to reconstruct a Platonic theory of art based on imitation seems to fly in the face of this fact.[1] It was not Plato but his successors beginning with Aristotle who exploited the idea of imitation in order to justify art.[2]

With the exception of Aristotle and Eratosthenes, who survives only in fragments, ancient critics seem to have agreed with Plato that poetry should edify. Yet ancient critical theory is surprisingly irregular in its treatment of the means whereby poetry should achieve this end. A good many rules and conventions concerning individual genres are preserved, and at least one essay—*On the Sublime*—examines the devices appropriate to a particular literary effect. But *On the Sublime* is unique. Its existence underscores the fact that in ancient criticism as a whole there exists a curious gap between what may be called the macroscopic and the microscopic aspects of the study of literature. The microscopic aspect—the analysis of language, of the figures of speech, of techniques for achieving desired effects, and so forth—was relegated to rhetoric. Although rhetoric obviously influenced criticism, the relationship between rhetoric and poetic remained indefinite. The *Ars poetica,* for example, is indebted to Cicero's *De oratore* for both general topics and particulars,[3] but Horace offers no guide as to the principles which determined his use of rhetoric. Evidently, he did not consider the matter sufficiently problematic to merit explicit discussion. The fact that it was a problem—and an important one—is evident from the subsequent course of ancient criticism. During the silver age, rhetoric played an increasingly important part in the analysis of the poets. By the fourth century A.D., rhetoric and poetic had become so thoroughly intermingled that there was no clear distinction between orator and poet. Macrobius asserted in the *Saturnalia* (V, i, 1) that "Virgil is to be considered no less an orator than a poet"; and the question "Was Virgil an orator or a poet?" became a standard topic for the debating exercises known as *controversiae*.[4]

That such a question could be asked indicates confusion rather than insight. It suggests that the professors of literature knew that there was some close and important nexus between poetic and rhetoric but were not sure what it was. Thus they had trouble deciding exactly where the one left off and the other began. Such vagueness became less satisfactory as criticism became more formal, and the period of classical decadence was one of formalism. Therefore, it is not surprising that a formula appeared during this period which purported to explain how poetics was related to rhetoric. Briefly, this formula asserted that "belles lettres" are characterized by a kind of favorable or unfavorable heightening. Such heightening was described in rhetorical terminology as either praise (when favorable) or blame (when unfavorable). For convenience I will call this formula "the theory of praise." Although it may seem arbitrary and clumsy to the modern reader, its virtues enabled it to survive until the end of the *Cinquecento* in Italy and for a considerably longer period elsewhere.

I. INCEPTION

Although Plato believed that poetry is dangerous to the harmony of the state, he did not favor its complete abolition. In the *Laws,* especially Books II and VII (659-61, 801ff.), he says much about the importance of community celebrations during which the citizen will be stimulated to virtue by choric songs. Plato described these songs as a kind of praise, and they represented the only type of poetry which he endorsed: ". . . it will be proper to have hymns and praises of the gods intermingled with prayers; and after the gods, prayers and praises should be offered to demigods and heroes, suitable to their several characters. . . . In the next place, there will be no objection to a law that the citizens who are departed and have done good and energetic deeds . . . should receive eulogies . . . a man should make a fair ending, and then we will praise him" (*Laws,* 801). Plato's approval of the poetry of praise is by no means casual. Similar statements occur frequently in the dialogues. In the *Republic,* after calling for the expulsion of poets who lead men to vice, Socrates excepts "hymns to the gods and praises of famous men" as "the only poetry which ought to be admitted into our state" (X, 607). In the *Protagoras* he advises using "the works of great poets" to instruct the young, for "in them are contained many admonitions, and many tales, and praises and encomia of ancient and famous men, which [the student] is required to learn by heart, in order that he may imitate or emulate them, and desire to become like them" (325-26).

These remarks are far from a full-scale theory of poetry, but they had considerable influence. They suggest that the poetry of praise is of special excellence. More than other types it encourages reverence and patriotism. In addition, Plato touches on two subjects of great importance in late classical and Renaissance poetics. The first is education, or *paideia.* The *Protagoras* stresses the utility of praise in forming character. Presumably reading eulogies of Ulysses, Alexander, Cyrus, or the heroes of Thermopylae will encourage schoolboys to become warrior-heroes themselves.

The second subject touched on by Plato is fame. The efficacy of the poetry of praise depends on its ability to arouse "emulation" or "imitation." The incentive that it offers is the prospect of immortality through verse. Plato is sometimes said to be opposed to poetry because of its tendency to stir the emotions. This is true only of emotion that he considered antisocial. The poetry of praise depends on an emotion—the hunger for fame—but it uses this emotion to strengthen the state by inculcating virtue. The idea that poets are the special custodians of fame is repeated by Horace, Cicero, and a host of other classical writers. The revival of the "cult of glory" during the Renaissance has been described in detail by Burckhardt. Plato was not responsible for this cult, but the dialogues certainly encouraged its growth.

Since Aristotle tended to ignore *paideia* in discussing poetry it might be thought that his contribution to the theory of praise is small. This is doubtless true if Aristotle can be separated from his commentators. Or, to put the matter more honestly, if Aristotle is read in terms of modern interpretations rather than sixteenth-century ones. To sixteenth-century commentators several key passages in the *Poetics* appeared to justify the theory of praise. Because these passages agreed with what the commentators had learned from other sources, they were often given disproportionate emphasis.

Aristotle's theory of the origin of poetry is one of the most frequently cited of these passages. After a period of undifferentiated "imitation,"

> Poetry . . . broke up into two kinds according to the differences of character in the individual poets; for the graver among them should represent noble actions, and those of noble personages; and the meaner sort the actions of the ignoble. The latter class produced invectives at first, just as others did hymns and panegyrics. . . . The result was that the old poets became some of them writers of heroic and others of imabic verse. . . . As soon, however, as Tragedy and

Comedy appeared in the field, those naturally drawn to one line of poetry became writers of comedies instead of iambs, and those naturally drawn to the other, writers of tragedies instead of epics, because these new modes of art were grander and of more esteem than the old (1448^b-49^a).

It is impossible to say how close Aristotle felt the relationship to be between the earliest forms—the panegyrics and invectives—and the literary types which evolved from them. However, it is clearly possible to emphasize the closeness of this relationship. Aristotle was thus pressed into service to justify a theory of genres in which praise and blame are central. Heroic poetry is the first step in the evolution of the original "panegyric"; and it, in turn, gives way to tragedy. Conversely, "invective" develops into "comic epic" like the *Margites,* satire, and finally into full-scale comedy. The following scheme appears to be intended:

Praise	Blame
Hymns and panegyrics	Invective
Heroic poetry	Comic epic
Epic	Satire
Tragedy	Comedy[5]

Aristotle's discussion of character can be related to this system of genres. The heroic and tragic poets, he says, show us men "better than" ourselves; and comic poetry "would make its personages worse . . . than most men of the present day" (1448^a). Rhetorically oriented critics interpreted Aristotle to mean that epic and tragedy present idealized figures. Since the devices of idealization are the devices of epideictic rhetoric, the reliance of epic and tragedy on praise seemed confirmed. Conversely, the devices for making men seem "worse than" average are the devices of blame, or denigration.

Finally, Aristotle's "better than" and "worse than" refer to moral qualities, for "the dividing line between virtue and vice is one dividing the whole of mankind" (1448^a). Didactic criticism assimilated the *Poetics* by assuming that the idealization of forms based on praise creates edifying pictures of virtue, while the forms based on denigration make vice seem unattractive.

The fragmentary nature of surviving Greek and Roman criticism makes it dangerous to generalize about any but the most widely held critical beliefs. However, there are a good many references to literature that appeared to later ages to confirm the idea that literary genres are based on praise and blame. Pindar's odes, for example, have an obviously encomiastic quality. Pindar refers to them as "praises prompted by gratitude . . . in requital for kindly deeds" (*Pythian Odes,* II, 16-18); and he begins the second Olympian with the question, "Ye hymns that rule the lyre; what god, what hero, aye, what man shall ye loudly praise?" Isocrates, a favorite during the sixteenth century, speaks of the epics and tragedies of the Trojan War as "celebrations" and "praise" (*Evagoras,* 6-7). In the *Pro Archia,* which was familiar to every Renaissance schoolboy, Cicero describes the *Annales* of Ennius as "praises" by which "not only the man praised, but the Roman people is exalted" (IX, 22). Whatever his personal theory of epic, Virgil provided a near-perfect illustration of Cicero's text through his dual celebration of Aeneas and the greatness of Rome.

The concept of comedy and satire as forms of rebuke—hence allied to the rhetorical technique of blame—is a natural one and is evident from Aristophanes (*Acharnians,* 644-45) through Lucilius (frag. 1030-34) to Horace (*Satires,* I, x; II, i) and Juvenal (first satire). It was common for historians of comedy to divide the form into the *comoedia vetus* and the *comoedia nova.* The first type, exemplified by Aristophanes, was described as bitter excoriation of folly and vice in living persons; while the second, typified by Menander, was a more tolerant ridicule of fictitious characters exemplifying middle-class folly or vice. These theories, Theophrastian in origin, were transmitted by Euanthius, Donatus, and other minor authors to the Middle Ages.[6]

None of the preceding references suggests a self-conscious literary theory. They suggest a general tendency, inherited from Plato and Aristotle on the one hand and primitive tradition on the other, to speak of literature in terms of praise and blame. However, there is a great deal of difference between a tendency and a critical system. The development of the theory of praise depended on the fusion of critical ideas with those of rhetoric. Therefore, we may turn briefly to rhetoric.

II. EPIDEICTIC RHETORIC

From Aristotle on, the standard authorities divided rhetoric into three departments: (1) judicial oratory, the oratory of the courts; (2) deliberative oratory, the oratory of the political assembly; and (3) epideictic or demonstrative oratory, the oratory of ceremonial occasions, commemorations, patriotic festivals, funerals, and the like. The first two types have little or no contribution to make to literary criticism, but the third is literary by its very nature.[7]

Aristotle's explanation of epideictic rhetoric (*Rhetoric,* I, 9) provides a convenient basis for discussion, although it must be supplemented by reference to later authors. For Aristotle and all of his successors the method of epideictic rhetoric is praise and blame. He thought chiefly in terms of praise of men but admitted the possibility of "frivolous" praise and praise "of inanimate things, or of the humblest of the lower animals" (*Rhetoric,* 1366^a29f.). Praise is defined (1367^b27) as "the expression in words of the eminence of a man's good qualities," and its object is said to be "Virtue and Vice, the Noble and the Base" (1366^a24). Much space is devoted to the nine virtues that orators should emphasize, but beyond admitting casually that "to praise a man is in one respect akin to urging a course of action" (1367^b36), Aristotle says nothing about the possible moral effect of the epideictic speech.

The standard form of the epideictic oration is the encomium. As explained by Aristotle and his successors this form involves much more than simple flattery. It is in some respects closer to biography than oratory. The body of the encomium is devoted to a summary of the life of the man being praised. It will usually begin with favorable notice of his nation, family, comeliness, and education. Such material should be secondary, however, to his noble deeds (*praxeis;* Lat., *gesta*).[8] While the subject's deeds are central, they need not be presented in the objective light of history. Instead, they should be "heightened" to make the praise more emphatic. Since the encomium is quite long, it will be leavened by pleasant digressions and embellishments. Obviously, the form is not restricted to oratory. On the one hand it is related to the "panegyrical biography" so popular in antiquity. On the other it has similarities to epic, as will become clear during the succeeding discussion.

Later authorities did not add much to Aristotle, but they reduced his prescriptions to formulae that could be used by even the most unimaginative student. Aphthonius, Menander, and the author of the *Ad Herennium* distinguish between three types of praise based on "goods of nature," "goods of fortune," and "goods of character" respectively.[9] The first two types are "external" and are employed in the *effictio* (Gr. *karakterismos*). The third is used in the *notatio* (Gr. *ethopoeia*). The *effictio* is the ancestor of the medieval and Renaissance blazon; and the *notatio* is related to the Theophrastian "character" as developed during the seventeenth century.

The existence of three kinds of personal praise gave rise to a controversy over their relative merits. If praise was to be morally instructive it had to concentrate on virtue. Did this not rule out the topics of the *effictio?* Cicero vehemently insisted that "family, beauty, strength, possessions, riches, and the rest which fortune gives, either externally or to the body, are not true praise, which should be given to virtue only."[10] Quintilian was willing to admit praise of externals, but "only as they are honorably used."[11] Most later authorities agreed that a full-scale encomium should include all forms of praise but should concentrate on "goods of character."

The most important innovation in epideictic theory after Aristotle was the idea that praise and blame should be didactic. Isocrates claimed that his *Evagoras* was a new kind of oration because it attempted "to eulogize in prose the virtues of a man" in order to stimulate "emulation for virtue" among the young. Cicero agreed (*De oratore,* II, 84, 342) that "true praise is due only to virtue," and Quintilian (*Institutio oratoria,* III, 7, 1) used the old Roman funeral oration as an example of the moral utility of praise. Since inciting to virtue is a form of persuasion, some rhetoricians suggested including the whole category under the political or legal branches of oratory. So considered, the purpose of epideictic oratory is not "display" but simply "virtue" or "the honorable," a formula appearing in several late classical rhetorical works.[12] Insistence on the moral utility of praise is still more obvious in late classical panegyrics. Pliny defended his servile flattery of Trajan with the argument that in it "good princes might recognize what they have done; bad, what they ought to have done."[13] And Julian the Apostate, a still more spineless hypocrite, boasted that praise makes good men "zealous to aim at a still higher level of conduct" and stimulates the morally weak "both by persuasion and compulsion to imitate that noble conduct."[14]

All rhetoricians ageed that the epideictic orator should cultivate an ornate style. According to the *Rhetoric* (1368^{a}) his special devices are "comparison" and "amplification." "Comparison" does not refer to simile or metaphor. It is a figure in which the subject of the oration is compared to paragons of the past. A soldier is compared to Alexander, a philosopher to Socrates, a wife to Penelope, and so forth. The point of the comparison will be that the orator's subject surpasses the paragon. This form of comparison is familiar in medieval poetry as the topic of "outdoing."[15]

Amplification is left somewhat vague. In Book I ($1368^{a}10$ff.) it is equated with "heightening," and in Book II ($1403^{a}17$ff.) it is defined along with "depreciation," its opposite, as "one type of enthymeme; viz., the kind used to show that a thing is great or small." In other words, amplification and depreciation are the techniques used to convert historical materials into praise or blame respectively. Later, the devices of amplification were codified. The most commonly mentioned devices are repetition (*interpretatio, frequentatio, expolitio*), periphrasis (*circuitio*), comparison (*similitudo, comparatio, collatio*), apostrophe (*exclamatio*), prosopopeia (*conformatio, fictio personarum*), digression, description (*effictio, notatio*) and affirmation by negation (*oppositio*).[16] Under the Latin titles of *dilatatio* and *diminutio* amplification and depreciation became fundamental to medieval poetics. About one-third of the *Poetria nova* of Geoffrey of Vinsauf, for example, is devoted to the figures of amplification.

The combination of didacticism and emphasis on amplification made late classical rhetoricians take an extremely offhand attitude toward historical fact. There is a nice distinction between exaggeration for the sake of moral edification and servile flattery, but practically speaking, it is academic. Almost any distortion could be justified by the claim that the orator is presenting "what ought to be" rather than "what is." Hence the biography of the subject tended to disappear behind a cloud of idealized vignettes, and considering the lives of some of the figures whose encomia have survived, this is probably for the best. As Julian the Apostate explained: "... to rhetoricians the art of rhetoric allows just as much freedom [as to poets]; fiction is denied them, but flattery is by no means forbidden, nor is it counted a disgrace to the orator that the subject of his panegyric should not deserve it. ... Orators assert that the advantage of their art is that it can ... marshal the power of words against that of facts."[17]

A final characteristic of epideictic theory is the proliferation of epideictic types. Aristotle had only discussed the encomium in detail. The *Progymnasmata* of Aphthonius, however, gives formulae which can be used for praising (or blaming) seasons, animals, plants, abstract ideas, and so forth.[18] *Ekphrasis* (heightened description) was particularly useful in such a program. It is the technique of "set pieces" such as the *locus amoenus* trope[19] and of descriptive poetry such as the *Mosella* of Ausonius.[20] The *De virginitate* of Aldhelm illustrates the technique of praising an abstract idea, while Statius' *Laudes Neapolis* is an example of the praise of cities. The paradoxical encomium—for example, Synesius' "Praise of Baldness"—was an especially popular variation on the epideictic pattern.[21]

Menander's *Peri epideiktikon* employs a classification by types rather than by subject matter. He begins with hymn, of which he lists nine subtypes. He then makes an elaborate survey of secular forms of praise which includes twenty-three basic topics, among them praise of a ruler (*basilikos logos*), epithalamion, funeral speech (*epitaphios logos*), panegyric, and birthday song (*genethliakos logos*). The distinctions between types need not concern us at present. What is important is that the types and formulae worked out by Menander and his fellow rhetoricians for epideictic speeches became standard topics for poetry. The significance of this fact was clearly perceived by Ernst Curtius. He remarked, "The majority of lyric themes, which the modern poet 'creates' out of his 'experience,' were included in the list of epideictic topoi by late antique theory. They were material for rhetorical exercises. And as such they were used in the teaching of poetry in the Middle Ages."[22]

In sum, epideictic theory began with a bias toward literary and poetic techniques. This bias became more pronounced as Greek and Roman cultures passed into their decadent phase. By the time of Statius—and even more by the time of Claudian, Ausonius, Fortunatus, and Sidonius—the distinction between a poem and an epideictic oration or "set piece" was often only metrical.[23]

III. LATE CLASSICAL AND MEDIEVAL FORMULATIONS OF THE THEORY OF PRAISE

The late classical period witnessed an outburst of critical and scholarly activity. A distinction should probably be made between the humanists and the commentators of this period. The humanists were in the mainstream of classical tradition. They were widely read, undogmatic, and generally philosophical in outlook. The commentators, on the other hand, tended to be narrow in outlook, increasingly eccentric in their approach to literature, and preoccupied with systems. During the Middle Ages the humanists were read and admired, but the commentators were quoted and imitated; and it is by them that the theory of praise was formulated.

The first extant author to state the theory of praise in other than general terms is Tiberius Claudius Donatus (fl. 4th C.), in the *Interpretationes Virgilianae*. Nothing about this work suggests originality. It is probable that despite his claim to the contrary, Donatus has simply restated a commonplace of his age. At any rate, he begins his commentary with the following declaration: "First and foremost we must know what matter (*genus materiae*) our Maro has taken. This is nothing other than epideictic (*laudativum*). It has been overlooked and hidden because while he ran through the acts of Aeneas using a marvelous epideictic form (*artis genere laudationis*), he is also shown to have included incidents from other forms. However these are not really alien to the elements of praise, for they were included to heighten the praise of Aeneas. If anyone wants to measure Virgil's genius, his morality, the nature of his speech, his knowledge, character, and skill in rhetoric, he must first learn whom he undertakes to praise in his poem. . . ."[24]

Donatus wrote with a sound knowledge of classical rhetoric. On the basis of this knowledge, he concluded that the *Aeneid* was written according to the prescriptions of the encomium. The word "matter" (*genus materiae*) refers not to the plot but the rhetorical category—epideictic—within which the *Aeneid* is included. The substance of the poem is the acts (*gesta*) of Aeneas, through which he is glorified. The narration of the acts is interrupted by pleasing digressions or passages composed in the style of other "matters"—that is, forensic or deliberative. As a well-trained rhetorician, Donatus properly insists that they are not extraneous but serve to heighten the praise. An important bit of epideictic lore is added in a later comment. Just as the encomium was supposed to inculcate virtue, the *Aeneid* is a storehouse of patterns which men from all walks of life can emulate.[25]

The principles set down by Donatus were soon repeated in the *Exposition of the Content of Virgil According to Moral Philosophy* by Fulgentius. This is a curious and, to modern tastes, absurd book, yet its influence was enormous, as Comparetti has shown in *Virgil in the Middle Ages*.[26] Its theories were still valued in the sixteenth century. Tasso's *Allegoria del poema,* written to silence puritanical critics of *Gerusalemme liberata,* uses Fulgentius-like methods. Two facts are significant about the *Exposition*. First, it is frankly, even slavishly, dedicated to extracting moral philosophy from Virgil. Hence its appeal to medieval critics. Second, it self-consciously uses the theory of praise to do this. Fulgentius assumes that Virgil consciously used epideictic formulae. In other words, he regards the theory of praise both as a critical device for discovering the moral content of poetry and as a set of prescriptions guiding the composition of didactic poems.

At the beginning of the *Exposition,* Virgil conveniently appears to Fulgentius in a dream. Mortals, it seems, are unable to pierce the dark veil of his allegory, and so he will assist them. Since the desire for such guidance is familiar even in the twentieth century, the modern critic can feel a measure of sympathy for Fulgentius as he cowers before the awesome bard. The first problem that Virgil clears up is the word-order of his opening line. His explanation hinges on the fact that *arma* is interpreted metaphorically as a reference to the virtue of fortitude. He says: "Although in following the rules of logical discourse (*dialecticam disciplinam*) one ought to mention the person first and then his attribute . . . because I have followed the rules for praise (*laudis materiam*) I have mentioned the excellence of the man before the man himself. . . . There may be many men, but not all are praiseworthy. Therefore I placed the virtue first [for which the man is to be praised]."[27]

The comment depends on a nice point of syntax. In an expository work—say, a treatise on ethics—the normal procedure would be from general to specific, from genus to species, or, in this case, from man to attribute. However, the *Aeneid,* says Virgil, is not a treatise but a poem of praise. Since praise emphasizes virtue rather than logical refinements, it is proper that virtue should come first. As the commentary proceeds, the full import of the approach becomes apparent. The substance of the poem remains the acts of Aeneas. Since, in a proper encomium each act illustrates a particular virtue, this soon leads to allegorical intepretation. The Cyclops episode, for example, shows youthful vanity overcome by good sense. The Dido episode becomes an illustration of a young man's triumph over lust; and the descent into Hades becomes an allegory of wisdom gained by philosophical study.

After Fulgentius little was added to the theory of praise until the paraphrase of the *Poetics* made by Averroes in the thirteenth century. Averroes labored under numerous difficulties, not the least of which was the fact that he had never read a Greek play and had only the haziest notion of what a tragedy was. Yet his paraphrase was accepted in Europe at face value.[28] It was translated into Latin in 1256 and survives in no less than twenty-three manuscripts scattered throughout Europe.[29] The prestige of the paraphrase is indicated by the fact that there existed a quite good translation of the *Poetics* made in 1278 by William of Moerbeke, but that this translation survives in only two manuscripts.[30] The subsequent history of the paraphrase indicates that it remained popular. It was published in 1481 by Philippus Venetus, thus becoming the first version of the *Poetics* to be printed. Other editions, most of them based on Latin translations of Hebrew versions, appeared in 1515, 1525, 1550, 1560, and 1574.[31]

The paraphrase begins with an emphatic reduction of all poetry to the epideictic category: "Every poem and all poetic discourse is blame or praise. And this is evident from examination of the poems themselves, which concern matters of will—the honorable or the base."[32]

Later the idea is developed in more systematic fashion. The following quotation will give an idea of the direction of Averroes' thought: "And because makers of representations and imitations intend through this [poetry] to impel to certain actions which involve the will and to repel [from others], those subjects will of necessity be . . . either virtues or vices. For all action and all morality is concerned with . . . virtue or vice. . . . And therefore the good poets occupied themselves in praise and not in blame. And conversely, the others in blame, not in praise. And therefore in imitation there are these two different modes. . . ."[33]

Averroes' ideas resemble those of Donatus and Fulgentius so closely that one is tempted to suspect a common influence. Had the paraphrase added only the magic name of Aristotle to the theory of praise it would be a significant document. It added something more. Donatus and Fulgentius were apologists defending a specific poem. At best their comments apply only to epic. The paraphrase, however, purports to discuss all literary genres and to give a general definition of imitation. In it the theory of praise is converted from a special plea for a single type of poetry into a general theory of criticism.

To follow the subsequent development of the theory of praise we must turn to Italy. There literary criticism tended to follow two independent lines. The early Florentine humanists drew on Platonic, Horatian, and late classical tradition. They frequently referred to epic and lyric as kinds of praise, but their references are rather like Plato's own—indicative of a bias rather than a self-conscious system. The inheritors of the Averroistic tradition, on the other hand, followed the Averroes paraphrase. The difference can be illustrated by contrasting Petrarch to Benvenuto da Imola and Coluccio Salutati.

Petrarch's fondness for praise is evident throughout his work. His fifth sonnet ("Quand'io movo i sospiri a chiamar voi") is an elaborate pun on Laura and Italian *laudare* and announces that the cycle will be divided between the lover's sighs and the praises of the lady. Drawing on Isidore, Petrarch traced poetry to praise of the gods; and, of course, he enthusiastically endorsed the idea that the poet is the custodian of immortal fame. His "Letter to Horace" is somewhat more explicit, for he wrote of the odes and satires, "You either excite your companions to virtue by singing deserved praise; or, slyly laughing at foolishness, bite at vice with dainty teeth."[34]

Benvenuto da Imola was less amusing but more systematic. He was something of a philosopher, for he had written an *Exposition* of Averroes' doctrine of the intellect.[35] He had also read the Averroes paraphrase. Confidently claiming "Aristotle's testimony" as his precedent, he asserted that it is "manifest to whoever contemplates the forces of poetry . . . that all poetic discourse is either praise or blame."[36] Later he cites "the commentary of Averroes" to prove that poetry is morally uplifting. His analysis of the structure of the *Divine Comedy* is particularly instructive. He believes that Dante is a supreme poet because "no other poet ever knew how to praise or blame with more excellence . . . he honored virtue and the virtuous with encomia, and lacerated vice and the vicious."[37] Viewed in these terms the *Divine Comedy* is a collection of epideictic vignettes. The *Inferno* is a long *vituperatio* or blame of vice. The *Purgatory* and *Paradise* are encomia of limited and perfect virtue respectively. Although the modern reader is likely to resent rhetorical explanations of great poetry, it is evident that praise and blame are broad enough categories so that men of Benvenuto's day—and of the sixteenth century as well—could think of them as the organizing principles of the *Divine Comedy* without feeling that Dante was thereby reduced in stature.

Coluccio Salutati (1331-1406) was a Florentine and the spiritual heir of Petrarch. This did not deter him from learning a good deal from the Averroists. The first book of the *De laboribus Herculis* is a little "ars poetica" heavily influenced by the Averroes paraphrase.[38] In fact, Salutati believed that the earliest poetry was "praise of divinity and virtue," and that modern poets are worthy to carry on the great tradition only because they "criticize vice . . . and celebrate virtue" in the way prescribed in "Averroes' little book."[39]

Several chapters of Salutati's art of poetry are devoted to reworking classical materials in conformity with the theory of praise. In Chapter II rhetoric and poetic are said to have the same "matter"—that is, to share the category of praise and blame. They are distinguishable because poetry uses "meter and imaginative and figurative discourse."[40] In Chapter XIII the tired classical definition of the orator (*vir bonus dicendi peritus*) is refurbished to apply to the poet who is "a perfect man skilled in praise and blame" (*vir optimus laudandi vituperandique peritus*). Even Horace is summoned to testify to the correctness of the theory of praise. The delight-instruction formula is explained in the following way: "The reprehension of vice may profit right away, but does not immediately please; praise pleases but does not immediately profit. Therefore blame is primarily for utility, praise for pleasure; although in a secondary way the former may please and the latter profit."[41]

IV. RENAISSANCE VERSIONS OF THE THEORY OF PRAISE

To trace all the ramifications of the theory of praise during the sixteenth century would be to write a small-scale history of Renaissance criticism. Therefore, the present survey makes no pretense of being complete. Its object is to sketch a few representative variations of the theory of praise and to demonstrate the continuity of this theory throughout the period.

The keynote of the period was struck by its most dazzling *uomo universale,* Lorenzo de'Medici, in a letter prefacing an anthology of Italian poetry which he prepared for Frederick of Aragon. Recalling Cicero's impassioned defense of literature in the *Pro Archia,* Lorenzo attributed the military and philosophical achievements of the ancients to the desire for the immortal fame conferred by the poet's praise. "Honor," he wrote, "is what provides nutriment for every art; nor are the minds of mortals inflamed to noble works by anything so much as glory."[42] To Lorenzo poets were "holy givers of praise" (*sacri laudatori*), and this note continued to dominate humanistic criticism. Indeed, in 1637, the last, and in some ways the noblest, humanist of them all, John Milton, would write, "Fame is the spur which the clear spirit doth raise . . . To scorn delights and live laborious days." That it was also for Milton "that last infirmity of noble mind" is simply a reminder of the precariousness of the humanistic compromise.

Corollary to the image of the poet as custodian of fame is the idea that the truest poetry is the poetry of praise. Critics who were sympathetic with the aims of the Florentine humanists commonly repeated this idea. Vida insisted that hymn and epic—praise of gods and heroes—surpassed all other forms of poetry, while Bernardino Daniello admitted that the philosopher-poet of his *Poetica* would often rise "like the melodious swan . . . from earth to heaven, carrying high the praises of another's virtue in sweet lyric song; or, excoriating vice . . . descend to the depths."[43] No critic of the period was destined to have more influence than Scaliger. In his *Poetics* he quite consciously invoked the Platonic-humanistic tradition to justify his high estimate of poetry: "Good fame is the reward of wise men. Thus Plato in the *Laws* made ill fame a punishment for crimes. And he says the same in the *Ion*. Poets make others what they are themselves. Thus by the art which makes them immortal they confer immortality on those whom they celebrate. So boasted Pindar; so sang Theocritus; and so say the rest."[44]

Sebastian Minturno was of the same generation and eclectic frame of mind as Scaliger. He too benefited from the "new criticism" generated by the rediscovery of Aristotle's *Poetics*. Even more than Scaliger, however, he sympathized with the ideals of the Florentine humanists. To him the basic poetic emotion is emulation (*aemulatio*), and emulation is the struggle to live up to the virtues of those who have been praised by the poets: ". . . emulation spurs good men to virtue that they may attain the praise and glory which they seek. . . . For those on whom poets or historians bestow the highest praise are indeed not without emulators."[45] At the end of the century, although the humanist tradition deteriorated, a few critics still defended it. Of these Tommaso Campanella is the most persuasive. In his *Poetics* he defends many lost causes—among them the cause of the poet-theologue—and he expresses special fondness for the poetry of praise: "If poetry is an art, it should have use in the republic . . . since it is concerned with the good rather than the truth for its own sake, it is an instrument of the legislator. Therefore it will praise good men and virtues and rebuke vice and evil men. Thus it will stabilize law and religion and pleasantly offer precepts to help the cause of the state and of amicable social relations."[46]

A more technical slant was given poetics by those critics who were concerned to reconcile it with rhetoric. Pontanus attempted to do this in the *Actius,* a dialogue on poetics composed at the end of the fifteenth century. The point of the dialogue is that both history and poetry rely on oratory. This observation leads Pontanus to many conclusions about both arts. One of the most interesting is that both are limited to two categories: "history and poetry both utilize the demonstrative [epideictic] category and also the deliberative, as is shown by their speeches and councils."[47] Again, both poetry and oratory "are forms of discourse . . . and they have praise in common, which is called the demonstrative genus, and also deliberations. . . ."[48] Since set speeches, councils and "deliberations" form only a small part of most poetic compositions, Pontanus' theory seems to emphasize epideictic rhetoric heavily. This is borne out by the remark that poetry favors "amplifications, digressions and variety"—an echo of the standard prescriptions for epideictic style.[49]

The revival of the *Poetics* naturally encouraged further discussion of praise and blame in literature. The Averroes paraphrase was a factor in this discussion, as may be demonstrated by references to Averroes in the commentaries. Partly because of the tradition encouraged by the paraphrase and partly because of the contents of the *Poetics,* all commentaries deal with praise and blame to some degree. Emphasis varies from Robortello and Castelvetro,[50] for whom epideictic concepts are secondary and enter chiefly in connection with the evolution of poetic genres, to Trissino, who referred frequently in the Aristotelian sections of his *Poetica* (Bks. V and VI, publ. 1562) to the theory of praise. Trissino's ideas are not new. His references to praise constitute a more sophisticated version of Averroes, supplemented by an acquaintance with literature which was both scholarly and practical, Trissino being a moderately successful poet.[51] The first poetry, we learn, was encomium and vituperation, from which arose the two basic 'genres' of poetry. Homer's *Iliad* and *Odyssey* were elaborations of encomium and the *Margites* of vituperation. Tragedy is the highest kind of praise, and comedy is a form of ridicule, treating vice which is not vile but merely ugly.[52] Lyric is halfway between these two forms: "such kinds of poem, that is, *canzoni, serventesi* and the rest, include both genres of poetry; that is, that of praise and admiration of better things, as in tragedy and heroic poetry, and that of execration and the blame of evil, as in comedy."[53] The result of the use of poetic devices is to create an "example, or an excellent idea, which men can imitate"—in other words, an idealized portrait.[54]

Praise continued to be discussed in connection with the *Poetics* as late as 1575. Alessandro Piccolomini's commentary, published in that year, begins with a fairly conventional attempt to place poetry among the sciences. Poetics, the art of poetry, is considered a technique (*techne*) and hence a part of the *Organon*. Its end (*fin*), however, is the improvement of mankind. This makes it a part of practical philosophy subject to the doctrines taught in ethics. In fact, "art would not be art if it did not hold some end in mind which serves and assists our lives."[55] Inevitably this leads back to the theory of praise: "While the species of poetry are diverse, they equally in their various kinds seek to bring utility and improvement to our life. By the imitation and praise of virtuous men we are inflamed and excited to virtue in order to become similar to those whose praises we heard. If we hear poetic imitation of the vices and crimes of the other sort and its expression is negative and in the form of blame, we immediately begin to be repelled and hate the vicious actions, far more excited by such imitations than by admonitions, no matter how well expressed."[56]

Many critics were unwilling to make the praise-blame formula as fundamental to poetics as it is for Piccolomini. Aristotle distinguished between six parts of drama—plot, character, diction, thought, spectacle, and melody (1450[a])—and this list was often used to organize discussions of poetry. When it was, only one of its six topics demanded treatment in terms of moral philosophy. This was character. Aristotle's term, *ethos,* and its Latin and Italian translations (*mores* and *costumi*) all point toward the ethical rather than psychological phase of character-portrayal. The way in which discussion of character led to discussion of praise is illustrated in Alessandro Lionardi's *Dialogue on Poetic Invention* (1554).[57] As the rhetorical term "invention" suggests, the dialogue is a self-conscious attempt to show how poetry and rhetoric (and history as well!) are related. As Lionardi approaches the topic of character his terminology becomes explicitly epideictic: "It is necessary that the poet know in what form and manner he ought to speak. . . . And he will take this perfection from the orator. If he treats characters or works either virtuous or vicious, he will have recourse to the demonstrative category of oratory, providing honors for virtues and dishonor for vice."[58] The extremely broad application of this principle is evident from Lionardi's list of "demonstrative" works. Among others he cites the *Symposium,* the funeral orations of Demosthenes and Plato, the *Cyropaedia* of Xenophon, and Petrarch's lyrics.[59]

Many others critics approached character in the same way. Giraldi Cinthio, for example, maintained, "In respect to conduct (*costume*) the office of our poet is to praise virtuous actions and rebuke vices and make them hateful through terror and pity. . . ."[60] Here the theory of praise leads to a definition of catharsis as the purgation of the desire to sin which Cinthio confidently attributes to "the definition which Aristotle gives of tragedy."[61] A similar position is taken by Tasso. His statement of the case is interesting for two reasons. First, it recapitulates the history that we have been following in the present chapter. And second, it was written in answer to Castelvetro. In effect it is a reaffirmation of the Christian humanist tradition. Tasso believed that character is made exemplary in literature by the techniques of praise and blame. Being essentially an epic poet, he was particularly concerned with the fate of this form. He concluded his rebuttal of Castelvetro by declaring: ". . . without doubt Castelvetro erred when he said that praise was not appropriate to the heroic poet, for if the heroic poet celebrates heroic virtue he ought to raise it to the heavens with his praises. And Saint Basil says that Homer's *Iliad* is nothing other than the praise of virtue; and Averroes has the same opinion in his commentary on poetry; and Plutarch. . . . Therefore, leaving aside the followers of Castelvetro in their opinion, we will follow the opinion of Polybius, of Damascus, of Saint Basil, of Averroes, of Plutarch, and of Aristotle himself."[62]

Tasso's remarks merit, I believe, special consideration. They confirm the history of the theory of praise as it has been presented in the present chapter. Moreover they are not the idle speculations of an academic critic. They are the comments of one of the great poets of the age, and they are obviously made with feeling. Tasso was not only aware of the tradition of praise, he valued it highly. It is fair to suppose that the *Gerusalemme liberata* reflects his feeling.

If we turn briefly to English critics of the latter half of the sixteenth century we find the same opinions that were popular in Italy. Golding's translation of the *Metamorphoses* appeared in 1567 at the beginning of the golden age of English literature. Its quality has, perhaps, been overrated, but its influence was felt from the age of Marlowe to that of Milton. Golding was at some pains to justify Ovid in view of his dubious reputation. His first defense, given in the epistle to Leicester, is that Ovid's myths are profound allegories. Ovid has not one but four levels of meaning. Of these the first three are related to natural philosophy but the fourth is moral. Golding insists that Ovid's character portrayal consists of ". . . pitthye, apt, and pleyne/ Instructions which import the prayse of virtues, and the blame/ Of vices . . ." (ll. 64-66). Later, in the epistle to the reader, the point is restated in slightly more elaborate form: ". . . under feyned names of Goddes it was the Poets guyse/ The vice and faults of all estates too taunt in covert wyse./ And likewise too extolle with prayse such things as doo deserve" (ll. 83-5).

Golding's remarks are elementary, but English critics were quick to improve their art by drawing on Italian sources. Both Spenser and Sidney were influenced by the theory of praise. George Puttenham, whose *Arte of English Poesie* appeared in 1589, based his classification of genres on praise and blame in the manner of such Italian critics as Trissino and Piccolomini: ". . . the chief and principall [type of poetry] is the laud, honour, and glory of the immortall gods . . .: secondly, the worthy gests of noble Princes, the memoriall and registry of all great fortunes, the praise of vertue, reproofe of vice, the instruction of morall doctrines, the revealing of sciences naturall & other profitable Arts, the redresse of boistrous & sturdie courages by perswasion, the consolation and repose of temperate myndes: finally the common solace of mankind in all his travails and cares of this transitorie life."[63] In this passage praise is the method of the "chief and principall" type, the hymn; and the second type is merely a paraphrase for encomium. In fact, Puttenham summarizes the standard rhetorical topics for encomium when he remarks in a later passage that princes and heroes were treated "by a second degree of laude: shewing their Princely genealogies and pedigrees, mariages, aliances, and such noble exploites, as they had done in th'affaires of peace and of warre. . . ."[64] Classical myths are considered as originally historical encomia.[65] And of poetry concerning the "inferiour sort" we learn that "inferiour persons with their inferiour vertues have a certaine inferiour praise. . . ."[66] Puttenham also discusses the poetry evolving from blame. In Chapters XIII through XVII of the *Arte of English Poesie,* satire, comedy and tragedy are grouped together as poetic types "reprehending vice."

Although it became unimportant in Italy, the theory of praise persisted in England. Milton, for example, commonly associated poetry and praise. The morning hymn of Adam and Eve in *Paradise Lost,* V, is a Miltonic symphony on the theme of "Laudate nomen." Milton thought of the elegiac poets that it was "the chief glory of their wit, in that they were ablest to judge, to praise, and . . . to love those high perfections which under one or other name they took to celebrate. . . ." And considering his own aspirations and talents he hoped, "with more love or virtue" to choose "the object of not unlike praises."[67] The last we hear of the theory of praise in English criticism is David Hume's offhand remark, "All polite letters . . . inspire us with different sentiments, of praise and blame."[68]

The theory of praise is one of the most persistent of critical traditions. Originating in the Greek ideal of *paideia,* receiving indirect—and doubtless unintentional—support from Aristotle's *Poetics,* it achieved the status of a system when combined with the technical lore of epideictic rhetoric. During the Middle Ages its effects are evident in both practice and theory. It received particular emphasis in the paraphrase of the *Poetics* by Averroes. It entered the Renaissance in two ways—first via late classical and medieval sources; and second via Averroes and such intermediary authors as Benvenuto da Imola and Salutati. In the early sixteenth century the late classical and medieval influences predominated. Later, Aristotle—and with him Averroes—became important. Finally there appeared eclectic critics who drew on the humanistic tradition but were also well-schooled in Aristotle. Minturno and Tasso are the best of these. Their work summarized some of the most typical ideas of Italian criticism at the moment of its decline and transmitted them to northern Europe. The theory of praise was transmitted in this way, and it continued to interest poets long after Italy had sunk into the sterilities of Marinism and the banalities of the Arcadia.

CHAPTER III

The Scope of Didactic Criticism

It is probably fortunate that during the sixteenth century poetry was continually under attack. Zealots, reformationists, counter-reformationists, Jesuits, Puritans, educators, politicians, and men in the street all at various times hacked lustily on the fair body of Lady Art, and critics were forced to range widely in order to reassemble her dismembered parts. The result was that criticism gained the status of a professional discipline. The richness of its material was immeasurably increased, and its major questions became codified, a fact reflected in such formal surveys as Francesco Patrizi's *Della poetica, la deca disputata* and Benedetto Fioretti's *Progynnasmi poetici,* both of which are organized around standard topics and develop them by quoting authorities *pro* and *con*.

Plato's attack on poetry in the *Republic* furnished its enemies with much of their ammunition. Therefore, early in the sixteenth century refutation of the Platonic charges became a standard part of the full-scale defense of poetry. The charges were codified under three headings. First there was the charge that poetry lies. Second there was the charge that poetry excites the passions and leads impressionable readers down the primrose path. Third there was the charge that poetry—being a third-degree imitation of reality—is inherently trivial; no matter how pleasing it may be, it is no fit occupation for the serious man.

In answering these charges didactic critics were forced to a theory of imitation explaining the relationship of poetry to history, ethics, and philosophy respectively. This fact is reflected in the organization of numerous Renaissance defenses and eulogies of poetry. Sidney's *Defense of Poetry* is a case in point. The work is organized on the pattern of the classical oration.[1] Its second section, which defines the character of poetry, devotes one of its paragraphs (#3) to the fact that philosophers have been poets, one (#4) to historians as poets, and six (#5-10) to the fact that under the titles of *areytos, vates,* and *maker* the poet has always been considered a teacher. Part V develops these ideas in detail by showing how the poet excels the historian (esp. # 18, 23, 24) and the philosopher (#20, 21, 22) and teaches virtue (#19, 20, 25, etc.). In Part VI, which corresponds to the *refutatio* of the classical oration, four major objections are listed. These are first, "that there [are] many other more fruitefull knowledges"; second, that poetry is "the mother of lyes"; third, that it infects us "with many pestilent desires"; and fourth that "Plato banished [poets] out of hys Common-wealth."[2] Answering these charges leads to reiteration in modified forms of the arguments in Part V: the poet teaches useful knowledge by moving to virtue; the poet is not a liar but transcends historical truth; right poetry does not arouse improper passions; and Plato only objects to the abuses of the poets. It is fair to say that the Platonic charges account for the basic organization and most of the substance of Sidney's argument.

A significant fact about Sidney's presentation of his case appears to have escaped notice. At the beginning of Part V he proposes "to weigh this latter sort of Poetrie by his works, and then by his partes . . . " (#17). The poetry referred to is that "fayning notable images of vertues, vices, or what els, with . . . delightfull teaching" (#16). The term *works* may be interpreted to mean "moral effects," and *parts* to mean *genres.* Sidney's transition from *works* to *parts* repeats these terms, parenthetically summarizing the gist of what has been said about *works:* "But I am content not onely to decipher him by his workes (although works in commendation or disprayse must ever holde an high authority), but more narrowly will examine his parts. . . ."[3]

Sidney's parenthesis recalls the theory of praise. It is casual—so casual that it can be overlooked—but its very casualness suggests how natural it was to Sidney and his readers. For the modern reader, however, it comes as a surprise. Praise is mentioned in Part V, but there is no suggestion before the transition sentence that Sidney's idea of *works* (moral effect) of poetry depends heavily upon praise and blame.

Yet Sidney is as typical of his age in drawing on the theory of praise to answer the charges against poetry as he is in selecting the charges themselves. Plato had specifically exempted the poetry of praise from banishment, and there was, as we have seen, a solid tradition associating poetry with epideictic rhetoric. It was natural for sixteenth-century critics to draw upon and develop the theory of praise when answering Plato's charges. To follow this development, and to understand how Sidney could think of his discussion of *works* in terms of "commendation and disprayse," we must examine the historical, ethical, and philosophical defenses of poetry as they were commonly formulated by Renaissance critics.

I. POETRY AND HISTORY

Plato's attack on poetry opens in Books II and III of the *Republic.* The burden of the remarks in these two books is that poetry lies because it spreads slander concerning the gods and heroes upon whose worship the ideal state is to be based. A typical expression of this sentiment is found in the dialogue between Socrates and Adeimantus, where the former explains what poems he would ban:

> Those, I said, which are narrated by Homer and Hesiod, and the rest of the poets, who have ever been the great story-tellers of mankind.
>
> But which stories do you mean, he said; and what fault do you find with them?
>
> A fault which is most serious, I said; the fault of telling a lie, and what is more, a bad lie.
>
> But when is this fault committed?
>
> Whenever an erroneous representation is made of the nature of gods and heroes,—as when a painter paints a portrait not having the shadow of a likeness to the original.[4]

It can be seen from these remarks that Plato does not specifically identify lying with fiction. In fact, Socrates has just commented, ". . . let the censors receive any tale of fiction which is good, and reject the bad. . . ." What seems to constitute the lie in the Platonic sense is the attribution of moral flaws to figures who are supposed to be ideal, as was the practice of both epic and tragic poets. On the other hand, the temptation to equate lying with the creation of fiction was naturally very great. Even in the quotation from the *Republic* the reference to "a portrait not having a likeness to the original" implies some sort of criterion whereby the poetic "lie" is related to deviation from historical truth; and this idea was inevitably emphasized by Aristotle's remark, "It is Homer who has chiefly taught other poets the art of telling lies skillfully," as well as by his equation of poetry and "making"—i.e., creating plots.[5] Thus in later attacks on poetry, the specifically Platonic charge of slander was broadened to include any perversion of truth, from making the gods seem undignified to the invention of fable.

Plutarch and Petronius agreed that one of the special virtues of the poet is his ability to lie convincingly.[6] However, zealous Christians often thought that the ability to lie was anything but a virtue. In his work on *The Vanity and Uncertainty of the Sciences* (1531; many later eds.), Cornelius Agrippa reminded his readers that "St *Austin* calls Poesie the Wine of Error, quaft only by drunken Doctors. St. *Jerome* also calls Poesie the Meat of the Devils."[7] For his own part, Agrippa suggested that poetry should be defined as *"the female Architect of falshood, and the preserver of idle and fond opinions."*[8] Not to be outdone, a native English Puritan complained,

"The writers of our times are so led away with vainglory, that their endeavor is to pleasure the humor of men; and rather with vanity to content their minds, than profit them with good example. The notablest liar is become the best poet; he that can make the most notorious lie, and disguise falsehood in such a way that he may pass unperceived, is held the best writer."[9]

If poetry lies, it is natural to turn to history as the best source of truth. This fact generated a standard debate in Renaissance criticism over the part which history should play in poetry.[10] On the one hand there are the principles outlined in Chapter IX of the *Poetics*. The poet, Aristotle says, is a "maker" of plots and hence a writer of fiction. The essence of poetry is "fable" rather than history, so that Herodotus versified would still be denied the name of poetry. Comedy is pure fiction, and even though tragedy utilizes traditional legends, it, too, is fictional because it is based on universal probability rather than the particulars of history. In fact, the *Antheus* of Agathon uses both fictitious names and incidents and yet manages to be an excellent tragedy. The subsequent elaboration of these ideas—with greater or lesser fidelity to Aristotle—is too involved to be discussed here, but it can be conveniently followed in Benedetto Fioretti's *Progynnasmi poetici,* Book V. In Chapter II of this Book, Fioretti cites numerous authorities, classical and modern, who insist that poets should base their works on history; and in the following chapter authorities are quoted who take the Aristotelian position in favor of fiction.

Only a few critics were willing to defend fiction *per se*. While many proclaimed the right of the author to invent fables, not until late in the sixteenth century do we find serious critics (like Mazzoni) insisting that fiction alone is the material of poetry. To a majority of Renaissance critics, including many who insisted on the need of "fable," the most noble forms of poetry are intimately related to history. The *Iliad,* for example, was generally considered historical. The critics cited by Fioretti (V, ii) as favoring the connection of poetry and history argue that their position is vindicated by the "eyewitness" accounts of the Trojan War by Dares and Dictys, which prove Homer's accuracy.[11] In similar fashion, the materials of the Greek and Roman tragedians were usually considered historical. Not only was there a long critical tradition to the effect that tragedy must be "grounded upon a true History, where the greatness of a Known Person, urging Regard, doth work the more powerfully upon the Affections,"[12] but there was also a widespread and venerable tradition of euhemerization—the theory that the classical gods and demi-gods were originally historical persons about whom legends gradually accumulated. Castelvetro and Bacon both subscribed to this idea, and Puttenham remarked concerning poems about the "great Princes and dominators of the world," "Such personages among the Gentiles were *Bacchus, Ceres, Perseus, Hercules, Theseus,* and many other, who thereby came to be accompted gods and halfe gods or goddesses (Heroes), & had their commendations given by Hymne accordingly, or by such other poems as their memories was thereby made famous to the posterities for ever after. . . ."[13]

Epic and tragedy are, of course, only two of many poetic forms, but they are the forms in which Renaissance critics were most interested, and they are also the forms in which the problem of "fable" is most evident. Most other forms—Patrizi listed sixty-four in his effort to prove that "favola" is unnecessary to poetry—are either occasional or in some other way closely related to real events, comedy being the major exception to the rule.[14] This fact is strongly reflected in critical judgments of the *Cinquecento*. Pontanus, following Quintilian, argued that poet and historian were closely related, the difference being that the poet has greater liberty to embellish and ornament his material.[15] A roughly parallel position was taken by such humanistic critics as Minturno, Tasso, Vossius, and Sidney. Other critics were less willing to compromise, and a tendency to vacillate between the claims of history and fable is particularly noticeable in commentaries on the *Poetics*. Robortello, for example, announced at the beginning of his commentary that "Since poetry has as its special material fictional and fabulous speech (*orationem fictam et fabulosam*), it is clearly a part of poetry's task aptly to make up fable and lies; and creating lies is not more proper to any other art than this one."[16] Yet in a later section he appears to advocate the use of history in poetry: "If events with the appearance of truth move us, true events will move us much more. Verisimilar events move us because we believe that a thing happened the way it might have happened. True events move us because we know a thing happened thus and so; therefore whatever power resides in verisimilitude, that power is wholly derived from truth."[17]

The reason for the inconsistency is apparent. Tradition sanctioned the use of history by poets, and it was regularly a postulate of defenses of poetry. On the other hand, fidelity to Aristotle seemed to require emphasis on fiction. Castelvetro sided with tradition when he described poetry as "deriving its whole light from history"[18] and made this a basic principle of his *Poetica d'Aristotele*. Occasionally, however, his text proved stronger than his principles, as when he asserted that "with good reason Lucan, Silius Italicus, and Girolamo Fracastoro in his *Joseph* are to be removed from the ranks of the poets and denied the glorious title of [writing] poetry; for they have treated material in their writing presented first by the historians, and when it was not treated first by historians, still, it happened first and was not imagined by them."[19] A similar uncertainty is apparent among critics who were strongly influenced by Aristotle. Scaliger admitted Lucan to the ranks of the poets on the assumption that verse, not fable, is the essence of poetry, but he also considered comedy the finest type of poetry because it is wholly "invented."[20] Ben Jonson was being a good Aristotelian when he wrote that the poet is "not he which writeth in measure only, but that feigneth and formeth a fable, and writes things like the truth."[21] Yet one of Jonson's most cherished articles of faith is that serious literature—especially tragedy—depends for its effect upon "truth of narrative," a fact which is most evident in the meticulous annotations to his *Catiline*.[22]

Typically, the contradictory claims of history and fable were settled by compromise. Fioretti and the majority of critics cited by him as favoring the use of history in poetry believed that the poet must select his material from history and then exercise "invention" to create new episodes, digressions, and other ornamental embellishments. This process is explained at length by Tasso in the second book of the *Discorsi* (1594). Tasso's first principle is that poetry—and especially epic—should be based on history. This will make it credible to the readers. Critics like Piccolomini, who defended fiction, and Mazzoni, who suggested that poetry is "phantastic imitation," are refuted. But poetry is not simply versified history. The poet should select an area of history that is half-legendary in order to allow himself ample scope for descriptions, inventions, and, above all, "the marvelous"—i.e., miracles, supernatural agents, and the like. As a poet faced with the problem of locating a suitable epic subject, Tasso found the crusades ideal. Their history was reasonably well-established, and there existed in addition to the history a large mass of fabulous, legendary, and romance material suitable for exploitation by the poet. Furthermore, the fact that the history involved was Christian history would make the epic marvels credible; they would be understood as miracles.[23]

Let us now recall Plato's admission of "hymns and praises of famous men" to the *Republic*. Of the many reasons for this license one is especially clear. Neither hymns nor encomia can be accused of lying. The former are wholly true, being based on theology, and the latter are as true as the records of history and the Platonic censor allow them to be. Rhetorical prescriptions for praise emphasized its reliance on history. The topics of *effictio* included such historical facts as race, nation, family, strength, and appearance of the person praised; while the *notatio* called for narration of his famous deeds. Practically speaking, the deeds (*gesta*) formed the major portion of the praise, giving it the form of a biography. Specific epideictic types such as the "praise of a ruler" (*basilikos logos*) or panegyric simply modified these topics to fit the specialized subject.[24]

Renaissance critics involved in the defense of poetry tended to follow Plato's lead. The simplest illustration of this is the tendency of discussions of poetry to emphasize hymns and praise of famous men, and to include as much poetry as possible under these rubrics. Gosson was an unimaginative moralist and his *School of Abuse* repeats the Platonic idea in its crudest form: "The right use of auncient poetry was to have the notable exploytes of worthy captaines, the holesome council of good fathers, and the vertuous lives of predecessors set down in numbers, and sung to the instruments at solemne feastes, that the sounde of the one might drag the hearers from kissing the cup too often, and the sense of the other put them in minde of things past, and chaulke out the way to do the like."[25]

This theory (if it can justifiably be called a theory) is worth noting only because it defines the extreme. A much more liberal argument is found in Patrizi's *Deca disputata,* in the chapter "Whether Poetry Can be Formed from History" ("Se d'istoria formar si possa poesia"). Here the reader is given a point-by-point rebuttal of Chapter IX of the *Poetics,* beginning with Aristotle's idea that Herodotus in verse would be history rather than poetry. After criticizing Aristotle's logic, Patrizi turns to the fact that much ancient poetry, including the poems of Homer, is based on history. To prove this he first cites evidence that the Trojan War really happened. Then, as further evidence, he quotes two passages in which Plato commends the poets who "praise many things which really happened."[26] Since the passages from Plato link ancient historical poetry with praise, it was logical for Patrizi to read it as praise. In the *Deca istoriale,* the part of Patrizi's work which traces the history of poetry, the same two passages are quoted to show that *Eroiche* (epics, particularly those of Homer) are essentially poems in praise of heroes that arouse men to virtue.[27] Thus the theory of praise is invoked by Patrizi to account for both the historical basis of poetry and the special ends to which the poet shapes his historical materials.

Although Patrizi applied Plato's comments to epic, their author appears to have had lyric forms—hymns and odes—in mind. This may explain why Renaissance comments on lyric often have an especially strong epideictic bias. Isaac Casaubon recalled Plato when he wrote of ". . . that poetry which the most ancient men used at the altars of the gods when they sang their praises. It cannot be doubted that this is the most ancient and noblest kind of poetry . . . and Plato seems to have understood this; when he expelled poets from the Republic, he only retained the writers of hymns. . . ."[28] And although Sidney does not mention Plato explicitly in this connection, the comment in the *Republic* is echoed in his definition of lyric as the form "who with his tuned Lyre and wel accorded voyce giveth praise, the reward of vertue, to vertuous acts . . . who giveth morrall precepts and naturall Problemes, who sometimes rayseth up his voice to the height of the heavens, in singing the laudes of the immortall God."[29]

The same influence is evident in a revival of the ancient distinction between melic and Doric poetry.[30] During the Renaissance the distinction was given a new and characteristic interpretation in which the major criterion was the difference between (noble) lyrics praising gods and heroes and (ignoble) ones dealing with love and the Good Life. Giordano Bruno suggested the myrtle and laurel as symbols of the two forms: "Those who sing of love boast and can boast of myrtle. . . . Those who worthily sing of heroic subjects can boast of laurel."[31] For Vossius the distinction resolved itself into the difference between song (*carmen*) and poetry (*poesis*): "Thus initially [poets] treated in part love not imagined (*fictos*) but true through *song;* while *poetry* seems in the beginning to have treated partly praise of god and partly the acts of outstanding men."[32] Gabriello Chiabrera is probably a more significant witness to the practical influence of Renaissance theory than either Bruno or Vossius. In his own day he was a highly-regarded poet, and his criticism seems to be a by-product of the problems which presented themselves to him during composition. His chief accomplishment was the perfection of the Italian Pindaric, and his discussion of the two forms of lyric (which may be termed *lyric* and *quasi-heroic*) shows that praise was an essential ingredient of the form which he preferred: " . . . we can affirm as true that the manner of poetry-writing which is called lyric is wholly of love and good times (*conviti*) and its material is that which has the power to delight. . . . I do not deny, however, that the lyric poet praises knights and noble personages. Nor is praise written in this manner to be placed outside of the confines of lyric which versifies with somewhat greater dignity, it is true, but not yet with the elevation of epic versifying."[33]

Among the English critics, Webbe suggests a division between the *vates,* who carries on the tradition of poetry as hymns and praise of famous men, and the *poeta,* who strives only to delight.[34] And the eclectic Puttenham places the "laud of heroes" in the highest category while love lyric is relegated to the meanest category (poems of "common solace"), ". . . used for recreation onely, [which] may allowably beare matter not alwayes of the gravest or of any great commoditie or profit, but rather in some sort vaine, dissolute, or wanton, so it be not very scandalous & of evill example."[35]

Most critics grudgingly accepted this "vaine, dissolute, or wanton" poetry because it comprised a very large proportion of the lyric production of the sixteenth century, but Quintilian had rejected love elegy from his curriculum and he was followed by many Renaissance educators. Certainly there was never any question about which type of poetry is the nobler.[36]

A curious reminder of the close relationship between history and praise in the sixteenth century is the tendency to emphasize the epideictic element in formal history. This was encouraged by the fact that many ancient biographies—the *Cyropaedia* is the example most frequently mentioned—are frankly "panegyrical."[37] That is, they are idealized rather than factual, and they are intended to instruct. Cornelius Agrippa took a page out of the rhetoric books when he defined history as "a Narration of Actions, either with praise or dispraise, which declares and sets forth the conduct and event of great things . . . for that by the examples of great things, it both incites the best of Men, out of a desire of Immortal Glory, to undertake great and noble Actions, and also for fear of perpetual Infamy, it deters wicked Men from Vice."[38] Pontanus made the same point in his dialogue *Actius,* where he described the historian as "assuming the character of a judge" in order to deal out praise and blame.[39] Both Pontanus and Agrippa are minor figures who wrote before Italian criticism had fully matured. Therefore, it is interesting that Scaliger also recognized the affinity of the historian to the epideictic orator: "The orator praises someone. He cannot do this without narration of life, family, and nation. This he shares with the Historian. The latter often adds maxims: as we read concerning Camillus, Scipio, Hannibal, Jugurtha, Cicero: and he, as it were, interposes his decrees."[40]

It is hardly necessary to add that the combination of poetry, history, and praise was important in Renaissance poetry, particularly epic. *Italia liberata dai Goti, Gerusalemme liberata,* the *Franciade,* the *Lusiads,* and *The Faerie Queene* all deal with quasi-historical materials, all have as one objective the glorification of nation or a ruling family, and all present the reader with idealized patterns of virtue.

From both the critical and practical standpoint, then, one result of the Platonic charge that poetry lies was a counter-stress on those of its forms which are historical. Since epideictic literature is by nature historical and since Plato had approved it, there was a natural tendency to include as much poetry as possible in the epideictic category.

II. ETHICS AND POETRY

The idea that poetry depends on history was occasionally valuable as a defense, but understood literally it is a critical strait-jacket. Only when modified by the ethical requirements which didactic critics agreed poetry should meet did it become a significant and flexible element of critical theory.

Plato's second objection to poetry—and for many enemies of poetry the most damning of all charges—was that poetry fails to inculcate moral virtue. Unlike philosophy, poetry arouses emotion, and poetic emotions, according to Plato, tend to be perturbing or hedonistic. Again, however, the poetry of praise is an exception. This type of poetry is no less "emotional" than other types, but the emotion that it arouses is socially useful. In the *Protagoras* the poetry of praise is admitted to the ideal curriculum because it creates images of ideal virtue and stimulates desire for emulation in the young: " . . . the words of the great poets . . . [the student] reads sitting on the bench at school; in these are contained many admonitions, and many tales and praises and encomia of ancient famous men which he is required to learn by heart in order that he may imitate them and desire to be like them."[41]

The emotion generated by praise is thus not "perturbation" but desire for virtue. Whether this desire is based on vanity—the desire to be glorified in poetry like the hero of the school poem—or something more inherently noble, it manifests itself in an effort to "imitate." These ideas are the same ones offered in justification of their speeches by epideictic orators like Isocrates, Pliny, and Julian the Apostate; and by theorists from Aphthonius and Menander to Cicero, Quintilian, and the rhetoricians of the classical decadence.[42] The epideictic oration based on praise selects an inherently noble man. It stresses moral qualities (the *notatio*) and thereby creates a pattern of virtue made particularly attractive through the use of a ceremonial style. The listener's admiration is aroused and, by a simple transition, his desire to imitate the man described. Citizens are made better in character and the state flourishes. Conversely, the oration of blame (*vituperatio*) creates patterns of vice and makes them so unattractive that the citizen desires to avoid them in his own life.

Plato's remarks in the *Republic* encouraged the wholesale transfer of these concepts into literary criticism. This resulted in a characteristic theory of poetic emotion and is reflected in a frequently repeated set of critical terms. While there is nothing like perfect consistency and specific terms vary from critic to critic and language to language, there is enough repetition to make it worth while to list them. The listing technique is admittedly sketchy, but it has the advantage of presenting the terms as mutually related, rather than in isolation from each other.

The poetic hero is usually described as an "image," "pattern," or "example" of virtue, with emphasis in epic on the virtues of fortitude, wisdom, and (in Christian poetry) piety.[43] In order to make the "example" attractive the poet clothes it with "magnificence" which, as Tasso explains, can be created by elevated conception or ornaments of style or both.[44] This creation in turn arouses "admiration"—a term which persists unchanged through Latin, Italian, French, and English criticism, and which was early associated with literary matters in a discussion by Cicero of the effects of an epideictic speech.[45] Finally, admiration begets "emulation" or the desire to "imitate" the poet's hero by conforming to the pattern of virtue which he exemplifies.[46]

A characteristic set of terms also became associated with forms of poetry deriving from *vituperatio,* but these are less uniform than the terms related to praise. For one thing, there was disagreement as to whether tragedy was a form of praise or of blame. The Aristotelian tradition, particularly after it passed through such distorting lenses as the paraphrase of Averroes and derivative works like Salutati's *De laboribus Herculis,* treated tragedy as a form of praise, a *carmen laudativum.*[47] On the other hand, the tradition deriving from Theophrastus and usually incorporated in sixteenth-century didactic criticism insisted that tragedy is an image of noble figures overwhelmed by catastrophe.[48] Since the catastrophe was interpreted as a consequence of the hero's moral flaw, the tragic form could be interpreted as an example warning against this flaw and consequently a derivative of *vituperatio.* As Sidney put it, "Tragedy . . . openeth the greatest wounds, and showeth forth the Ulcers that are covered with Tissue, that maketh Kings feare to be Tyrants, and Tyrants manifest their tyrannicall humors."[49] After the numerous variations and inconsistencies of Renaissance theories of tragedy are admitted, there is enough uniformity to warrant mention of a few particularly common terms. The didactic critic usually interpreted the tragic hero as an "example" or "image" less noble than the epic hero since his excellence is diminished by his tragic flaw. The treatment of the protagonist is by a form of "rebuke" (the term is Puttenham's) which is designed to create "abhorrence" or "horror" in the audience.[50] Frequently catharsis was explained as the purgation of the desire to sin by means of "horror" or "terror," and occasionally this idea was read into the *Poetics.*[51] Comedy is a lesser from of "rebuke" which uses "ridicule" to expose minor "vices and follies" and make them unattractive.[52]

The term "example" is the most important of those listed in the preceding paragraphs and was pervasive in sixteenth-century discussions of literature. Even history was frequently valued not so much for its facts as for its examples of virtue and vice, as preface after preface testifies.[53] At the beginning of the sixteenth century Savonarola attempted to demonstrate that the distinguishing technique of poetry (the "poetic syllogism") is example.[54] His purpose was to deflate the pretensions of poetry by assigning to it the weakest of all forms of proof. Later critics often circumvented this problem by treating example as a rhetorical rather than a logical device. In the *Organon,* example is an imperfect form of syllogism which cannot be used for rigorous demonstrations. However, in rhetoric, where the purpose is persuasion rather than formal proof, example is one of the most effective of devices. Since moralists wanted to reform society rather than speculate on niceties, they felt that poetry's use of example made it especially excellent. Speaking of early poetry Minturno remarked that "the people had to be instructed and made virtuous; not by the precept of the philosophers but by examples, which not historians but poets provided."[55] Generally, the didactic critics of the sixteenth century agreed with Minturno. Varchi believed that poetry's "means or instrument is example";[56] and whereas he admits that example is a weak logical form, he insists on its power to move to virtue. Tasso boasted that "the highest end [of poetry] is to aid mankind with an example of human actions."[57] Giordano Bruno divided poets into philosophers and those who praise noble spirits "celebrating them and making them into an exemplary mirror (*specchio exemplare*) for political and civil acts."[58] Sidney's poet also "coupleth the generall notion with the particuler example";[59] and Milton spoke of poetry as "teaching over the whole book of sanctity and virtue, through all the instances of example."[60]

To the rhetorician, example can be either a limited figure of speech, useful in clarifying a hard point, or something much broader which might be labeled an *exemplum* or exemplary narrative. It is in the latter sense that "example" became an important sixteenth-century critical term. When the exemplary narrative is considered as a self-sufficient unit—that is, a separate speech—it is necessarily epideictic. It cannot be forensic or deliberative, for it has no relationship to legal problems or parliamentary debate. More important, the process of composing an exemplary narrative is that of composing an epideictic oration. The rhetorician who makes an exemplary narrative from the life of a great man must do two things. First he must relate the important facts of his biography using as a guide the topics of the *efficio* and *notatio*. Second, the author must present the facts in such a way as to stress their excellence, and he does this by using the techniques of praise. The result, if carried out fully, is a work such as the *Cyropaedia* of Xenophon or the *Evagoras* of Isocrates. For convenience, I will call the poetic form of exemplary narrative a *pictura*.[61]

It is already clear that when Renaissance critics speak of "example" in poetry, they usually mean exemplary narrative or *pictura*. Several other terms were also used in the sense of *pictura*. Citation of a few of the more common ones will illustrate the ubiquity of the concept, as well as the diverse traditions that appeared at the time to justify its use in criticism. There is, for example, a very close relationship between *pictura* and the analogy between poetry and painting which is found in Simonides, Horace, Petronius, and other classical writers. Daniello wrote, ". . . Poetry was compared by the wise ancients to a picture; and the picture was said to be nothing other than a tacit and mute poem; and conversely, poetry [was] a speaking picture. Just as the imitation of the painter is done with styli and brushes, and with diversity of colors . . . so, that of the poet is done with the tongue, with the pen, with numbers and harmonies."[62] The quotation indicates that the common element in poetry and painting is the image of the subject. The visual image is created with brush and color, while the verbal image must be created by description or biographical details or both. Minturno, making the same comparison, equated the *imago* of the painter with the *exemplum* of the poet, stressing the poet's ability to create moral patterns: ". . . the excellent painters are to be imitated, so that—just as they depict their subjects as more handsome than they are, intent on expressing an image (*imaginem*) both proper and verisimilar—the poet (as I have often advised), intent on describing men who are magnanimous, timid, industrious, base, mild, wrathful, and the rest . . . , seeks for himself an *example* (*exemplum*) from its respective species. Thus in Achilles Homer depicted warlike and ferocious power; and in Aeneas Virgil depicted piety and fortitude."[63]

If the *pictura* was often compared to a literal picture, it was also frequently compared to the image in a mirror. The analogy, usually attributed during the Renaissance to Cicero, was actually derived from Euanthius, who described comedy as "an imitation of life, a mirror of custom, an image of truth" and "a mirror of everyday life . . . for just as by looking in a mirror we discover the lineaments of truth, so by the reading of comedy we painlessly discover an imitation of life and customs."[64]

The basis of this metaphor is the same as that of the speaking picture. Both a portrait and a mirror present an image that is comparable to that of the *pictura*. Minturno made this point when he defined the imitator as one who "represents everything to you in a mirror," which presents "not the living thing but images of things."[65] But the mirror is more specialized than the speaking portrait. Because *mirror* connotes self-examination, a search for faults, it is particularly appropriate to a form like comedy which reflects daily life in order to correct its vices and follies. This is the sense intended by Euanthius, and it is the sense in which the metaphor enters *The Mirror for Magistrates*. The magistrate who peered into this immense and rather cloudy mirror was expected by its authors to discover his own faults and set about correcting them before his life became material for yet another dismal addition to the work.[66]

Another term for *pictura* is *idea*. Because of its Platonic associations *idea* inevitably suggests *idealization* and is thus opposite in implication to *mirror*. In its literary sense *idea* can signify both a mental image (analogous to the physical image of the picture and mirror), and the essence of that image. The two meanings fuse in the following remark by Giraldi Cinthio, where the reference to painting emphasizes the connection between *idea* and *pictura:* ". . . it seems to me that Virgil . . . imitated the excellent painters, who, wishing to form a single image which would represent female beauty, looked at all the beautiful ladies they could: and from each one took the best features . . . as many as seemed to them to suffice to create the Idea which they had in their soul. . . ."[67] On the one hand, Virgil's imitation is a portrait of Aeneas created through narration of his background and noble exploits. On the other, it is a composite of perfect features corresponding not to an historical figure but to the "idea" of epic nobility. Aeneas is thus an example of ideal nobility. Trissino was so far in agreement with this line of thought that he spoke of "an example, or excellent idea,"[68] using the two terms as synonyms. One of the questions raised in Patrizi's *Deca disputata* is whether Homer "formed Agamemnon and the other kings and captains according to the Idea of good Kings, and of good Shepherds of the people."[69]

Perhaps the most elegant term used during the sixteenth century as a synonym for *picture* is *idol* or *eidolon*. This term, which was presented as something of a novelty by Mazzoni in his second *Defense* (1587) of Dante, was traced by him to Plato's *Sophist,* and explained as meaning a feigned poetic image.[70] It is characteristic of "phantastic" poetry, which is concerned more with the credible than the true, and it is a corollary of Mazzoni's belief that poetry is a subcategory of sophistic. For Tasso the eidolon was a characteristic of "icastic" poetry (poetry based on probable truth) rather than phantastic poetry, and derived from dialectic rather than sophistic. He further explained the term by equating it with "making of images," "speaking picture," and "idea" in the Platonic sense.[71] It is clear, then, that Tasso's eidolon is a synonym for *pictura* used with special reference to the problem of poetic truth. At least in Tasso's usage it is a way of affirming that poets do not lie—that the *pictura* is based on the truth of history and/or morality.

The two concepts of historical narrative and example of virtue or vice meet in *pictura*. They are present because *pictura* has the two epideictic functions of imitating an individual and creating a pattern that will arouse emulation or abhorrence. The two functions are not, however, entirely compatible. In order to create patterns of virtue and vice the poet must often distort history. As Cinthio pointed out, the epic hero is not so much an historical personage as a composite of perfect parts, an ideal rather than a fact.

Attempts to reconcile truth and morality led to a second phase of the theory of example that may be called idealization. Idealization is inherent in all forms of praise. It is simply the result of the use of the epideictic technique of "heightening." The enemies of poetry often complained that—while poetry may not lie—it is guilty of gross flattery; while its defenders replied that idealization is essential if poetry is to be truly exemplary. Vossius argued that the detractors "say that no kind of men is more pestilent than flatterers, and no kind of men flatter more exquisitely than poets. . . . But not all praise is to be considered flattery. Often praises are deserved and worthy . . . in order that others may be excited [to make themselves] a similar example."[72]

Idealization was important because it created a link between the historical *pictura* and the fictional narrative. It was frequently introduced into criticism by the assertion that authors show men "not as they are but as they ought to be." Speaking of those very hymns and encomia which Plato admitted to the *Republic*, Minturno said that "we do not know whether [their subjects] were really as described; but we believe that they are described in the way in which they ought to have existed."[73] Trissino went somewhat further. He believed that poets intentionally write impossibilities ". . . to leave an example, or excellent idea, which men can imitate; and the example ought always to be much more excellent than that which commonly exists."[74] Castelvetro disagreed with the theory of idealization, but grudgingly admitted that, "Some believe that . . . poets and painters imitate things as they ought to be, and make them more excellent than they really are or can be . . . so that they may be an example on which people . . . ought to pattern their actions."[75]

It should be apparent that the license to write "what ought to be" rather than "what is" constitutes a justification for historical fiction. In terms of the logical categories so frequently invoked by sixteenth-century critics, pure fiction is related to sophistic and consequently is "falsehood made to seem like truth." On the other hand, to relate historical events in terms of "what ought to be" is to describe them according to the probabilities of moral philosophy. For instance, history teaches us that tyrants are sometimes successful, but moral philosophy teaches us that they ought to be failures. If the poet modifies history to make it accord with this principle, he cannot be accused of lying in the simple sense of the term. His narrative is related to dialectic rather than sophistic, and its deviations from history are instances where truth of particulars has been sacrificed for the higher truth of moral universals. For this reason humanistic critics regularly invoked the theory of idealization to justify poetic fictions. Campanella traced the invention of fable to the idealization that became necessary as poets turned from celebration of gods and heroes to more mundane subjects: ". . . it was [then] necessary to depict [their subjects] not as they were but as they ought to be. From this, fable (*favola*) evolved, in which—imitating truth—one heightens the virtue of someone, and the evil when one is critical—as Virgil did in Aeneas and Dido. Furthermore, since it was impossible to rebuke openly the vices of tyrants, it was necessary to describe them by means of fable understood only by the wise.[76] Sidney would have been in complete accord with these sentiments. Although he recognized that poets often employ history, he treated the material of poetry as a means to a moral end. Consequently, if a fiction could be as instructive as true history, it deserved to be read. The *Cyropaedia* was just the kind of historical fiction that Sidney admired, and he asked his opponents. "Now would I fayne know, if occasion bee presented unto you to serve your Prince . . . why you doe not as well learn it of *Xenophons* fiction as of the others verity . . .?"[77]

Occasionally such ideas led to a broadening of the genre of "historical poetry" to the point where it included fiction as well as history. Puttenham, for example, told his readers that "the Poesie historicall is of all other next the divine most honorable and worthy . . ." and went on to explain there are "three sorts" of history, "wholly true, and wholly false, and a third holding part of either." Thus, ". . . the good and exemplarie things and actions of the former ages were reserved only to the historicall reportes of wise and grave men. . . . These historical men neverthelesse used not the matter so precisely to wish that al they wrote should be accounted true . . . considering that many times it is seene a fained matter or altogether fabulous, besides that it maketh more mirth than any other, works no lesse good conclusions for example then the most true and veritable, but often times more. . . ."[78]

Such theories encouraged the defenders of poetry to more positive assertions. Instead of apologizing for poetic fictions, they attacked historical truths, claiming that history is at best a stringing together of facts about a worthy man or nation, but most typically a narration of suffering, war, and crime. For every Agricola there were a hundred Caligulas. Historians, of course, claimed that their discipline was moral, but as Sidney pointed out,

> . . . the best of the Historian is subject to the Poet; for whatsoever action, or faction, whatsoever counsell, pollicy, or warre strategem the Historian is bound to recite, that may the Poet (if he list) with his imitation make his own; beautifying it both for further teaching, and more delighting . . . But the Historian, beeing captived to the trueth of a foolish world, is many times a terror from well dooing, and an incouragement to unbrideled wickednes.
>
> For see wee not valiant *Milciades* rot in his fetters? The just *Phocion* and the accomplished *Socrates* put to death like Traytors? The cruell *Severus* live prosperously . . . *Sylla* and *Marius* dying in theyr beddes? . . . Historie . . . indeede can affoord your *Cipselus, Periander, Phalaris, Dionisius,* and I know not how many more of the same kennell, that speede well enough in theyr abhominable unjustice or usurpation.[79]

The depth of Sidney's conviction is emphasized by the strength of his language, but he is no more severe with history than Chapman. The "epistle dedicatory" to the translation of the *Odyssey* reduces the historian to "a poore Chronicler of a Lord Mayors naked *Truth* (that peradventure will last his yeare)" while poetry has the capacity to create a living body and a soul, ". . . wherein, if the Bodie (being the letter, or historie) seems fictive, and beyond Possibilitie to bring into Act: the sence then and Allegorie (which is the soule) is to be sought: which intends a more eminent expressure of *Vertue,* for her loveliness; and of *Vice* for her uglinesse, in their several effects. . . ."[80] In this quotation, the fundamental element remains the exemplary moral purpose. The idea of a "fictive historie" is touched on, and ultimately, behind the "expressure of *Vertue,* for her lovelinesse;

and of *Vice* for her uglinesse" is the idea of poetry as an idealizing medium which incites to virtue and repels from vice.

Two other concepts in the quotation will bear further consideration. The first one is the attitude toward verisimilitude revealed in the phrase, "beyond Possibility to bring into Act," and the second is the relationship between *example,* which we might expect from the context, and *allegory,* which is the word Chapman used.

The problem of verisimilitude is related to the rivalry between history and poetry. Chapman, translating a poem in which many episodes do violence to even the most simple-minded credulity, was forced to stress the excellence of the moral instruction in the hope of atoning for the impossibilities. This was an extreme position. The majority of critics, although they did not insist as strongly as Ben Jonson on "truth of narrative," stressed the need for preserving the illusion of truth. This position is in part foreshadowed by the discussion of "probability" in the *Poetics.*[81] However, Renaissance discussions usually ignored the *Poetics* in favor of the rhetorical theory of probability as the science of utilizing the beliefs of the crowd to gain assent or conviction.[82] This is far from the idea of aesthetic harmony that modern readers find in Aristotle, but it is the idea that Castelvetro and his French disciples of the seventeenth century invoked to justify their "rules"; and it is what readers of Horace thought was the point of the opening lines (the image of the woman-fish) of the *Ars poetica.*

Verisimilitude, however, often meant more than rhetorical probability. To Platonists, for example, it could mean the manipulation of fact to conform to *idea,* the reality behind the phenomenal. Another common view, perhaps inspired by Quintilian, was that verisimilitude is the "imitation" of the great works of the ancients, since these have demonstrated by the mere fact of survival their hold on the reader's mind. And another view was that the poet achieves verisimilitude merely by using his eyes—by being true to "Nature" as he sees it. This is a scientific view (albeit a debasement of Renaissance scientific theory). It was sometimes combined with the other views, as when Milton pondered "whether the rules of Aristotle . . . are strictly to be kept, or nature to be followed" in the composition of epic.[83]

There is in fact a confusing variety of definitions of verisimilitude. Most of the confusion vanishes, however, if we consider objective rather than method. For while authors disagreed on how to achieve conviction, they agreed that some sort of conviction is necessary if the poet is to succeed. Didactic critics went further. For them "willing suspension of disbelief" would have been wholly inadequate. Only if the audience *actually believes* that the events depicted are true will it be persuaded that the poet's moral lessons have practical application. Therefore, even in fiction the poet should pay lip-service to history by referring to famous men and events. The legendary history advocated by Tasso not only saves the poet from the charge of lying; it also helps to persuade the audience of the truth of the narrative and thereby insures effective moral instruction. The doctrine is a complex one in which realism, idealization, and didacticism are inextricably mixed, but throughout it testifies to the seriousness with which Renaissance critics regarded literature.

III. POETRY AND PHILOSOPHY

The question of the relationship of poetry to philosophy is complicated by two facts. First, Renaissance authors thought of philosophy in terms of Aristotle's division of the sciences. If a critic insists that poetry is a part of philosophy, the reader has to be sure which philosophy he means. The occasional suggestion that poetry is a part of theoretical philosophy has been dealt with in Chapter I. At present we need only be concerned with the way in which poetry reflects moral philosophy; that is, politics, economics, and ethics. Second, poetry can reflect moral philosophy in two quite different ways. When we say that poetry is "didactic" we normally mean that it is exemplary. This theory was developed during the Renaissance in response to attacks of moralists on poetry and has already been examined. The third of Plato's charges creates a different problem. To call poetry a third-degree imitation is not to deny that it can be exemplary. It is a way of saying that poetry is inherently trivial. It may be useful as a device for instructing the young and keeping the masses docile, but it is no fit occupation for the wise man engaged in the pursuit of the Good and the True.

The argument that poetry offers a great deal of miscellaneous information (*doctrina*) in a pleasing manner is unsatisfactory. No matter how much geography can be extracted from the *Odyssey,* Strabo is more reliable and more comprehensive. Schoolchildren and women may prefer Homer, but the serious student will soon go on to better things.

Moreover, the poetry most frequently attacked by the philosophers was fabulous poetry. In works like the *Odyssey,* the *Aeneid,* and the *Metamorphoses* the *doctrina* is all but concealed by the fable. For such poetry a special defense was needed. The most common one is suggested by Chapman's idea that in the *Odyssey,* "if the Bodie . . . seemes fictive, and beyond the Possibility to bring into Act: the sence then and Allegorie . . . is to be sought." Chapman's appeal to allegory is understandable in the light of Renaissance feeling about verisimilitude. There can be no question of credibility in the *Odyssey,* which shares with the *Metamorphoses* the honor of being the most incredible of classical poems. But the comment is more than special pleading. In suggesting that Homer has concealed important knowledge beneath his marvelous fables, Chapman is answering the philosophical objections to poetry in a way that ignores *doctrina* and focuses on the very heart of Homer's poem, the fable.

Allegory, was, in fact, the standard answer of didactic critics to the charge that poetry is insufficiently philosophical. Daniello, who was especially concerned with the problem of the poet versus the philosopher, expressed his conclusions through the ancient metaphor comparing fable to a veil covering useful doctrine: ". . . the poet, covering some useful teaching under various fictions and fabulous veils, arouses the spirits of the listeners or readers through their hearing, and draws them to him. . . ."[84] The same comparison is found in the commentary on Alciati's emblem, "In Deo laetandum," where it is included as part of an extended definition of poetic allegory.[85] Poetry, we are told, is a kind of enigma in which truth is concealed by obscure or figurative language. There are three kinds of truth that are so concealed—physical (or scientific), ethical, and theological. The first type of truth is illustrated by Homer's depiction of Jove, Juno, Neptune, and Pluto, who represent the four elements in continual strife. The second type is revealed in the fables of Pallas and Mars, where the attempts of the passions to control the reason are represented. Finally, the fables of Coelus, Rhea, and Saturn are theological allegory in which Coelus is divine essence, Rhea, divine life, and Saturn, divine mind. The reason for these allegories is that the early poets wished to keep the people ignorant of holy mysteries.[86] The commentator quotes Cicero and Lactantius as his authorities; he might also have mentioned Augustine's *City of God*.[87] Other sources include such Neoplatonists as Proclus and Maximus Tyrius, who seems to have influenced Nash's belief that "Poetrie [is] of a more hidden & divine kinde of Philosophy, enwrapped in blinde Fables and darke stories, wherein the principles of more excellent Arts and morrall precepts of manners . . . are contained."[88]

The idea of allegory was widespread during the Renaissance because of its usefulness as an answer to philosophers, but it is a very ancient critical doctrine that antedates more rational theories of poetry; and before examining its rhetorical aspect, we should at least take brief note of its history. It originated, apparently, in primitive traditions concerning the divinity of the poet. The Greeks, for example, believed that their ur-poets, Apollo, Amphion, Linus, Orpheus, were either demi-gods or divinely inspired, and evidently similar ideas clung to the art of poetry in the comparatively rationalistic atmosphere of Plato's day. Early poets had miraculous powers. They were able to create cities, to move rocks and trees, to lead men from barbarism, and even to charm the powers of hell. They (and their successors also) wrote under the influence of a divine furor that seemed madness or drunkenness to the uninitiated, but was really the inspiration of a god.

The inheritors of these traditions naturally sought occult knowledge in mythology and early poetry.[89] Homer, Hesiod, Ovid, and Virgil were eventually allegorized, and by the fourth century, the *Psychomachia* of Prudentius initiated the long series of consciously constructed allegories discussed by Professor C. S. Lewis in *The Allegory of Love*.[90] During the Middle Ages the allegorical tradition flourished since it was often the only practical way of defending the use of pagan poets in the schools and also since the church, herself, stressed allegorical exegesis in the reading of the Old Testament. Dante's use of allegory need hardly be mentioned except as a reminder of the overpowering prestige which *The Divine Comedy* and the *Convivio* lent to allegory.

In the Renaissance, the popularity of allegory is attested by commentaries like Boccaccio's *Genealogia deorum* and Salutati's *De laboribus Herculis,* by numerous allegorical exegeses of Dante, Petrarch, Ovid, Homer, and Virgil, by the composition of allegorical poems like *The Faerie Queene,* and by commentaries like Harington's on Ariosto or Tasso's exposition of the *Gerusalemme.* Indeed, whether or not he was wholly sincere, Tasso provided a good sample of the Renaissance reading of epic when he described it as "like an animal in which two natures are joined; it is composed of imitation and allegory."[91] And so the matter rested until the combined demands of rationalism and the Protestant desire for "one simple, appropriate, and certain literal sense" in scripture gradually discredited allegorical literature.[92]

The foregoing sketch does scant justice to the complex history of the allegorical genre, but it will, I believe, be sufficient as a reminder that there existed a tendency, independent of rhetoric, which served to emphasize whatever allegorical features might develop from the relationship between rhetoric and poetry. If we now turn to rhetoric, we see allegory from a different but significant perspective. It has already been shown that one common response of critics and writers to the ethical charges against poetry was the theory of example whereby poetry was treated as an idealized image of good or an exaggerated picture of vice. Such an image is bound to be ambiguous. To what extent is it to be exemplary? And when does example cease to be example and become allegory? The confusion of the two terms is illustrated in Wilson's *Arte of Rhetorique* under the heading "of enlarging examples by copy." To explain "enlarging," Wilson cites legends of famous heroes. These are, first of all, taken from poetry rather than history. Second, they are called "fables" and "poetical narrations" as well as examples. Of Ulysses, Wilson says: ". . . what other is the painfull travaile of *Ulisses,* described so largely by *Homer,* but a lively picture of mans miseries in this life. And as *Plutarch* saieth: and likewise *Basilius*

Magnus: in the *Iliades* are described strength, and valientnesse of the bodie. In *Odissea* is set forth a lively patterne of the minde."[93]

In a discussion of *example* we might expect to find Ulysses treated as a paragon of wisdom or fortitude, but from this quotation, as well as from Wilson's literary terminology, it is clear that the term has been inadvertently extended to mean what is normally meant by allegory. The point is confirmed by the other figures cited by Wilson. Instead of examples, he lists a series of fables—Jupiter, Icarus, St. Christopher—all interpreted as allegories.

If example naturally tends to develop into allegory, this tendency is particularly strong in the case of the *pictura*. The subject matter of the *pictura* is the deeds of an individual. Since it is supposed to cause emulation of the virtue which it depicts, the individual deeds become exemplary. If these are selected and arranged to reflect various aspects of the central virtue, the narrative becomes true philosophical allegory. Justice, for example, can be represented simply by the stock exemplary figures of David, Trajan, or Constantine.[94] If, however, the idea of justice is to be developed philosophically, the protagonist must confront a series of situations in which its several aspects can be embodied. This procedure is the one which Spenser consciously followed in composing Book V (*Justice*) of *The Faerie Queene*. Spenser's *pictura* is fictitious, but it is developed through the same techniques as the *Cyropaedia* of Xenophon and the *Evagoras* of Isocrates. In the tale of Artegal, the sequence of virtuous deeds (the *gesta*) illustrates various special facets of justice. Since the deeds are "invented" they are not "history" but "fable" or "poetical narration."[95]

An extended example of this approach is provided by Tasso's explanation of *Gerusalemme liberata*. According to Tasso, Godfrey is more than an example of wisdom, piety, and fortitude, the three standard epic virtues of the sixteenth century. Faced with the practical necessity of making his poem conform to the stereotyped exemplary *pictura* in order to satisfy his persecutors, Tasso asserted that it is an allegory of the mind (Godfrey) and the body (the Christian army) attempting to attain "civil felicity." Within this large framework, each episode has a special significance. The love of Tancred and the anger of Rinaldo represent the ever-recalcitrant passions of love and wrath. The magician Ismeno signifies the force that seeks to delude "opinion," while Armida is temptation appealing to the appetite. Even the enchantments have allegorical meaning. The fire, the whirlwind, and the monsters are fallacious arguments which make honorable undertakings seem impossible; while the flowers, fountains, brooks, and nymphs are false syllogisms which make delights of the sense seem good.[96] In sum, reading the *Gerusalemme* as an example in which each episode is also exemplary converts it into an elaborate allegorical lesson in psychology.

Tasso's reading has another important effect. Whereas the poem is a romance on the literal level, with many digressions and many important characters who divert the reader from Godfrey, the allegorical reading wrenches it forcibly into the pattern of a unified biography of a representative man. This is by no means accidental. Recalling Plutarch's insistence that epic presents an "image of human life," Tasso maintained that, "since epic imitation is never anything but a resemblance and image of human action, the allegory of the epic poets is usually a metaphor (*figura*) of human life. . . . Now, the *Comedy* of Dante is a metaphor of the contemplative man, and the *Odyssey* [also] . . . but one sees civil life adumbrated throughout the *Iliad;* and again in the *Aeneid*. . . ."[97]

Underneath its veil of fable, then, Tasso's poem is a *pictura*. It is the unified biography of a single man who is a pattern of virtue. His famous deeds form the basis of the narrative. These, and the actions of minor characters, digressions, and fabulous episodes have an allegorical meaning. When properly understood they embody a systematic philosophy.

Tasso's interpretation of *Gerusalemme liberata* is, of course, a piece of *ad hoc* reasoning. One suspects that Bacon was right when he observed of many allegorical renderings, "I doe rather think that the fable was first, and the exposition devised, then that the Morall was first, and thereupon the fable framed."[98] On the other hand, it cannot be doubted that many critics took allegory seriously and saw in it a way of asserting the superiority of the poet over the philosopher. It was, for example, standard rhetorical doctrine that the orator had to use "fables" in order to make the rabble understand his point.[99] The idea rests on the assumption that teaching is best accomplished through poetic devices rather than bare exposition. It was enthusiastically adopted by Sidney: ". . . the Philosopher, setting downe with thorny argument the bare rule, is so hard of utterance, and so mistie to bee conceived, that one that hath no other guide but him shall wade in him till hee be olde . . . for his knowledge standeth so upon the abstract and generall . . . [a poet] . . . coupleth the generall notion with the particuler example. A perfect picture, I say, for hee yeeldeth to the powers of the minde an image of that whereof the Philosopher bestoweth but a woordish description. . . ."[100]

The same idea was frequently expressed by the metaphor of the sugar-coated pill or the honey-smeared glass, in which "fable" is the sweet covering and philosophy the bitter medicine. This metaphor, it should be observed, is parallel to the one in which the fable is a veil covering the lesson beneath, but the two images have almost directly opposite implications. In the veil-metaphor, the lesson is something desirable but intentionally concealed from the reader; in the honey-metaphor, the lesson is something which the reader must be taught but which would normally repel him. Thus the honey-metaphor repeats the idea that poetry is superior to philosophy. Derived from Lucretius, it appeared in such diverse Renaissance contexts as Daniello's *Poetica,* Minturno's *De poeta,* Campanella's *Poetica,* the third stanza of the *Gerusalemme,* Alciati's *Emblemata,* and elsewhere.

The attractiveness of the outer covering of poetry—the sweetness of the sugar coating—was often considered not only justifiable, but the very resource that makes poetry superior to all other disciplines.[101] By extension, this idea provides the context for emphasis on the delight element in poetry as it appears in such morally serious critics as Tasso and Fracastoro. To stress the fact that poetry delights does not mean that poets are hedonists or that poetry can be separated from morality. Rather, it means that "teaching" is too harsh a word for the pleasant process of instruction by poetry. For example, in the early *Discorsi dell'arte poetica,* Tasso said, "I admit what I think true and what many would deny; that is, that delight is the end of poetry."[102] This raises the question of what is delightful in poetry, and Tasso answered the question in several ways. Sometimes it is clever fable; sometimes it is aesthetic unity; sometimes it is fine style. All of these particulars delight insofar as they partake of the same quality—beauty. At this point, Tasso's Platonism enables him to reconcile morality with pleasure, for, like a good student of the master, he held that ". . . whatever is good is beautiful; and, reversing the order, whatever is beautiful is good."[103] The practical effects of this idea are everywhere evident in *Gerusalemme liberata,* which not only abounds in beautiful lyric passages but also is one of the great Renaissance celebrations of virtue.

Tasso's equation of goodness and beauty constitutes an answer to the philosophers which goes beyond allegorical exegesis. It is adumbrated in Aristotle's idea of poetic universality. According to Butcher, Aristotle held that art "passes beyond the bare reality given by nature, and expresses a purified form of reality disengaged from accident. . . ."[104] This idea implies much but it was the classical Neoplatonists who developed the most explicit argument against the doctrine of imitation found in the *Republic.* Plotinus, for instance, proclaimed the superiority of the fine over the mechanical arts because the former "do not simply imitate the visible, but go back to the reasons from which nature comes. . . ."[105] That is, when the carpenter makes a chair or the cobbler a shoe, he imitates the models that he finds all about him; but when the poet imitates an object, he attempts to ascend to the divine idea that is its archetype, and the result is consequently more "real" than an artifact.

Such an idea shifts the concern of the artist from moral and philosophical matters to essence. He may choose external objects as a point of departure but these are not his basic concern. If they were, he would be like the artisan. What he seeks is the idea, and in consequence he turns inward from the object to his mental conception of the object, which is closer to the archetype and was stamped there by the creator like a seal on wax, to use Ficino's metaphor.[106]

What this meant for Renaissance criticism can be seen in Giraldi Cinthio's claim that painters and poets create their pictures by collecting perfect elements from various sources and then combining them according to "the Idea which they have in their soul."[107] Minturno was equally Neoplatonic. In his discussion of imitation he rejected the ideas advanced in the *Republic.* Instead, he proposed three "kinds" of imitation of which the better (*praestantior*) kind is by means of the *species,* or "type," of the object; he believed, "it seems to me that nothing can be expressed very emphatically (*dilligenter*), whose true species does not reside in the soul of the imitator."[108] Sidney, too, was influenced by the Neoplatonists: ". . . that the Poet hath that *Idea* is manifest, by delivering them forth in such excellencie as hee hath imagined them."[109]

The fullest sixteenth-century expression of the concept is to be found in Fracastoro's *Naugerius.* Fracastoro defined the object of poetry as "the idea of the Beautiful." Like many Neoplatonists, he believed that his theory was adumbrated in the *Poetics,* and he claimed Aristotelian precedent for defining the poet as one who imitates things "not as they happen to be, sustaining many imperfections, but as they ought to be, having contemplated the universal and most beautiful idea of their maker."[110] Unencumbered by the particulars of science, the poet looks to the ultimate source of things and produces a golden world of truth far transcending the laborious and imperfect truths of the discursive philosopher.[111]

A corollary to the type of Platonism illustrated by Fracastoro is a theory of style in which ornament is functional—not a sugar-coating but the resource that expresses the poet's most profound insights. The poet who has glimpsed the "universal and most beautiful idea" must translate his vision into effective expression. To do so he must utilize the full resources of rhetoric. Fracastoro advised the poet who has discovered the "idea" to seek "all the beauties, all the ornaments of speech" and "to omit none of those devices which make speech perfect and simply beautiful."[112] More specifically, the poet must use the figures and "colors" of style, and in particular, the devices of amplification and "heightening," which lend special sublimity to a subject. Writers concerned with narrative poetry added that digressions enhanced the subject (Cinthio's defense of romance draws on this idea)[113] and treated them as a special form of amplification. Viperanus, for example, explained the fall of Troy, the wanderings of Aeneas, the death of Dido, the funeral games, and the description of Hades as "amplification" of the fable of the *Aeneid* and added, "Epic must be amplified by many episodes, for if it is not expanded by digressions, it will be sterile and flat, deprived of all delight and pleasure."[114] In discussing amplification, Viperanus compared poets to "orators, especially in the epideictic genre" (*Oratores, praesertim in genere demonstrativo*).[115] Since amplification is part of the technical vocabulary of epideictic rhetoric, and since digressions were treated as a particularly appropriate form of amplification,[116] we may detect in the preceding remarks a last echo of the theory of praise.

Although distasteful in an age dominated by aestheticism, the didactic theory of literature was tough-minded, well-informed, and remarkably comprehensive. The form which it took owed much to Plato's charges and their reformulation by his zealous disciples in church, assembly, and schoolroom. At I have tried to show, its positive features also owe much to Plato. In admitting the poetry of praise to his ideal republic and his ideal school, he encouraged the use of epideictic concepts in criticism. The problems of orator and poet are different, but many ideas first developed in epideictic rhetoric were transferred directly to poetry; and many others furnished hints as to the methods whereby poetry could be defended. When Sidney casually described the effect of poetry as "works in commendation or disprayse," he touched on a tradition that is almost forgotten now but was deeply involved in the sixteenth-century understanding of how poetry achieves its goals.

CHAPTER IV

The Major Literary Genres

When Aristotle announced in the first paragraph of the *Poetics* that he intended to "treat of poetry itself and of its various kinds, noting the essential quality of each," he suggested the possibility of studying the great works of the past for the purpose of discovering the rules and principles inherent in each form. Alexandrian criticism carried this work forward, but its potentialities were not fully exploited until the sixteenth century. Francesco Patrizi's *Della poetica, la deca istoriale* (1586) is a landmark in the history of scholarship.[1] It is a self-conscious history of poetry, making use of the mass of information recovered by humanistic research in the century before its compilation, and is the forerunner of such works as Tiraboschi's *History of Italian Literature* and Warton's *History of English Poetry*. Patrizi's history is essentially a genre-study intended to instruct the moderns in the true aims and techniques of each type: ". . . founding ourselves on history, we will be discovering the arguments and the uses of ancient poetry, and recovering from the uses the true ends, and from the ends the true forms, and from these the variety and the materials. . . . These things informed the poetry of the outstanding men of those times and can inform [poetry] in the future; and we will be forming an art of poetry based on them so that others can understand them well and can form praiseworthy new poetry."[2]

Modern scholarship has developed the historical approach with great skill and sophistication. We have histories of epic, tragedy, comedy, satire, pastoral, ode, sonnet, and other more specialized forms such as topographical poetry, tragicomedy, Senecan tragedy, revenge play, and comedy of manners. In fact, the proliferation of specialized studies suggests one weakness in the approach. This is the idea that each literary type is autonomous and self-perpetuating, and that it can therefore be studied in isolation from other types.

The deductive approach to literary genres rests on quite different assumptions, although it, too, finds its precedent in the *Poetics*. In his second paragraph Aristotle assigns poetry to the *genus* of imitation and proposes three *differentiae* for imitative arts—the medium, the objects, and the manner or mode. These *differentiae* not only distinguish poetry from other imitative arts such as music or painting; they also distinguish the individual genres of poetry. "Medium" refers to the use in poetry of rhythm, speech, and melody and their various combinations. In Aristotle's scheme "medium" supplies *differentiae* for epic, "elegiac imitations," drama, and dithyramb. "Object" refers to the status of the characters imitated, whether "better than" or "worse than" average. It provides *differentiae* for epic and tragic poetry on the one hand, and comic and satiric poetry on the other, and is an important concept in Aristotle's description of the initial division of literary genres (*Poetics,* $1448^{b}24$-$49^{a}6$). "Mode" refers to the way in which the poet presents his material. He can speak in his own voice, as in pure narrative; he can present characters acting for themselves, as in drama; or he can use a "mixed" method as did Homer.

The difficulty of applying Aristotle's *differentiae* is notorious. It puzzled Renaissance critics and has continued to vex modern students of the *Poetics*. The most satisfactory explanation of what Aristotle intended is that by Gerald Else.[3] However, we need not at present be concerned with the "true" meaning of the *Poetics*. Since our concern is with Renaissance criticism we need only note that Aristotle furnished sixteenth-century critics with non-historical principles upon which to base theories in which each major literary form was defined not in isolation, but *in relation to* other forms.

The present chapter will examine the Renaissance theory of genres with special attention to the way in which examples cited by critics illuminate this theory. It makes no pretense of replacing the work of historical critics on specific genres, but may be considered a supplement and in some ways a control for this work. Because Renaissance critics were particularly interested in the genres of epic, tragedy, and lyric, it will concentrate on these, offering a few supplementary remarks on comedy and satire.

I. THE RANKING OF GENRES

Sixteenth-century critics agreed that poetry may be broken down into the major categories of epic, dramatic, and lyric, but there was a good deal of controversy over the relative merits of the three. Critics who followed Plato and Aristotle in deriving poetry from hymns to the gods and encomia of heroes tended to ignore Aristotle's belief that evolution is a progressive movement from lower to higher forms and to rank hymn as the highest of all forms of poetry. It was generally conceded when the matter arose that the psalms are the most excellent of all poems and David the prince of poets. As Campanella wrote: ". . . since the republic has God as its end, preserver, and creator, our first poem will be sacred, as psalmody, and hymnody. Not only David but Orpheus and Homer sang praises—he of God, the others of the gods."[4]

The Renaissance evaluation of hymn results partly from piety and partly from the use of *differentiae* based on the imitator's object. If the highest type of poetry known to Aristotle is that imitating men "better than" average, poetry imitating the inconceivable excellencies of God will be more noble still. "Object of imitation" became the controlling factor in Renaissance comments on the high, mean (i.e., middle), and humble styles:

> The matters therefore that concerne the Gods and divine things are highest of all other to be couched in writing; next to them the noble gests and great fortunes of Princes, and the notable accidents of time, as the greatest affaires of war & peace: these will be all high subjectes, and therefore are delivered over to the Poets *Hymnick* & historicall who be occupied either in divine laudes or in *heroicall* reports. The meane matters be those that concerne meane men. . . . The base and low matters be the doings of the common artificer. . . . So that in every of the sayd three degrees not the selfe same vertues be egally to be praysed nor the same vices egally to be dispraised . . . but every one in his degree and decencie, which made that all *hymnes* and histories and Tragedies were written in the high stile, all Comedies and Enterludes and other common Poesies . . . in the meane stile, all *Eglogues* and pastorall poemes in the low and base stile. . . .[5]

Schematically, this yields the following system:

High Style	*Mean Style*	*Base Style*
Hymns	Comedies	Eglogues
"heroicall reports"	Enterludes	pastorall poemes
tragedies	common Poesies	

Although hymns are the "highest of all other [matters] to be couched in writing" the most important distinctions are those *between* the three styles. Hymn, epic, and tragedy all employ the high style because all are in the "better than" category of imitation. As Vernon Hall has demonstrated this arrangement is in harmony with Renaissance thought about social classes, and it is extremely widespread.[6] Because hymn is a very specialized form of poetry, Renaissance critics generally paid lip-service to its merits and then devoted major attention to the other two forms in the high style, epic and tragedy.

Traditionally, epic had been considered the noblest form of poetry and the *Aeneid* the greatest of epics. The rediscovery of the *Poetics* forced critics to take into account Aristotle's preference for tragedy, and in this case

Aristotle's own *differentiae* were invoked to refute their originator. If poetic excellence is a function of the object of imitation, the character of the poet's protagonist determines the status of his form. Epic and tragic characters were both of noble rank. However, didactic critics sharply differentiated between them. The epic hero was to be a "pattern" or "idea" of nobility whose exploits would arouse emulation. On the other hand, the tragic hero must have a flaw. Aristotle had taught that the flaw could be minor—an error of judgment—but in the sixteenth century it was generally felt that the flaw should be a moral failure and the catastrophe the instructive consequence of the failure. Daniello thought that it was "criminal rather than pitiable or fearful" to show "just and virtuous men changed into vicious and unjust men by adversity of fortune."[7] With a fuller understanding of Aristotle, Tasso still insisted that "tragedy demands characters neither [wholly] good or bad, but of a middle condition . . . epic on the other hand needs the sum of virtue in its characters."[8] This being the case, tragedy is a lower form than epic, although both are in the high style.

The formal characteristics of epic and tragedy appeared to confirm this opinion. Believing that unity, definition, and intensity are major artistic virtues, Aristotle preferred tragedy to epic. However, he admitted that "epic poetry has . . . a great—a special—capacity for enlarging its dimensions. . . . The epic has here an advantage, and one that conduces to grandeur of effect . . ." (1459^b17-31). Sixteenth-century critics felt that "grandeur of effect" was just the characteristic that should distinguish the highest literary style. Unlike tragedy, epic permitted amplifications, digressions, marvels, and ornament. Quintilian's comparison of epic to an ocean was expanded until the epic poet became a minor god creating "a sea, a form and image of the universe."[9] In Tasso's enthusiastic description the epic poet is a cousin to the "supreme Artificer" and creates a "little world" having all the variety, life, and wonder of the great world around him.[10] Since the epic hero is more noble than the tragic hero and the epic form more grand than the tragic, most critics unhesitatingly ranked epic above tragedy.

II. EPIC

Examination of Renaissance comments about epic shows that whatever else they believed, almost all critics agreed that epic is a form of praise. In the early period the idea appears as a commonplace derived from writers like Cicero, Donatus, Fulgentius, or Averroes. Politian quoted St. Basil to prove that "all of the works of Homer consist in praise of virtue."[11] Commentators on the *Poetics* found in Aristotle's discussion of the evolution of poetry from archetypal forms of praise and blame a confirmation of the idea and a means of exploiting it. Robortello, for example, explained that of the two primitive types of poetry, one was "abusive and humble; the other given to praise and grave" and added that the *Odyssey* and *Iliad* are the prime examples of the second sort.[12] Castelvetro followed suit,[13] and Trissino called the Homeric poems "grave and given to praise of great works and glorious deeds."[14] This is not a false interpretation of Aristotle, but it emphasizes the element of praise rather more strongly than appears justifiable from the context of the passage in the *Poetics*. Other critics were still more emphatic. Minturno stated simply that "Homer composed the *Iliad* in praise of Achilles; and the *Odyssey* in praise of Ulysses."[15] Patrizi spoke of "heroic poems" as "recounting the deeds of various heroes with the object not only of praising and exalting . . . but also to move others with an example."[16] Campanella described epic as a form in which "the praises of heroes are sung and examples of all kinds of men are intertwined."[17] Among English critics, Camden lamented that King Arthur "could find no panegyrist for his virtue";[18] while Puttenham concluded his survey of poetic genres with the claim, "So have you how the immortall gods were praised by hymnes, the great Princes and heroicke personages by ballades of praise called *Encomia,* both of them by historicall reports [i.e., epics] of great gravities and maiestie. . . ."[19]

The idea that epic is a kind of praise involves more than commonplace-book generalizations. It influenced the way that Renaissance critics read classical epics and the way that Renaissance epic poets thought about such matters as subject, plot, characterization, and style. To illustrate, we may turn from theory to literary works.

Xenophon's *Cyropaedia* has already been mentioned to illustrate the Renaissance concept of fiction. It was extremely popular during the sixteenth century and was translated into the major European vernaculars as well as into Latin.[20] Its special appeal is indicated by the fact that Philemon Holland, its second English translator, prepared his version under commission from King James I as a courtesy book for Prince Henry.[21] Xenophon's biography of Cyrus was universally considered an exemplary portrait. Castiglione listed it along with Plato's "perfect republic" and Cicero's "perfect orator" as a precedent for his image of the perfect courtier.[22] Machiavelli believed that Scipio achieved excellence by practicing in his life the "chastity, affability, humanity, and liberality" that he found portrayed by Xenophon.[23] Puttenham compared the *Cyropaedia* to Plato's *Republic,* the *Odyssey,* and More's *Utopia;* and the Earl of Sterling compared it to Sidney's *Arcadia.*[24] Perhaps the most remarkable series of references to the *Cyropaedia* is in Sidney's *Defense,* where it is mentioned eight times and coupled with the poems of Homer and Virgil as providing a pattern of virtue and a guide to Princes.[25]

The popularity of the *Cyropaedia* is understandable. It illustrates in a simple and direct way the theories advocated by didactic criticism. First, it is, as Sidney remarked, "an absolute heroicall poem."[26] That it is in prose is beside the point; in this it resembles other "prose epics" such as the *Aethiopian History* of Heliodorus or the *Arcadia* of Sidney himself.[27] Second, it is an epideictic *pictura* utilizing the topics of praise to create a model for imitation. Cicero had called Cyrus an "image of just rule," and sixteenth-century rhetorical critics like Alessandro Lionardi unhesitatingly placed the *Cyropaedia* in the category of epideictic compositions.[28] Cornelius Agrippa recognized (and characteristically, scorned) both the influence on poetry and the exemplary nature of the work: "*Xenophon* wrote the Story of *Cyrus,* not as he was, but what he ought to have been; propounding him as a true Pattern and example of a Just and Heroick Prince. Hence it comes to pass that many apt to feign by Nature, and using industry therewithal, have applied themselves to write those Romances of *Morgant, Morgalona, Amadis, Floran, Tyran, Conamor, Arthur, Lancelot, Tristram;* generally unlearned, and worse than the mad Dreams of Poets."[29]

At the beginning of the *Cyropaedia,* Xenophon comments on the excellent constitution of Persia. He also praises the salutary Persian habit of hunting. The family and childhood of Cyrus are then described. While still a child Cyrus displays such abnormal wisdom that he is appointed judge. He is also an outstanding athlete and remarkably courteous and humble. Visiting his grandfather he lectures the old man on the evils of drink. Soon he is given a military command. He prepares to aid the oppressed Medes, subjects of his uncle Cyaxares. Book I ends with a Platonic dialogue between Cyrus and his father Cambyses on the nature of the ideal leader.

Books II through VII chronicle the military exploits of Cyrus. In Book II he organizes his army. He is a kindly commander and encourages friendly competition among the troops. Soon he conquers Armenia by clever strategy. In Book III he spares the captured King of Armenia after listening to the arguments of the King's son Tigranes. In Book IV another conquest is described. This time Cyrus fights against the Abyssinians, who are always superior to him in manpower. Because of his piety (his watchword is "Zeus our saviour and our guide") and his prudence, he defeats them. Now his uncle Cyaxares becomes jealous of his success and the two are temporarily alienated.

In IV, vi, there is the first of several digressions. The Assyrian deserter Gobryas tells of the murder of his son and the threats to his beautiful daughter by his king. A much longer digression begins in Book V. Cyrus' spoils include the beautiful Lady Panthea. The lady is chaste and Cyrus respects her virtue. He places her in the care of a lieutenant after a leisurely dialogue on love in which the lieutenant scoffs at those who are ruled by passion. Soon the lieutenant makes passionate advances to Panthea and she complains to Cyrus, who is amused by the weakness of the lieutenant. Panthea's husband is then summoned. He fights valiantly, is slain, and Panthea nobly commits suicide (VII, iii).

The major action of Book V concerns hostilities between Cyrus and the Assyrians. In Book VI, Cyrus prepares for the greatest battle of his life—that between his forces and the Assyrian army. He constructs many new weapons including scythe chariots and mobile siege towers and uses camels as a new type of cavalry.

Book VII is the climax of the story. It opens with an ornate description of the beauty of Cyrus' troops as they march forward in the sun. Then the Assyrians close in. Their huge army threatens to engulf the Persians. Cyrus' troops waver, but at the crucial moment, and after a final "Zeus our savior and guide," he begins the war paean and his men take heart. There is a furious battle. Cyrus' horse is killed under him, but he is unhurt. He gains a decisive victory and advances on Babylon, which he takes by diverting the river and entering via the dry river bed. His humane occupation of Babylon ends the book.

In Book VIII the government of Cyrus is described. It is based on virtue, responsibility and, especially, temperance. Although Cyrus always appears magnificently dressed on state occasions (VIII, iii, 1-25), his magnificence is merely to help his government command respect. A digression in this book tells how one of Cyrus' freedmen gives his wealth away to avoid the worry of possessions (VIII, iii, 37-50). After stabilizing his throne, Cyrus revisits his uncle Cyaxares, is betrothed to his daughter, and thereby becomes heir to the Median throne.

The final authentic part of Book VIII describes the death of Cyrus. He is very old. He is warned of death in a vision. He gathers his sons about himself, arranges for the succession, plans his burial, and, like Socrates, discusses immortality. Finally he shakes hands and dies amid universal sorrow. In an apocryphal section added to the work after Xenophon's death, the decline of the Persians is described.

From the preceding summary it can be seen that the *Cyropaedia* is a "panegyrical biography" tailoring the facts of history to the requirements of encomium. Technically speaking, it is allied to "praise of rulers" (*basilikos logos*) since its subject is a prince rather than a "private person." Book I celebrates his nation, parents, and "childhood acts" which presage future greatness. Books II-VII are an idealized résumé of his heroic acts with emphasis on military victories and, consequently, the virtue of fortitude. Book VIII concentrates on his qualities as governor and places major emphasis on wisdom. The work closes with a description of his "good death." These are the standard topics of the epideictic orator. They are "praise" rather than biography because they are idealized. In conformity to the epideictic requirement that the orator concentrate on "goods of character" rather than "goods of fortune," Xenophon has consistently stressed virtue. Even the unpromising topic of "praise of nation" illustrates a moral point: the greatness of Persia is ascribed to its enlightened constitution rather than to its location, resources, or climate. Later, we are repeatedly told that when Cyrus fights, his victories are the result of superior discipline and strategy rather than brute force. The constitution of the empire that Cyrus establishes furnishes proof of his excellence as a governor, and his easy death is treated as the reward of a virtuous and temperate life.

In order to present his pattern of virtue, Xenophon had to rewrite a good deal of history. His willingness to deviate from fact provides a good illustration of the sort of "heightening" condoned by epideictic rhetoric. Xenophon's primary source was the first book of the *History* of Herodotus. His most important deviations are as follows:

1. The "constitution" of Persia is invented.
2. The simplicity, temperance, and piety of the Persians is really Spartan.
3. Tigranes is fictitious—he is modeled on Socrates.
4. Cyrus' military organization and tactics are Spartan, not Persian.
5. Media was not ceded to Cyrus as a dowry but conquered by treachery.
6. Cyaxares, Cyrus' uncle, is a foil to Cyrus, for he is intemperate, undisciplined, jealous, and lecherous.
7. Panthea and her husband are fictitious.
8. The conquest of Egypt (merely mentioned) was really achieved by Cyrus' son.
9. Cyrus' constitution is largely imaginary, although it has some historical basis.
10. Cyrus actually died a violent death fighting the Massagetae.

None of these deviations is so much a contradiction of history as a "heightening" of it. For example, the fact of Cyrus' acquisition of Media is not challenged; it is modified, however, in order to remove the stigma of treachery. Xenophon's motive for revising history is obviously not flattery; Cyrus had been dead well over a century when the *Cyropaedia* was written. The true motive is didactic. Each modification emphasizes exemplary features of Cyrus or suppresses less admirable ones.

In addition to being an ideal, semi-historical character, Cyrus is a prince and a military commander. Had he been of the non-noble class he would have been admired by Renaissance critics, but he would not have been compared to the heroes of Homer and Virgil. Sixteenth-century theorists gave lip-service to the idea of the self-made hero in the commonplace argument that personal achievement is the sole measure of worth, but they did not select their epic heroes from the lower classes. As in the *Cyro-*

paedia, the hero is given the best of both fortune and character. Cyrus is a prince and a warrior; he is naturally courteous, and he believes in *noblesse oblige* to such an extent that when playing with his boyhood friends he selects games in which he knows they are his superiors. His nobility is then illustrated by his deeds. He leads his armies to glorious victories; he resists the snares of drunkenness, lust, cruelty and vanity. He enjoys philosophy and writes a model constitution. In fact, he is so perfect a model that he was sometimes praised by writers who found Homer's heroes puzzling or even reprehensible. Achilles, Agamemnon, and Ulysses have too many flaws to be readily fitted into the category of the exemplary hero, but the *Cyropaedia* is a simple and obvious celebration of virtue.

Xenophon's method of development involves techniques often used in Renaissance epic. First, the episodes are arranged chronologically, strung together on the thread of the hero's life. Second, the major episodes—the battles—have rudimentary dramatic progression, each battle being more dangerous than the preceding one. A rudimentary suspense is created which increases until the climactic battle with the Assyrians. Third, thematic unity is achieved through the device of making each episode exemplify a specific virtue. Instead of telling the reader that Cyrus was temperate, Xenophon illustrates this fact by Cyrus' refusal to drink wine at his grandfather's banquet. His chastity is illustrated by his refusal to violate the virtuous Panthea. His mercy is shown by his pardon of the King of Armenia; his piety, by his prayers to Zeus. Finally, Xenophon's title means, literally translated, "The Education of Cyrus." Evidently the reader is to discover that Cyrus matures as a result of his experiences. The work is, therefore, the world's first *Bildungsroman,* a forerunner of Renaissance epics like the first two books of Spenser's *Faerie Queene,* and a distant and staid predecessor of Fielding's *Tom Jones.*

Numerous digressions complicate this basically simple pattern. Their most obvious function is to add a pleasing variety to the *Cyropaedia.* A biography of eight books, if uniformly devoted to a parade of virtues, would be intolerably monotonous.[30] A second reason for the digressions is that they provide parallels and contrasts to the main plot. Cyaxares, the dissolute ruler, becomes more and more futile while Cyrus, the temperate ruler, gains ever greater glory. The puritanical lieutenant fails to understand himself and is forced to an embarrassing recognition of his frailty, while the more mature Cyrus is able to withstand temptation. Other digressions enable Xenophon to represent virtues that Cyrus cannot display. Tigranes illustrates how much eloquence can accomplish when addressed to a benevolent monarch. Panthea is also exemplary. She is a paragon of womanly virtue in some respects parallel to Cyrus. The tale of her tribulations recalls similar digressive stories of female virtue in distress in Tasso and Spenser.

Finally, the *Cyropaedia* is a success story *par excellence*. The epic hero can encounter much adversity, but he must emerge triumphant in the end. According to history Cyrus died violently among the Massegetae. According to Xenophon he died discussing immortality with his friends. The parallel to Socrates is doubtless intentional and an attempt to interject into the description of the death of Cyrus some of the idealism of the *Phaedo* and Xenophon's own *Memorabilia*.

The extent of Xenophon's debt to formal rhetoric is impossible to determine, but in the *Cyropaedia* he created a model that rhetoricians could only praise. The techniques by which he sketched out the education of his ideal leader are those of the epideictic orator, tailored to the requirements of a long work intended for reading rather than public delivery. Having the virtues of familiarity, simplicity, and moral seriousness, they were naturally attractive to literary critics. Not only was the *Cyropaedia* accorded the status of an epic, but true epics were reinterpreted—often drastically distorted—in conformity with the ideal that it defines. The most obvious case in point is the *Aeneid*. There seems to be general agreement today that Virgil's handling of his material is literary rather than exemplary. He is interested in his narrative first, and the celebration of Roman ideals and the *gens Julia* is a secondary theme. Just for this reason the *Aeneid* could not be read objectively by critics of the succeeding age. It had to be rationalized, and the process was carried out by showing that, appearances to the contrary, Virgil composed the poem using the same techniques observed in the *Cyropaedia*.

The *Exposition of the Content of Virgil* by Fabius Planciades Fulgentius has already been cited as an illustration of the development of the theory of praise. It begins with a demonstration that the *Aeneid* is a work of praise (*laudis materiam*) rather than logic.[31] This being the case, its major episodes must be treated as the *gesta* of the epideictic orator. Since the *gesta* are supposed to illustrate the virtues that make the orator's subject praiseworthy, the episodes of the *Aeneid* must also be exemplary. The result is predictable. Book I of the *Aeneid* becomes an allegory of birth (shipwreck) and entry into a life of pain. Juno is the goddess of birth; Aeolus, perdition. Books II and III depict the naïve imagination and perils of childhood. The Cyclops, for example, represents youthful vanity conquered by good sense (Ulysses), and Polyphemus is the threat of "lost reputation" ("apolunta femen quod Latine perdentem famam dicimus") appropriately avoided by Aeneas when he escapes. The death of Anchises represents the end of parental authority, and Book IV shows youth enjoying independence. Aeneas-Everyman, like his remote descendant Lusty Juventus, gives way to lust (Dido), until intellect (Mercury) frees him. Then the flame of love turns to ashes (Dido's pyre). In Book V the hero returns to the example of his father and devotes himself to valorous exercise (the funeral games). In Book VI, the most obscure of the twelve books, Aeneas seeks wisdom (in the temple of Apollo) and plunges into philosophical studies that are symbolized by the descent into Hades. There the hero learns the secrets of things. Time (Charon) guides him over the troubled waters of youth. He sees the quarrels that divide men (Cerberus) and learns of the future. He recalls and reflects on passion (Dido) and affection (Anchises). With this the first half of his life—his education—is complete.

In Book VII the hero attains Ausonia (increase of good) and takes Lavinia (*via laborum*) as his bride. In VIII he allies himself with Euander (*bonus vir*) and learns from him how virtue (Hercules) triumphs over vice (Cacus). In the remaining four books Aeneas is clad in the arms of the spirit (the arms of Vulcan) and combats the vices that attack him. Turnus is rage and is led first by drunkenness (Metiscus) and then by stubbornness (Iuturna; i.e., *diuturna*). He is assisted by blasphemy (Mezentius) and folly (Messapus). Wisdom finally triumphs.

Incapable of responding to the narrative appeal of the *Aeneid,* Fulgentius made it over in the image of the panegyrical biography. The most striking result of the process is the revision of the structure of the poem. Instead of beginning *in medias res,* the revised *Aeneid* begins with the birth of the protagonist, which is followed by a series of allegorical examples of the trials of youth. Since the hero eventually achieves maturity by successfully passing these trials, his story is a *Bildungsroman* as well as a biography. In all of these respects it resembles the *Cyropaedia,* but the effect is greatly complicated by the exegetical sleight-of-hand needed to give the interpretation a veneer of credibility. Whereas the *Cyropaedia* has a single, explicit meaning, the *Aeneid* must be understood in two quite different ways. The narrative is the apparent meaning, but it is only a veil concealing the "true" meaning beneath. The apparent meaning is particular, while the true meaning is universal, "according to moral philosophy." By the same token, the hero has two distinct characters. In the narrative he is Aeneas, a legendary figure whose exploits led to the founding of high Rome. In the allegory, however, he is Everyman, and his experiences are those which are encountered by men in every age and country. While the legendary hero displays resourcefulness by saving his followers from the Cyclops, Aeneas-Everyman provides an object-lesson in the control of vanity by wisdom. Likewise, when the great warrior exhibits courage by defeating his adversary in single combat, Aeneas-Everyman teaches how rage can be controlled by reason. Both levels demonstrate the greatness of the hero, but the allegorical level is the one which makes the *Aeneid* a true classic, suitable for

Christian as well as pagan readers. By the end of the poem, the whole spectrum of virtues from humility and chastity to fortitude and wisdom has been demonstrated,[32] and Aeneas has been rewarded for his righteousness by complete success. It may be added that the allegorical interpretation of the epic combats necessarily makes them into "battles for the soul"—examples of the psychomachia—and that the psychomachia remained an extremely popular feature of medieval narrative and drama and Renaissance epic.

The debt of the *Aeneid* to history is less simple than that of the *Cyropaedia* but it is of the same kind. Tradition, myth, archeology, scholarship, and *belles lettres* supplied material for the poem, and both Livy and Plutarch grudgingly admitted the legends of the age of kings to a place in formal history.[33] Whatever Virgil may have felt about the validity of his sources, later critics almost unanimously accepted Aeneas as a true historical character and believed that there was an historical basis for the main outlines of the *Aeneid*. Virgil's additions were considered either amplifications or inventions justified by gaps in the tradition. Like Xenophon, Virgil idealized, but it was generally agreed that he did not falsify essential facts. A secondary historical element was recognized in Virgil's topical references. Just as elements of the *Cyropaedia* are based on Spartan rather than Persian traditions, many events in the *Aeneid* must be understood as allusions to the Rome of Augustus. Topical allusion remained a standard device of Renaissance epic. Ariosto sings of Ippolyte d'Este, Tasso celebrates Alphonso II, and Spenser, Elizabeth and Leicester.[34]

In addition to satisfying the demands of historical truth, Aeneas has the noble status required of the epic hero. Being "goddess born" he is more than princely. Yet his career does not depend on gifts of fortune. At the beginning of the *Aeneid* fortune is against him. His race has been defeated, his city burned, and he himself is an exile. What he achieves is gained by character alone and in the face of overwhelming odds. His major deeds are military, but in the later books his virtues as a statesman are revealed; and throughout the poem his *pietas* is kept constantly in the reader's mind. The parallel to the *Cyropaedia* is completed by Fulgentius' emphasis on the element of success. Aeneas wins his kingdom despite the ire of the gods and the lures of Dido. The walls of high Rome are predicted if not raised, and Aeneas-Everyman achieves everything necessary to sainthood except formal canonization.

To move from the straightforward methods of the *Cyropaedia* to the astonishing excursions of Fulgentius behind the Virgilian veil is to move from the neat rationalism of the Greeks to the fantastic world of romance. As the work of Fulgentius illustrates, this world was not entirely a product of Gothic ignorance. It could be more charitably described as a product of too much knowledge—of a value system that had become so obsessive that it compulsively made over the past into its own image. The *Aeneid* is not and never was a simple poem, but read today, it reveals a calmness, a clarity of vision, a sense of harmony and design that are clearly and essentially classic in Goethe's sense of the term. None of these qualities is stressed by Fulgentius. The elements which he seeks are not intrinsic to the poem but to the culture of the Middle Ages and the poem must yield to the culture. Instead of lamenting this fact we might do well to attempt to see the poem as Fulgentius and his successors apparently saw it. If we do, we are immediately struck by its variety, indirection, ornament, and obscurity. It becomes, in fact, the first and greatest of the medieval romances and the foremost precedent for the Renaissance understanding of epic.

Of all sixteenth-century epics, none better illustrates the continuity of the Fulgentius tradition than Edmund Spenser's *Faerie Queene*. Spenser had the humanist's admiration for Virgil.[35] He knew the poetry intimately, referred to it, paraphrased it, imitated it, and as early as the *Shepherd's Calendar* admitted having Virgilian aspirations. Yet to the untutored reader the epic that he wrote seems astonishingly un-Virgilian. The most fantastic adventures of Aeneas seem prosaic when compared to the exploits of the Red Cross Knight, Britomart, or Sir Calidor. The exotic lands visited by Virgil's traveler appear almost commonplace if set beside Spenser's Arthurian dream-world with its dark forests and enchanted bowers, its endless plains and mysterious castles, and its population of monsters, fairy-folk, heroes, witches, personified vices, brigands, maidens in distress, and simple shepherds. The difference in tone is paralleled by the difference in method. In place of Virgilian narrative we have Spenserian allegory. *The Faerie Queene* begins in the abstract world of the famous "twelve moral virtues," which, if not Aristotelian, are certainly derived from the treatises of the moral philosophers. Clearly, these differences, which seem glaring today, were not so apparent to Spenser. The explanation is that Spenser thought of Virgil in terms not essentially different from those of Fulgentius. Far from being a perversion of the *Aeneid, The Faerie Queene* is, by Spenser's standards, an imitation of it.

The first point on which Spenser and Fulgentius agree is the idea that epic is a kind of praise. The gloss on the October *Shepherd's Calendar* remarks that ". . . if the Poet list showe his skill in . . . higher veyne and more Heroicall argument . . . there be many Noble and valiaunt men, that are . . . worthy of his payne in theyre deserved prayses."[36] The sonnets prefacing *The Faerie Queene* contain no less than ten distinct deferences to the idea of poetry—and especially *The Faerie Queene*—as praise.[37] Finally, the poem itself begins with the promise to

. . . sing of Knights and Ladies gentle deeds;
Whose prayses having slept in silence long,
Me, all too meane, the sacred Muse areeds
To blazon broad emongst her learned throng. . . .[38]

Fortunately, Spenser was a poet who liked to talk shop, and we can gain a fairly accurate notion of what he meant by "prayses" by referring to his letter to Raleigh. Whatever the relation between the letter and the completed portion of his poem, the letter shows what he hoped to write and thus has considerable critical relevance.[39] The points that Spenser emphasizes most strongly are his desire to create a series of exemplary heroes and his faith that in so doing he is following classical (and Virgilian) precedent:

. . . I have followed all the antique Poets historicall, first Homere, who in the Persons of Agamemnon and Ulysses hath ensampled a good gouvernour and a vertuous man, the one in his Ilias, the other in his Odysseis: then Virgil, whose like intention was to doe in the person of Aeneas: after him Ariosto comprised them both in his Orlando: and lately Tasso dissevered them againe, and formed both parts in two persons . . . vertues of a private man, coloured in his Rinaldo: The other named Politice in his Godfredo. By ensample of which excellente Poets, I labour to pourtraict in Arthure, before he was king, the image of a brave knight, perfected in the twelve private morall vertues . . . which is the purpose of these first twelve bookes.

The passage has the true Fulgentian ring. The "antique Poets historicall" were inspired teachers leading men to virtue by example. Their interests lay not in the particular but in the universal—the moral qualities needed by the governor and the "private man." There is no hint in the passage of the enthusiastic response of one great poetic talent to another, just as there is no hint of awareness of the gulf separating the poems and their interpretation. Later, Spenser cites the *Cyropaedia* as another precedent. Doing this entails a transition from poetry to prose and from works of genius to one of skillful mediocrity, but, as we have seen, the whole weight of tradition appeared to justify it. The only question that occurs to Spenser is whether Plato's *Republic* is a better model than Xenophon's biography of Cyrus, and this question is easily answered by appeal to the theory of example: "For this cause is Xenophon preferred before Plato, for that the one in the exquisite depth of his iudgement, formed a Commune welth such as it should be, but the other in the person of Cyrus and the Persians fashioned a governement such as might best be: so much more profitable and gratious is doctrine by ensample, then by rule. So I have laboured to doe in the person of Arthure. . . ." Like Fulgentius, Spenser distinguishes between an exercise in dialectic—"doctrine by rule"—and the rhetorical method of example. The latter is the poet's method since it leads to effective social reforms. Arthur will be Spenser's supreme example and will unify *The Faerie Queene* in the same way that Cyrus unifies the *Cyropaedia.* Meanwhile, in order to illustrate fully the twelve virtues that comprise Arthur's "magnificence," there will be twelve lesser heroes, one for each of the projected books.[40] The bewildering, almost chaotic diversity that resulted from carrying this plan into practice is notorious, but, at least in the letter to Raleigh, Spenser seems untroubled by doubts. The plan ingeniously provides for the kind of *discordia concors* that the Renaissance found especially delightful, and all of its elements contribute to the end of fashioning "a gentleman or noble person in vertuous and gentle discipline."

Spenser's dominant concern in his letter is the explanation of how philosophical ideas are translated into narrative. His emphasis on the abstract is so strong that one is tempted to consider *The Faerie Queene* a thinly disguised courtesy book. In fact, the purpose of Castiglione's *Courtier* is the same as that of *The Faerie Queene,*[41] and one of the precedents mentioned by Castiglione is Xenophon's *Cyropaedia.*[42] However, there is an essential difference. *The Faerie Queene* is "an historicall fiction," for like his predecessors, Spenser felt that an epic poem must be based on history as well as philosophy. The history of Arthur was ideally suited to the purposes of an epic poet in search of a subject. Its validity, though often questioned, was attested by medieval chronicler and Tudor propagandist alike.[43] Being legendary, it afforded ample opportunities for poetic inventions; and being English it was perfectly suited to the celebration of *Respublica.* Being Christian, it provided a credible context for epic marvels.[44] Finally, in the larger historical pattern there was room for the topical allusions sanctioned by Virgil. If Aeneas resembles Augustus, Arthur glorifies the Tudor line and resembles Leicester; Gloriana and Belphoebe resemble Elizabeth; and the lesser characters have innumerable topical connections.[45]

The practical consequence of Spenser's theory is exemplified in Book I, which is based on the St. George legend. This gives Spenser a hero whose career is fixed in outline but obscure in detail. The elements which cannot be altered are the saintliness of the protagonist and the fact that he saves a virgin by slaying a dragon. On this "historical" frame, Spenser creates a tapestry-like series of episodes most of which are pure invention and come under the heading of poetic license. Following the practice that Fulgentius had attributed to Virgil, Spenser translates the somewhat vague notion of saintliness into an elaborate doctrine of holiness. The Red Cross Knight personifies this virtue, and to praise him will be to encourage emulation of it in the reader. The episodes that form the plot are like the *gesta* of the encomium. They illustrate the hardships that beset the devout and the way in which these hardships can be overcome. The very first episode, the slaying of Error, illustrates the triumph of sincere devotion over confusion.

The moral also holds good on the topical level, for the devout Protestant learns that with faith and resolution he can withstand the perils of Catholic propaganda. Other episodes—the giant Orgoglio, the cave of Despair, the House of Holiness, and the fight with the dragon—have similar allegorical and topical meanings. Taken together, they provide the reader with a fairly systematic review of the whole doctrine of holiness. Because Spenser's hero is a knight, the plot material is appropriately heroic, and from it the psychomachia with its cognate notions of the Christian soldier and the full armor of Christ develops as naturally as it does in the *Gerusalemme liberata*.[46]

Spenser's organization deserves further comment. So much has been written about the lack of straightforward development in *The Faerie Queene* that the basic simplicity of Spenser's method is worth stressing. Despite the complexity of the poem as written, it is theoretically no more involved than Xenophon's *Cyropaedia*. Arthur's adventures, though separated by wide narrative gaps, are in chronological order. The order is undisturbed by narrative of prior action because Spenser was no more capable than Fulgentius of appreciating Virgil's use of *in medias res*.[47] The individual books are also for the most part chronological, although the sense of orderly sequence is blurred by digressions. In Books I and II, the simple plot form encouraged by the analogy between epic and encomium is relatively obvious. The tests invented for the Red Cross Knight and Sir Guyon follow one another chronologically, growing progressively harder as Books I and II approach their climaxes. Since both heroes are imperfect, a certain amount of suspense is generated. Moreover, since both mature as a result of passing their trials, their stories assume the familiar *Bildungsroman* pattern. St. George, for example, proceeds from the relatively simple tests represented by Error (Canto i) and Sansfoy (ii) to the more difficult ones represented by Orgoglio (vii) and Despair (ix), which are only passed with the aid of Arthur and Una. The visit to the House of Holiness (x) is the culmination of his education and could not have occurred earlier since, lacking appropriate experience, he could not have understood or apperciated it. This event, rather than the cave of Despair, corresponds to Aeneas' descent into Hades as interpreted by medieval and Renaissance critics. The final test is the climax of Book I. The slaying of the dragon corresponds on the level of narrative to Cyrus' defeat of the Assyrians and Aeneas' defeat of Turnus. Allegorically, it is a still greater achievement. The dragon symbolizes evil, and its defeat foreshadows the ultimate Christian triumph—the defeat of Satan by Christ.[48]

The digressiveness of *The Faerie Queene* is, properly considered, a corollary of its chronological organization. Ariosto and Tasso furnished Spenser's precedents, but his reason for imitating them was the idea that digressions and amplifications relieve the monotony of the *gesta* that form the basic matter of epic. The theory had been used by the Italians to defend romance,[49] and we have already noted the digressive tendency of the *Cyropaedia* and the Fulgentius *Aeneid*. The equation of digression and delight is evident in Spenser's defense of historical fiction as a form "which the most part of men delight to read, rather for variety of matter, then for profite of the ensample," and in his later remark that "many other adventures are intermedled, but rather as Accidents, then intendments. As the love of Britomart, the overthrow of Marinell, the misery of Florimell, the vertuousnes of Belphoebe, the lasciviousnes of Hellenora, and many the like." The same tradition encouraged Spenser's use of the marvelous and his ornate style. The Spenserian stanza, with its involved rhetoric and elaborate musical effects, is an English equivalent of the magnificent style that Tasso advocated in his criticism[50] and exemplified in the *Gerusalemme liberata* and that he considered a modern vernacular equivalent of Virgilian grandeur. Spenser learned a great deal from Ariosto and Tasso, but critical tradition encouraged him to think of the *Aeneid*, itself, as a romance; and he admired the Italians for their ability to adapt Virgilian techniques to the vernacular rather than for their innovations. The assurance with which he invokes "the antique poets historicall" in his letter to Raleigh is a measure of the continuing influence during the sixteenth century of the idea of epic as praise.

III. MINOR RAMIFICATIONS OF EPIC

Probably the most distinctive feature of epic theory from Fulgentius to Spenser is its emphasis on the abstract. This led to a broadening of the definition of epic and a tendency to equate poetic unity with unity of theme. The *Aeneid*, for example, could be considered either a celebration of a man or a celebration of the virtues personified by the man. And if such virtues as fortitude and wisdom are appropriate for epic celebration, why not others? Rhetoric books such as the *Progymnasmata* of Aphthonius taught that any intrinsically excellent idea could be praised, and the lists of examples ranged from prudence, temperance, justice, and eloquence to skill in medicine and knowledge of military affairs. By the same token, if epic is essentially a celebration of virtue, why is it necessary to exemplify the virtue in a single dominant protagonist? Campanella appears to have recognized two distinct forms of epic, one unified around a dominant character, and the other unified around a dominant theme illustrated by a great many characters: "The heroic poem can treat such things [as abstractions], nor is unity or magnitude absent when similar elements are grouped together for one end and in exemplary fashion. . . . For men who are of the same nation and are related to telling the founding and fortune of a single republic create unity; and likewise, characters who are exemplary of the same virtue, although they are gathered from different nations, create unity, as in *The Triumph of Modesty* all are [examples of] modesty."[51]

As long as a literary work treats a character conceived as historical, it is likely to retain at least a rudimentary sense of human reality. However, when it becomes a "praise of abstractions" such as justice, temperance, or liberality, its relationship to human reality becomes vague. Spenser's epic, for all its richness, tends to the abstract. Books II and V of *The Faerie Queene* treat temperance and justice respectively, personifying these qualities in protagonists whose historicity is of the most tenuous kind. Book III (the legend of chastity) is still less historical. Like the "Triumph of Modesty" described by Campanella it is unified by a theme which is illustrated by several characters. Britomart is the nominal protagonist, but Amoret and Scudamour, Belphoebe and Timias, and Florimell all illustrate aspects of chastity; while Malbecco and Hellenore serve as foils illustrating the evils of lechery. The adventures of these characters are "Accidents" according to Spenser, but they are not digressions in the sense of being unrelated to the book as a whole. They permit Spenser to treat phases of his theme that would otherwise have to be omitted. Obviously, for example, the ideal of chastity culminating in marriage illustrated by Amoret and Scudamour would have been impossible to treat had Book III been limited to Britomart or Belphoebe.

But praise of abstractions is only one possible variant of epic. Among the topics commonly recommended by epideictic rhetoric are praise of nation and praise of nature. If the most basic requirements of epic are elevation of subject and high moral purpose, both topics have epic potentialities. The verse chronicle, a Renaissance inheritance from the Middle Ages, was sometimes given epic status on the grounds that it celebrated the nation, was in verse, and taught patriotism. Webbe included Christopher Ocland's *Proelia Anglia* in the category of heroic poems, while Puttenham called Harding "a Poet Epik or Historicall," and Meres ranked Spenser and Warner together as "our chief historicall makers."[52] There are also non-historical ways to celebrate the nation. For example, *Polyolbion,* Michael Drayton's endless topographical poem, was considered an epic by William Drummond.[53]

Still further removed from praise of heroes is praise of nature. Idealized nature descriptions began to appear as separate poems during the late classical period. The surviving examples are obviously influenced by epideictic formulae but are either short "set pieces" or topographical works like the *Mosella* of Ausonius. Theoretically, however, praise of nature has epic potentialities, and those potentialities were encouraged by Christian works treating nature as the awe-inspiring book of God. With a bow to the psalms as well as to critical theory, Campanella taught that after praising the gods directly in hymns, "Men then sang animate things as effects of the great God, for they are means to know him and praise him, it being impossible to please an artisan more than by looking on his works with admiration and declaring to others with what virtue and mastery they are made."[54] Because Campanella moves from the highest to the lowest forms of poetry, we may assume that he felt the praise of God's works to be as noble as heroic poetry. The nobility of nature poetry was frequently stressed in Renaissance discussion of the *Georgics*.[55]

A particularly clear example of nature poetry with epic pretensions is James Thomson's *Seasons* (1730 and later). The background of *The Seasons* includes the *Georgics, Paradise Lost,* seventeenth-century topographical poetry, Newtonian science, and Deism.[56] Rhetorically speaking, its most important precedent is the commonplace epideictic topic *laus quattuor temporum,* which originated during the late classical period and passed into the Renaissance in music, painting, and literature. Thomson's development of the topic is significant because it so clearly attempts epic stature in its length, division into books, and its use of Miltonic blank verse and rhetoric. In accordance with epideictic prescriptions Thomson attempts far more than external description. Just as encomium is justified by its moral effect, operating through the admiration of the protagonist created in the audience, so Thomson tries throughout to create admiration and awe for the objects that he describes. Such admiration naturally leads to admiration for the Creator, and Thomson's poem tends to fall into a series of descriptions interrupted by passages in praise of God—a literal application of Campanella's advice, "look on his works with admiration and declare to others with what virtue and mastery they are made." In Thomson's concluding "hymn" the subjects of the poem are brought together, and—with an assist from Adam and Eve's "morning prayer" (*Paradise Lost,* V, 153-208)—commanded to join in praising God. The brooks will "attune" His praise (l. 48); the sea will "sound His stupendous praise" (l. 54); light will "write with every beam His praise" (l. 69); and the poet, joining praise and humility, must confess,

I cannot go
Where Universal Love smiles not around,
Sustaining all you orbs, and all their sons;
From seeing Evil still educing Good,
And better thence again, and better still,
In infinite progression. But I lose
Myself in Him, in Light ineffable!
Come then, expressive Silence, muse His praise (ll. 111-18).

There is an important residue of this technique in *The Prelude.* The mingling of description and moral reflection, and their supposed interrelationship, suggests a refinement of Thomson as much as it suggests a radically new departure.

IV. ADMONITORY EPIC AND TRAGEDY

One apparently unavoidable characteristic of systematic criticism is the tendency of its terminology to assume a life of its own. The need for clear definition gives rise to distinctions which are of the system rather than the literature being investigated. Eventually, the distinctions come to be regarded as profound truths to be observed by all authors who aspire to literary excellence, and the resulting literature is held up as proof of the rightness of the system. Both neoclassic and romantic criticism illustrate this tendency, and it is, therefore, not surprising to find it manifested in sixteenth-century criticism.

The epideictic category treats techniques of blame (*vituperatio*) as well as praise and defines blame as the opposite of praise. While praise creates examples of the good, blame creates examples of evil by showing vice in an unfavorable manner. While praise stimulates emulation, blame stimulates repugnance and results in a catharsis which is a purging of the desire for evil.[57] The neat division between the two forms suggests that since there is a form of epic based on praise, there should be an equal and opposite form based on blame. For convenience this form may be called admonitory epic. Renaissance moralists occasionally interpreted the *Iliad* as an admonitory epic since its hero exemplifies a vice (wrath) rather than true epic virtue as depicted in Ulysses and Aeneas.[58] The protagonist of the admonitory epic could be either wholly depraved or stained with a single flaw. An utter villian should be depicted by reversing all of the formulae of praise; while the flawed protagonist like Achilles may be admirable in most respects so long as his flaw is appropriately punished.

Admonitory epic and tragedy are closely related. Because didactic critics were less concerned with *differentiae* based on "mode of imitation" than those based on "moral purpose" and "object of imitation," they were willing to label narrative poems tragedies and certain forms of drama heroic poems. Lucan's *Pharsalia,* for example, was called an epic by some critics and a tragedy by others.[59] Conversely, because the heroic play deals with "examples of virtue, writ in verse" which move to admiration, it was described by Dryden as "an imitation, in little, of an heroic poem."[60] And if Dryden could imagine a drama with epic characteristics, William Davenant could boast of having divided his epic poem *Gondibert* into acts and scenes like drama.[61]

Two distinctions commonly served to differentiate epic and tragic forms.

The first is a moral one. The tragic forms—whether narrative or dramatic—were to be devoted to the instructive treatment of vice. The point was made by classical authors like Euanthius, who traced both tragedy and comedy to festivals where "men of evil habits" (*male viventes*) were rebuked.[62] Despite the fact that Aristotle, followed by Averroes, had derived tragedy from forms of praise, the idea of tragedy as rebuke of vice persisted. Campanella asserted that the tragic function was "to reprehend the vices of tyrants."[63] Puttenham put the issue clearly when he listed tragedy among the poetic forms by which "vice and the common abuses of man's life were reprehended," and distinguished between tragedy and the other forms of "reprehension" (i.e., comedy and satire) by the nobility of the subject matter of tragedy.[64] Sidney praised "high and excellent Tragedy, that openeth the greatest wounds, and sheweth forth the Ulcers that are covered with Tissue; that maketh Kinges feare to be Tyrants, and Tyrants manifest their tirannicall humors."[65] And Hamlet so far trusted this theory as to base his effort to catch the King's conscience upon it. It may be noted that the public confession which Hamlet expects his play to bring about is an extreme form of the moral theory of catharsis.

The second means of distinguishing between epic and tragic forms was the success or failure of the protagonist. Poetic justice is an essential ingredient of any didactic theory of literature: to arouse emulation the epic hero must succeed; to generate abhorrence the tragic hero must fail. Sidney contrasted epic and tragedy in the following way: ". . . you see *Ulisses* in a storme, and in other hard plights; but they are but exercises of patience and magnanimitie, to make them shine the more in the neere-following prosperitie. And of the contrarie part, if evill men come to the stage, they ever goe out (as the Tragedie Writer answered to one that misliked the shew of such persons) so manacled as they little animate folkes to followe them."[66] At the end of the seventeenth century, the same concept was invoked by Dryden to explain the dramatic possibilities of the story of Antony and Cleopatra: ". . . the chief persons represented were famous patterns of unlawful love; and their end accordingly was unfortunate. All reasonable men have long since concluded, that the hero of the [tragic] poem ought not to be a character of perfect virtue, for then he could not, without injustice, be made unhappy; nor yet altogether wicked, because he could not then be pitied."[67] The casual tone of Dryden's remarks—his offhand reference to opinions held by "all reasonable men"—indicates the commonplace nature of his principles. The protagonists are noble but imperfect—"patterns of unlawful love"—and their end "accordingly was unfortunate."

Perhaps the best example of the overlapping of epic and tragedy is John Milton's *Paradise Lost*. During the early 1640's Milton drafted a series of outlines for a work on the subject of the Fall. These are preserved in the Trinity Manuscript, and they make it clear that he originally planned a tragedy rather than an epic.[68] The fact is often explained with the passing observation that Milton was following the pattern and tradition of the medieval mystery play. If this were true it would be surprising, considering Milton's humanistic prejudice against the Middle Ages and his slighting reference to "the Adam of the motions" in *Areopagitica.* However, it is not true. Milton selected a subject which had been popular among medieval authors, but he planned to treat it according to the best principles of Renaissance literary theory. He selected dramatic form because, like Grotius and Andreini before him, he interpreted Adam's story as one of failure and Adam as an example of vice rather than virtue—hence a tragic not an epic hero. Even when Milton had written the work as an epic it bore unmistakable marks of tragedy, for the ten books of the original (1667) edition fall clearly into five two-book units reproducing the five-act structure of classical tragedy.[69] In 1674 Milton issued a second edition of the poem in which the ten books had been further divided to make twelve. The revision is an obvious bid to make the work more "epic," but it did not eliminate the ambiguities, and the true genre of *Paradise Lost* was debated for the remainder of the seventeenth century. Invoking the same principle that had guided Milton when he had made the outlines in the Trinity Manuscript, Dryden insisted that, ". . . his subject is not that of an Heroic Poem, properly so called. His design is the losing of our happiness; his event is not prosperous, like that of all other epic works. . . ."[70] The controversy persisted into the eighteenth century, so that Addison felt compelled to begin his discussion of Milton with the assertion that "I shall waive the discussion of that point which was stated some years since, Whether Milton's *Paradise Lost* may be called an heroic poem?"[71]

Addison defended *Paradise Lost* on the basis of the Longinian critical principles that were already transforming European criticism. He believed that the earlier debate had been the result of "general discourses" that "turn chiefly upon words." In place of such sterile discourses he appealed to impressions, arguing that *Paradise Lost* is sublime in style and, therefore, epic, no matter how ambiguous its form. This mode of defense would probably have confused Milton as much as it would have confused the sixteenth-century Italians from whom he derived his critical ideas. Like the Italians, Milton had a high regard for definition, consistency, and system; and consideration of the reasons "turning chiefly upon words" which justified the epic form of *Paradise Lost* will clarify the relationship between positive epic, admonitory epic, and tragedy.

In the first place, Biblical paraphrase was traditionally considered "epic." Beginning with Juvencus, there were numerous poetic renderings of Biblical material, among them, Claudius Victor's *Comentarii in genesin* (5th cent.), Avitus' *De spiritualis historiae gestis* (c. 500), Dracontius' *De laudibus Dei* (c. 500), and later, the Anglo-Saxon *Genesis B*. Such productions merged naturally with less strict paraphrases and adaptations during the Renaissance, including Tasso's *Il mondo creato,* and DuBartas' *Semaines*.[72] The writers of Biblical paraphrase persistently claimed epic status. Juvencus, Sedulius, and Aldhelm open their works with the claim that they are treating an entirely new subject and one intrinsically better than that of Homer or Virgil.[73] The tradition persisted. In Chiabrera's first dialogue on poetry it is suggested that Tasso's *Il mondo creato* is an epic; and Harvey wrote in his copy of Gascoigne's *Certayne Notes of Instruction*, ". . . Sallustius Bartasius in the French language [is] a divine Homer."[74] Milton doubtless had such precedents in mind when he decided to use epic form for *Paradise Lost.*

In the second place, both Adam and Satan can be considered appropriate figures for admonitory epic. Since the *Iliad* was sometimes considered "admonitory" it is probably significant that Milton claims at the beginning of Book IX (where Adam "falls") that his argument is "not less but more heroic than the wrath of stern Achilles." At any rate, Adam corresponds to the admonitory hero who has excellent qualities but is brought to ruin by a single flaw. Whether Adam's flaw is his naïveté—his "fugitive and cloistered virtue"—or "uxoriousness," it brings on the tragic catastrophe and this completes the admonitory pattern.

Satan is the second type of admonitory figure. He is of "noble" rank and is formed according to Aristotle's advice in the *Rhetoric* to reverse the topics of praise in order to form the *pictura* based on *vituperatio*. Thus Satan possesses in a negative way all of the qualities of the epic hero. His nobility is apparent from his divine origin (cf. the topics of ancestry and birth), his awesome appearance (physical endowments), and his courage (endowments of character). It is the perversion of these qualities into their negatives which makes him despicable. Instead of being prince in heaven, he is king of hell. Instead of shining with celestial light, he grows gradually blacker. His impressiveness, which would be magnificence in the virtuous hero, becomes haughtiness, political chicanery, and bluster. This reversal of qualities has been elaborately documented as part of the recent campaign to rescue *Paradise Lost* from the romanticists who believe that Satan was Milton's secret hero. One point—small but instructive—may be added. The epic hero is usually shown to act on his own initiative, unassisted by "gifts of fortune." This pattern is reversed in Satan's acts. Each time Satan accomplishes something noteworthy—the rising from the burning lake, the opening of the gates of hell, the trip across chaos—Milton is careful to indicate that he does so only with the indirect aid of God, whose plans he is unwittingly furthering.

Satan is integrated into Milton's poem in two ways. First, he has a dramatic part to play in Book IX. His actions prior to Book IX are a preparation for the temptation. Second, he is related to the *theme* of the epic as distinguished from its plot. Just as Amoret illustrates one phase of chastity in Book III of *The Faerie Queene,* Satan illustrates one phase of the central moral issue of *Paradise Lost,* disobedience of God's commands. Through his soliloquies we learn that disobediance of God is a violation of the fundamental laws of our being and that hell can be a mental state as well as a physical place. Equally important, Satan defines the extreme form of disobedience. Because of this his fall is complete, and his triumphs only serve to plunge him deeper into despair. Conversely, Adam falls but repents, and by the end of the poem he has regained a measure of his former harmony with God.

In the twelve-book version of *Paradise Lost* the admonitory elements are still present, but Milton's revisions encourage a reading that emphasizes structural features characteristic of the *Cyropaedia* and *The Faerie Queene.* The more these features are stressed, the more *Paradise Lost* comes to resemble the positive rather than the admonitory epic. As a positive epic hero, Adam is an example "to imbreed and cherish in a great people the seeds of virtue and public civility." His story assumes features of the *Bildungsroman.* He begins life with a virtue that is perfect but untried. He is troubled by the first overt manifestation of evil (Eve's dream, described in Book V) and prays for assistance. He is accordingly "educated" by Raphael. In the course of talking with Raphael he reveals certain weaknesses. He criticizes God's workmanship in constructing the solar system and shows proneness to uxoriousness (Book VIII). These weaknesses are dangerously close to sins, but they are converted by the Angel into opportunities for further instruction. By the beginning of Book IX, Adam has received a short but pointed series of lessons in theology, morality, ontology, cosmology, and psychology, and his education is complete. Now, if ever, he is prepared to stand against the wiles of the Tempter.

At this point it is useful to recall what has been observed concerning the "positive" epic. Usually Adam's fall is considered the climax of *Paradise Lost.* But if Milton's twelve-book revision is interpreted as an effort to make the work into a true epic on the traditional pattern, the fall cannot be climactic. It is a terrible setback, but it is no more decisive than the "storms and hard plights" that Sidney tells us make the success of Aeneas the more glorious, or the encounters of the Red Cross Knight with Orgoglio and Despair. In fact, it resembles these encounters closely since the fall itself involves pride, and it leads, in Book X, to despair. A reading which conforms to the apparent intent of the twelve-book revision of the poem must seek the climax in an act that converts defeat into victory and leads forward to the triumphant closing dialogue with Michael. Clearly, this act occurs in Book X when, assisted by Eve and "prevenient grace," Adam repents, confesses, and seeks forgiveness. It is this action that most emphatically differentiates the fallen Adam from the fallen Satan and exemplifies the "better fortitude of Patience and Heroic martyrdom unsung" which Milton felt to be the highest epic virtues. After Adam's prayer, the tone of the poem rapidly becomes more positive. Just as the Red Cross Knight is "cheered" at the House of Holiness after his bout with Despair, Adam is cured of his perturbations by Michael's history lesson. At the end of this history, Adam is so awed by the wonderous design of Providence that he regards the fall itself as a *felix culpa*—a sin whose good results outweigh its evils.[75] Nominally, the expulsion from Paradise is a punishment, but this, too, is transformed as Michael assures Adam that the practice of virtue will enable him to possess "a paradise within thee happier far" than the physical Eden that he must leave.

In addition to "imbreeding virtue" and "allaying perturbations," Milton felt that the epic should "celebrate in glorious and lofty hymns the throne and equipage of God's almightiness."[76] It is entirely fitting that the climactic passage of Book XII of *Paradise Lost* should be a celebration of "goodness infinite, goodness immense!/ That all this good of evil shall produce. . . ." Milton has faced honestly the darkest truths of human experience. They have caused his poem to veer perilously close to tragedy—in fact only if he had been less honest could Milton have avoided the tragic elements—but they are here subsumed and transformed. God's greatest miracle and His highest praise is not that He brings light out of light and good out of good, but that He brings good from evil and light from the darkness of human failure.

Clearly, it is only a short step from admonitory epic to tragedy. The idea that tragic drama creates instructive examples of vice has been treated so often and so well that extensive illustration would be superfluous. Willard Farnham has traced the evolution of this idea from the medieval "fall of princes" story, exemplified by Chaucer's *Monk's Tale,* into the sophisticated forms of Elizabethan tragedy. Lilly Bess Campbell has called attention to the importance of the *Mirror for Magistrates* in crystallizing English notions of how tragedy should be written. She has also performed an important service for students of Shakespeare by pointing out how his tragic heroes consistently become victims of a passion that is both a moral failure and psychological disurbance.[77]

The burden of such studies is that Renaissance tragedy usually treats a figure of noble status, a king, prince, or military commander. The plot is based on true or legendary history, and the artist freely shapes the historical materials to suit his purposes. The hero's tragic flaw is a moral one, often treated as a psychological disorder. The action moves toward a catastrophe that is the result of the flaw and in some sense a punishment for it. The catastrophe warns the audience against the flaw exemplified. Because of the hero's rank, tragedy is especially useful for instructing magistrates and members of the nobility. Melpomene, the personified tragic Muse of Thomas Heywood's *Apology for Actors,* boasts that she

> . . . held in awe the tyrants of the world
> And played their lives in public theatres,
> Making them fear to sin, since fearless I
> Prepared to write their names in crimson ink
> And act their shames in eye of all the world.

And Heywood, writing *in propria persona,* insisted that "if we present a Tragedy, we include the fatall and abortive ends of such as commit notorious murders, which is aggravated and acted with all the art that may be, to terrify men from the like abhorred vices."[78]

To these observations we need only add that the technique—as opposed to the object—of tragedy was defined by rhetorically oriented critics as "reprehension" or *vituperatio.* Puttenham devotes three chapters of the *Arte of English Poesie* (XIII-XV) to poetry in which "vice and the common abuses of mans life was reprehended." These include satire, comedy, and tragedy, and his summary of tragedy is a particularly clear example of the rhetorical point of view: ". . . the bad and illawdable parts of all estates and degrees were taxed by the Poets in one sort or an other, and those of great Princes by Tragedie in especial, & not till after their deaths . . . to th'intent that such exemplifying (as it were) of their blames and adversities, being now dead, might worke for a secret represension to others that were alive, living in the same or like abuses. . . ."[79] That this idea had practical consequences for the drama is suggested by a play like Shakespeare's *Richard III,* which is an almost literal transfer of the topics of *vituperatio* from the pages of the rhetoric book to the stage. The topics of *effictio* include praise of nation, family, birth, and appearance. Shakespeare could not "reverse" the first three of these topics without appearing unpatriotic, but he made the most of the fourth. Not only is Richard's physical deformity emphasized, but throughout he is described with the imagery of animals. He is "made up . . . so lamely and unfashionable/ That dogs bark at me as I halt by them" (I, i, 21-23); and in Act I, alone, he is called "minister of Hell" (ii, 46); "foul devil" (ii, 50); "hedgehog" (ii, 101); "toad" (ii, 148); "abortive, rooting hog" (iii, 228); and "poisonous bunch-back'd toad" (iii, 246), to cite only the most prominent examples.

Like the encomium, the *vituperatio* concentrates on deeds revealing moral qualities. If the *Cyropaedia* is a panegyrical biography, *Richard III* is a negative biography. Although it is dramatic rather than narrative, it has structural features like Xenophon's work.[80] Historically, Shakespeare's play stretches from the death of Henry VI (1471) to the death of Richard (1485). From the mass of material available, Shakespeare selected episodes illustrating the various evil deeds by which Richard gained and attempted to retain the throne of England. One of the scenes—the wooing of Anne—is pure invention and serves to illustrate Richard's hypocrisy and craft. The murder of Clarence illustrates his treachery; the interview with the Lord Mayor and citizens of London, his Machiavellian politics; the murder of the princes, his cruelty; the ghost-scene (V, iii), his cowardice and despair. These episodes are arranged chronologically and, more emphatically than the episodes of the *Cyropaedia,* they form a continuous action leading to the Battle of Bosworth Field. The final action as far as the protagonist is concerned is his death. This is the opposite of the "good end" which Xenophon invented to crown the life of his ideal hero. Richard dies in battle, knowing his cause is lost, and at the hands of his arch-enemy.

Supplementing and underscoring the use of the topics of *vituperatio* is a constant stream of invective hurled at Richard throughout the play. It is particularly significant that Queen Margaret, who is a choral character and the source of a great deal of this invective, was largely Shakespeare's invention. She obviously "heightens" the *vituperatio* and might be compared to epic embellishments of history for the purpose of heightening the praise of the hero.

Marlowe's *Jew of Malta* is another play which makes uninhibited use of the topics of *vituperatio*. Indeed, Marlowe's Jew is such a repulsive creature that it has been suggested that Marlowe meant him to be a comic figure, perhaps a satire on Elizabethan villains. Jonson's Sejanus is a close kin to Shakespeare's Richard and Marlowe's Jew. He, too, is a monster of depravity. The play in which he figures tends to become a series of episodes strung on the thread of his rising fortune in which he is given an opportunity to display ambition, lust, vanity, cruelty, treachery, and a host of other vices. When the inevitable catastrophe has occurred, Jonson leaves his audience with an admonition underscoring his exemplary purpose: "Let this example move th' insolent man/ Not to grow proud and careless of the gods. . . ." Jacobean dramatists often used *vituperatio* so freely that their tragedies became condemnations of society at large. The technique—evident in plays like Webster's *Duchess of Malfi* and Ford's *'Tis Pity She's a Whore*—makes for a curious blend of tragedy and satire with affinities to such bitterly satirical comedies as Machiavelli's *Mandragola* and Ben Jonson's *Volpone.*

The techniques of *vituperatio* are most obvious in tragedies that deal with total depravity, whether individual or social. They are far less apparent in tragedies whose protagonists are essentially noble figures brought to ruin by a single flaw. In fact, rhetorical criticism is of very limited assistance in the analysis of plays like *Hamlet* or *Othello*. It can provide some useful information about the dramatist's language, but its prescriptions are far too limited to cast much light on structure or characterization. A gifted rhetorician might conceivably have produced a work resembling *Richard III*. On the other hand, only a mature dramatist, drawing on resources undreamed of in the pages of Menander and Cicero, could have created the succession of tragedies extending from *Julius Caesar* to *Antony and Cleopatra*.

V. LYRIC

Renaissance lyric is more obviously influenced by epideictic rhetoric than any other genre. This is partly because of the natural tendency of lyric expression to assume the form of praise. Inevitably, the formal rhetorical theory stressed in the Renaissance curriculum continued to be an important influence when the schoolboy had become a courtier and was turning his hand to sugared trifles and idle sonnets, the fruits of his leisure hours. Criticism reinforced this influence. There is a good deal of Renaissance comment on the nature of lyric poetry, and almost all of it contains references, sometimes brief, sometimes elaborate, to the theory of praise. Religious poems had been defined as "praise of the gods" from the time of Plato, and Menander gives formulae for several types of hymn in his *Peri Epideiktikon*. Beginning with Statius, Roman poets consciously used epideictic formulae for short occasional lyrics, and it needs no elaborate argument to prove that a good many love lyrics are simple, undisguised praise of a lady. Among the critics, Minturno taught that the function of lyric was "properly in praising and praying";[81] while Campanella wrote, "Since some outstanding men were worthy of praise on account of excellent benefits to the people and virtue shown at death or in some outstanding deed—as in the case of saints and heroes—therefore hymns and odes were invented and the songs which we sing to the lyre."[82] Vossius took the same view,[83] and Sidney observed that the lyric "with his tuned Lyre, and well accorded voyce, giveth praise, the reward of vertue, to vertuous acts. . . ."[84]

Lyric, like the epideictic oration, arouses the hearer to admiration and emulation. Sidney believed that lyric was "most capable and most fit to awake the thoughts from the sleep of idlenes to imbrace honorable enterprises."[85] Minturno summarized the point neatly: "It seems to me that whoever is praised by such pleasant song either in company or during festivities is inflamed to doing what will gain more praise. And whoever hears it is excited to emulate him who merits so much praise, since both men believe that praise is the highest reward of virtue. . . . [Lyric] stimulates men to honorable and excellent acts."[86]

The idea that lyric is a poem praising gods or heroes is clarified by the examples that the Renaissance critics cite to illustrate lyric excellence. Inevitably the key examples, and the ones almost never missing from discussions of lyric, are David, Pindar, and Horace. At times David was considered an imitator of classical poets, as when Lodge claimed that "David was a poet, and . . . his vayne was in imitating (as S. Ierom witnesseth) Horace, Flaccus, and Pindarus."[87] More often, David was considered superior to the classical poets and even their model, as when Christ in *Paradise Regained* explains,

> . . . our Psalms with artful terms inscrib'd,
> Our Hebrew Songs and Harps in *Babylon*
> That pleas'd so well our Victors ear, declare
> That rather *Greece* from us these Arts deriv'd;
> Ill imitated, while they loudest sing. . . .[88]

We are thus led to a definition of the better type of lyric as a form based on praise and imitating the psalms or the odes of Pindar or Horace. To refine this definition and to understand the way in which it can be modified to include love lyric, it will be necessary to examine in more detail the traditions of the religious poem—i.e., psalm and hymn.

The influence of the psalms on lyric theory is considerable. From the time of Josephus and Origen, Christian writers have been fond of tracing classical forms in the Bible. Jerome is a common source for the idea. In his preface to the *Chronicle of Eusebius,* for example, he remarks that Deuteronomy, Isaiah, the Song of Solomon, and Job "as Josephus and Origen tell us, were composed in hexameters and pentameters. . . ."[89] And he makes a special reference to the psalms in a letter to Paulinus of Nola: "David, who is our Simonides, Pindar, and Alcaeus, our Horace, our Catullus, and our Sirenus all in one, sings of Christ to his lyre."[90] The centuries between Jerome and the Renaissance produced nothing to weaken Jerome's thesis. Milton called the Song of Solomon a "divine pastoral drama," Revelation a "high and stately tragedy," and Job a brief epic.[91] Although the modern reader might quarrel about Revelation and Job, the case for the psalms as lyrics is quite strong as long as their metrical regularity is not insisted on.[92]

Because the psalms are so successful as lyrics, they have been a living influence during every period of religious enthusiasm. The earliest Latin hymns were modeled on them. Later, imitation of the psalms was the formative element in the style of the sequences of the eleventh century and after. The finest product of the Franciscan revival is the *Laudes creatu-*

rarum, which is modeled directly on the psalms.[93] Finally, the psalms form the basis of Calvinist hymnody and, therefore, had special influence during the Protestant Reformation in England, a fact reflected in the great number of metrical paraphrases of the psalms made between 1550 and 1650.[94]

In view of their influence, the critical interpretation of psalm and hymn is of considerable importance, and on this subject there is almost monotonous uniformity. Despite their heterogeneity they are almost always called poems of praise. St. Augustine's comment on Psalm CLXVII is the *locus classicus* for the idea: "'Praise the Lord,' he saith, 'for a Psalm is good.' . . . The 'Psalm' is praise of God. This, then, he saith, 'Praise the Lord, for it is good to praise the Lord.' . . . Wilt thou then sing a Psalm? Let not thy voice alone sound the praises of God, but let thy works also be in harmony with thy voice."[95] Since the psalms are described in the Vulgate as "hymns sung by David,"[96] it is not surprising to find that Augustine defines hymn as a form which "consisteth of three things: song, and praise, and that of God. Praise, then, of God in song is called a hymn."[97] Commentators, popularizers, critics, and artists from Isidore of Seville to George Wither were content to follow Augustine's lead.[98]

The venerable and unequivocal definition of hymns and psalms as poems of praise was bound to encourage this element in secular lyrics. Even before the age of the *stil novo* Latin and vernacular poets employed epideictic themes. Many examples provided by Geoffrey of Vinsauf for his *Poetria nova* are frankly epideictic—the notorious lament for Richard is a case in point. Popular poetry employed themes of praise in a less self-conscious way. According to students of the genre, Troubadour *canso* alternates naturally between praise of the lady and lament.[99] The poets of the *stil novo* inherited many of the motifs of praise used by the Troubadours. Yet they were not mere imitators, for they infused the materials of their French predecessors with a spirituality that was new to secular lyric. Theology, allegorical methods of reading scripture, speculations on the nature and destiny of the soul, quasi-Platonic explorations of love, and (in the case of Guittone d'Arezzo) scholastic rationalism all contributed to the new lyric, and it is reasonable to assume that along with religious themes, the *stilnovisti* assimilated the standard interpretations of the way in which the religious poet should express himself.

Karl Vossler's work on Dante and his milieu is in many respects dated, but his emphasis on the Fransciscan revival still seems right.[100] It calls attention to the part played by the *laudesi*—writers of religious "praises" in the vernacular—in preparing the way for the *stilnovisti.* The *laudesi,* of whom Jacopone da Todi is today the best known, discovered that the most exalted spiritual experiences can be expressed in direct, passionate language.[101] Inverting this technique, the *stilnovisti* describe human love in terms suggesting intense spirituality. Cino da Pistoia addressed his love as "my sweet god" ("dolce mio dio") and prayed to Lady Selvaggia with the astonishing comment, "In your hands, my sweet Lady, I deliver up my dying spirit" ("Nelle man vostre, dolce Donna mia,/ Raccomando lo spirito che moure").[102] Dante's Beatrice, it has been pointed out, is so nearly a Christ figure that editions of the *Vita nuova* were censored in Italy during the Counter-Reformation;[103] and Petrarch explicitly compared the birth of Laura to the birth of Christ.[104]

Such expressions are, in themselves, a form of praise, and there is ample evidence that the *stilnovisti* were conscious of the fact. Despite the fact that the *Vita nuova* is about equally divided between the glories of the lady and the miseries of the lover, Dante speakes of it in Section XVIII as though it were wholly praise: "I proposed to take for my material always that which would be praise of this most gentle lady. . . ."[105] Petrarch is equally emphatic. The fifth sonnet of the *Canzoniere* strikes a keynote of the work in its pun on the similarity between the name *Laura* and the Italian word for praising, *laudando:*

> When I sigh out, calling to you
> And your name, which Love wrote in my heart,
> Praising begins to be heard on every side—
> The sound of the first sweet syllable of your name. . . .[106]

Petrarch continued to think of his sonnets as praise even when he regretted having written them. Toward the end of his life he described them as "inane little songs filled with the false and obscene praise of females."[107] That writers of the sixteenth century continued to regard the Petrarchan sonnet as a kind of praise is shown by the comment on Petrarch written by Bernardino Tomitano in 1545: "Petrarch praises his lady throughout the *Canzoniere* in respect to the nobility of her family, her intelligence, and her spirit. . . . So that most of his sonnets are to be placed in the epideictic category (*genere dimonstrativo*) . . . the words, the letters, the syllables, the very articles, not to mention the whole verses and poems of the poet [are] full of the praise of Laura. . . ."[108]

Tomitano's brief summary of the topics of praise used by Petrarch (family, intelligence, spirit) suggests that one important feature of the *stil novo* was less obvious to sixteenth-century rhetoricians than to modern historical scholars. There are many references to such matters as the nobility and beauty of the lady in the work of *stilnovisti,* but these are less significant than might be expected. In fact, it has been suggested that lack of emphasis on externals is a defining characteristic of the *stil novo*.[109] The Italian poets were more interested in "goods of character" than in "goods of nature" or "goods of fortune." We know that the ladies celebrated by

Guido Cavalcanti, Dante, and Petrarch are paragons of *bellezza,* but it is their *virtù* that the poets emphasize. Even ruby lips, golden hair, lily skin, ivory teeth, and jewel-like eyes tend to become outward manifestations of an inward grace.

The *stilnovisti* were not content with direct praise of the lady's virtue. They also emphasized it indirectly by showing its ennobling effect on the lover. The troubadours had employed this device in a limited way by suggesting that love begets gentility in the lover, but in the poetry of the *stil novo* the effect of love is more profound. It is Beatrice's *virtù* rather than her *gentilezza* which Dante eventually comes to imitate. Thus, his rejection of the god of love need not be read as a palinode in which the love of the lady is also rejected. The proper sequel to the *Vita nuova* is the *Paradiso,* where Dante is reunited with Beatrice in the world of spiritual perfection to which she has led him. Petrarch's sonnets to Laura follow the same pattern. There is the traditional emphasis on *gentilezza:* "the honest appearance and the courteous reasoning,/ The words which it heard,/ Have made gentle a base heart" (cclxx, 81-83). But there is also the newer orientation: "My faithful and dear leader/ Who led me in the world, now leads me/ By a better path to an untroubled life" (ccclvii). And yet more emphatic,

> O happy that day when, departing the earthly prison
> I leave this heavy, frail, and mortal dress
> Broken and scattered in the dust.
> And from such thick and mournful shades
> I fly so high in the beautiful serenity of heaven
> That I see my Lord and my lady! (cccxlix)

A natural corollary to praise of the lady's virtue is the development of an allegorical bias. Epic tends to become allegorical because it is a praise of virtue as well as of a quasi-historical hero. The same is true of love lyric. In the first place, the sonnet lady has a kind of historical vagueness that is analogous to the legendary quality of the epic hero. Beatrice, Simonetta, Délie, Stella, and Shakespeare's "dark lady" remain enigmatic despite the ingenuity of numberless scholars, and it would seem time to admit that the Renaissance sonnet writer had a better reason than modesty for not being explicit about his subject. The slightly vague, generalized quality of the sonnet lady is the result of the desire to objectify. If the subject were a particular woman, the poem describing her would tend to become either a list of banalities or gross flattery. Since the subject is ambiguous—*based on* history but not limited to it—the poet speaks with a double voice. To the lady he is a passionate lover; to his larger audience he is the creator of an image of ideal womanhood.

The stereotyped pattern of the sonnet cycle as a whole reinforces the allegorical effect. The same event, repeated from cycle to cycle, eventually becomes impersonal. It is no longer a biographical detail but a convention. Its meaning—if it is to have any—must come from its suggestion of a general truth or experience. The death of the sonnet lady, for example, became a convention early in the history of the Italian sonnet cycle. Its repetition was justified by allegorical exegesis, which explained it as the symbol of a mystic death to the world marking the transition of the lover from carnal to spiritual values. In the words of a recent critic, it "corresponds in the medieval mystique to the death of human reason in seizure and ecstasy of the mind; to the death, in sum, of Rachel, who died mystically through raising herself to the summit of contemplation."[110]

Lyric allegory persisted from the age of the *stil novo* until the sixteenth century. The very title of Dante's *Vita nuova* invites allegorical interpretation. A sample of full-scale allegorical interpretation is supplied by Dante in his analysis of the *canzoni* of the *Convivio,* where the critical method parallels the methods of biblical exegesis—with due allowance for the difficult distinction between "poets' allegory" and allegory of theologians. The members of the Florentine Academy brushed aside such distinctions in their search for an esoteric religion, adumbrating Christianity, in the poetry and mythology of the ancients. Some of their enthusiasm is evident in the sonnets of Lorenzo de'Medici, who opened his cycle with the death of the lady and justified himself with the observation that "if love has in itself that perfection which we have already remarked, it is impossible to come to that perfection without dying first." Later he added that "the beginning of true life is the end of the life which is not true"[111]—an apparently intentional allusion to the Christian devotional tradition. During the sixteenth century, critics continued to regard lyrics as allegories. Because of the variety of traditions that they inherited their comments varied widely, ranging from detailed exegesis, such as Daniello's reading of a Petrarch *canzone* as an allegory of the poet's allegiance to philosophy and theology,[112] to Gascoigne's rather hazy remark, "If I should undertake to wryte in prayse of a gentlewoman . . . I would either finde some supernaturall cause . . . or discover my disquiet in shadowes *per Allegoriam*. . . ."[113] Most sixteenth-century authors would probably have agreed with Gabriel Harvey that Petrarch is a poet "whose ditty is an Image of the Sun voutsafing to represent his glorious face in a clowde."[114]

In considering the debt of the love lyric to the tradition of praise, it has been necessary to ignore one major motif, the lover's description of his pains. This motif is not harmonized with the epideictic element in lyric, any more than the penitential psalms are consistent with the definition of psalm as *Laus Dei*. However, the sonnet writers often used it as oblique praise. The lady's power is illustrated by the way in which her slightest action—even an accidental glance—can plunge the lover into despair or raise him to ecstasy. Moreover, the lover's pains and the lady's cruelty are always somehow delightful. According to Petrarch love is a "sweet trouble" which "sweetly consumes me"; its pains are "delicious hardships," and a whole sonnet (cxxxii) is devoted to the paradox of love as "a living death or a delightful bane."[115] Lorenzo de'Medici says that his love-agonies were so pleasurable that they gave him a reason for desiring to live when he was imprisoned and life seemed hopeless.[116] The paradox of pleasurable pain is a commonplace in the love lyric of the sixteenth century. The reason for its popularity is partly love of wit for its own sake, but another factor is the need to reconcile the lover's pains with the celebration of the lady. If the pains were really painful and the lady really cruel, the lover might seem to be criticizing her rather than singing her praises.

The patterns and motifs of the *stilnovisti* persisted throughout the high Renaissance. Like their predecessors, the sonnet writers of the sixteenth century wrote lyrics combining historical, exemplary, and allegorical levels of meaning. Perhaps the most distinctive new feature of their work is their tendency to substitute a Platonic quasi-religion for the earlier Christian framework. The Platonic ladder as described by Bembo in the *Cortegiano,* Scève in the *Délie,* and Spenser in the *Fowre Hymnes* came to be a standard symbol for love's effects. Spenser, in fact, reconverted the love lyric into hymn. His *Fowre Hymnes* trace the influence of love from delight in physical beauty to a final mystic glimpse of

> . . . that soveraine light,
> From whose pure beams al perfect beauty springs,
> That kindleth love in every godly spright,
> Even the love of God. . . .[117]

If Petrarch and David were models for the love lyric and hymn, Pindar was the great model for the secular lyric.[118] Horace was widely admired and imitated along with Anacreon in lyrics on such shady topics as the pleasures of wine and the Good Life. But after the Aldine edition of Pindar (1513) writers of secular lyric increasingly aspired to the heady sublimity of the formal ode. When the difficulties of imitating Pindar became evident, as they did to poets like Gabriello Chiabrera and Ronsard, the poets returned to simpler "Horatian" forms but attempted to infuse them with Pindaric spirit. Marvell's "Horatian Ode" celebrating Oliver Cromwell is an English example of the amalgam.

One feels that the attempt to imitate Pindar was for the most part unfortunate. In the first place, Pindar was insufficiently understood. Certain externals of his technique could be imitated—his triads, his irregular lines, his myths, and his "enthusiastical manner" as Dryden called it. But Congreve pointed out in his *Discourse on the Pindarique Ode* (1705) that Abraham Cowley, the most assiduous English imitator of Pindar, interpreted Pindar's complexity as simple rhapsodic freedom. Pindar himself, says Congreve, followed rules and laws. The full explanation of Pindar's forms did not come until the nineteenth century; and explanation of his use of imagery, myth, and musical (rather than logical) unity has been heavily indebted to the interest of modern poets and "new critics" in these matters.

Failing in understanding, Renaissance poets were forced to interpret the Pindaric in terms that fitted their own conception of what poetry should accomplish. Since Pindar's odes are occasional and ostensibly devoted to "celebration," they were interpreted as encomia. They were distinguished from the straightforward rhetorical form of encomium by the sublimity of their style, the elevation of their subjects and the poetic furor that begot them. Renaissance authors were not interested in athletic victories, but they were interested in hymns and praises of kings, nobles, outstanding public figures, military victors, and patrons. These themes, treated according to the epideictic topics and elaborately varied in imitation of Pindar's supposed freedom, were the dominant themes of Pindaric as written by Luigi Alamanni, Ronsard, Benedetto Lampridio, Gabriello Chiabrera, John Southern, Ben Jonson, Abraham Cowley, and John Dryden. Gilbert Highet says of Ronsard's odes, "most of them . . . are merely encomia"; and he characterizes the use of the form in the late sixteenth and seventeenth centuries as follows: "Most of the Pindaric odes written in the baroque period were not musical but ceremonial. With the aid of Pindar, poets celebrated the births, marriages, and deaths of the nobility and gentry; the accessions, coronations, birthdays, jubilees, and victories of monarchs; the founding of a society, the announcement of an invention, the construction of a public building, any public event that expressed the pomp and circumstance of the age."[119] Inevitably, literary theory encouraged would-be Pindars and their cousins, the would-be Horaces, to move from celebration of men to celebrations of institutions and abstractions. Cowley celebrated the Muse and Destiny as well as the more conventional subjects. Even the female sex eventually received Pindaric tribute. The finest English Pindaric of the seventeenth century, Dryden's "To the Pious Memory of . . . Mrs. Anne Killigrew," manipulates the topics of elegy to celebrate feminine virtue.[120]

VI. LYRIC AND COMEDY

Because of their subjects, hymns and odes were considered to have an elevation comparable to that of epic and tragedy and were therefore to be in the "high style." Love lyric was a different matter. Since its subject was not noble in the technical sense it was assigned the middle style. This does not mean that it was considered less "artistic" than epic. In fact, because of its brevity and lack of narrative or dramatic structure it should be more finely wrought than higher forms of poetry.[121] Tasso explained, "The style of lyric, then, although not so magnificent as the heroic, must be much more flowery and ornate. This form of flowered speech (as the rhetoricians affirm) is a property of the middle style (*mediocrità*). The style of lyric should be flowery because the person of the poet appears more frequently [than in epic] and because the materials which are treated are for the most part materials which would remain base and low if unornamented by flowers and wit (*scherzi*)."[122]

Tasso here stresses the two *differentiae* which we have seen to be major factors in the system of epic and tragic genres. These are the *differentiae* of "object of imitation" and "moral end." His first point is that in lyric the "person of the poet" often appears. Since the lyric poet is usually not noble and almost never heroic, decorum requires that he be treated in a style less grand than that reserved for gods, heroes, and princes. The second point is that erotic love is intrinsically "base and low." It is not the lowest possible subject. In certain circumstances it can lead to mystic vision, but it is intrinsically less edifying than epic combats or the fall of great men from high station. "Heroic love," it may be noted, is quite different from the love depicted in the sonnet cycles as comparison of the *Gerusalemme liberata* to the *Canzoniere* will quickly demonstrate. Thus both subject and "object" of love lyric are inferior to these elements in forms reserved for the "high style."

In the *Arte of English Poesie,* Puttenham observes that ". . . all Comedies and Enterludes and other common Poesies of loves and such like [are] in the meane [i.e., middle] style."[123] The quotation suggests that comedy is related stylistically to lyric. The basis of this linkage is that comedies, like lyrics, deal with the middle class rather than with kings and princes. The idea can be traced to the Theophrastian distinction between comedy and tragedy and was transmitted by late classical grammarians and scholiasts to the Middle Ages. In his essay on comedy and tragedy, Euanthius points out that the earliest comedy—the "old comedy"—began as satire of individual citizens who were identified by their proper names. The "new comedy" according to Euanthius continued to satirize citizens but did so in a more universal manner. Fictional names were substituted for proper names, the characters tended to become "types" rather than specific individuals, and the satire became less abusive.[124] This defines the practice of Menander, Plautus, and Terence, and it is the practice prescribed by Renaissance critics. According to Puttenham, comic poets properly treated ". . . sometimes of their owne private affaires, sometimes of their neighbours, but never medling with any Princes matters nor such high personages, but commonly of marchants, souldiers, artificers, good honest housholders, and also of unthrifty youthes, yong damsels, old nurses, bawds, brokers . . . and therefore tended altogither to the good amendment of man by discipline and example."[125]

Puttenham's remarks not only indicate the tendency of Renaissance theory, they also describe a good deal of Renaissance practice. Comic writers like Ariosto, Machiavelli, Ben Jonson, and Molière, who were imbued with neoclassic doctrine, seldom gave major parts to comic characters of more than a middle-class rank. Shakespeare was much freer in his choice of subjects, but he, too, concentrated on the middle class. *The Comedy of Errors, The Taming of the Shrew,* and *The Merry Wives of Windsor* are fairly strict middle-class comedies. *Twelfth Night* and *As You Like It* include members of the ruling order, but the focus of attention is on members of the lower class of nobility and middle-class characters. *Measure for Measure* is restricted in a similar fashion: the Duke of Vienna is a *deux ex machina* and during most of the action he is disguised as a friar.

If comedy was associated with lyric in regard to style, it was associated with tragedy on moral grounds—another instance of Renaissance disregard of "mode of imitation." Like tragedy, comedy was considered a form that rebukes vice. Euanthius traced comedy to festivals at which the Athenians, "when they wished to publicize men of evil habits . . . published their vices along with their individual names. . . ."[126] Isidore said of comedians, "they rebuked the vices of all men; nor was it forbidden to describe the worst ones or to reprehend the sins and habits of anyone."[127] Although the new comedy was less personal, its object remained the reprehension of the sins and follies of the middle class.

This view of comedy is the one most often taken during the sixteenth century. Castelvetro asserted that "comic writers . . . ridiculed and made fun of vices and [foolish] actions."[128] Lodge pointed out that tragedy and comedy have a common basis in their use of "reprehension" and differ in respect to gravity: "[comedies] had theyr beginning with tragedies, but their matter was more pleasaunt, for they were suche as did reprehend, yet *quodam lepore*."[129] Sidney repeats these ideas with emphasis on the moral purpose of the comic form: "Comedy is an imitation of the common errors of our life, which he [the poet] representeth in the most ridiculous and scornefull sort that may be; so as it is impossible that any beholder can be content to be such a one."[130] Ben Jonson, too, accepted the standard Renaissance theory of comedy. He believed that "the parts of a comedy are the same with a tragedy, and the end [correction of vice] is partly the same."[131] There is a bitter streak in Jonson's comedy that suggests the same quality in Machiavelli and Molière. Although he did not revert to the proper names of "old comedy," he did at times revert to the bitter abuse associated with that form. This intensifies the element of *vituperatio* in his work. In the preface to *Everyman Out of his Humour,* Jonson compared to a scourge rather than to the pleasant instrument of correction described by Lodge:

> I will scourge those apes;
> And to these courteous eyes oppose a mirror,
> As large as is the stage whereon we act
> Where they shall see the time's deformity
> Anatomized in every nerve and sinew,
> With constant courage and contempt of fear.[132]

Considered in moral terms satire is an obvious cousin to the type of comedy described by Jonson. Castelvetro distinguished between comedy and satire on the basis of the intensity of the rebuke. Comedy makes fun of its characters, but satirists are "critics (*biasmatori*) of vice who do not make fun of it."[133] Campanella frankly used the term *vituperatio* to describe satire and defined its end as "execration of vices."[134] Puttenham summed the matter up by saying, "The first and most bitter invective against vice and vicious men was the *Satyre*. . . . [Poets] made wise as if the gods of the woods, whom they called *Satyres,* or *Silvanes,* should appear and recite those verses of rebuke, whereas in deede they were but disguised persons under the shape of Satyres. . . .[135] In sum, the criterion of "object or imitation" led Renaissance critics to associate lyric and comedy, since both were considered imitations of "middle" subjects; while the criterion of "moral purpose" led them to the quite different but equally emphatic association of comedy with tragedy and satire.

The system of genres which has emerged from the preceding discussion may be presented schematically as follows:

Forms Based on Praise	*Forms Based on Blame*	*Style*	*Subject Matter*
Hymns Epic "Encomia of heroes," Ode	"Admonitory epic" Tragedy	High Style	Gods, Heroes, Members of the Nobility, Great Men, Great Occasions, Noble Abstractions
Love Lyric Occasional Poetry	Comedy (Horatian Satire?)	Middle Style	Middle Class; The "Person of the Poet," Middle Class Occasions (Birth, Marriage, Death, etc.)

Poetry on Humble Men and Conditions (Pastoral?)	Early Satire; Vituperative Satire	Humble Style	Members of the Lower Class (Shepherds, Farmers, Artisans, etc.), Oblique References to the Great (As in *The Shepherd's Calendar*)

It would be wholly erroneous to maintain that this system is the only one which was suggested during the Reanaissance. Many critics ignored it completely and others made important variations of their own. Yet it was extremely widespread. Influenced by the distinctions of epideictic rhetoric, it satisfied the requirement that the major forms of literature be clearly oriented toward instruction. It appeared consistent with a good deal of literary tradition inherited from the Middle Ages, and it also appeared to conform to the *Poetics* as that work was commonly interpreted. It enabled the critic to see the major genres in relation to one another rather than in isolation, and it thereby emphasized the unity of poetic art. It also influenced literary practice. It helped the artist apply to literary composition the rhetorical techniques that he had learned in school and it did this in the areas of invention, plot-construction and characterization as well as diction. It certainly did not give him final answers, but it provided a starting point from which he could begin to explore the questions.

CHAPTER V

Occasional Poetry

When Sir Philip Sidney's muse advised him, "Look into thy heart and write," she spoke more than she knew. Following her advice, Sir Philip discovered inspiration, but he also found a considerable array of rules, moral ideals, models, conventions, commonplace sentiments, and techniques within which the inspiration was contained. A little more than two hundred years later the advice of Sidney's muse became a cardinal principle of romanticism. Goethe, Wordsworth, Shelley, and Baudelaire looked into their hearts, but what they found was different from what Sidney had found. The romantic heart was not a storehouse of conventions and traditions but a refuge from them. The heart had its reasons, the imprisoned soul had its intimations of immortality, the Aeolian harp played without conscious effort, and the buried life sent airs and floating echoes from the soul's subterranean depth. True poetry was to be a journey into the self and the poet an explorer of the darkness at the center of life. Poetry itself tended increasingly toward lyric. According to the Spasmodic poets of England and Edgar Allan Poe in the United States, the long narrative poem was a contradiction in terms; at best the epics of the past are a series of lyric outbursts set like jewels in a drab narrative framework.

By corollary occasional poetry came to be considered a kind of betrayal of the muse. Occasional poems were not subjective. Instead of looking into his heart the occasional poet usually looked into the purse of his patron for inspiration and handbooks of rhetoric for techniques. Wordsworth was pilloried for his productions as poet laureate; to Browning he was a lost leader who sold out, Judas-like, for a handful of silver and a riband to stick in his coat. Southey, because he had so little to betray, was treated with ridicule rather than rebuke and, lacking wit himself, was the occasion of immense wit in Byron. Since the beginning of the nineteenth century the occasional mode has almost vanished from serious poetry. Tennyson's

"Ode on the Death of the Duke of Wellington," Whitman's "When Lilacs Last in the Dooryard Bloom'd," and Allen Tate's "Ode to the Confederate Dead" are brilliant exceptions which stand out all the more because they have so few rivals.

During the Renaissance, however, occasional literature was highly valued. Poets and critics agreed that literature had an important social mission. The great forms like epic and drama dealt with legendary or historical figures and produced generalized patterns for emulation or admonition. The occasional forms dealt with contemporary events and living (or recently living) figures. They were particularly suited to arousing patriotism, stimulating interest in specific institutions or events, teaching admiration for a particular ruler, or demonstrating the existence of virtue in the society in which the reader actually lived. Book III of *The Faerie Queene* depicts love in the legendary and idealized setting of Spenser's Arthurian England. Real love—love experienced by living Elizabethans—is celebrated by Spenser in two occasional poems, the "Epithalamion" and the "Prothalamion." *The Faerie Queene* has its topical allegory pointing toward the historical reality of the Elizabethan court, and the "Epithalamion" has its mythological allusions that point toward the romantic world of legend and ideal types, but these need not obscure the essential difference. The epic centers on experience higher than and removed from everyday life; the occasional poem is begotten by a real and contemporary event.

To appreciate the full range of Renaissance poetry it is necessary to abandon the romantic prejudice against occasional literature. It is true that library shelves groan beneath the weight of laments over forgotten men, praises of insignificant municipalities, and encomia representing black-hearted villians as shining examples of Christian piety. However, it is also true that poets like Tasso, Ronsard, Spenser, Jonson, Donne, and Milton frequently wrote in the occasional mode and produced compositions of great artistic merit. To ignore these compositions or to try to pretend that they are not occasional is to miss or distort an important expression of Renaissance ideals.

The present chapter begins with a brief survey of occasional types. Since the life of man is short, it does not attempt to examine them all in detail. Instead, one of the richest types, funeral elegy, is selected as representative, and the chapter continues with an analysis of the standard topics and patterns of funeral elegy. The two chapters that follow relate theory to practice. In Chapter VI several funeral elegies are examined. Each has some claims to literary merit in its own right and together, the elegies illustrate the ways in which a skillful Renaissance poet could adapt the topics to varying circumstances and objectives. In Chapter VII two compositions—Donne's *Anniversaries*—serve to demonstrate the remarkable potentialities of the form when used by a major artist as the height of his creative power.

I. THE OCCASIONAL TYPES

Although occasional poetry is as ancient as poetry itself, during the late classical period its forms were codified in works like Menander's *Peri Epideiktikon,* and taught as types of epideictic oration. The formulae were elaborated and modified by later rhetoricians but, as Theodore Burgess has demonstrated in his *Epideictic Literature,* the continuity of the formulae is far more striking than the modifications. Reference to Appendix I, where the lists compiled by Menander and Scaliger are reproduced, will confirm this point. We may take it as fact that from the second century B.C. until well into the seventeenth century the formulae were essentially static. When poets like Statius, Claudian, or Ausonius wrote occasional poetry they followed the formulae with such elaborations and inventions as their talents permitted. Renaissance critics recognized their use of the formulae and were inclined to look for the same formulae even in works like the Homeric hymns and the odes of Pindar. Renaissance poets drew both on the formulae and the late classical models when composing original occasional poems.

In the *Arte of English Poesie,* Puttenham lists the more important occasional types. His list is less elaborate than that compiled by Scaliger but its convenience outweighs its relatively minor oversights. In the quotation below standard rhetorical labels for the types are given in brackets:

Chapter XII

[hymn]: The gods of the Gentiles were honoured by their Poetes in hymnes, which is an extraordinarie and divine praise, extolling and magnifying them for their great powers and excellencie of nature in the highest degree of laude.

[genealogicon]: Wherefore to praise the gods of the Gentiles for that by authoritie of their owne fabulous records they had fathers and mothers, and kinred and allies, and wives and concubines, the Poets first commended them by their genealogies or pedegrees.

[peplasmenos logos]: their marriages and aliances, their notable exploits in the world for the behoofe of mankind.

[mythikos and physikos]: [The hymns reporting acts of the Gods] such of them as were true were grounded upon some part of an historie or matter of veritie, the rest altogether figurative & mysticall, covertly applied to some morall or naturall sense, as *Cicero* setteth it foorth in his bookes *de natura deorum* . . . therefore the Gentiles prayed for peace to the goddesse *Pallas;* for warre . . . to the God *Mars;* . . . for issue & prosperities in love, to *Venus* . . . etc.

[Christian hymn]: But with us Christians . . . we cannot exhibit overmuch praise, nor belye him in any wayes, unlesse it be in abasing his excellencie by scarsitie of praise, or by misconceaving his divine nature, weening to praise him if we impute to him such vaine delights and peevish affections as commonly the frailest men are reproved for: namely to make him ambitious of honour, jealous and difficult in his worships, terrible, angrie, vindicative, a lover, a hater, a pitier . . . as in effect he shold be altogether *Anthropopathis*.

[Chapters XIII-XV treat satire, comedy, and tragedy as "reprehensions" of vice. These are not occasional and are considered in the preceding chapter on the major genres.]

Chapter XVI

[encomium, laus, laudatio]: the Poets . . . [were] bound next after the divine praises of the immortall gods to yeeld a like ratable honour to all such amongst men as most resembled the gods by excellencie of function . . . by more then humane and ordinarie vertues shewed in their actions here upon earth. They were therfore praised by a second degree of laude . . . thereby came to be accompted gods and halfe gods or goddesses (*Heroes*), & had their commendations given by Hymne accordingly.

[sub-categories]: [The Poet writes] sheweing their high estates, their Princely genealogies and pedegrees, mariages, aliances, and such noble exploites, as they had done . . . to the benefit of their people and countries. . . .

Chapter XX

["Of lesser praise"]: In everie degree and sort of men vertue is commendable, but not egally . . . for continence in a king is of greater merit then in a carter . . . wherefore the Poet in praising the maner of life or death of anie meane person did it by some litle dittie, or Epigram, or Epitaph, in a fewe verses & meane stile comformable to his subject.

Chapter XXIII

[triumph]: those of victorie and peace are called *Triumphall*.

[encomium]: Those that were to honour the persons of great Princes or to solemnise the pompes of any installment were called *Encomia;* we may call them carols of honour.

[epithalamion]: Those to celebrate marriages were called songs nuptiall or *Epithalamies,* but in a certaine misticall sense, as shall be said hereafter. [Ch. XXVI expatiates on the epithalamion as a celebration and incitement to virtuous love as distinguished from "loose and fickle affection," but it leaves us wondering what the "mysticall sense" may be, since the description of the origin and function of the parts of epithalamion is anything but delicate.]

[genethliaca]: Others for magnificence at the nativities of Princes children, or by custome used yearely upon the same dayes, are called songs natall, or *Genethliaca*. [See also Puttenham's Ch. XXV.]

Chapter XXIV

[Puttenham mentions lamentations of nations or cities over defeat in war and lamentations of lovers; however, major stress falls on funeral poetry.]

[epicede]: . . . the lamenting of deathes was chiefly at the very burialls of

the dead, also at monethes mindes and longer times, by custome continued yearely, when as they used many offices of service and love towardes the dead, and thereupon are called *Obsequies* in our vulgare . . . funerall songs were called *Epicedia* if they were song by many, and *Monodia* if they were utttered by one alone.

Chapter XXVIII

[epitaph]: An Epitaph is but a kind of Epigram only applied to the report of the dead persons estate and degree, or of his other good or bad partes, to his commendation or reproch, and is an inscription such as a man may commodiously write or engrave upon a tombe in few verses, pithie, quicke, and sententious, for the passer-by to peruse and judge upon without any long tariaunce. So as if it exceede the measure of an Epigram, it is then (if the verse be correspondent) rather an Elegie then an Epitaph, which errour many of those bastard rimers commit, because they be not learned.[1]

The major difference between Puttenham's list of occasional forms and the list compiled by Scaliger is organization. Scaliger devotes a separate chapter to each of the more common forms. Puttenham groups the forms in larger chapters dominated by the idea of common function. Chapters XII and XVI deal with praise of gods or men. Chapter XXIII treats poems arising from festive occasions such as military victories, marriages, and birthdays. Finally, Chapters XXIV and XXVIII describe poems of lamentation with particular stress on funeral elegy.

To attempt a simplification one step beyond that of Püttenham we may say that occasional types fall into three general categories—poems praising or blaming a person, poems of lament, and poems praising or blaming non-personal subjects such as cities, rivers, or abstract virtues. The first group employs the topics of personal praise as explained in Aristotle's *Rhetoric* and formalized by his successors. The types are differentiated on the basis of subject and occasion. All poems about gods are hymns. The appearance of the god is given in the form called *physikos logos; mythikos logos* recounts his legendary exploits; and the *genealogikos logos* tells of his ancestry. Praise of a ruler is *basilikos logos;* of a noble figure (not necessarily a king), *encomium*. A speech to one departing is a *propemptikos logos;* a marriage hymn is an *epithalamion;* a funeral oration, an *epitaphios logos*. In each form the basic topics of praise are adapted to the subject and the occasion. Poems dealing with non-personal subjects are labeled according to subject. Most rely heavily on description.

Rhetoric text books such as the *Progymnasmata* of Aphthonius treat epideictic forms as though they can be written according to formula and without much attention to guiding principles. Practically, however, the poet's guiding principles are extremely important and determine how he uses the formulae. Thus the "Lay of Fair Eliza" in Spenser's *Shepherd's*

Calendar is fairly simple flattery; it may be considered praise embellished by elaborate mythological allusions. But this approach would not suffice for the image of Belphoebe in *The Faerie Queene*. Here flattery has given way to the desire to create an exemplary pattern or *pictura*. The lady's beauty is important but it is more than idealized physical attractiveness. Following the conventions of the *stil novo* and numerous Platonic poets of the sixteenth century Spenser makes Belphoebe's beauty an outward symbol of her spiritual graces. If the reader forgets this fact he misses an important level of Spenser's meaning.

The same point may be illustrated in two descriptive poems, one by Ben Jonson and the other by John Donne. A very large percentage of Jonson's poetry is frankly occasional. His elegy on Penshurst follows the conventions for praising a country estate. After contrasting Penshurst with ostentatious houses "built to envious show" Jonson praises its climate, the forest surrounding it, the fields with their farm animals, the ponds brimming with fish, and the orchard. He next describes the happy peasants who "salute" the lord and lady with gifts, and then Penshurst's "liberal board." This is followed by reference to noble visitors, "domestic economy," and the gentility and virtue of the lord's children. Except for occasional mythological allusions, Jonson's description is circumstantial. The reader finishes with a fairly good sense of the "historical" Penshurst. Jonson was no less preoccupied with moral teaching than earlier didactic poets, but he seldom sacrificed the sense of reality for the sake of a moral. Instead he preferred to idealize, and this is the strategy of his elegy on Penshurst. Beyond the clearly delineated historical or "true" setting are hints of pastoral innocence, the golden age, and, perhaps, a suggestion of Eden. These make the poem more than a piece of flattery and lead the reader to significant moral reflections.[2]

By contrast, Donne's "The Calm" seems written from the top down. It is an *ecphrasis*—a description of nature—but its metaphorical meaning is much more important than its literal one. The calm described by Donne is a psychological rather than a natural state; the history crystallizes out of the poet's mood in the manner of an objective correlative. Because of the manifold religious and moral ramifications of the imagery the reader loses interest in the external situation; and, indeed, it is hard to say how important it was to Donne. Although both "To Penshurst" and "The Calm" are excellent poems, each is defective if judged by the standard of the other. Jonson's is cold or trivial or rank flattery if we judge it with "The Calm" as norm; while with "Penshurst" as norm, "The Calm" becomes obscure, undisciplined, crabbed, and exaggerated. Whereas "Penshurst" ends with a graceful apostrophe to the estate, "The Calm" ends with a paradoxical meditation on human impotence:

How little more alas
Is man now, then before he was? He was
Nothing; for us, wee are for nothing fit;
Chance, or our selves doth still disproportion it.
We have no power, no will, no sense; I lye,
I should not then thus feel this miserie.[3]

The two poems are variant developments of epideictic topics. The first emphasizes the historical phase of the total *pictura,* and the second emphasizes the symbolic or moral phase. In both the full range is present, but Jonson seems to start, like a good empiricist, with "things" while Donne starts with "spirit."

II. THE TOPICS OF ELEGY

Poems of lamentation are considerably more complicated than poems of simple praise or blame. They include primarily the types of funeral poetry, ranging from brief epitaph as in the *Greek Anthology* to poems of the length and complexity of Donne's *Anniversaries.* Their influence extends to poems that are not usually considered occasional. For example, the sonnet cycles treating the death of the lady frequently employ the topics of funeral elegy.

The near impossibility of differentiating between the various formal types of funeral poetry such as epitaph, epicede, elegy, and monody has been amply demonstrated.[4] Renaissance authorities are inconsistent and often contradictory in their terminology. For practical purposes, we may take as norm the longer funeral piece, known variously as epitaph, epicede, naenia, or funeral elegy, using the term "funeral elegy" as the most convenient label.

To Greek rhetoricians, the funeral elegy was composed of three main sections, the *epainos,* the *threnos,* and the *paramuthia.*[5] These are respectively the praise of the individual, the song of lament, and the consolation. Although they could be separate compositions, they were most commonly combined, with the last two topics subordinate to the first.[6] Scaliger's formula for the funeral elegy is a convenient introduction to its chief features:

Epitaph is either recent or at anniversaries [*anniversarium*]. In recent, these are the parts: Praise, demonstration of loss, lamentation, consolation, exhortation. At anniversaries all these [are present] except lamentation. For no one weeps for a man dead one or two years. . . . Praises [are] not only of the dead man but of death itself—as in my epitaph on those who died at Vienna in the war against the Turks. The demonstration of loss begins calmly and then with more excited narration in which elaboration and amplification increase the desire for what has been lost. From this part [proceed] immediately [to] lamentation, for since such a noble pledge of glory has been lost, there is nothing else to do but mourn. After this proceed to consolation. Reflect that, although the king is dead, this great loss can be mitigated by the virtues of his successor. You will relate the successor's praise in a most emphatic but brief section. . . . The poem should be closed with exhortations: it is not so much a matter of their being mourned as it is that their present felicity, which shelters their survivors, be treated with due gravity, to further the emulation of their virtues, minds and deaths.[7]

A natural progression of *mood* imposes itself on most funeral poetry, as Scaliger's instructions show. The poem that Scaliger describes will have a definite movement from dejection to consolation. It will open with a brief summary of the greatness of the individual (*praise*), and then develop the same material in much more detailed form (*demonstration of loss*) through biographical detail heightened by the devices of amplification. Recalling the deeds of the dead person intensifies the grief of the survivors and leads to a lament. Grief is then consoled, and the poem ends on the exhortation that the audience imitate the virtues of the subject of the poem.

This is a clear enough description of the emotional pattern of the funeral elegy. It holds good for the majority of Renaissance examples of the genre. However, there are still unanswered questions. Who, for example, is the real subject of the poem? The consolation is not addressed to the dead but to the living. Likewise, what is the point of the poem? Is it to praise the dead, to allow the mourners a kind of emotional catharsis, to comfort them, or to incite to virtue? Another possibility is that the poet, himself, is both subject and object of the funeral elegy—that the form may really be a lyric of personal grief. Frequently the poet speaks in the first person in the funeral elegy.[8] Or else, the poet may consider himself a "representative mourner."[9] When he does, the resolution he achieves may be taken as standing for the community's resolution of its grief. This possibility is attractive, but it fails to explain the prominence given to praise of the dead person and to moral exhortation, two topics which appear to contradict a cathartic theory of elegy.

The fact that the funeral elegy was always considered an epideictic type has already been mentioned. This resolves the problem by making it clear that praise is the essential element of the form. If consolation were the most important element, funeral elegy would be deliberative rather than epideictic, since *consolatio* was generally classified in the former category. On the other hand, if the poem were primarily a lament with the object of offering either the poet or his audience emotional catharsis, the positive elements of the poem would become subordinate to the negative ones. Threnody can be considered epideictic—a complaint or *vituperatio* against the order of things—but whether considered rhetorically or psychologically, it has no place for the elaborate praise of the *demonstratio,* the philosophical reasoning of the consolation, or the positive and hortatory ending.[10] Naturally, the balance between praise, lament, and consolation varies with individual elegies, but in the majority, the first is dominant and the latter two subordinate.

Scaliger's instructions make the subordination evident. The elegy begins with personal praise, and the lament is a logical consequence—hence dependent on it: "Since such a noble pledge of glory has been lost, there is nothing else to do but mourn." Without the praise, the lament would be unmotivated, and conversely, the more hyperbolic the praise, the more intense the mourning. Grief, however, must be assuaged. *Consolatio* often involves a summary of the virtues of the deceased, but its major function is to persuade the mourner that his sadness is unnecessary. It changes the mood of the elegy from negative to positive. Since the lament involves complaining against the order of things which includes death as its inevitable end, *consolatio* celebrates orthodoxy. "Immoderate grief is impious" was a standard argument of classical consolation, and was greatly amplified by Christian authors. It is an important one since to write a poem questioning the order of things without answering the questions would be to insult the deceased rather than to praise him.[11]

The exhortation that ends the elegy is the poet's bow to the moral seriousness of epideictic forms. Praise has shown the virtues of the deceased and his earthly rewards. Consolation has shown the eternity of his fame among men and predicted his speedy transfiguration. He, therefore, stimulates emulation in every way. In case any reader is too dense to see the point, the poet must end with a passage that will "further the emulation of their virtues, minds, and deaths."

Personal praise, as distinguished from direct flattery, consists of recounting the life of the individual according to the familiar topics of encomium. In the *Arte of Rhetorique,*[12] Wilson divides the topics of praise into "things" "Before his life; in his life; and after his death." The "before his life" category includes realm, shire, town, parents, and ancestors. The "in his life" category includes birth and infancy, childhood, "the stripling age, or springtide," manhood, old age, and death. Under the heading of "stripling age" the studies, companions, and deportment of the individual are to be treated. Manhood and old age concentrate on "prowesse doen" and "pollicies and wittie devises" respectively, a formula that recalls the traditional epic virtues of fortitude and wisdom. Death is a particularly important topic: "At the time of his departing, his sufferaunce of all sicknesse, may much commende his worthinesse. As his strong heart, and cheerfull pacience even to the ende, cannot want great praise. The love of all men towards him, and the lamenting generally for his lacke, helpe most highly to set forth his honour."[13]

Closely connected with the topics are the commonplaces, although these are not mentioned in Wilson's discussion. Expressions of inadequacy and comparisons are the most frequent of these. In the first, the poet remarks that the greatness of his theme far surpasses his capabilities, and he only continues with divine aid or because of an overpowering emotion or the insistence of others.[14] In the second, the poet compares his subject to parallel cases in antiquity and concludes in each instance that his own subject surpasses the historical example.[15] In the most fulsome type of praise, comparison and parallel are frequent, and corollary devices like allusion, hyperbole, and dilation are used with greater or lesser restraint, depending on the poet.

Indirect patterns of praise are furnished by the lament. In Scaliger's explanation the lament is a natural result of praise of the dead and subordinate to it. Many funeral poems concentrate on lament and this is especially true in classical and classicizing poetry.[16] The function of lament is explained by Wilson: "the love of all men towards him, and the lamenting generally for his lacke, helpe well most highly to set forth his honour." Naturally, the poet is a participant in the general mourning.

The desolation appropriate to lament is conventionally expressed in one of two ways: first, there are exclamations, expressions of sadness and descriptions, largely drawn from classical poets, of the despairing extravagances of the mourners. They weep, tear their clothing, smear ashes on their faces, moan loudly, and so forth. A more elaborate pattern is that which arises from the questioning of the order of nature. "Why did it have to happen?" quickly becomes generalized into "Why were we put here to suffer needlessly?" The question can be asked in several ways. The mourner can accuse fate and the gods; he can withdraw; or he can express the sudden loss of a healthy, "normal" outlook in terms of a reversal of the usual patterns of life. If the poet is speaking in his own person, this requires a good deal of introspection and personal comment. If, as in many pastoral elegies, the poet is speaking as poet, he will question the worth of art or the effort necessary to produce it.[17] In "Lycidas," for example, Milton begins with a reference to his immaturity as a poet, and in the first "movement" of the poem he asks whether sporting with Amaryllis is not preferable to plying the thankless shepherd's trade in a vain pursuit of fame. Milton is not neglecting Edward King or digressing. Since he is speaking as poet, he naturally expresses grief in questions about the significance of art in a world subject to mutability.

Another expression of negation is the topic "nature reversed." Instead of questioning his own values, the poet may impose his despair on the external world. Even today, the funeral in literary stereotype generally occurs in the rain or against a gloomy setting. During the Renaissance there was more than an inarticulate sense of sympathy between man and nature. The theory of correspondence postulated a reciprocal relationship between the microcosm of the mind, the macrocosm of nature and society, and the stellar cosmos. A reversal of normal patterns in any one of these spheres could be expressed as a reversal of normal patterns in the others—for example, Hamlet projects despair in the image of the world as an unweeded garden. Pastoral poetry—"Lycidas" illustrates the convention—normally symbolizes negation by images of natural disruption: the sterility of the earth in winter, blights that ruin the crops, weeds that choke out useful plants, or other disruptions of the idyllic world. In other poetic types there is a corresponding adjustment of the negations. Poetry with political subject matter, for example, can express negation as an unsettling of regular political patterns—the untuning of the base string of degree, the possibility of revolt or defeat in war, and so forth. Other reversals include cosmic disruption. Planets shoot from their spheres, comets appear, or eclipses threaten. Such disorders are commonplace in poems lamenting the death of a great person, as are natural disruptions in the form of floods, earthquakes, or violent storms. The Biblical description of the Passion is the precedent for many of these reversals, but the number of possibilities is endless. Finally, the topic of nature reversed is closely related to what may be called the topic of community. Often the elegist speaks as a representative of a grief-stricken community. For several reasons, of which the natural elegy-tendency to hyperbole is only one, he claims that a whole city or nation—even, all mankind—is involved in the loss of the deceased.

The third element of the funeral poem, the consolation,[18] was treated by rhetoricians as an independent form related to the deliberative rather than the epideictic category. When used in funeral elegy, it retained its emphasis on logical persuasion. Wilson taught in the *Arte of Rhetorique* that there are two basic methods of consolation: ". . . they use two waies of cherishing the troubled mindes. The one is, when we shewe that in some cases, and for some causes, either they should not lament at all, or els be sorie very little: the other is when we graunt that they have just cause to be sad, and therefore we are sad also in their behalfe, and would remedie the mater if it could be, and thus entering into felowship of sorowe, we seeke by and litle to mitigate their greefe."[19]

Wilson's second method of consolation ("fellowship") explains the connection between *consolatio* and lament. The writer of a lament is not expressing merely personal emotion; he is giving voice to the grief of all the mourners, hence providing the common ground on which they can share their grief. The first method of consolation ("showing causes") is more important. Beginning with Cicero and Seneca several standard arguments were developed to deal with the problem of death. The usual Renaissance consolation is a tissue of these arguments. Wilson used the most common ones in his example of *consolatio*. They may be summarized as follows:

1. He is not dead, but in heaven.
2. Death is common to all mankind.
3. He made a good end.
4. Do not complain; immoderate grief is impious.
5. Life is a debt to be repaid.
6. He would not return to earth if he could; he is happier in heaven.
7. He welcomed death; he did not fear it.
8. Neither wealth, strength, nor beauty can withstand death.
9. He has passed from a wretched life to a secure haven.
10. A longer life would have increased his sins; as it was, he died virtuous.
11. The good die young, and length of life is unimportant.
12. He died for our sins; we did not deserve to keep him.
13. A good short life is better than a long, ordinary one.[20]

III. PAGAN AND CHRISTIAN FORMS OF ELEGY

Although all of Wilson's topics are capable of amplification by classical and Biblical material, by far the most important point, and the one to which Wilson constantly returns, is the Christian consolation of immortality. The use of this topic is one of the distinguishing features of Christian funeral poetry. Immortality is frequently mentioned in classical elegies, as in Virgil's fifth eclogue,[21] but it is not heavily stressed. Classical ideas about after-life are vague and rather gloomy in comparison to the assured and optimistic notions which Christians have about heaven. Bishop Jewel, commenting on *First Thessalonians,* advised: "We are not . . . forbidden to mourn over the dead; but to mourn in such sort as the heathen did we are forbidden. They, as did neither believe in God nor in Christ, so had they no hope of the life to come. When a father saw his son dead, he thought he had been dead forever. He became heavy . . . rent his body, cursed his fortune, cried out on his gods. O my dear son (saith he), how beautiful, how learned and wise and virtuous wast thou! Why shouldst thou died so untimely. . . . Thus they fell into despair and spake blasphemies. . . . But why may not Christians mourn and continue in heaviness? [Because] . . . they that depart this life are not dead, they are not gone for ever as the heathen imagined."[22]

Because of this basic difference there is a strong contrast between the styles of Christian and classical funeral elegy, and the contrast illustrates the remarkable degree to which style is a reflection of general cultural factors. Nothing could be more striking, for example, than the contrast between the

Panegyricus of Paulinus of Nola, an elegy on the death of an eight-year-old boy and the "first Christian funeral elegy";[23] and a roughly comparable pagan poem, the "Epicedion Glauciae Melioris" (*Silvae,* II, i) of Statius.[24] Each poet faces a similar problem, the celebration of the death of a young child. This is quite difficult because the biographical details and virtuous acts are lacking which usually comprise the bulk of the funeral elegy. Indeed, Statius' poem is a kind of *tour de force.* One of its purposes was doubtless to show the skill of the rhetorician in treating an unpromising theme. Paulinus, on the other hand, was passionately sincere.

Statius' elegy follows the standard pattern. After thirty-five lines of lament (1-35) he describes the boy's appearance (36-68), his attractive character (69-105), his youthful deeds (106-36), his virtuous death (137-57), and his funeral (158-82). This is followed by the consolation (183-234).

Despite its efficient technique, the poem is a failure. Statius never adequately comes to terms with death. He announces that the dead boy is fortunate because he has been freed of fear of death, but this is hardly a consolation. The reader is more impressed by the gloomy descriptions of Hades and the moments when a genuine lyric cry of pain over the shortness of life bursts forth. The poem offers few reasons for optimism, but its despair is still moving: "Whatever comes into the world, must fear its death. We will all die. We will die! Aeacus shakes his urn with his gigantic arms."[25]

Few would claim that Paulinus has the talent or the polish of Statius, but his deficiencies in this respect are offset by his intense conviction. His poem contains the commonplace parts of elegy, being composed of praise, lament, and consolation. The praise, however, seems very brief in proportion to the length of the poem. It is restricted to the first thirty-six lines of a work of more than six hundred lines. Lament enters the poem in the form of frequent exclamations of grief, but the bulk of the poem is based on the argument that "he is not dead but in heaven." The consolation is extremely long because Paulinus felt compelled to prove the truth of the Christian idea of immortality before showing Celsus in heaven. His arguments are those of the early Christian apologists modified to fit the requirements of the elegy form. The conclusion of the poem is strictly conventional. Celsus becomes a paragon of virtue. His death has provided an opportunity to reaffirm Christian truth. He is now in heaven, and all who wish to join him will imitate his spotless life.[26]

The contrast between Paulinus and Statius can be further illustrated by a comparison of their treatment of the immortality theme. The slave boy of Melior plays in a gloomy Virgilian underworld far more appropriate to literary tradition than to a poem that promises consolation. Blaesus, a deceased friend of the family, will meet the boy and "show the joys of mild

Elysium—the unflowering boughs, the silent birds, and the pale flowers on drooping stems."[27] Celsus, on the other hand, enjoys the perfect happiness of the Christian heaven: "he plays in Paradise in a perfumed grove with the children of Bethlehem whom evil Herod struck down for spite, and weaves crowns, the rewards of honored martyrs."[28]

Both Paulinus and Statius use digressions to amplify their subjects. In both cases this is necessary because of the lack of biographical material. In Paulinus, however, the digressions, no matter how clumsy, are related to the intent of the poem. The reader *must* be convinced of the truth of Christianity before he will accept the immortality of Celsus. Most of Paulinus' digressions are necessitated by the proofs which he offers. They, therefore, lead back to the poem's central idea, making it theoretically (if not aesthetically) unified. In Statius, on the contrary, the digressive elements lead away from the central idea. Statius' chief device is the use of mythological parallel. For example, he expands the fact that Melior loved the dead boy even though he was adopted, by making it into the thesis, "natural children are necessary; adopted children are a source of joy." This he supports with references to Achilles and Chiron, Achilles and Phoenix, Pallas and Acoetes, Dictys and Perseus, Bacchus and Ino, and Romulus and Acca.[29] Such mythological parallels account for much of the bulk of Statius' elegy.[30] They are non-functional since they distract the reader from the true subject. Yet Statius wrote with a full command of classical literary tradition, whereas Paulinus was already in the shadow world between the late classical period and the Middle Ages.

Comparison of Paulinus and Statius demonstrates that different approaches to consolation give rise to at least two modes of elegy, a Christian one where lengthy and complicated digression is possible without a loss of (technical) unity, and an essentially pagan one, which, because of its inability to answer positively the questions raised by death, tends to move away from the central idea rather than toward it. This fact is particularly apparent in the poems compared because both treat the death of a child. A few very skillful classical poems change digression from a vice to a positive virtue. It becomes a means of "changing the subject"—of diverting attention from the ugly and unanswerable fact of death to the beauties of nature and art. Milton touched on this device in the flower passage of "Lycidas." When the coffin of the dead shepherd is concealed under masses of flowers, the poet experiences momentary relief. However, Milton was a Christian poet. The relief soon proves illusory, and he must move forward from the empty coffin to the final triumphant vision of Lycidas in heaven.

Classical poets who lacked Milton's assurance occasionally dallied with the false surmise which Milton rejected. This is especially common in the epitaphs of the *Greek Anthology*. Martial's epitaph on a young girl (V, xxxvii) is also a good example, although marred by a clever ending that is omitted in the following translation:

The girl sweeter to me than aged swans,
Softer than the lamb of Tarentine Galaesus,
More delicate than the shell from the Lucrine lake;
To whom you would not prefer Eastern pearls,
Or the polished ivory of Indian herds,
Or the first snow and the untouched lily;
Whose hair surpasses the fleece of Baetic flocks,
The knotted hair of Rhine and the golden dormouse;
Whose breath is as sweet as the roses of Paestum,
As the first honey of Attic combs,
As a lump of amber warm from the hand;
Compared to whom the peacock was unsightly,
The squirrel unlovable, the phoenix too frequent,—
Now Erotion lies, still warm, on a fresh pyre,
Whom the bitter decree of the wicked fates
Carried off in her sixth year—and that incomplete—
My love and joy and delight.[31]

Here the grief is unmistakable and affecting. The technique is understatement. Martial tells us very little about the girl; his only rhetorical topic is her beauty, which is suggested by a series of "outdoing" comparisons emphasized by parallelism of clause and phrase. These factors make the reader conscious of the poem as lyric. Caught up in its artistry he is willing to forgive the fact that Martial never resolves the grief through explicit consolation.

Martial is successful because the brevity of the epitaph allows him to evade issues for which he has no adequate solution. It is not surprising to find his technique employed in the more formal long funeral elegy. The first elegy on Maecenas is an example. Although the poem is not particularly good—it is even denied its time-honored place in the *Virgilian Appendix* by Fairclough, the Loeb editor—its ending is interesting. Unable to offer convincing consolation, its author turned to the *Greek Anthology* for ritual phrases and images that might replace philosophical resolution:

Now what can I do? Earth hold his bones lightly
  And gently balance your weight on his body.
Always will we give you wreaths, always perfumes,
  And never thirsting you will ever bloom.[32]

The same technique is used in the pastoral elegy, where the conventionalized beauty of the surroundings, the innocence of the speakers, and the elaborate formal tradition all combine to make the grief impersonal. In Virgil's song of Mopsus (Eclogue V), for instance, we find a pastoral modification of the topic of "nature reversed"

> . . . Since the Fates took you,
> Pales herself has left the fields and Apollo has departed.
> Often in the furrows where we planted barley grains
> Ill-starred darnel and sterile oats arise;
> In place of the sweet violet and the gleaming narcissus
> The thistle and thorn with sharp spines now grow.[33]

Even while we recognize that this is a conventional topic of negation, we are involved in the beauty of the expression. It is irrelevant to complain that the author has not provided a transition from negation to affirmation. Virgil has not "explained away" grief but he has helped his reader to forget it.

Praise, lament, and consolation are the three major components of funeral elegy. The latter two are subordinate to the first and provide indirect patterns of praise which supplement the direct ones. In the case of consolation, there is an intimate connection between stylistic patterns and the moral commonplaces available to the poet. Since the next chapter will be an analysis of several funeral poems in terms of these patterns, it will be useful to summarize them:

1. Patterns emerging from the topics of personal praise:
    a. Simple praise of accomplishments, family, beauty, etc.
    b. Praise of the individual as exemplar of virtue.
    c. Use of stylistic methods of amplification (comparison, allusion, hyperbole, expression of inadequacy, etc.)
2. Indirect patterns developing from lament:
    a. Exclamations and expressions of sadness.
    b. Loss of faith in self or in world order (nature reversed).
    c. The assertion that all society or all nature mourns (community).
3. Indirect patterns emerging from consolation:
    a. Expressions of faith, especially in immortality (this entails assertion of the goodness of the dead person).
    b. Resolution by art (changing the subject).

This grouping, it should be noted, is analytic. In most funeral poems the topics are mixed, and even a rudimentary sense of poetic economy encourages reference to several topic simultaneously. In the quotation from Virgil's song of Mopsus, for example, pastoral convention is used to express loss of faith in the world order and at the same time to adumbrate the final artistic resolution. This complicates analysis but also enriches the literary work.

CHAPTER VI

Varieties of Elegy

The Renaissance poet who set himself the task of commemorating the death of a friend or patron could select from an almost embarrassing richness of material. Living in an age sensitive to genres, types and modes of literature, he did not need to create new forms but could select from already existing ones the form best suited to the expression of his attitude. The poet in this situation is not a romantic bard who must remain silent until some overpowering inspiration gives him a new vision of reality. He is more like an architect creating inspired new structures by selecting from the components that are the stock-in-trade of the profession. The economics of literary activity being what they are, this situation has drawbacks as well as attractions. Much Renaissance poetry is simply a dull rehash of commonplaces. On the other hand, much of it is technically more assured and aesthetically more satisfying than all but the most successful romantic poetry.

The range of possibilities open to the Renaissance elegist was large. The simplest type of funeral poem is the epitaph, in which the artist's full resources are employed to produce the illusion of artlessness. Two other forms, still essentially classical, are the art elegy—a consciously artificial form illustrated most obviously by pastoral elegy—and the elegy stressing moral (usually stoic) virtue. In Christian elegies, the rewards of immortality become important. The elegist can emphasize the historical subject of the poem and console the mourners with visions of a better life to come; or he can treat the "soul" or "idea" of the deceased, as Donne does in his *Anniversaries*. Finally, there is the special case of poems on the Passion. These employ elegy topics in a way which adds significantly to the understanding of personal elegy.

In the present chapter, poems of each type are examined. Although emphasis is on typical rhetorical patterns, consideration is given to the relationship between them and the artistic whole within which they operate.

This is important because in successful poetry the part can never be adequately explained in isolation from the larger design. The format of the quotations in the present chapter is slightly different from that of previous chapters. Because the discussion involves aesthetic considerations, foreign language quotations are given first in translation and followed by the originals.

I. CLASSICAL TYPES

The *Greek Anthology* provided the basic models for Renaissance epitaph. Pontanus wrote a whole series of epitaphs (*De tumulis*) imitating the *Anthology*.[1] Other writers, like Michael Marullus, imitated Martial's practice of scattering epitaphs through collections of epigrams.[2] Sir Thomas More followed the latter practice in his epigrams and bequeathed it to his English successors.[3] Of these Ben Jonson is without doubt the most noteworthy. Jonson was inspired by the spirit as well as the conventions of classical literature. More than any of his contemporaries he was able to translate this spirit into the forms and idiom of the English language. His sense of poetic craftsmanship doubtless contributed greatly to his success, for the polished simplicity of the typical *Anthology* epitaph is the reverse of artlessness. Jonson's skill is evident in his epitaph on Elizabeth, Lady H—:

> Would'st thou heare, what man can say
> In a little? Reader, stay.
> Under-neath this stone doth lye
> As much beautie, as could dye:
> Which in life did harbour give
> To more vertue, then doth live.
> If, at all, shee had a fault,
> Leave it buryed in this vault.
> One name was *Elizabeth;*
> Th' other let it sleepe with death:
> Fitter where it dyed, to tell,
> Then that it liv'd at all. Farewell[4]

In the first couplet the poet calls attention to his basic strategy, which is brevity. This is to be expected. Not only is the epitaph form traditionally brief, but its typical method of treating death is by the avoidance of topics requiring lengthy development. The brevity has the general effect of litotes—it implies beauties and virtues that it does not describe. Insofar as the poem is a success it suggests the grief of a poet so affected that he dare not think too closely on the characteristics of the dead lady. The restraint of the style becomes a manifestation of inner restraint before the fact of death.

The element of restraint controls the development of the positive topics of praise.[5] For the long and often elaborate lists of graces and good deeds which personal praise normally demanded, Jonson substitutes generalization. Yet the topics are present in germinal form. "Bodily beauty" is responsible for the most memorable couplet in the poem (ll. 3-4). It very lightly modifies the grief by hinting at the Neoplatonic idea of the immortality of beauty. The connection between this topic and the second (gifts of character) is stressed by the parallelism of the two couplets in which they are mentioned. Lines five and six suggest that Elizabeth's beauty was an outward sign of her virtue. Here the advantages of the epitaph form are obvious. The standard elegy, in which beauties and virtues are mechanically listed, it likely to end by insulting the reader's credulity. Epitaph avoids the problem of verisimilitude by avoiding particulars. Lines three to six of Jonson's poem are, literally speaking, hyperboles. However, because they are extremely general the reader is not invited to measure them against practical experience. They emerge as graceful tributes rather than exaggerated flattery.

Brevity is also the strategy of the negative elements in the poem. In longer funeral pieces—for example, the elegies on Lady Jane Pawlet and Venetia Digby—Jonson employed the topics of lament to express profound grief and the topics of consolation to resolve this grief. Such material requires a form that is large enough for the topics to be developed effectively and capable of articulation, so that one section can be balanced against the other. The epitaph form has neither of these characteristics. In Jonson's epitaph on Elizabeth the lament has been reduced to a restrained sadness that is suggested without ever being made explicit. Consolation is also implied. We are never told that Elizabeth has gone to a better life or lives on as a pattern of virtue. Death is a simple fact. It must be accepted. It cannot be questioned.

The tone of finality is especially striking in lines eight to twelve. These lines are not intended to convey intense emotion. If they did, they would violate the condition of the poem's success. The idea that death is a terminus is expressed in two statements to the reader. Both advise against asking about Elizabeth's life. The first elaborates the commonplace *de mortuis nihil nisi bonum,* while the second advises against attempts to recover the family name of Elizabeth. Now that she is dead, it makes no difference who she was.

The concluding *farewell* completes the poem aesthetically. The strategy of brevity culminates in a curt, single-word sentence that occupies only one metrical foot of the short tetrameter line. After it, there is nothing left to say. The *farewell* is all the more effective because of its *Greek Anthology* associations. The reader's attention is subtly shifted from life to literature—

from the pain of personal loss to the impersonal world of art. Combined with other elements—especially the chant-like tetrameter couplet—it creates an effect of aesthetic distance. The reader does not see death but a picture of death. His grief is "contained" in a formal artistic pattern. Probably all funeral poetry has something of this effect, but it is never so strong as in the case of *Greek Anthology* epitaphs and their imitations. The shift from life to art is the special virtue of the successful examples of the genre and certainly contributes to Jonson's success.

Renaissance funeral poems that imitate the longer classical elegy are generally less attractive than epitaphs imitating the *Anthology*. Frequently there is a tasteless mixing of Christian and classical elements that makes the reader sympathize with Dr. Johnson's strictures on "Lycidas," if not with their appropriateness to that particular poem. An example of such mixed poetry is the elegy "On the Death of Lucia Faustina" ("In Obitu Luciae Faustinae") printed in *Carmina poetarum nobilium,* an anthology of neo-Latin poetry published in Milan in 1563.[6] The first two sections of this poem are primarily lament. Since pagans and Christians express grief in similar fashion no serious conflict arises form the poet's use of classical imagery to describe Lucia's Christian mourners. In the third section, however, difficulties arise. While describing Lucia's funeral the poet asserts that she has been taken to heaven. The idea is a commonplace of funeral elegy. Normally it introduces the formal consolation: the deceased has gone to a happier life; therefore, the survivors should rejoice. Lucia's elegist, however, cannot forego an opportunity to display his familiarity with Ovid. He exclaims:

O mourners, do you not know the thefts of Jove? Or what,
    Who, how often and how many there were in ancient times?
Do you not know of the gold of Danae and the swan of Leda?
    But I, loving too much, remember his crimes.
Do you wish me to speak of Europa, or Io struggling with the horns.
    Or Ganymede himself—the thefts of Jove?
And I could mention six hundred more. . . .

(Furta Jovis miseri, ignorantis, qualia, quot, quae,
    Quanta olim priscis temporibus fuerint.
Nescitis Danaes aurum, Cycnum quoque Ledae?
    At scelera ipsius novi ego amans nimium.
Vultisne Europam, aut luctantem cornibus Io,
    Seu Ganymedem ipsum, furta Jovis, referam?
Sexcentasque alias memorem. . . .)[7]

After this, the poet simply cannot refer his poem to Christian context without blasphemy. He has created an impossible situation by attempting to remain "classical" in a case where antiquity and Christianity cannot meet. Following the standard rhetorical formula for "heightening" a situation (in this case, the bearing off of a girl to heaven), the poet has compared it to parallel cases in classical mythology. In consonance with this controlling blunder, the poet ends with a clumsy and unconvincing reference to after-life: he dreams of seeing the girl in a valley, and in what is surely one of the most fatuous of recorded Virgilian borrowings, he cries,

> O how should I speak of you, Valley: You alone by a
> direct path
> Lead onward to the Elysian fields.
>
> (O quam te memorem vallis. tu tramite recto
> Una ultro campos ducis ad Elysios.)

Such a poem richly deserves the obscurity in which it has languished for hundreds of years. The excuse for mentioning it here is that it illustrates the dangers of attempting to mix Christian and classical modes. Many humanistic poets ignored the dangers, and a few—like Sannazaro and Milton—were successful. Many, however, failed as miserably as Lucia's elegist. The obvious solution was to maintain purity of type—to select either the classical or Christian mode and stick to it.

In the previous chapter it was observed that one characteristic feature of classical elegy is the weakness of its consolation. The classical elegist lacked the optimistic faith in immortality which is an article of Christian dogma. Therefore, he was committed to a restrained treatment of the negative topics of elegy arising from the lament. If his grief were too extravagant or his questioning of the order of things too profound, the result would be a poem of despair rather than affirmation or acceptance. Renaissance poets were aware of this fact. Their imitations of classical elegy avoid extravagant expressions of despair such as those permitted in devotional poetry. Even so, they tend to be somewhat negative, and their typical answer to the problems raised by death is stoic resignation.

Ronsard's "Épitaphe de Claude l'Aubespine" is a good example of a relatively simple imitation of classical elegy.[8] It includes the topics of praise and lament but suppresses consolation. Its general effect is negative, and its conclusion is the rather somber observation that we must accept the inevitable. A pastoral note is introduced via a probably inevitable pun on *aubespine* (i.e., hawthorn). This is the only unconventional feature of the poem.

The praise of Aubespine is kept rather general. Other of Ronsard's elegies, such as that on Monsieur d'Annebault or the shorter "Épitaphe de François de Bourbon," make considerable use of biographical detail.[9] Such detail is irrelevant to the "Epitaphe de Claude d'Aubespine" because Ronsard does not present Aubespine as a paragon of virtue to be imitated by readers of the poem. We learn first of Aubespine's vitality, which is expressed pastorally, in terms of flower imagery, and connected to the motif of the dying rose. He was

> in the flower of his age;
> [He] flourished like a young rose
> Blossoming at daybreak on the bough
> Which a storm arising at midday
> Strikes to the ground and makes a plaything of the wind. . . .
>
> (en son âge plus beau
> Qui florissoit comme une ieune rose
> Dessus la branche au poinct du iour esclose,
> Que la tempeste à midy s'eslevant
> Fainst à terre & fait iouët du vent. . . .)[10]

Later we learn that he was a lover of the muses, " . . . for you loved the troup of the sister Muses when you lived here. . . ." (". . . car tu amois la trope/ Des Muses soeurs quand icy tu vivois. . . ."), and that he had great "vertu."[11] Both of these traits are qualities of character. They conclude the overt praise in the poem. A fuller delineation of Aubespine's merits would be pointless unless he were proposed as a model.

Stylistic ornaments supplement the direct praise by "heightening" the stature of Aubespine and the devotion of his mourners. The most important ornaments are classical allusions and parallels. The speaker in the poem (Aubespine's wife) is an "errant dryad"; Aubespine is taken on a voyage by Charon to a hell ruled by Pluto; Calliope is invoked "her lyre in her hand" ("la lyre au poing"). In two cases the allusions are developed into passages of several lines. In the first a parallel is drawn between the dryad and Orpheus: just as the latter charmed Hades by the sweetness of his lament, so the dryad will charm it a second time with her weeping. But she surpasses Orpheus because she does it,

> Not like him to have my wife again,
> But, dear husband, only to see you
> And to know if bold death
> Has robbed you down there of your handsome face
> And your beautiful eyes. . . .
>
> (Non comme luy pour ma femme r'avoir,
> Mais cher mary, seulement pour te voir,
> Et pour sçavoir si la mortelle audace
> T'a desrobé là bas ta belle face
> Et tes beaux yeux. . . .)[12]

In the second instance the parallel is between Alcestis, who was willing to die for her husband, and the dryad who would like to do the same for Aubespine.

There are naturally many negative elements in the poem. The dryad shows much personal grief. She is "disheveled, alone, melancholy . . . weeping" ("eschevelée, seule, pensive . . . pleurant.") In imitation of the classical mourner,

> With pointed nails she scratches her breast
> And striking the air with continual lamentation
> Names the gods and the cruel stars,
> Tears her hair and overcome with madness
> Makes this complaint against Death [himself].
>
> (D'ongles poinctus sa poitrine elle entame,
> Et frappant l'air de cris continuels,
> Nomme les Dieux & les Astres cruels,
> Rompt ses cheveux, & de fureur attainte
> Contre la Mort pousse telle complainte.)[13]

She wishes for death; she frequently bursts into despairing exclamation (Las! je trespasse . . . ; A! fiere Mort . . . ; etc.); and she compares herself to a nightingale whose feeding ground has been unexpectedly mowed by the harvester. The modes of expressing personal sadness are, however, limited. After exclamation (he is sad!), statement (he says he is sad), and description (he looks and acts sad), the poet must find new material or become repetitious. Consequently, secondary themes of lament are developed.

The first of these is the simple accusation of fate which has taken away the dead person. In Ronsard's poem, the motif is expressed through a *vituperatio* of Death. Death and his minions are "deaf, cruel, wretched . . . harsh, criminal" ("sorde, cruelle & malheureuse . . . dure, felonne"). The dryad exclaims, "These cruel ones have neither eyes nor hearts, tendons, muscles or veins to be moved by human prayers" ("ces cruels n'ont pas/ Ny yeux, ny coeurs, tendons, muscles ny veins,/ Pour se flechir par les prières humaines").[14] In this exclamation the tendencies latent in the motif began to appear. Death is part of the universal human experience. To despair over the fact of death is to question the value of life itself.

Ronsard also uses the topic of "nature reversed" to embody the dryad's despair. Death has destroyed her personal happiness. The microcosm of her soul has been desolated, and this desolation is reflected in her view of the macrocosm of nature. It is, she discovers, a world of cruelty and death. To enquire whether the defects that she finds are real or merely symbols of mental suffering is irrelevant. Is the world of Denmark really an "unweeded garden" or is it Hamlet's melancholy that makes him see it as one? Nature is the setting for the elegy on Aubespine, and Ronsard, like many another literary artist, used setting functionally to intensify the central theme of his poem. At first the nature-reversed theme is presented as a simile. The dryad compares death to men who destroy the idyllic pastoral world:

In such a way the little birds plumeless in their nest
Are customarily seized by the shepherds before their sweet songs
Are heard from bush to bush.

(Les oisillons dedans leur nid sans plume
Par les Pasteurs ont ainsi de coustume
Estre ravis, ainçois que leurs beaux sons
Soient entendus de buissons en buissons.)

Later, death is compared to a destructive storm:

In such a manner one sees, in a bitter storm,
The grain overturned in its young growth
And bent them down on the earth without hope
Before the warm weather has ripened its ears.

(Ainsi voit-on sous la tempeste dure
Les bleds versez en leur ieune verdure,
Et sans espoir contre terre accropis
Ains que le chaut ait meury leurs espis.)

Finally, the desolation of nature is expressed as a literal truth:

The rivers wept at your passing,
And the broad Seine, parting its huge course,
Which surrounded your mansion with its waves,
Groaned in its wavy depths for you.
The pretty flowers lost their colors for you;
Autumn, struck by extreme sorrow,
Became winter! The forests clothed
In a green cloak were stripped bare for you.
Everything changed. The rocks and forest
Mourned you: So did the Kings,
Princes and Nobles who had knowledge
Of your virtue from your earliest infancy.

(De ton trespas les fleuves ont pleuré,
Et Seine large au grand cours separé,
Qui ta maison entournoit de ses ondes,
En a gemy sous ses vagues profondes.

Les belles fleurs en ont perdu couleur:
L'autonne atteint d'une extreme douleur
Devint Hyuer! les forest habillées
D'un manteau verd, en furent despouillées.
Tout se changea: les rochers & les bois
T'ont regreté: aussi ont fait les Rois,
Princes, Seigneurs, qui avoient cognoissance
De ta vertu dés ta premier enfance.)[15]

The abandonment of simile here intensifies the sense of grief. The speaker is so carried away that she no longer distinguishes between inner and outer experience. Objective reality has become a mirror for her passion. What began as a conventional lament is transmuted into genuine—though not necessarily great—poetry.

The elegy has no formal consolation. Horace's "levius fit patientia/ Quidquid corrigere est nefas" neatly expresses classical resignation before the inevitable, and Ronsard ends on the true Horation note:

It is necessary to die. For to all that lives
There is a day predestined for its death.

(Il faut partir: car toute ce qui est né,
Est pour mourir un jour predestiné.)

If this is not particularly uplifting, it is true to the spirit and limitations of the classical mode. Doubtless the survivors of Aubespine were well satisfied.

Considered as an attempt to come to terms with death, Ronsard's elegy has the same inadequacies as the elegies of Statius. A much more impressive example of the possibilities of the classical type is the "Elegy . . . on the Early Death of Albiera Albitia" (*Elegia . . . in Albierae Albitiae immaturum exitum*) by Angelo Politian. This poem is one of the most celebrated of neo-Latin funeral pieces. Its success is indicated by the fact that George Chapman paraphrased it for an elegy on the death of Prince Henry in 1612, over a century after its composition.[16]

Politian's elegy employs an almost unique method of amplification. Instead of heaping comparison on comparison, classical parallel on parallel, Politian "amplifies" his material by inventing a myth to explain the fever that caused Albiera's death. Certain medieval and early Renaissance poems use mythology to embellish descriptions of historical events, but Politian's chief models were Ovid, Statius, and Claudian.[17] His orientation is pagan rather than Christian. Like Ronsard he offers no elaborate consolation, but unlike Ronsard he accepts fully the challenge to provide a substitute. His mythological machinery diverts attention from death to the literary treatment of death. Thus, despite its length, his elegy relies on the strategy of "changing the subject" observed in Jonson's imitation of *Greek Anthology* epitaph. This is probably not accidental. Albiera died at the age of fifteen and on the point of marriage.[18] Her death involves the kind of pathos that was favored by the authors of the *Greek Anthology*.

The structure of the poem is skillfully adapted to its subject. Since Albiera died before any noteworthy accomplishments it would have been difficult to "celebrate" her through a chronological series of virtuous deeds. Instead, Politian arranged his material into alternating expressions of affirmation and negation. The general movement is not toward simple affirmation but toward a mean between the two extremes. Part one (pp. 259-61)[19] is a lament on the death of Albiera. It ends when the poet, following Statius' elegy on his father, invokes the dead girl as his muse:

> You, who were cause of so much sorrow to me,
> [Must] now speak to the stricken bard as his sad Muse.
>
> (Tu mihi nunc tanti fuerit quae causa doloris,
> Attonito vati moesta Thalia refer.)

Part two (pp. 261-62) is a narration of events connected with Albiera's last day of health. It emphasizes her beauty and grace and contains some very appealing description. In direct contrast, part three (pp. 262-65) describes Febris, Politian's goddess of fever, in a personification that concentrates on her repugnant characteristics. It ends as Febris visits Albiera's bed and causes a mortal sickness. Part four (pp. 265-66) contains the consolation of Albiera to her husband and ends with her death. Part five (pp. 267-68) describes the mourners and the funeral ceremonies; and part six (pp. 268-69) is a four-line epitaph on the *Greek Anthology* model. The poem thus alternates rhythmically from negative to positive moods and ends in resignation.

The topics of direct praise are introduced in the initial lament via a description of Albiera's beauty. Its imagery echoes the flower-imagery of the sonnet cycles:

> To [her] alone nature gave whatever she has of charm;
> To [her] alone grace gave whatever she has.
> Her fairness was suffused with a sweet blush, like
> White lilies mixed with red roses.
> Her happy eyes sparkled like a shining star
> Whence Love often brought its torches kindled. . . .
>
> (Uni quicquid habet, dederat natura decoris,
> Uni etiam dederat gratia quicquid habet.
> Candor erat dulci suffusus sanguine, qualem
> Alba ferunt rubris lilia mixta rosis.
> Ut nitidum laeti radiabant sidus ocelli,
> Saepe amor accensas rettulit inde faces . . . [p. 260]).

Later, this image develops into a comparison of the dying girl with a flower:

But death was beautiful, like a light sleep . . .
Thus languish white lilies gathered by a virgin hand
And crowns woven of snowy roses.

(Sed formosa levem mors est imitata soporem . . .
Virginea sic lecta manu candentia languent
Liliaque & niveis texta corona rosis. . . .)

and:

Where now those eyes shooting forth starry flames;
Alas, where those lips like Punic roses?

(Lumina sidereas ubi nunc torquentia flammas,
Heu ubi Puniceis aemula labra rosis? [p. 268])

Politian also uses topics of praise based on character. A lengthy passage describes Albiera's skill as a dancer:

Albiera outshines the other nymphs with her beautiful features
And from her face sheds a wavering light.
The air ruffles her hair streaming down over her white back,
Her dark eyes sparkle with sweet fire . . .
Speechless, youths and old men watch Albiera. . . .

(Emicat ante alias vultu pulcherrima nymphas
Albiera, & tremulum spargit ab ore iubar.
Aura quatit fusos in candida terga capillos,
Irradiant dulci lumina nigra face . . .
Attonita Albieram spectant iuvenesque senesque . . . [p. 262]).

Later Politian displays Albiera's "strong heart, and cherefull pacience even to the ende," as the rhetoricians put it. With her dying glance, Albiera contemplates her young husband ("I die a virgin . . . you have nothing but the title of husband") ("discedam virgo . . . coniugii nil nisi nomen habes . . ."), and seeing that he is grief-stricken, she consoles him:

O Sigismund, part of my soul, if the last words
Of your wife have any authority for you
Cease, I pray, your crying. I lived, I finished life's course,
And now my fate calls me far from you.

(Pars animae Sismunde meae, si coniugis in te
Quicquam iuris habent ultima verba tuae,
Parce precor lacrymis, vixi, cursumque peregi,
Iam procul a vobis me mea fata vocant [p. 266]).

Since this topic illustrates a feminine virtue, i.e., regard for one's husband, Albiera might be considered a moral example. However, the suggestion is kept very light, and the reader is never explicitly urged to imitate her. In the only other extensive reference to her virtue Politian's indifference to the didactic function of praise is especially clear. Albiera's physical beauty is described in concrete terms and at some length. But the beauties of her spirit, her virtues, are enumerated in a list that gives the effect of hurried summary:

> . . . honor and a face white with tender modesty,
> And decorum and propriety, blushing shyness,
> Unstained faith, a merry laugh, virtuous manners,
> Modest bearing and straightforward simplicity.
>
> (. . . honor & teneri iam cana modestia vultus,
> Et decor, & probitas, purpureusque pudor,
> Casta fides, risusque hilaris, moresque pudici,
> Incessusque decens, nudaque simplicitas [p. 261]).

Style contributes much to the celebration of Albiera. The mere length of Politian's elegy is noteworthy, and it is probable that he was enough of a rhetorician to take pride in his ability to amplify an unpromising subject. He relies heavily on classical allusion and parallel. Albiera is compared to Diana when her hair is unbound; to Venus when it is combed back. She surpasses her peers "as Lucifer with his shining face obscures the lesser stars" ("quam Lucifer ore/ Purpureo rutilans astra minora premit"). Later, at her funeral, "Not otherwise did the Trojan mothers weep at the funeral of Hector" ("Non secus Hectoreo Troianae in funere matres/ Fleverunt . . .").

The elaborate personification of fever deserves special attention, for it is the most prominent feature of the poem. Politian's vocabulary is generally classical. Even the funeral ceremony is described ambiguously enough to pass for its pagan counterpart. Realism would be fatal to the carefully wrought artificiality of this technique. Therefore, Politian softened the harsh fact of death by introducing an obvious and striking fiction. As Albiera is being applauded for her grace and beauty, Rhamnusia, goddess of death, sees her. Rhamnusia then visits Febris, the horrible patroness of fever whose mouth vomits pestilence and who is surrounded by such figures as Lamentation, Cries of Agony, Sobs, Fear, Delirium, and Thirst (pp. 262-63). Having been told of the happy girl "ignorant of her future lot" ("sortisque ignara futurae"), Febris visits her as she sleeps and infects her with a deadly illness (p. 264). Albiera cries for help, but no medicine avails. The course of the fever is described (p. 265) and then Albiera's death. About ninety lines, or approximately one-third of the elegy, are taken up by the episode.[20] The effect is like that of the fictional and marvelous elements in historical epic. Intrigued by the poet's invention we cease to be shocked by the cruel reality that he is describing.

Patterns of lament are also important in the elegy. Expressions of grief are frequent. Exclamation, for example, is used constantly: "alas, in vain . . . you accuse the stars"; "Ah, sorrow"; "alas, I am silent"; "ah, grief"; etc. (heu, frustra . . . sidera damnas; proh dolor; heu . . . taceo; ah dolor . . . ; etc.) (pp. 259-61). The motif of death silencing the poet also appears:

> Alas, not sounding sweetly my strain, I mention not strife
> and the trumpets,
> And offer my sad lament to the black pyre . . .
>
> (Heu nil dulce sonans taceo iam bella, tubasque,
> Et refero ad nigros carmina moesta rogos. . . .)

The survivors are, of course, inconsolable. They swim in tears, rend the air with laments and otherwise manifest deepest sorrow. With what he might have thought daring originality, Politian makes Sigismund's grief too deep for tears:

> You, pitiable man, have neither the tears nor words of the mourners;
> Stunned, your voice is frozen in your numb mouth.
>
> (Non lacrymas miserandus habes, non verba dolentum,
> Attonitus pigro torpet in ore sonus [p. 267]).

Later, Sigismund wishes for death, "to follow the devout spirit, but his brothers prevent him" ("ut manes prosequerere pios./ Sed prohibent fratres"). For others, the conventions established by pagan mourners are sufficient:

> Who, who now does not know the cries of the sad mourners
> And the words of parents repeated in the midst of such evils?
> Her brother drenches his face with tears, and her sad sister
> Tears her hair and scratches her tender cheeks with her nails. . . .
>
> (Quis nunc quis gemitus miserorum & verba parentum
> Nesciat in tantis heu repetita malis?
> Ora rigat lacrymis frater, rumpitque capillos
> Moesta soror, teneras & secat ungue genas . . . [p. 267]).

More intense negation is introduced through expressions of despair, accusations of the gods and variations on the "nature reversed" theme. Near the beginning of the poem the poet describes life as a hopeless effort to escape all-conquering death:

Bitter death seizes all with a pitiless hand. . . .
Ah, the sadness! Go now and place your faith in prosperity
  Which Fortune gives and takes with fickle hand.
Be bold and heap up triumphs gained from a conquered enemy;
  The laurel-wreathed head must bow to death.
Erect buildings splendid with columns of Greek marble;
  Fate will drag you from it with her swift hand.
Trust in wit and beauty and the strength of youth;
  Behold, Albiera lies undone by heavy death.

(Mors cuncta immiti carpsit acerba manu. . . .
Ah dolor, i nunc & rebus confide secundis,
  Quas Fortuna levi fertque refertque manu.
Tolle animum & victo molire ex hoste triumphos,
  Laurigerum morti subjiciere caput.
Erige Taenareis radiantia tecta columnis,
  Parca tamen rapida te trahet inde manu.
Ingenio, formae, validae confide iuventae,
  Albiera ecce gravi morte soluta iacet [p. 261]).

Later there is a long apostrophe to the cruel goddess who is unmoved by beauty and youth, which culminates in a cry of despair that is limited to a single line following the death of Albiera: "I now believe the gods themselves can die" ("Credo ego iam divum numina posse mori"). This line might be considered the emotional crisis of the poem. It is reinforced by a vivid description of the events preceding Albiera's death. Albiera has been consoling Sigismund with the usual commonplaces about death. Her speech is obviously intended to be moving, but its effect is almost totally canceled by her sudden hopeless cry:

Alas, I am seized! Live for me, and I, though dead, will live in you.
  Already my heavy eyes grow dark in death.
And now, farewell, my husband; farewell my dear parents.
  Alas, I am taken far from here, hidden in the dark night.

(Heu raptor, tu vive mihi, tibi mortua vivam,
  Caligant oculi iam mihi morte graves.
Iamque vale o coniunx, charique valete parentes.
  Heu procul hinc nigra condita nocte feror [p. 266]).

Despair, darkness, fear of the unknown—these are the basic elements of Politian's treatment of death. They are not particularly Christian, but they are still effective because they catch the essence of a universal emotion.

The consolation offered by Albiera is cleverly made to serve a double function. It presents several commonplaces of consolation (I died young, "unstained" ["nullis sordida de maculis"]; I will be famous; I have the satisfaction of knowing that I will not survive my husband; I have escaped old age; etc.); and it also illustrates Albiera's piety. Yet it does not lead to affirmation. Politian's final answer to the problems raised by Albiera's death is resignation. The need for stoic self-control is emphasized in the descriptions of the funeral ceremonies and again in the "breve carmen" that ends the poem:

Beneath this marble lies the beautiful body of Albiera.
No other gravestones are worthy of such honor.
Her body ennobles the tomb; her spirit the stars.
O what great glory and praise have illuminated
the heavens.

(Hoc iacet Albierae pulchrum sub marmore corpus.
Nulla quidem tantum marmora laudis habent.
Exornat tumulum corpus, sed spiritus astra.
O quanta accessit gloria, lausque Polo [p. 268]).

The lines recall the epitaphs of the *Greek Anthology*. The formalism of the expression, the balanced clauses, the curtness of the *adjunctio* in the third line, and the use of epitaph formulae all combine to create the effect of finality. The intentionally formulistic reference to immortality in the third line harmonizes perfectly with this effect.

Politian's elegy defines the limit to which the purely classical funeral poem could be taken while maintaining its effectiveness. One step further and Albiera would disappear in a cloud of myth; she would be absorbed into the fictional elements of the poetry. Without the myth, however, Albiera's death would become merely another example of the need for stoic self-control in the face of the inevitable, a lesson which classical elegists taught several times over and which Ronsard and his contemporaries frequently repeated for their Renaissance audience.

II. TYPES STRESSING VIRTUE

We may now pass to a more obvious type of funeral poem—the type in which the individual is treated as a paragon of virtue. Here the use of praise to flatter or console is supplemented by its use in creating a desire to imitate virtue. Usually the virtue is illustrated by the noble deeds of the deceased, but occasionally it is presented by generalizations, or by a few representative examples. One restriction on the form is important. Since the praise is to lead to virtue, virtue must be shown to have its own rewards. Fame and the efficacy of example in society are possibilities, but along with these, Christian ideas of immortality are important. Therefore, the stoicism of the type of elegy previously examined becomes modified. Sadness is permissible, but consolation is essential. If the gloom of lament were not dispelled by the vision of the rich rewards of virtue, elegy might popularize escapism. Instead of Christian soldiers, the state might breed Horatian epicures sipping their Falernian wine amid lyre players and Greek singers. On the other hand, the existence of a consolation permits a more extensive use of the themes of negation than is common in the classical type. The stronger his eventual answers, the more profoundly the poet can question the nature of things. In some of the most complex funeral pieces such as Donne's *Anniversaries* this questioning becomes so prominent that it all but obscures the other elements of the elegy.

Ronsard's funeral elegy on Roc Chasteigner[21] is a good example of the simpler type of moral elegy. The plan of Ronsard's poem is straightforward. The topic of personal praise is introduced in the third line, when Chasteigner is described as among "The great heroes in Hades who still engage in military games" ("les grands Heros, qui encore là-bas/ Vont exercant le mestier des combas"). After the introduction there is a brief six-line treatment of the topics of "ancestry" and "physical endowments," followed by an equally brief summary of "virtues of character":

. . . he was of such a race
That no one surpassed it in noble blood;
He was so handsome, gallant, and perfect
That Nature might have made him
As a portrait of beauty for the world. . . .

He had a heart so warm and generous
That from infancy he was chivalrous. . . .

(. . . il fut de telle race
Qu'en noble sang personne ne la passe.
Il fut si beau, si galliard & parfait
Que la Nature au monde l'avoit fait
Pour un portrait de beauté. . . .

Il eut le cour si chaud & genereux
Que dés enfance il fut chevalereux. . . .)

Like a good rhetorician Ronsard devotes the bulk of the elegy (85 of 117 lines) to a chronological summary of Chasteigner's deeds. Barely past "his earliest childhood" ("sa premier enfance"), he fought against Spain. Later he was wounded at Mirande and made a captain of infantry. He fought in the Piedmont and defeated a boasting Spaniard in a tournament. Wounded frequently, he continued to advance in prestige. He was "chosen from one hundred thousand as Lieutenant of the Duke de Longueville ("Choisi entre cent mille/ Pour Lieutenant du Duc de Longueville"). Finally,

> . . . alas! by a fatal and harsh bullet
> He had his brain and head shattered,
> Losing his life and his winged youth.
>
> (. . . las! d'un plomb fatal & dur
> Il eut ceruelle & teste escrabouillée
> Perdant sa vie & sa ieunesse ailée.)

Thus the body of the poem summarizes Chasteigner's exploits in chronological sequence from birth to death. The narrative has almost no digression. The image created is true—i.e., historical—in contrast to the fictionalized image created by Politian. The total sense is one of heroic triumph. We might be dealing with the argument of an heroic poem rather than a funeral elegy.

Because of its emphasis on the admirable and successful achievements of Chasteigner, the poem is positive in mood and the portrait invites emulation. Chasteigner's exemplary function is stressed in the conclusion of the elegy. The passer-by is invited to place flowers on the tomb and to recite the following exhortation to his children:

> . . . a good death makes a man triumphant,
> Overcoming Death, when the excellent record
> Of his virtues is written in history
> Serving as an example and public model
> That a good subject should die for his King.
>
> (. . . un beau mourir rend l'homme triomphant
> Domtant la mort, quand la belle memoire
> De ses vertus est escrite en histoire,
> Servant d'exemple & de publique loy
> Qu'on bon suiet doit mourir pour son Roy.)

In more complex types of moral elegy lament is usually more prominent than it is in Ronsard's elegy on Chasteigner. Superficially these types resemble classical elegies that end with stoic resignation. There is, however, a major difference. No matter how negative they become, elegies emphasizing virtue are committed to some explicit positive resolution. The resolution does not have to be Christian, nor does immortality have to be a part of the consolation. A poem on a soldier, for example, can be limited solely to social references (his services to the state, his immortal fame, etc.), and it can emphasize that limitation by a parallel limitation of imagery. Obviously, however, if a poem asks theological questions, theology must answer them.

The type of poem that resolves negation in social terms may be illustrated by the Latin Pindaric "On The Death of Adornus" ("In obitu Adorni") by Benedictus Lampridius, who is credited with having introduced the Pindaric into neo-Latin poetry.[22] The poem has all of the trappings of the formal ode—its digressions, its complicated metrics, its elevation, and its obscurity. It ranges from the Trojan War to sixteenth-century Italy, and somehow it manages to achieve a genuine and somber tone at times resembling Tennyson's "Ode on the Death of the Duke of Wellington."

Adornus is praised for his achievements as a warrior and statesman. A long section of the poem (ll. 125-95) is devoted to a speech made by him which reveals his concern for the state, for the condition of Italy (torn by civil war), and, incidentally, his eloquence; for Adornus combined the heroic virtues of wisdom and courage. Finally, religious matters enter the poem but in a manner accommodated to the over-all social orientation. Adornus is deeply concerned over the continuing success of the Turks and tries to warn his audience of the threat that they represent to Christendom.

More interesting is the development of negative patterns. We have observed how the theme of nature reversed is developed by the use of pastoral imagery. In the poem on Adornus the negation is in social terms. All Italy suffers in the loss of Adornus:

> . . . alas! We Italians
> Are overwhelmed by returning shade
> Now that the light of Adornus
> Is extinguished. . . .
>
> (. . . heu tenebris
> Itali repetitis involvimur
> Postquam extinctus Adorni
> Fulgor. . . .)

The extension of this image leads to one of the most effective and frightening pictures in the poem. Moved by the thought of death, the writer contemplates contemporary Italy:

> . . . everywhere the bones
> Of citizens slain in battle rot;
> Often the rustic farmer
> Dulls his tools on them.
> And wherever he fixes his plow,
> In place of a fertile field he penetrates
> A bitter grave, and the earth, reddening,
> Oozes still pitiable gore.

And who mentions these things with a dry face?
And the towns consumed in sudden flames?
I have seen mothers, when they fled
The lawless enemy, throw themselves
Exhausted into rivers turbid with blood,
Swimming with the right hand, and with the left
Holding their miserable children,
Their hair dishevelled, screaming piercingly.

(. . . ubique putrefiunt
Ossa oppetentum vulnere civium,
Saepe quibus doluit sua rusticus
Cultor arma obtundit.
Nam quacumque infigit aratrum
In dura campo busta pro feraci
Incidit, tellusque rubens cruores
Exudat, adhuc miserandos.
Ecquis ore diserat
Haec sicco, aut rapidis oppida in ignibus
Absumpta? Matres vidi ego
Dum fugerent nefandum
Hostem, fluviis sanguine turbidis
Sese projicere ausas
Dextra trahentes, et sinistra
Infelicia pignora,
Passis crinibus, et querela acuta.)[23]

The painful scene is made still more intolerable by the impiety of the enemy:

Horror prevents one from saying
How the insolent army
Has stained the altars with impious slaughter. . . .

(Horror loqui vetat,
Quin aras etiam exercitus insolens
Foedavit impia nece. . . .)[24]

Except for this vivid elaboration of the topic of "society reversed" the poem is fairly conventional. There are the usual complaints against the cruel Parcae and against the gods: "Alas, again the gods in high heaven deliver us into misfortune!" ("eeheu, nos iterum Dii/ In damna tradunt Caelo ab alto"). Such references are doubtless elegant from the literary standpoint, but they severely limit the type of consolation that the poet can offer. If the gods are sadists who delight in causing suffering of the kind described by Lampridius, there can be no suggestion that they are literary symbols or foreshadowings of the Christian God. Nor can the poet invoke Christian ideas of immortality without the risk of blasphemy. Adornus, himself, was a Christian and the society described is a Christian one. Yet the author treats his subject with resolutely classical images and allusions.

Since the consolation of immortality would be inappropriate, Lampridius emphasizes the consolation of fame: the virtue of Adornus has been amply rewarded by the fame which he has gained. If we accept the humanistic belief that fame is a satisfying reward for achievement, we accept the consolation. However, the cult of fame is hard to accept in the twentieth century, and even during the Renaissance it was something of a hothouse growth. To many humanists from Petrarch to Milton, fame was in the last analysis a delusion. It was good as a stimulus to virtue, but, as Petrarch learned from St. Augustine in the *Secretum,* it clouded the real issue by turning men's aspirations from heaven to earth and from virtue pure and simple to heroic (sometimes even criminal) exploits.[25] In the end, time conquers fame but virtue is immortal. We can understand what Lampridius was attempting without feeling that it is entirely satisfying. The images of war's brutality and society turned on itself are the most memorable in the poem. It is almost as though Lampridius were asking whether, in the strife-torn Italy of his day, life had any moral significance.

III. CHRISTIAN TYPES

To move from secular to explicitly Christian elegy is to move from a world of well-made, often beautiful villas to a world of Gothic cathedrals—sometimes structurally weak, sometimes ungainly, but almost always touched with mystery. Despite his classicism, Ben Jonson evoked this world in his longer elegies, a fact that explains why they seem more "metaphysical" than his other poems. His formal ode on the deaths of Cary and Morison provides a striking contrast to the elegy by Lampridius on Adornus. The elegy to the memory of Shakespeare is noteworthy for its introduction of literary topics into the frame of the funeral poem; and his epicede on Venetia Digby is of interest because its motto is from the introduction to Book V of Statius' *Silvae* and invites comparison to Statius' epicede on Priscilla (V, i). Of all the elegies, however, the "Elegy on the Death of the Lady Jane Pawlet" most clearly exploits the possibilities of Christian funeral poetry.

Overt praise in the elegy for Lady Jane is presented in a conventional manner. Specific acts of Lady Jane are not recorded, but Jonson includes a generalized list of her virtues. First there is praise of the family:

> Shee was the Lady *Jane,* and *Marchionisse*
> Of *Winchester;* the Heralds can tell this:
> Earl *Rivers* Grand-Child—serve not formes, good Fame,
> Sound thou her Vertues . . . (ll. 19-22).[26]

The last line shows that Jonson remembered his rhetoric and wished to make a distinction between praise treating "gifts of fortune"—in this case "nobility of family"—and that treating virtue. The virtues are duly "sounded" from line thirty-nine to line sixty-two. In a couplet neatly summarizing the topics of personal praise, Jonson asserts, "What Nature, Fortune, Institution, Fact/ Could summe to a perfection, was her Act!" This is followed by a quasi-realistic character sketch of Lady Jane in the form of a witty—almost metaphysical—description of her attitude toward death:

> . . . when they urg'd the Cure
> Of her disease, how did her soule assure
> Her suffrings, as the body had beene away!
> And to the Torturers (her Doctors) say,
> Stick on your Cupping-glasses, feare not, put
> Your hottest Causticks to, burne, lance, or cut:
> 'Tis but a body which you can torment,
> And I, into the world, all Soule, was sent! (ll. 49-56)

Jonson's wit would obviously be out of place in a serious elegy based on classical models. Yet in the Christian context it has a curious appropriateness. The assurance of immortality makes Lady Jane contemptuous of her transient suffering. Even before Jonson's formal consolation, the reader is made to share an optimistic feeling toward death. The direct praise ends with Lady Jane comforting her husband and son in a manner reminiscent of Politian's Albiera. The sadness of the mourners is turned by Lady Jane's heroic bearing into enthusiasm and applause.

In addition to having praiseworthy characteristics Lady Jane is an example of virtue. For Jonson she exemplifies "that Contention, and brave strife/ the Christian hath . . ." (ll. 95-96); and contemplation of her can lead other Christians to the rewards which she has gained. Yet Jonson insists that he has not violated historical truth in order to create his pattern:

> . . . calling truth to witnesse [I'll] make that good
> From the inherent Graces in her blood!
> Else, who doth praise a person by a new,
> But a fain'd way, doth rob it of the true (ll. 35-38).

Jonson felt that the historical existence of a praiseworthy trait is a vitally important factor in making it credible. Excessive adulation, by offending the reader's sense of verisimilitude, robs the poem of its ability to teach; while creation of a wholly fictitious picture or—what is similar—praise of what is unworthy, is downright immoral.[27]

Jonson's stylistic devices are, as elsewhere in his work, beautifully controlled. In comparison to the stylistic devices of the poems previously considered they are unobtrusive, but this adds to their grace. The occasional hyperbole emerges from the context with the effect of sincerity. Jonson's statement that he is unequal to praising Lady Jane is his most obvious rhetorical flourish. Even this commonplace is put to fresh use:

> It is too neere of kin to Heaven, the Soule,
> To be describ'd! Fames fingers are too foule
> To touch these Mysteries! We may admire
> The blaze, and splendor, but not handle fire! (ll. 29-32)

The lines are not merely another inexpressibility conceit but a statement defining the limits of the poem, and, in the final analysis, the limits assigned by Jonson to the domain of art. Both as rationalist and neoclassicist Jonson suspected the extravagant claims that earlier humanists had made for poetry, as well as the extravagant poetry that had resulted from the attempt to live up to these claims. In some elegies the avowed intent of the poet *was* to give the soul its name, but Jonson elected to avoid such "Mysteries" in favor of the certainties of the here and now.

Jonson's use of lament is neatly adapted to the general purpose of making Lady Jane an example to her survivors. The elegy includes the conventional exclamations and descriptions of grief, but they are consistently softened. The pale ghost referred to in the poem's introductory section suggests restrained sadness rather than anguish. The poet's own grief ceases to be real when he asks Fame to write Lady Jane's epitaph on his breast so that ". . . I, who would her Poet have become,/ At least may beare th'inscription to her Tombe" (ll. 17-18).[28] It would be wrong to consider these lines a grotesque failure of sensibility. The wit is an intentional strategy to prevent the emotion from becoming so intense as to modify the poem's positive and exemplary tone. Later a more genuine note of grief is introduced in the form of the topic of nature reversed. Instead of being creative, the world becomes for the poet a place of universal death:

> If you can cast about your either eye,
> And see all dead here, or about to dye!
> The Starres, that are the Jewels of the Night,
> And Day, deceasing with the Prince of light,
> The Sunne! great Kings, and mightiest Kingdomes fall!
> Whole Nations! nay, Mankind! the World, with all
> That ever had beginning there, t'[h]ave end! (ll. 85-91)[29]

In pagan elegy and in elegies emphasizing the consolation of fame, "nature reversed" darkens the mood of the poem and threatens to lead to despair. There is none of this pessimism in Jonson's elegy, for no sooner is the theme introduced than its effect is canceled by the triumphant affirmation of immortality that ends the poem:

> . . . but for that Contention, and brave strife
> The Christian hath, t[o]' enjoy the future life,
> Hee were the wretched'st of the race of men:
> But as he soares at that, he bruiseth then
> The Serpents head: Gets above Death, and Sinne,
> And, sure of Heaven, rides triumphing in (ll. 95-100).

Jonson has asked the hardest questions that death can raise and has given the answer of faith. Even today the poem is moving. It might be added that Jonson's Christianity is only one factor in his success. Many sincere Christian funeral poems of the period are failures. In Jonson's elegy the elements are fused into an artistic whole. Praise, lament, and consolation are not merely parts of a conventional formula to be followed for its own sake. They are components of a unique poetic design, and their full significance is only evident when they are related to that design. Praise of Lady Jane illuminates the concept of virtue. Her highest praise is that in the end, contemplation of her leads the poet and the reader to a reaffirmation of Christian truth. The lament becomes a means of raising questions that can only be answered by Christian faith. In a sense, it demonstrates the necessity of faith. The pessimism of "nature reversed" thus leads directly to the assertion of man's superiority to his human condition; and death, instead of being a supreme horror, becomes capable of semi-humorous treatment.

As we have observed, the limits of Jonson's elegy are defined by his refusal to treat the "soul" of Lady Jane. Several Renaissance authors consciously attempted what Jonson refused to do. The best examples are not formal elegies but sonnet sequences that treat the death of the lady. In these the elegy patterns are worked out in elaborate detail and the spiritual qualities of the lady are depicted by means of the symbolism developed by the writers of the *stil novo.* Lorenzo de'Medici, Ronsard, and Scève all wrote sonnet cycles on the death of the lady, but all looked to Petrarch's *Canzoniere* as their supreme model. Despite their anti-Petrarchan vein the metaphysicals, too, drew on the *Canzoniere,* and modern scholarship is making it clear that their debt was large.[30]

The *Canzoniere*[31] may be divided into two sections. The first is devoted to Laura while she is alive. It has a rudimentary "plot" based on the poet's experiences from the time that he first fell in love to Laura's death. A good deal of the first section consists of direct praise. Laura's physical beauty is delineated and her *virtù* is emphasized. In the first part of the *Canzoniere* the *virtù* is predominantly social. The word *gentilezza* is a good one to use here, for it calls attention to the combination of social grace, modesty, propriety, honor, and Christian virtue stressed by Petrarch. It has an elevating effect on the lover similar to the effect of courtly love; he becomes more sensitive and refined, but the nature of his love is unchanged. It remains basically a combination of sentiment and natural instinct.

The poems of direct praise (e.g., xxx; xxxvii, 81-112; lxxvii; cxxvii; etc.) employ the whole range of rhetorical devices for "heightening" description. Exclamation, comparison, allusion, and hyperbole are used with astonishing virtuosity. Laura is depicted against the backdrop of nature reborn in the spring, of the sunlight sky, and of the starry spheres. Imagery of light and darkness, of precious stones and metals, mythological imagery, and topical references are all summoned to contribute to Petrarch's celebration. His use of religious symbolism is especially important, both for its direct effect in the first part of the *Canzoniere* and for the additional significance that it gains after the second part has been read. Laura is frequently compared to an angel (e.g., xxxvii, 89-96; lxiii; lxxii; xc; cxxiii), although she is at this point merely *angelica,* not *angelicata.* She is regularly compared to the sun and in ways that emphasize the Christian associations of the sun image; she is called divine, addressed in prayers, and referred to as a phoenix, a standard Christ symbol. At times the poet's love for Laura is shown explicitly competing with his love of God (e.g., lxiii, lxviii). Occasionally the love seems, at least to the modern reader, to verge on idolatry. Laura's birth is called a miracle and (iv: "Que' ch'infinita provvidenza") compared to the birth of Christ. At one point (xvi) Petrarch compares his efforts to find ladies who remind him of her to the efforts of a pilgrim at Rome to discover the face of Christ by looking at the Veronica. In sonnet xcv he compares his own love to the love of Mary Magdalene and Peter for Christ; and later he finds an analogy between Laura and God:

Just as eternal life is the sight of God
 Nor does one suffer nor can suffering be
 Thus, my lady, sight of you makes me
 Happy in this, my brief and fragile life.

(Sì come eterna vita è veder Dio,
 Nè più si brama, nè bramar più lice,
 Così me, donna, il voi veder felice
 Fa in questo breve e fraile viver mio [cxci]).

More commonly, however, Laura's love has the effect of improving the lover's character. If it does not intensify his faith, it at least purifies his thoughts:

There is no base desire which is felt here,
But love of honor and virtue. Now when before
Were basest thoughts by highest beauty slain?

(Basso desir non è ch'ivi si senta,
Ma d'onor, di vertute. Or quando mai
Fu per somma beltà vil voglia spenta? [cliv])

Petrarch's handling of religious images, allusions and concepts in the first half of the *Canzoniere* creates a striking effect. The material is present but submerged. The poet's world is vibrant with spiritual meaning, but he is so preoccupied with immediate realities that he fails to see what becomes obvious to the reader. The poet is revealed as a denizen of the City of Man, incapable because of his own passion of seeing the splendor of the City of God which is concealed in the secular world. His world is similar to the dark forest of Milton's *Comus,* which is both a "dungeon of innumerable boughs" and a pastoral world, its sky illuminated by the stars, its earth generating the miraculous herb haemony, and its river the abode of the semi-divine Sabrina. In the second part of the *Canzoniere* a dramatic reversal takes place. The physical object of love has been removed. Laura is dead. Therefore the poet's love must rise above natural instinct seeking physical gratification. The religious element gradually becomes dominant. The lady is no longer "angelic"; she is a *donna angelicata.* It is the City of God that now interests the poet, and the City of Man recedes ever further into the background. The change is so emphatic that symbolic interpretation is necessary: the death of Laura is both the cause and symbol of a mystic death to the world and has the same implications as the death of Beatrice in the *Vita nuova* or of Simonetta in Lorenzo de'Medici's cycle.[32]

Naturally the second part of the *Canzoniere* contains little extended praise of Laura's beauty. Laura no longer has physical existence. Moreover, her *virtù* is presented in a new light. *Gentilezza* is meaningful only in human society. Laura is now in heaven, and she embodies the supreme perfections of the transfigured spirit.

The "plot" of the second part of the *Canzoniere* is the story of the poet's gradually maturing spiritual knowledge. At first he feels overwhelmed by the pain and grief of loss. However, as he gropes for consolation, he realizes that Laura has a mission in life more important than arousing love:

God, who so soon removed you from the world,
Displayed [in you] such great and noble virtue
Only to inflame our love [of it].

(Dio, che sì tosto al mondo ti ritolse,
Ne mostro tanta e sì alta virtute
Solo per infiammar nostro desio [cclxx, ll. 99-101]).

At this point, the memory of Laura is simply a means of mitigating grief. Yet the image which the poet invokes is not that of the living Laura. She has already undergone a transformation, and when he imagines her she has taken on the beauty of heavenly spirits:

The lady more beautiful and graceful than ever
Appears before me as up there
Where she knows her beauty most pleases.
This is one pillar that upholds my life. . . .

(Più che mai bella e più leggiadra donna
Tòrnami inanzi, come
Là dove più gradir sua vista sente.
Questa è del viver mio l'una colonna . . . [cclxviii, ll. 45-48]).

Later he experiences moments of calm when he recognizes that even Laura's "sweet harshness and calm rejection full of chaste love and piety" ("dolci durezze e placide repulse piene di casto amore e di pietate") were "the root of my health, which otherwise would have been lost ("la radice di mia salute, ch'altramente era ita").[33] Still later, in one of the climactic passages of the cycle, Petrarch's despair gives way to a passionately affirmative vision of fulfillment after death, a fulfillment made possible by Laura:

I fly on the wings of thought to heaven. . . .
Now my heart trembles with a sweet chill,
Hearing her, for whom I have grown pale,
Say to me: Friend, now I love and honor you,
Because you have changed your manners and your habits.

(Volo con l'ali de'pensieri al cielo. . . .
Talor mi trema 'l cor d'un dolce gelo,
Udendo lei per ch'io mi discoloro,
Dirmi:—Amico, or t'am'io et or t'onoro,
Perc'ha'i costumi variati e 'l pelo [ccclxii]).

The element of spiritual growth is somewhat obscured in the *Canzoniere* by Petrarch's psychological realism. That is, the poet's change of heart is a long and painful process. He vacillates, cries for grace, rebels, despairs, attempts to return to the past, and only gradually does affirmation replace negation. Nevertheless, the over-all pattern is unmistakable.

In courtly love tradition, turning to God meant rejecting the lady; hence poems of courtly love often ended with a palinode. Neither Dante nor Petrarch followed this tradition. Both poets depicted love as an experience that becomes constantly deeper and richer as the lover's spiritual understanding matures. Consequently, both poets imagined themselves reunited with their ladies in heaven. Beatrice and Dante meet in the *Purgatorio* and continue together until the closing cantos of the *Paradiso*. Petrarch also looks forward to reunion with Laura. Why then does the *Canzoniere* end with a hymn to the Blessed Virgin?

Petrarch's final *canzone* has been interpreted in two extreme ways. It has been explained as a palinode in which the poet abandons all forms of human love—the result of either genuine conviction or the desire to end on a safely religious note; and it has been explained as daring fusion of Laura *with* Mary.[34] The second of these interpretations is doubtless preferable, since it allows one to take the *canzone* seriously, but both interpretations are unsatisfying. The palinode theory fails to distinguish between the two types of love which the poet expresses for Laura in the two parts of the *Canzoniere*. The first is secular and human. It has beneficial results in that it encourages *gentilezza,* but among its corollaries are physical passion, vanity, desire for temporal fame, and neglect of spirit. It is this love that the poet rejects. The hymn to Mary completes the rejection, and it is presented not as a negative withdrawal *from* temptation, but as a recognition of the fulfillment of love which becomes possible as the poet transcends human limitations. In this respect it is comparable to Dante's rejection of the God of Love after the death of Beatrice in the *Vita nuova*. Likewise, the fact that the final poem of the *Canzoniere* is addressed to Mary rather than Laura does not mean that Petrarch confused the two. It is simply a means of shifting emphasis from Laura as exemplar of Christian values to a supreme symbol of the whole Christian system. Again there is a parallel in Dante's work. In the final cantos of the *Divine Comedy* Beatrice yields to St. Bernard, yet no one has suggested that Dante intends either a rejection of Beatrice or a fusion of Beatrice and Bernard.

In Ben Jonson's elegy on Lady Jane Pawlet, contemplation of the individual leads naturally to contemplation of Christian truth. The highest praise of Lady Jane is that her manner of life and death becomes a way of leading those who mourn her to God. This movement is repeated on a much larger scale in the *Canzoniere*. But Petrarch goes further. Because the second part of the *Canzoniere* involves conscious affirmation of spiritual values implicit in the symbolism of the first part, the poem embodies discovery as well as growth. Petrarch learns that it was the spiritual Laura whom he really loved from the beginning; and the reader discovers that the world of commonplace experience is radiant with the light of the spirit. That this is a conscious process is indicated by the recurrent contrast in part two between the flesh as veil and the spirit as reality (cccii, cccxxix), between in the world as prison and heaven as freedom (cccxlix), between death in life and life from death (cclxxix; cccxxxi, 25-36). In sonnet cclxxxix Petrarch thanks Laura for "high wisdom,/ Who with her lovely face and sweet distain/ Made me, burning with passion, consider my health." (Lei ne ringrazio e 'l suo alto consiglio,/ Che col bel viso e co' soavi sdegni/ Fècemi, ardendo, pensar mia salute.") The most explicit "discovery" of the true nature of Petrarch's earlier love for Laura is sonnet cccxlviii:

> O high and rare prodigy of women,
> Now in the face of Him who sees all
> I can see my love and that pure faith
> For which I spilled so much ink and tears,
> And find that my love for you on earth
> Was the same as it is now for you in heaven,
> And I never wished other from you
> Than the splendor of the Sun shining in your eyes.
>
> (O de le donne altero e raro mostro,
> Or nel volto di Lui che tutto vede
> Vedi 'l mio amore, e quella pura fede
> Per ch'io tante versai lagrime e 'nchiostro;
> E senti che vèr te il mio core in terra
> Tal fu qual ora è in cielo, e mai non volsi
> Altro da te ch 'l Sole de li occhi tuoi.)

It is important to bear in mind the spiritual orientation of the second part of the *Canzoniere* when considering its style. Hyperbole is one of Petrarch's most characteristic methods of "heightening" Laura's praise. Jonson had refused to "foul" the soul by attempting to capture it in poetry. Petrarch, however, was quite consciously trying to capture the soul of Laura. This fact has some importance for the history of poetry because Petrarch's reputation as a lyricist kept alive the tradition of lyric as multi-dimensional and tinged with mystery at a time when other literary forms were being reduced to the banality of neoclassic formalism. At any rate, in the second part of the *Canzoniere* the historical Laura recedes into the background to make way for the *donna angelicata* who visits the poet, counsels him, reproves him, and is seen by him in the high spheres of heaven. The image of Laura is an idealized memory and is derived from the same "libro della memoria" that furnished Dante with the materials for the *Vita nuova*.[35] However, the reader is never reminded of this fact. He is constantly encouraged to take the poet's visions as though they really happened. The historical Laura is thus caught up in the figure created by the poet's imagination. Insensibly, she is transformed into a spiritual ideal; or, to put the matter differently, she becomes a "soul." Since hyperbole, like paradox, can be a specialized technique for transcending the limits of language and suggesting what would otherwise be inexpressible, its use in the second part of the *Canzoniere* is not only appropriate but necessary.

Theological symbolism is a special type of hyperbole as used by Petrarch. To understand its functions in the second part of the *Canzoniere* we need to recall that to praise the soul is to praise more than such virtues as piety, modesty, temperance, and the like. It is to praise the God in man. For example, both Beatrice and Laura are described as miraculous, "the great new miracle which appeared to the world in our days" ("L'alto e nuovo miracol ch'a'dì nostri apparve al mondo").[36] The statement at first seems to be mere rhetorical extravagance. Yet it is intended seriously. The soul *is* a miracle. To say so is not hyperbole but simple Christian truth. In fact, nothing short of the term miracle can accurately express the poet's meaning. Petrarch's allusions to Christ and the Virgin Mary also contribute to the description of Laura's "soul" by the kind of analogy that explains particulars by reference to an archetype. It is proper to say that the transfigured Laura is *like* the Blessed Virgin; but it would be blasphemy to assert equivalence. Dante also used analogy in this way. In the *Vita nuova* there is an extended parallel between Beatrice and Christ. Although this analogy troubled the literary censors of the Counter Reformation, it is not blasphemous unless the reader insists that Dante asserts equivalence between his lady and the Saviour.[37]

Lament understandably bulks large in the second part of the *Canzoniere*. The poet's sorrow is proportionate to his love. The first sonnet of the second part announces the death of Laura amid conventional exclamations of grief: "Alas, the beautiful face; alas, the sweet glance; alas, the graceful bearing . . . alas, the way of speaking . . ." (Oimè il bel viso, oimè il soave sguardo, oimè il leggiadro portamento . . . oimè il parlar . . ." [cclxvii].) Sighs and tears fill many of the poems. In none, perhaps, do the tears fall more copiously than in the following:

> My eyes, exhausted from searching for you in vain,
> Leave no place dry near them.
>
> (Gli occhi miei stanchi lei cercando invano,
> Presso di sè non lassan loco asciutto [cclxxxviii]).

These are conventional manifestations of grief. They can be found in most of the funeral poems already considered. Of greater interest are those passages in which the negation is expressed in general terms. Petrarch's frequent wish to die, which enters *canzone* cclxviii ("It is time to die;

I have already waited longer than I should wish . . .") ("Tempo è ben di morire, et ho tardato più ch'i'non vorrei . . ."), is not striking in itself. It is a commonplace of funeral poetry. In its usual form the desire for death is purely negative—a suicide impulse. Overwhelmed by despair the poet wishes to end his pain in the dreamless sleep of death. However, the *Canzoniere* employs the motif in a different way. Because Laura's transfiguration is heavily emphasized, the desire for death becomes the expression of a desire to rejoin her in paradise. This robs it of some of its negative connotations. Instead of being a desire to *escape from* something intolerable, it is a desire to *rise to* something good. Other negative motifs are modified in the same way. Not despair but desire for final truth causes Petrarch to exclaim, "No longer follow changing and fallacious thought, but sure and certain [knowledge] which leads to a good end" ("Non seguir più penser vago, fallace, ma saldo e certo ch'a buon fin ne guide!" [cclxxiii]). The attitude is particularly clear in the following variation on the *contemptus mundi:*

Miserable world, unstable and wayward!
He who places his hope in you is wholly blind;
For my heart was taken and is held by you
So that it is now earth, and bone no longer is joined
to nerve.
But the better form, which still lives
And will always live in high heaven—
Of its beauties I become ever more enamoured.

(Misero mondo, instabile e protervo!
Del tutto è cieco ch'in te pon sua spene;
Che'n te mi fu 'l cor tolto, et or se'l tene
Tal ch'e già terra e non giunge osso a nervo.
Ma la forma miglior, che vive ancora
E vivrà sempre su ne l'alto cielo,
Di sue bellezze ogni or più m'innamora . . . [cccxix]).

And again, in a passage where the parallel between Laura and Christ is stressed:

Every day until I follow my dear
And faithful guide appears to me more than a thousand
years. . . .
Nor should I fear the threats of death,
Which my King suffered with more heavy pain
To make me follow strong and constant. . . .

(Ogni giorno mi par più di mill'anni
Ch'i segua la mia fida e cara duce. . . .
Nè minnaccie temer debbo di morte,
Che 'l Re sofferse con più grave pena
Per farme a seguitar constante e forte . . . [ccclvii]).

The final sonnet of the sequence begins with the exclamation, "I am lamenting my past life which I wasted in loving a mortal thing . . ." ("I'vo piangendo i miei passati tempi/ I quai posi in amar cosa mortale . . ." [ccclxv]). The "mortal thing" is not Laura but her unreal self which has died, leaving only her immortal soul.

Contemptus mundi leads naturally to the topic of nature reversed. Sonnet cclxxii, for example, describes the world as a wasteland ravaged by death:

Life flies by and does not stay one hour,
And death follows after with gigantic strides
And things present and past
Trouble my mind, and the future also. . . .

(La vita fugge e non s'arresta una ora,
E la morte vien dietro a gran giornate,
E le cose presenti e le passate
Mi dànno guerra, e le futore ancora. . . .)

In sonnet ccxcix the poet takes up the *ubi sunt* theme. *Canzone* cccxxiii expands it into an image of universal death. The poem is composed of scenes supposedly witnessed by the poet alone at his window. After seeing an animal torn to pieces by hounds, a ship sink, a tree felled by lightning, and a fountain surrounded by nymphs and muses swallowed by the earth, the poet watches as a "graceful and beautiful lady" ("leggiadra e bella donna") is poisoned by a snake. The lady, of course, reminds the poet of his personal loss, and he laments, "alas, nothing but death in this harsh world!" Later, in an apostrophe to Death, "nature reversed" appears in the form of the pathetic fallacy:

Death, you have left the world without its sun,
Obscure and chilled, Love blind and weak,
Grace stripped bare, and beauties sickened. . . .
. . . you have destroyed the fairest flower of virtue:
Now that the first excellence has been destroyed, how can
there be a second?

The air and earth and sea should weep
    For mankind which without her
    Is like a field without flowers, or a ring without a gem. . . .

(Lasciato hai, Morte, senza Sole il mondo,
        Oscuro e freddo, Amore cieco et inerme,
        Leggiadria ignuda, le bellezze inferme. . . .
    . . . svelt' hai di vertute il chiaro germe:
    Spento il primo valor, qual fia il secondo?
Pianger l'aer e la terra e 'l mar dovrebbe
    L'uman lenaggio, che senz' ella è quasi
    Senza fior prato o senza gemma anello . . . [cccxxxviii]).[38]

Yet the negation is a transient mood. Like the desire for death it evolves toward the more commonplace Christian feeling that all mortal things are subject to change and the only permanence is in God.

In the first *canzone* of Laura's death (cclxviii), Petrarch laments, "What skill with words could depict my lamentable condition?" ("Qual ingegnio a parole/ Porìa aguagliare il mio doglioso stato?"). This is the first instance of the inexpressibility conceit that was used so frequently in formal funeral elegy. It is particularly appropriate for the *Canzoniere* since Petrarch writes *qua* poet as well as *qua* lover. When his world is shattered by the death of his lady he naturally expresses his disillusionment as a loss of faith in his ability: "She who made me speak is dead. . . I cannot . . . make bitter and crude rhymes sweet and limpid" ("Morta colei che mi facea parlare. . . . Non posso . . . Rime aspre e fosche far soavi e chiari" [ccxciii].) Along with conventional professions of inadequacy there are other, more radical uses of the inexpressibility conceit that tend to transform it from a correlative of despair into an affirmation. Thus, meditating on Laura's memory, Petrarch observes that he has been able to "adumbrate" ("ombreggiare") one or two of her "praises" ("lode"), but

. . . now that I come to the divine part
Which was a brilliant and brief Sun to the world,
The impulse, the genius, and the art prove inadequate.

(Ma poi ch'i'giungo a la divina parte
Ch'un chiaro e breve Sole al mondo fue
Ivi manca l'ardir, l'ingegno e l'arte [cccviii]).

In the very next sonnet, the feeling develops into an almost mystic rejection of poetry for silent contemplation: "Who understands truth knows in silence that she surpasses all speech, and then sighs, 'Blessed then the eyes that saw her alive.'" ("Chi sa pensare il ver, tacito estime/ Ch'ogni stil vince e poi sospire:— Adunque/ Beati gli occhi che la vider viva!—"). Taken together such expressions form an important *motif* in the second half of the *Canzoniere.*[39] This motif might be called "the strife between death and art," and it is resolved before our eyes by the poet's refusal to stop writing. Each poem is a testament to his resolution. In the most literal sense the artistic success of the *Canzoniere* represents the poet's triumph over his loss of faith in art, hence over his despair.

The motifs of consolation used by Petrarch need little comment. The central one is the consolation of immortality. Because of his faith that Laura lives and that he will eventually rejoin her, the poet is able to show that each negation prepares him for a higher affirmation. At first, it is despair which causes him to view the world as a wasteland. Toward the end of the *Canzoniere* it is his anticipation of the life to come which makes him impatient and contemptuous of mortality.

IV. POEMS ON THE PASSION

Renaissance poems on the Passion embody many of the characteristic features of funeral poetry. It might be said that they are constructed by means of the same rhetorical formulae. However, it would be just as true to say that they provide a kind of archetype, and that Christian elegies are in some measure adaptations of this archetype. The second explanation is, I believe, most fruitful. All men are the sons of God; and the good Christian is expected to model his own imperfect life on the life of Christ. Because Christ is the archetype and the good Christian only an imitation, Christ fulfills in his historical life ideals which Christians can only approach distantly. This results in a curious but typical feature of poems on the Passion. Statements which are metaphorical in the conventional elegy became literal truths when applied to Christ. Laura is *like* a phoenix, but Christ *is* a phoenix resurrected from the ashes of his death. Laura is *like* a sun, but Christ *is* the light of the world. Laura is *like* "the fairest flower of virtue," but Christ *is* the essential principle of virtue. The poet must *imagine* Laura in heaven as a *donna angelicata,* but Christ's ascension is a matter of history and is recorded in the most true of all histories, the New Testament.

Sannazaro's "Lament on the Death of Christ" ("De morte Christi . . . lamentatio") is an essentially pious work with a heavy overlay of classical references.[40] Christ is "rector of Olympus" ("Olympi rector")[41] and, like Jove, a "thunderer" ("tonans"). He is mourned not by the three Marys but by "blue Triton" ("caeruleus Triton"). He does not visit a Christian hell but "the vast depths of Cocytus" ("vastas lacunas Cocyti") with their "raving furies" ("furias hiantes") and "waves of Phlegethon" ("Phlegethontis unda"). Such references, while they may impair the effect of the poem for the modern reader, make it interesting to the student of Renaissance literature.

Since he is writing a lament, Sannazaro makes no effort to list Christ's noble deeds according to the standard formula for praise. He does, however, employ indirect methods of praise. A parallel is drawn between Christ and Hercules, and it is pointed out that Christ is by far the greater hero. Christ's great labor was the Harrowing of Hell, undertaken out of love for man:

> The creator and sure intelligence of the Supreme Father,
> Who at his back controls the huge reins of the world;
> What if he had not voluntarily undergone such great labors,
> And by his death bought human life
> So that after death he gave the light of eternal life
> To souls unstained by the black waves of Phlegethon,
> And summoned them to share his works and kingdom:
> So great his love and glory in saving human kind.
>
> (Quid si non tantos subiisset sponte labores,
> Humanamque sua pensasset morte salutem
> Ille sator rerum, & summi mens certa Parentis,
> Qui nutu ingentes mundi moderatur habenas?
> Ut tandem intactos picea Phlegethontis ab unda
> Post obitum aeternae donaret munere lucis,
> In partemque suorum operum, regnique vocaret:
> Tantus amor generis servandi, & gloria nostri [ll. 62-69]).

Christ's charity is also mentioned (ll. 80-81), and, by way of warning, the terrible power which he will wield on the Day of Judgment.

In consonance with emphasis on lament, negative elements are prominent.[42] Early in the poem the poet commands his readers to look on the crucified Christ:

> Behold, and weep full rivers of tears.
> Alas, the crime; alas, the cruel and impious deed!
>
> (Adspicite, & plenos lacrimarum fundite rivos.
> Heu scelus, heu crudele nefas! [ll. 14-15])

This involves a graphic description of the Passion itself. Although Sannazaro's Latin is too artificial to achieve the intense and brutal realism of fifteenth- and sixteenth-century paintings of the Passion, it is evidently motivated by the same deep need to realize the event in all of its human detail. Sannazaro exclaims,

Behold the breast pierced by the pitiless steel,
The breast, and the gory hands, and the face
Smeared with blood, and the bleeding head and the torn
hair. . . .

(Adspicite immiti trajectum pectora ferro,
Pectora, foedatasque manus, perfusaque tabo
Ora, cruentatumque caput, crinesque revulsos . . . [ll. 11-13]).

As far as Sannazaro was concerned the description was simply a summary of historical fact. If there is any higher meaning in the scene described it must be implicit in the same way that the higher meanings of the Bible are generated from the literal narrative. The technique might be described as "realism." The classical trappings—the ghosts wailing in the streets, the mourning nymphs and sea-gods, the allusions to the gods and regions of classical mythology—are simply embellishments. Tasteful or not, they are within the limits of poetic license as understood by humanists of the *Cinquecento*.[43]

Sannazaro's description of the physical upheavals accompanying the crucifixion is a special case of the "nature reversed" topic. In the elegies previously considered the topic is an extended metaphor for the shock and grief following the death of the poet's subject. However, in the *Lamentatio* the metaphor becomes historical truth. The details mentioned by Sannazaro are derived from the New Testament (Matthew 27: 45-54). The sincere Christian cannot doubt that they actually occurred. Thus, the sun that was metaphorically extinguished at the death of Laura is literally extinguished at the moment of Christ's death. And the world metaphorically desolated at the moment of the death of Aubespine or Albiera is literally devastated by the death of Christ. Sannazaro's description combines its historical material with the classical embellishments previously mentioned:

[The earth] embraces his bloodless limbs in its bosom,
And shaken, gives voice to its heavy complaint;
The sun itself declares its sorrow, now hiding
Under a cloud, marking its head with obscure darkness.
You, also, O moon, cover your shapeless cheeks and pale face,
And present your final tribute to your Thunderer,
Cutting the golden beams from your yellow head
And shedding warm tears into the damp night.
Moreover, the story goes that ghosts left their broken tombs
And wandered through the streets in new shapes,
And the arisen shades wailed in the streets in the night
And filled remembered dwellings with their lament.

What more? Did not the fury of the sea
Seem to raise huge floods and roll up mountains of water,
Threatening to cast down cities and drag the earth into the deep?
And then blue Triton, raising his head from sounding caves,
Blew loudly with his horn over the ocean
And told sailors with a terrible voice
The Father of Nature, its King and Lord, was dead.
Did these hands cement the bonds of the vast world?
Is all that rests or moves the work of them?

([Tellus] . . . exsanguesque sinu complectitur artus,
Et tremefacta, graves testatur murmure questus.
Testatur sol ipse suum sub nube dolorem
Iam latitans, atraque notans ferrugine frontem,
Tu quoque deformesque genas, pallentiaque ora
Contegis, inferiasque tuo das, Luna, Tonanti,
Auratum flavo tondens de vertice crinem,
Et lacrimas uda fundens in nocte tepenteis.
Nec minus abruptis fama est exisse sepulcris,
Perque vias errasse novis simulacra figuris:
Excitasque umbras medias ululasse per urbes
Sub noctem, & notos questu implevisse penates.
Quid? non & pelagi rabies adtollere fluctus
Immanes visa est, monteisque evolvere aquarum,
Dejectura urbes, terrasque haustura profundo?
Quum simul & caput undisonis emersus ab antris
Caeruleus Triton rauco super aequora cornu
Constreperet, nautasque horrenda voce moneret,
Naturae cecidisse Patrem, Regemque, Deumque.
Haene manus vasti junxerunt foedera mundi?
Harum opus est, quodcumque jacet, quodcumque movetur?
[ll. 21-41]).

Like the conventional funeral poem Sannazaro's *Lamentatio* ends on a positive note. The horror and grief of the crucifixion are modified by Christ's heroic conquest of hell and eventually disappear in the image of Christ the King returning to heaven. Emphasis shifts at this point from Christ to his mission. Christ's Ascension is as much a matter of history as his crucifixion; therefore, no very elaborate argument is needed to convince the reader. Instead, Sannazaro reminds the reader that he is involved in Christ's triumph. Through Christ all Christians have an opportunity to receive the grace necessary to salvation:

That King, moved by love of his human brothers, forgetting
their crimes,
Mindful of his promises, will enter into friendly hearts,
And renew your souls, preferring them to temples.

([Rex ille] oblitus scelerum, cognatae stirpis amore,
Promissique memor, menteis intrabit amicas,
Vestraque posthabitis recolet praecordia templis [ll. 112-14]).

As might be expected, this leads to a picture of the blessed in heaven.[44] Here as elsewhere in the poem the metaphors of the personal elegies become simple truths. Laura is an incentive to virtue and she leads Petrarch toward God. However, she is not equivalent to the Virgin or Christ, and to suggest that she is involves metaphor. Christ, on the other hand, provides both a pattern for all men to imitate and the grace necessary to salvation. No metaphor is involved in the consolation of Sannazaro's "Lament."

George Chapman's "Hymne to our Saviour on the Crosse"[45] is a stimulating poem that treats the Passion in a way quite different from the *Lamentatio*. Because the differences are so great, it may be well to begin by listing a few similarities. First of all, both poems are sparing in their direct praise of Christ. In both, the aspects selected for particular emphasis are Christ's love and mercy. Both use the comparison of Christ to the epic hero; in Chapman, Christ is "Like our Champion Olympian,/ Come to the field gainst Sathan, and our sinne:/ Wrastle with torments, and the garland winne . . . thornes mixe with thy bowes/ Of conquering Lawrell . . ." (ll. 18-23). Both have the comparison of Christ to the sun (Chapman, ll. 243-51). In both, the negative themes of lament are extensively developed. In Chapman's "Hymne," instead of the gospel accounts of natural upheaval, there is a description of society plagued by religious faction (ll. 31-92) and abuse (ll. 94-122). "Society overturned" takes the place of "nature reversed." Again, the consolation is similar in both poems. Contemplation of the Passion makes Chapman realize how great are man's potentialities. Sannazaro stressed man's opportunity to gain immortality. Chapman naturally mentions this (ll. 200-12) but stresses the way in which Christ's Passion provides grace, enabling man to grow spiritually in this life:

T'enable acts in us, as the next howre
To thy most saving, glorious sufference
We may make all our manly powres advance
Up to thy Image . . . (ll. 161-64).[46]

Finally, both poets express contempt for purely worldly things. Sannazaro condemns wayward man, warns against sin and describes hell in lurid imagery. Chapman cavils against sin (ll. 179-207) and remarks that ". . .

these formes of earth,/ Beauties and mockeries, matcht in beastly birth: We may despise . . ." (ll. 164-66). This is later expanded into a remarkable Neoplatonic section on the seduction of the soul by the body (ll. 227-42). There are also frequent references to damnation.

The differences between the two poems are striking but hard to define with precision. Sannazaro's strategy is indicated by his repetition of the command *adspicite*—"Behold." He attempts to form a detailed picture of the Passion following his Biblical source and stressing visual images. Chapman avoids the specific and the visual. He gives no description of Christ on the Cross. He shows, as a matter of fact, little interest in the human phases of the Passion, and his mention of "torments rarefied farre past the sunne" (l. 234) merely calls attention to the absence of graphic description of these torments. Instead of describing hell as Sannazaro had done, Chapman contents himself with abstract references. And Sannazaro's vision of the blessed gazing over the ramparts of heaven at the damned "Whom the band of angels and the fortunate crowd of the devout could scarcely watch with dry eyes" (ll. 101-2) gives way in Chapman to a general reference to the "joyes of heaven" (l. 92) and "holinesse and heaven" (l. 51).

These contrasts can be explained in several ways. Chapman's Protestantism was less anthropomorphic than Sannazaro's Catholicism; hence his hesitancy to stress the human aspects of the Passion. Chapman was also more interested than Sannazaro in philosophical issues; hence his tendency to substitute philosophical digression for word pictures.

But the most satisfactory explanation is that suggested by Chapman himself near the end of the poem. Speaking of the effect of faith, he praises the man "who inward is" (l. 252) and possesses "one thought of joy" (l. 261) which

> Makes all things outward; and the sweetest sin,
> That ravisheth the beastly flesh within;
> All but a fiend, prankt in an Angels plume:
> A shade, a fraud, before the wind a fume (ll. 265-68).

The contrast between "inwardness," which is reality, and "outwardness," which is illusory and evil explains many characteristic features of the poem. Chapman makes little use of visual imagery because it beguiles the reader with outward show at the expense of inward truth. The contrast is also involved in the long passage on religious controversy. Disputes have arisen to divide Christians, says Chapman, because the outward trappings of dogma have become more important than faith. The truths of faith are always apparent to "our eternall truth-exploring soule." This being the case, there is no need for controversy. The highest Christianity is allegiance to this inner sense of truth: ". . . true pietie weares her pearles within,/

And outward paintings onely pranke up sinne . . ." (ll. 41-42). Later Chapman extends these ideas:

> All Churches powres, thy writ word doth controule;
> And mixt it with the fabulous Alchoran,
> A man might boult it out, as floure from branne . . . (ll. 61-63).

Apparently, even lesser breeds without the law can discover truth if they will only separate it from the outward husk (the branne) that covers it. The doctrine is compounded of about equal portions of rationalism and the notion of the "inner light." It may be compared to Donne's ideas in the satire "Of Religion," and in some measure anticipates the argument in favor of religious sects in Milton's *Areopagitica.*

The contrast between inwardness and outwardness explains Chapman's criticism of those who observe outward forms of virtue without being virtuous. These men practice "A tricke of humblenesse . . . Professe all frailties, and amend not one" (ll. 118-19). It also clarifies Chapman's description of the soul. This begins with a comparison of the soul to Narcissus,

> . . . who being amorous
> Of his shade in the water (which denotes
> Beautie in bodies, that like water flotes)
> Despisd himselfe, his soule, and so let fade
> His substance for a never-purchast shade (ll. 236-40).

Here the body, the outward or physical part of man, becomes a "shade," while the soul is "substance." Just as religious controversies arise when more attention is paid to dogma than to inward truth, so corruption begins when man prefers his physical to his spiritual self. The fact that the soul is "substance" is emphasized by Chapman in a passage borrowed from Ficino.[47] The source of all being is God, who is like a sun whose rays are "to radiance fir'd, in that pure brest of his" (l. 248). These rays pour down on man. Although they are diminished as sun's rays are weakened by passing through air, they are the light of the soul, and their influence determines whether man will incline to heaven or earth (l. 250).

To conclude, Chapman uses the rhetorical topics of praise, lament and consolation. His poem has many similarities to Sannazaro's *Lamentatio* and is generically related to the personal funeral elegy. Its distinctive qualities are a by-product of Chapman's philosophy rather than the result of basically new literary techniques. This philosophy is markedly dualistic. Although Chapman uses Platonic images and even paraphrases Ficino at one point, his chief affinities are with seventeenth-century Protestant rationalists.

The foregoing observations will, I hope, suggest the range and seriousness of Renaissance occasional poetry. They also provide a striking illustration of the fact that literary forms have intrinsic meaning. They are not bottles which determine the shape of anything poured into them, but neither are they lumps of clay subject to every whim of the artist. To use an extremely inadequate analogy, they might be compared to the models used in geometry to illustrate various kinds of deformation. These models can only be distorted in a limited number of ways. In the process of distortion the parts of the model retain a consistent relationship with one another, so that if one angle increases, another diminishes proportionately. If the geometer becomes impatient with the model and attempts arbitrary distortions, he ends with a tangled piece of wreckage. By the same token, successful poetry depends on the artist's respect for the intrinsic capacities of his form.

According to romantic theory form is a by-product of inspiration. This theory has encouraged the production of some of the great poems of the language. However, it has also tended to impoverish poetry. Romantic poetry is not formless. It is rather a series of variations on a few basic lyric forms. The price exacted by romanticism has been the loss to literature of non-lyric forms. In this respect the Renaissance poet had more freedom—because he had a wider range of choices—than the romantic poet. Examination of a few typical Renaissance elegies suggests that in abandoning the sense of the integrity of form and the corollary sense of writing as a craft the poet loses something of real value.

CHAPTER VII

The Idea of Elizabeth Drury

John Donne's *Anniversaries* on the death of Elizabeth Drury are among the most extraordinary poems of the earlier seventeenth century. They have been called personal lyrics, religious meditations, gross flattery, and even allegorical comments on the career of Queen Elizabeth. They have been used to illustrate the perversity of Donne's style, to show the influence of science on the Jacobean mind, to prove that the writers of the *stil novo* were the spiritual fathers of the metaphysicals, and to suggest that Donne's mysticism is essentially medieval. Almost the only approach that has not been exploited is the one suggested by their title. An *anniversary,* according to Scaliger, is a formal epideictic type.[1] It may be defined as a funeral elegy composed annually to commemorate someone's death. The first *anniversary* will be a regular elegy and include the standard topics of praise, lament, and consolation. Later *anniversaries* will include praise and consolation, but will not emphasize lament; for, Scaliger remarks, "no one continues to lament a man who has been dead for one or two years."[2]

An approach to Donne's *Anniversaries* based on their rhetorical background is illuminating in two ways. First, it brings into focus the diverse elements of the poems and thereby simplifies many problems of interpretation. Second, it helps to deepen understanding of the rhetorical topics themselves. For both reasons, examination of the *Anniversaries* provides an appropriate conclusion to the study of the theory of praise and its manifestations in Renaissance literature.

I. THE CONTEMPORARY SUCCESS OF THE ANNIVERSARIES

Before examination of the *Anniversaries,* the question of their contemporary success must be answered. Critics from Edmond Gosse on have argued that the poems were contemporary failures.[3] If this is so, if they were incomprehensible or repugnant to the Jacobean audience, then they do not deserve treatment in a study that is concerned with the traditional and commonplace rather than the unique. There are, however, several facts which indicate the *Anniversaries* were very successful.

Foremost among these is the number of editions of the *Anniversaries*. The first edition of the *Anatomy* (the first *Anniversary*) was published in 1611. Its careful punctuation and spelling indicate that Donne took the trouble to prepare the printer's copy.[4] In 1612 the *Anatomy* was reissued together with the *Progresse,* and these remain the only *Anniversaries* that Donne composed. It has been suggested that adverse criticism of the two poems (especially the first) discouraged Donne from continuing. However, if the first *Anniversary* aroused intense opposition, it is hard to understand why Donne reissued it a year after its first appearance. And if Donne, himself, felt the *Anatomy* to be a failure, it is still harder to explain why he wrote the *Progresse* in a similar style. The matter becomes all the more remarkable when it is recalled that the *Anniversaries* are the only two poems that Donne issued separately during his lifetime,[5] and that they are, if length is any criterion, his most ambitious finished poems.

At any rate, if the age had agreed that the poems were failures they would have been forgotten as quickly as the other funeral pieces of the period. Yet, instead of being forgotten they were republished twice in Donne's lifetime. The first of the later editions appeared in 1621 and the second, in 1625. Evidently Jacobean readers thought enough of the poems to justify their resurrection ten years after their first appearance. Sir Herbert Grierson has noted that the editions of the '20's are increasingly careless. This may mean that they were pirated. If so, evidence for the success of the *Anniversaries* is all the stronger. A printer would hardly bother to steal a poem for which there would be no market. Finally, biographers have traced the remarkable kindness of Sir Robert Drury toward Donne from the time of Donne's poems on Elizabeth.[6] If the pieces appeared to Jacobeans to be "blasphemous" or tasteless flattery, then Sir Robert must have been a monumental blockhead to be taken in by his flatterer and to allow the publication of the *Progresse* after the *Anatomy* had been universally decried.

Another indication of the popularity of the *Anniversaries* is the amount of comment which they stimulated. The surviving references to the poems suggest something like a genuine Jacobean literary controversy. Perhaps unfortunately, Ben Jonson's biting criticisms, made during his visit to Drummond in 1618, stand out. They are understandable in terms of Jonson's literary theories, as will be shown later. For the present it need only be remarked that the *Anniversaries* had a strong impact on Jonson. Otherwise he would not have been talking about them in such emphatic language six years after their appearance.

The first favorable comments on the *Anniversaries* occur in the laudatory

"Praise of the Dead and the Anatomy" and "Harbinger of the Progresse" which preface them. These were probably written by Joseph Hall. Since Hall was at the time under Sir Robert Drury's patronage they must not be given too much weight. More persuasive evidence is furnished by the fact that Donne defended the *Anniversaries* in no less than three letters written in 1611 and 1612, and at considerable length. Finally, two of Donne's elegists, writing in 1631, singled out the *Anniversaries* for special praise. Endymion Porter asked, ". . . tell mee, if a purer Virgin die,/ Who shall hereafter write her Elegie?"[7] And Jaspar Mayne began his tribute by asking,

> Who shall presume to mourn thee, Donne, unlesse
> He could his teares in thy expressions dresse,
> And teach his griefe that reverence of the Hearse,
> To weepe lines, learned, as thy Anniverse,
> A Poeme of that worth, whose every teare
> Deserves the title of a severall yeare.
> Indeed so farre above its Reader, good,
> That wee are thought wits, when 'tis understood,
> There that blest maid to die, who now should grieve?
> After thy sorrow, 'twer her losse to live;
> And her faire vertues in anothers line,
> Would faintly dawn, which are made Saints in thine.[8]

Whatever their poetic merits, Mayne's verses show that Donne's *Anniversaries* were remembered and admired almost as a touchstone of metaphysical wit. They also suggest an interesting possibility about the development of metaphysical style. Since the *Anniversaries* were the only poems by Donne generally available before the collected edition of 1633, they must have exerted an especially strong influence on readers and poets unable to refer to the manuscript poems. If so, the *Anniversaries* must have been particularly important in popularizing Donne's literary style.[9]

A final bit of evidence for the success of the *Anniversaries* is the number of echoes of the poems to be found in Donne's later work and that of his contemporaries. Evelyn Simpson has discovered several passages in the *Essays in Divinity* which are reminiscent of the *Anniversaries;*[10] and the notes in Sir Herbert Grierson's edition of Donne's poems cite many phrases and images later used in the sermons. The effect of Donne's work on his contemporaries can be illustrated by the case of George Chapman. Chapman had competed with Donne in the composition of a funeral elegy on Prince Henry and had come off a distinct second best. Two years later he wrote *Eugenia,* a funeral poem on the death of Lord Russell, his patron's father, announcing, ". . . Anniversaries that (for as many yeares as God shall please to give me life and facultie) I constantly resolve to performe to his Noblest Name and Vertues."[11] In his first "vigil" Chapman asks, "How then will this poore remnant of your powres/ This cut up quick *Anatomie* of yours/ This *Ghost* and shallow of you be preserv'd?"[12] Both passages echo Donne's *Anatomy of the World*. Perhaps to the impoverished Chapman the anniversary scheme appeared an ideal method of giving the patron a gentle yearly reminder of his debt to the Muse. Ben Jonson also seems to have been influenced by Donne, despite the critical reservations expressed to Drummond. In the "Elegy on Lady Jane Pawlet" the lines "serve not formes, good Fame,/ Sound thou her vertues, give her soule a Name" employ one of the most striking images of the *Anatomy*.[13] And the description of Lady Jane's ascent to heaven seems to owe something to Donne's *Progresse:*

> And now, through circumfused light, she lookes
> On Natures secrets, there, as her owne books:
> Speakes Heavens Language! and discourseth free
> To every *Order,* every Hierarchie!
> Beholds her Maker! and, in him doth see
> What the beginnings of all beauties be. . . .[14]

Among other compositions that show direct influence of the *Anniversaries,* William Drummond's *Cypress Grove,* Richard Brathwaite's *Anniversaries upon his Panarete,* Henry King's "Anniversary," and Habington's "Elegy upon . . . Henry Cambell" might be mentioned. In the light of this evidence, it is proper to conclude that the *Anniversaries* were not failures but quite notable contemporary successes.

II. DONNE'S DEFENSE: THE ANNIVERSARIES AS PRAISE

Any adequate interpretation of the *Anniversaries* must take into account Donne's defense of them. In 1611 he wrote to Sir G. F.:

I hear from *England* of many censures of my book, of Mistress *Drury;* if any of those censures do but pardon me my descent in Printing any thing in verse, (which if they do, they are more charitable than my self; for I do not pardon my self, but confesse that I did it against my conscience that is, against my own opinion, that I should not have done so) I doubt not but they will soon give over that other part of that indictment, which is that I have said so much; for no body can imagine, that I who never saw her, could have any other purpose in that, then that when I had received so very good testimony of her worthinesse, and was gone down to print verses, it became me to say, not that I was sure was just truth, but the best that I could conceive; for that had been a new weaknesse in me, to have praised any body in printed verses, that had not been capable of the best praise that I could give.[15]

And in two almost identical letters dated 1612 he told Gerrard:

Of my Anniversaries, the fault that I acknowledge in my self, is to have descended to print any thing in verse, which though it have excuse, even in our times, by men who professe, and practice much gravitie, yet I confesse I wonder how I declined to do it, and do not pardon my self. But for the other part of the imputation of having said too much, my defence is, that my purpose was to say as well as I could: for since I never saw the Gentlewoman, I cannot be understood to have bound my self to have spoken just truths, but I would not be thought to have gone about to praise her, or any other in rime, except I took such a person, as might be capable of all that I could say. If any of those Ladies think that Mistris *Drewry* was not so, let that Lady make her self fit for all those praises in the book, and they shall be hers.[16]

In both letters Donne divides the issue into two parts: first, the propriety of printing the poems, and second, the propriety of the contents. Critics who have asserted that his letters show Donne felt the *Anniversaries* to be failures have overlooked this division, for Donne only admits that he made a mistake in printing them. His regret may be sincere. However, it may be affected. The period is full of gentleman-authors who print only because some zealous (and mythical) admirer has issued a garbled version of their poems, or who pass off their tortuous sonnets as idle trifles.

Donne's defense of the content of the *Anniversaries* is unequivocal. He begins with the charge that he has "said too much." This can only be a reference to complaints of rank flattery such as are still made by readers of the poems. He replies that since he has never known Elizabeth, he cannot be bound to "just truth." The argument is surprising. Modern readers are likely to take it as a roundabout admission of insincerity. "I cannot be understood . . . to have bound my self to have spoken just truths" seems to imply "I *can* be understood to have spoken unjust exaggerations." Yet Donne intends his comments as self-justification, not confession.

The problem can be solved by reference to the theory of praise, and as a first step in this direction it is necessary to show that the *Anniversaries* should be considered poems of praise.

The letters are clear enough on the point. In both of the passages quoted Donne asserts that his object is to praise Elizabeth. The first letter indicates that the *Anniversaries* are "the best praise that I could give"; and in the second Donne insists that "I would not be thought to have gone about to praise her . . . except that I took such a person, as might be capable of all that I could say."[17] The title of the *Anniversaries* also supports the contention that they are poems of praise, since, as we have seen, an *anniversary* is a formal epideictic type.[18]

The evidence of the poems is conclusive. The *Anatomy of the World* begins with references to celebration and praise:

When that rich Soule which to her heaven is gone,
Whom all do celebrate, who know they have one,
(For who is sure he hath a Soule, unless
It see, and judge, and follow worthinesse,
And by Deedes praise it? (1-5)

And the poem concludes:

. . . . if you
In reverence to her, do thinke it due,
That no one should her praises thus rehearse,
As matter fit for Chronicle, not verse;
Vouchsafe to call to minde that God did make
A last and lasting'st peece, a song . . . (457-62).

The prefatory poem is especially interesting, for it shows that to at least one contemporary Donne's purpose was crystal clear:

Enough is us to praise them that praise thee,
And say, that but enough those prayses bee,
Which hadst thou liv'd, had hid their fearfull head
From th'angry checkings of thy modest red . . . (21-24).

And:

. . . O happy maid,
Thy grace profest all due, where 'tis repayd.
So these high songs that to thee suited bin
Serve but to sound thy Makers praise, in thine,
Which thy deare soule as sweetly sings to him . . . (33-37).

In addition to stressing the idea of praise, the second quotation recalls the fact that personal praise often evolves toward praise of God. The *Anatomy* is a praise of Elizabeth which ultimately serves "but to sound thy Maker's praise." This explains the similarity, noted by Professor Louis Martz between the *Anniversaries* and Jesuit devotions.[19] However, the similarity should not be stressed too heavily. Elizabeth is Donne's chief concern throughout both poems, and the praise of God is a secondary theme, almost a by-product of the fact that praise of any created object is indirect praise of its Creator.

If the *Anatomy of the World* is a poem of praise, it follows that the *Progresse* is also one. The prefatory "Harbinger to the Progresse" asserts,

Since thy [Donne's] aspiring thoughts themselves so raise
That more may not beseeme a creatures praise,

> Yet still thou vow'st her more; and every yeare
> Mak'st a new progresse, while thou wandrest here;
> Still upward mount; and let thy Makers praise
> Honor thy Laura, and adorne thy laies (31-36).

It is thus quite proper—in fact almost mandatory—to read Donne's poems in the context of the theory of praise.

To understand Donne's defense of the *Anniversaries* in his letters we need only recall that epideictic compositions owe a double allegiance to history and morality, and that specific works tend to stress one or the other element. Since Donne had never seen Elizabeth but had had "very good testimony of her worthinesse," he could not base his praise on biographical particulars. His term "just truth" is a reference to biographical particulars. "Just" has the common Renaissance meaning of "precise" or "specific"; and "truth," the meaning of "historical truth" in contrast to "moral truth." To compensate for the lack of historical detail, Donne stressed the moral aspect of praise. As he wrote in 1611, "When I had received so very good testimony of her worthinesse, and was gone to print verses, it became me to say . . . the best I could conceive." Such praise emphasizes ideal virtue and encourages emulation; in fact Donne remarked in 1612, "If any of those ladies think Mistress Drewery was not [as depicted], let her make her self fit for all those praises in the book, and they shall be hers."

Donne's letters, then, attempt to justify his treatment of Elizabeth by reference to the moral level of praise. There is certainly nothing "blasphemous" about this. One of the characteristic features of the epideictic *pictura* is its use of ideal patterns.

At this point a gloss is possible on Ben Jonson's criticism of the *Anniversaries.* To Drummond he remarked, "That Donne's 'Anniversary' was profane and full of blasphemies. That he told Master Donne if it had been written of the Virgin Mary, it had been something; to which he answered that he described the idea of a woman and not as she was."[20] Believing "truth of history" to be a prime essential of serious poetry, Jonson naturally objected to the method employed in the *Anniversaries.* He also believed that the effort to picture the soul necessarily "fouls" it. The proper approach to the mysteries of spirit (except in the divinely inspired revelations of the Bible) is via its manifestations in historical experience. On the other hand, while Donne agreed that the soul was "incomprehensible" he refused to allow this fact to "deterre/ Mee, from thus trying to emprison her . . ." (469-70). The difficulty of realizing the ideal merely spurred Donne to more zealous efforts.

The method by which the incomprehensible is made comprehensible, at least to the imagination, is by analogy to the familiar. Jonson knew this as well as Donne, but Donne was much bolder in his use of analogies. Therefore it is important to remember that the dazzlingly various analogies of the *Anniversaries* have a single purpose. In them Elizabeth's soul (or "idea") becomes what I. A. Richards calls the "tenor" of the image. The "tenor" is defined by several "vehicles" that have pre-established religious significance.[21] As in the *Vita nuova* and in the *Canzoniere* of Petrarch, this involves the constant use of parallels between the subject and the figures of Christ, the Blessed Virgin, and even God. Recent discussions of the *Anniversaries* have referred to Elizabeth as a "logos," a type of Christ, or an adumbration of the Virgin or Astraea.[22] Like God, Elizabeth creates a world in which ". . . all assum'd unto this dignitie,/ So many weedlesse Paradises bee . . ." (81-82). And like Mary, ". . . shee . . . could drive/ The poysonous tincture, and the staine of *Eve,*/ Out of her thoughts, and deeds . . ." (179-81). However, such references do not require us to think of Elizabeth as God or the Virgin any more than "my love is like a red, red rose" means that Burns is in love with a flower. They are "vehicles" for a "tenor"—the soul of Elizabeth—which is otherwise incomprehensible. Nor does Donne suggest that Elizabeth is far more virtuous than anyone else. There is nothing startling about the assertion that the virtuous Christian cultivates the image of God in his soul. What is unfamiliar is the difficult way in which Donne puts his point, and the necessity of remembering the "tenor" in the super-abundance of "vehicles."

To return to the *Conversations with Drummond,* Jonson, both as neoclassicist and as Catholic sympathizer writing after the Council of Trent, sought historical embodiment of the virtues of Elizabeth. The only historical, or "justly true," embodiment of Donne's *pictura* whom Jonson could think of was the Blessed Virgin; and he apparently assumed that Donne began his praises with the Virgin in mind and then applied the result to Elizabeth. If this were true, the *Anniversaries* would certainly be blasphemous. However, it is not true. Jonson's critical principles blinded him to techniques that other seventeenth-century poets used as a matter of course and that Hall understood perfectly in his prefatory poems.

III. THE OLD-NEW WORLD IMAGE

The title page of the *Anatomy of the World* offers an immediate challenge. The image suggested by *anatomy* is that of a medical dissection. Donne could not resist exploiting this connotation and does so in the rather gruesome conclusion to the poem:

> But as in cutting up a man that's dead,
> The body will not last out, to have read
> On every part, and therefore men direct
> Their speech to parts, that are of most effect;

So the worlds carcasse would not last, if I
Were punctuall in this Anatomy;
Nor smells it well to hearers, if one tell
Them their disease, who faine would think they're well (435-42).

However, *anatomy* has meanings other than medical. During the sixteenth and seventeenth centuries it was used to mean any systematic analysis, as in *The Anatomy of Abuses* and *The Anatomy of Melancholy*. Donne used the word in this sense in his title. The most striking fact about the organization of the *Anniversaries* is their use of topical—i.e., analytical—rather than chronological development. Very few occasional poems use this method, but Quintilian sanctions it in his discussion of praise in the *Institute*,[23] and it is a natural enough variation of the basic theme. As Martz has pointed out, devotional works of the period were usually topical. Donne may have been imitating their organization, but it seems more likely that the *Anniversaries* and the devotional tracts resemble one another because of a common source—epideictic formulae.

Donne's title is still confusing. Normally the elegist names his subject in his title, but Donne called his poem *The Anatomy of the World*. Apparently there is a sense in which understanding the "decay of the world" helps the reader to understand Elizabeth. It would be convenient to assume that the poem is based on the imagery of correspondence, and that the world referred to by Donne is a macrocosm symbolizing the microcosm of Elizabeth's soul. Unfortunately, the problem is not so simple, for Elizabeth is a paragon of virtue. If Donne were using correspondence in the conventional way, the "world" corresponding to Elizabeth would be harmonious, beautiful and productive.

The difficulty can only be removed by close examination of the way in which the word "world" is defined in the *Anatomy*. Donne explained the word in some detail, but his explanation has been overlooked because of confusion about his organization. It is usually assumed that the *Anatomy* is in seven sections—an introduction, five "meditations," and a conclusion.[24] The first meditation deals with mortality, the second with mutability, the third with loss of proportion, the fourth with loss of color, and the fifth with loss of heavenly influence. This analysis is not quite accurate. The five meditations are sub-divisions of three larger units that make up the body of the poem. The first major unit is announced by the structural couplet, "Her death hath taught us dearely, that thou art/ Corrupt and mortall in thy purest part" (61-62). The second begins with "For the worlds beauty is decai'd, or gone,/ Beauty, that's color, and proportion" (249-50). And the last begins, "Nor in ought more this worlds decay appeares/ Then that her influence the heav'n forbeares"

(377-78). The poem thus moves from physical through aesthetic to spiritual aspects of the world. The first and second units have two sub-divisions each (mutability, corruptness; color, proportion); and the third is devoted to a single topic (loss of heavenly influence).

The difference between a three- and a five-part division of the body of the poem may seem at first trivial, but it is not. For present purposes, the three-part division is important because it calls attention to a long digression imbedded in the section of the poem dealing with mutability and corruptness. Critics who insist on a five-part division assume that the first section begins with line 91, which announces, "There is no health; Physitians say that wee . . ."; and that all of the preceding material is part of a somewhat rambling introduction. However, as has been shown, the first unit begins with the structural couplet of lines 61-62. Therefore, the intervening material (ll. 63-90) is digressive. Once this is recognized the function of the digression is readily understood. The structural couplet announces the first two meditations on the "world." But the reader must understand what "world" the poet is discussing or he will miss the point. Lines 63-90 define and explain Donne's "world" and are therefore vital to a proper reading of the poem:

> Let no man say, the world it selfe being dead,
> 'Tis labour lost to have discovered
> The worlds infirmities, since there is none
> Alive to study this dissection,
> For there's a kinde of World remaining still,
> Though shee which did inanimate and fill
> The world, be gone, yet in this last long night,
> Her Ghost doth walke; that is, a glimmering light,
> A faint weake love of vertue, and of good,
> Reflects from her, on them which understood
> Her worth; and though she have shut in all day,
> The twilight of her memory doth stay;
> Which, from the carcasse of the old world, free,
> Creates a new world, and new creatures bee
> Produc'd: the matter and the stuffe of this,
> Her vertue, and the forme our practice is:
> And though to be thus elemented, arme
> These creatures, from home-borne intrinsique harme,
> (For all assum'd unto this dignitie,
> So many weedlesse Paradises bee,
> Which of themselves produce no venemous sinne,
> Except some forraine Serpent bring it in)

Yet, because outward stormes the strongest breake,
And strength it selfe by confidence growes weake,
This new world may be safer, being told
The dangers and diseases of the old:
For with due temper men doe then forgoe,
Or covet things, when they their true worth know (63-90).

Probably the most important lines in this passage are 75-76. They explain that the poem will deal with not one, but two "worlds." The first is an "old" world, which is the world as it existed during Elizabeth's life. When she died it ceased to exist; metaphorically, it became a "carcasse." It was succeeded by a "new" world, which is created by her memory and formed on the pattern of her virtue. The new world is the world of the present, the world occupied by Donne and Elizabeth's other mourners. It is the real world of the poet and his society. In view of this fact, the widespread notion that the images of decay and the references to the "new philosophy" in the *Anatomy* simply represent Donne's response to a contemporary crisis becomes untenable. These images and references depict the old world. The new world—the world in which Donne lives while he writes the poem—has not "decaied" because of Elizabeth's death. In fact it is in some sense a "weedlesse paradise."

Donne's two worlds are not, of course, to be taken literally. They are variations on the conventional elegy topic of "community," according to which the elegist claims that a whole city, or a society, or even the world at large is affected by the loss of the person being celebrated. While Elizabeth lived she provided an example of virtue that symbolically unified the world of her acquaintances. Just as Laura was "di vertute il chiaro germe," and the hands of Sannazaro's Christ "vasti junxerunt foedera mundi," so Elizabeth was "The Cyment which did faithfully compact,/ And glue all vertues" (49-50); and the old world was Elizabeth's palace, of which Donne says, "Her name defin'd thee, gave thee form and frame" (37). The image is hyperbolic but not particularly difficult. Its serious meaning is that of the familiar passage from the *Devotions:* "The Church is *Catholike, universall,* so are all her Actions; *All* that she does, belongs to *all.* When she baptizes a child, that action concerns mee; for that action is thereby engrafted to that *Head* which is my *Head* too, and engrafted into *body,* whereof I am a member. And when she *buries a Man,* that action concerns me. . . . And man's death diminishes me, because I am involved in *Mankinde. . . .*"[25]

Donne's next step greatly complicates interpretations. The topic of "community" is fused with the topic of "nature reversed." The old world symbolizing Elizabeth's admirers before her death is said to be a "carcasse" in the last stages of decay. Donne answers the objections to writing a poem for the inhabitants of a dying world in lines 63-78. Elizabeth's death has two effects. First, it makes her admirers aware of the true nature of the world which had seemed so adequate while she lived. Overwhelmed by grief, they realize that life is treacherous and corrupt, the world (i.e., the old world) a place of darkness, pain, and death. Second, the process of disillusionment produces a new level of moral awareness. Elizabeth's mourners turn from the illusions of the temporal world to the truths of spirit. Symbolically, they become inhabitants of a new and better "world." Since they are led to this world by Elizabeth's memory, she is described as a creator and a producer of "new creatures." Since the new world is based on spiritual awareness, it is compared to a "weedless Paradise" free of "venomous sin."

The descriptions of the sterility and decay of the "old" world are the most vivid parts of the poem. Donne elaborated them with inexhaustible ingenuity, drawing on every phase of contemporary thought. His references to the new science are a case in point. Although the modern reader is comfortably aware that the revolutionary discoveries of the new science foreshadowed the triumph of scientific method, Renaissance laymen often felt that they only proved the inadequacy of human reason. If doctrines supported by tradition, authority, and common sense could be demolished overnight, what faith could be placed in man's ability to discover truth? And if Aristotle, Ptolemy, and Galen were wrong, what assurance could Galileo, Copernicus and Harvey have of being right? The "new philosophy" of the *Anatomy* does not establish certainties; it "calls all in doubt." Since it is based on the use of reason to study nature, it demonstrates the corruption of reason and the unknowable mystery of nature. It thus establishes the futility of life lived according to the standards of the "old world." Donne used up-to-date imagery to make the corruption of the "old world" vivid to contemporary readers. But his essential "meaning" is as commonplace as "Now we see as through a glass darkly." Elizabeth has given her mourners a knowledge more adequate than the fallible truths of science. Although they do not see perfectly, they at least are aware of how dark their glass really is. Their education will be perfected when they enter heaven as reborn souls and see truth face to face. As Donne says in the *Progresse:*

> Why grasse is greene, or why our blood is red,
> Are mysteries which none have reach'd unto.
> In this low forme, poore soule, what wilt thou doe?
> When wilt thou shake off this Pedantery,
> Of being taught by sense, and Fantasie?
> Thou look'st through spectacles; small things seeme great

Below; But up unto the watch-towre get,
And see all things despoyl'd of fallacies (288-95).

So much for the basic meaning of the old-new world image. To stop here, however, is to miss the striking implications of Donne's poem. The old-new world image is not a grotesque attempt at wit. It was chosen deliberately, and has rich literary and theological connotations.

Several critics have remarked on Donne's affinity to the Italians of the *dolce stil novo,*[26] and there is a group of critics who trace metaphysical style to the Petrarchan conceit.[27] Donne's familiarity with Petrarch needs no demonstration, and his knowledge of the *Divine Comedy* is attested by a letter that criticizes Dante at some length.[28] Moreover, ever since Miss Ramsay's *Les doctrines médiévales chez Donne,* there has been talk about the parallel between Dante's journey into Paradise and that depicted in the *Progresse.*[29] Mario Praz, however, is alone in suggesting that the *Anatomy* is indebted for more than "Petrarchan hyperbole" to the *dolce stil novo.* To him, the sonnets of Sannazaro furnish a key to the old-new world image.[30] This suggestion is illuminating but needs, I believe, a minor qualification.

In the "Harbinger," Hall advises,

. . . let thy Makers praise
Honor thy Laura, and adorne thy laies (35-36).

Clearly, the Jacobean looked to Petrarch rather than Sannazaro for a parallel to Donne's poem. The most obvious similarity lies in the fact that both Donne and Petrarch treat the death of the lady. Moreover, from Dante on, the image of the "new life" into which the lover is brought because of the death of the lady is conventional. The fullest explanation of the convention is found in Lorenzo de'Medici's commentary on his sonnets. There we find that death is a transition from old to new life, and has been so treated by Homer, Virgil, and Dante.[31] While the lady of the sonnet cycle makes a literal transition, the lover makes a figurative one. Lorenzo's controlling metaphor is his comparison of the lady to the sun. When the sun sets (i.e., the lady dies), the ensuing darkness symbolizes the poet's realization of the dark and dreary nature of this world. Memory becomes his only consolation.[32]

What Dante expressed in the image of an old and new life, Petrarch in images of *contemptus mundi* and beatitude, and Lorenzo in the contrast between night and day, Donne presents by the image of an old and new world. And just as the "book of memory" ("libro della memoria") guided Dante, Petrarch, and Lorenzo, so Donne's new world is "created" by the memory of Elizabeth[33] and perpetuated by her poet.

Literature, however, is not the original source of the image. It is based on a traditional religious metaphor. From the time of the earliest apologists, the Christian conversion, and baptism in particular, was described as a second birth—an entry into a new life or a new world. This type of rebirth is suggested throughout the *Anatomy* in the baptism image, the image of the "weedless paradise" (for baptism removes the stigma of original sin; hence, ingrained corruption), and in other cases; while man's third birth—death—is the subject of the *Progresse*.[34] Since the Christian after conversion usually lived on in the world of mortals, he was said to "live in the world but not of it," and this is exactly how Elizabeth's mourners respond to her death. Although they live "in" the old secular world that they occupied before her death, they are "of" the new world. Donne's imagery might be compared to the description of the mode of life of early Christians found in the *Letter to Diognetus:*

. . . although [Christians] live in Greek and barbarian cities alike, as each man's lot has been cast, and follow the customs of the country in clothing and food and other matters of daily living, at the same time they give proof of the remarkable and admittedly extraordinary constitution of their own commonwealth. They live in their own countries, but only as aliens. They have a share in everything as citizens, and endure everything as foreigners. Every foreign land is their fatherland, and yet for them every fatherland is a foreign land. . . . It is true that they are "in the flesh," but they do not live "according to the flesh." They busy themselves on earth, but their citizenship is in heaven.[35]

IV. THE STRUCTURE OF THE ANATOMY

Placing the old-new world image in an historical perspective is essential to an understanding of the *Anatomy* but does not fully answer the question with which the present chapter began—in what sense does the *Anatomy* constitute the praise of Elizabeth? Having clarified Donne's basic image, we can proceed to an examination of the structure of the poem and, on this basis, attempt an answer. The poem may be outlined as follows:

I. (1-60) Introduction: Elizabeth's death shocks us into realizing the defects of the old world.

II. (61-248) Physical decay of the world: ". . . thou art/ Corrupt and mortall. . . ."

- a. Explanation of the old-new world image (63-90).
- b. Mortality of man (microcosm) (91-190).
    1. Lament for the mortality of man in the old world (91-174).
    2. Elizabeth as departed principle of health (175-84).
    3. Consideration of Elizabeth teaches how to escape the world by religion (185-90).

c. Corruption of the world (macrocosm) (191-248).
   1. Lament for corruption of old world (191-218).
   2. Elizabeth as departed principle of stability (219-38).
   3. Consideration of Elizabeth teaches how to escape the "world's infection" (239-48).

III. (249-376) Qualitative (or aesthetic) decay of the world: ". . . beauty, that's color and proportion. . . ."

a. Loss of proportion—*i.e.,* rational order (251-338).
   1. Proportion is gone from the old world (251-308).
   2. Elizabeth as departed principle of proportion. (309-26)
   3. Consideration of Elizabeth teaches the need for acting "fitly and in proportion" (327-38).

b. Loss of color—*i.e.,* aesthetic order (339-76).
   1. Lament for loss of color in old world (340-60).
   2. Elizabeth as principle of perfect beauty (361-70).
   3. Consideration of Elizabeth teaches us to avoid trying ". . . with bought colors to illude mens sense . . . (370-76).

IV. (377-434) Spiritual decay of the world: ". . . her influence the heav'n forbeares. . . ."

   1. Loss of heavenly regenerative influence—*i.e.,* the Platonic "circuitus divinus (377-98).
   2. Elizabeth as a spiritual force on earth (399-428).
   3. Consideration of Elizabeth teaches contempt for the world, and love of ". . . those rich joyes, which did possesse her heart . . ." (429-34).

V. Conclusion: It is best to speak of Elizabeth in verse rather than in "chronicle" because verse is preserved in the memory, as is clear from the example of the song of Moses.

What can be said about the *Anatomy* on the basis of its structure? In the first place, each section announces the realization, caused by the shock of Elizabeth's death, that some vital factor is missing from the old world. During Elizabeth's life it seemed to be present because Elizabeth manifested it, and her complacent admirers assumed it to be *of* the temporal world instead of *in* it. With Elizabeth gone, the wretchedness of the world is harshly apparent. The poet expresses his grief and disillusionment in a lament that is amplified by the topic of "nature reversed." But the lament is not entirely negative. If it conveys disillusionment it also conveys the healthy Christian knowledge that, in the light of spiritual understanding, the temporal world is false and corrupt.

These ideas are presented in the *Anatomy* in a survey covering all aspects of the world and fully realizing the implications of the word, *anatomy.* First the physical world, both microcosm, and macrocosm, is examined from a generally scientific—i.e., physical—standpoint. Medicine, astronomy, and geology are shown to support the idea that the physical world is mortal and decaying. The theory of correspondence may be invoked at this point to give the passage an additional layer of meaning. The physical aspects of the world are known by the lower (sensory) powers of the soul or the Platonic *anima prima.* Next, the world is examined in terms of qualities. Donne separates the qualities into those which are perceived by the rational—especially mathematical—faculty and those which are more distinctly aesthetic. Proportion and order can be understood logically. "Color" is not so easily defined. Donne's term is probably related to the Thomistic concept of "claritas" and is almost certainly a cousin to the Renaissance image of the "various light" of nature.[36] In terms of the correspondence of world to soul, this section is referred to the *anima secunda* or reasoning soul. Finally, the spiritual world is dealt with. Since the early days of Christian Platonism, the fecundity of the earth had been accounted for by the postulate of a divine emanation or "circuitus divinus" that filtered downward from God to earth and then rose again to unite with God.[37] The faculty in the soul that responds to this influence is the *mens.* It is an intuitive faculty and the highest one that man possesses. Together, the three major units of the *Anatomy* consider the world from the major points of view possible to the philosopher of Donne's time—physical, qualitative, and spiritual. By correspondence, they also survey the sensory, rational, and intuitive powers of the soul that perceive this world.

A glance at the outline of the *Anatomy* will show that each sub-section has three parts. These are closely related to the three basic topics of funeral elegy. Section II, *b,* for example, consists of a lament, a eulogy of Elizabeth and a consolation, each of which is limited to the topic of mortality. Since the other sub-sections have an identical structure *The Anatomy of the World* may be said to follow the rhetorical topics of funeral elegy. However, instead of being a continuous poem like the elegies previously examined, it is divided into topical sections in accordance with the method suggested by the word *anatomy.*

The sequence of lament, eulogy, and consolation calls for further comment. The usual arrangement of these topics was eulogy-lament-consolation. This arrangement is based on cause-effect: the nobility of the subject is the cause of the lament and the negative tone of lament makes the consolation necessary. The virtue of the scheme is that is leaves no doubt that the deceased person is the central subject of the poem.

Donne's reversal of the eulogy-lament sequence creates ambiguity. Instead of appearing as a normal human response to a particularly grievous loss, Donne's lament seems to be a complaint over the real decay of a real world. The ambiguity is increased by Donne's avoidance of direct references to Elizabeth in the laments. On the other hand, Donne's treatment has a logic of its own. Our immediate reaction to death is not eulogy but grief. The grief manifests itself in the sudden consciousness of some deficiency in the "world" of the poem. By a transition that is metaphorically, if not logically, acceptable, Donne suggests that the deficiency is only evident because Elizabeth has died; and from this it follows that Elizabeth originally exemplified the virtue that is missing. Thus, in the lament, Elizabeth is defined negatively by what is missing. The lament awakens memories of Elizabeth, and these lead to a tearful eulogy of her as a paragon of whatever virtue happens to be the poet's subject at the moment. The reference is still to the Elizabeth of the "old world"—that is, to the girl as she lived. Therefore, each eulogy ends with the refrain, "Shee, shee is dead. . . ."

The emotional pattern is completed in the consolatory sections, which are the antitheses of the laments. In these the conventional consolatory topics, and in particular the joys of future life, are omitted in favor of a demonstration of the effects of Elizabeth's memory on her mourners. Thus, each section becomes a threefold description of Elizabeth's "idea" through lament, eulogy, and explanation of how Elizabeth leads us to virtue. In that Elizabeth is treated as an individual, the primary epideictic aim—praise of the subject—is achieved. In that she is treated *sub specie aeternitatis,* as a principle of virtue emanating from the source of virtue, her praise fulfills both the exemplary requirement and the possibility of merging praise of the individual with praise of God. The *Anatomy* may not be as immediately satisfying as the lyrics of the *dolce stil novo,* but it has a comparable richness and breadth of vision.

V. THE STRUCTURE OF THE PROGRESSE

The *Progresse of the Soule* seems in every way a simpler piece than the *Anatomy*. Critics who have condemned the latter poem have often praised the former. Yet some confusion has developed concerning the relation of the *Progresse* to Donne's other work. According to one theory, advanced first by Grierson,[38] the *Progresse* is intended as a companion to the *Anatomy,* and the two poems together constitute a complete meditation in which *contemptus mundi* contrasts with the joys of heaven. Milton's companion poems *L'Allegro* and *Il Penseroso* have been suggested as parallels.

Two facts militate against this theory. First of all, there is *contemptus* material in abundance in the *Progresse*. Second, Donne thought of the two poems as parts of a series rather than companion pieces. In the *Anatomy* he says:

Accept this tribute, and his first yeares rent,
Who till his darke short tapers end be spent,
As oft as thy feast sees this widowed earth,
Will yearely celebrate thy second birth,
That is, thy death . . . (447-51).

And in the *Progresse,*

Immortall Maid, who though thou would'st refuse
The name of Mother, be unto my Muse
A Father, since her chast Ambition is,
Yearely to bring forth such a child as this (33-36).

Evidently, Donne used the term *anniversary* in the conventional rhetorical way. The *Anatomy* and the *Progresse* are the first two installments of a series to be continued until the poet's death. The objection that Donne did not write a third anniversary and, therefore, must have believed that the first two form a unit does not hold in view of his very specific promise in the second *Anniversary* to produce a third. The project seems to have been abandoned, probably because Donne has becoming increasingly preoccupied with his preparations for the ministry.

A second suggestion concerning the *Progresse* is that its title alludes to the earlier and fragmentary "Progresse," which was to trace the soul of heresy through a succession of sinners until it finally reached Queen Elizabeth.[39] There are intriguing parallels between the poems, but they hardly justify reading the second as a semi-official retraction of the first. The earlier poem is a fragment of a satiric epic, while the later one is a fairly straightforward occasional piece. Even the similarity of title is dubious, since the title page identifies the earlier poem as "METEMPSYCHOSIS *Poema Satyricon,*" and Jonson, speaking to Drummond, recalled it not as a "progress" but as Donne's "Transformation or Metempsychosis."[40] Jonson put the earlier "progress" in its proper place. It is a playfully cynical, even libertine, adaptation of the Pythagorean doctrine of souls to political and religious satire. It has no relationship to the *Progresse of the Soule.*

Other theories about the *Progresse* can best be considered on the basis of the structure of the poem. The poem has nine clearly-defined sections. These are indicated by marginal notes in the first edition. There is room for disagreement regarding the sub-divisions of the major sections, and the divisions made here will be explained below.

I. (1-44) Introduction.

II. (45-84) "Disestimation" of the world; i.e., *contempus mundi.*

- a. The world is rotten (45-64).
- b. Elizabeth was a pattern of perfection on earth (65-80).
- c. Consideration of Elizabeth teaches us to hate this world (81-84).

III. (85-156) Death.
- a. The process of death (*memento mori*) (85-120).
- b. Elizabeth's perfect composition made her seem immortal (121-46).
- c. Consideration of the fact that Elizabeth died teaches us that we all must (147-156).

IV. (157-250) The soul in the body and released from it (physical "incommodities").
- a. The soul is imprisoned in the body (157-78).
- b. Released, it has marvelous powers (179-219).
- c. Elizabeth represented perfect soul in perfect body (220-246).
- d. She calls us to heaven (247-50).

V. (251-320) Knowledge in the body and out of it.
- a. Here, all things are dark (251-94).
- b. After death, all is known perfectly (295-300).
- c. Elizabeth, knowing virtue, knew everything (301-14).
- d. She calls us after (315-20).

VI. (321-382) Society here and in heaven.
- a. Society here is corrupt (321-38).
- b. Society in heaven is perfect (339-55).
- c. Elizabeth was a pattern for a perfect society (356-79).
- d. Desire to join her society leads us to heaven, for accidental joys occur there; but first, essential joys (380-82).

VII. (383-470) Essential joy here and in heaven.
- a. We have no permanent essential joys here (383-434).
- b. The sight of God is essential and lasting joy (435-46).
- c. Elizabeth formed God's image in her heart while living (447-67).
- d. She is in heaven, who was as close as man comes to essential joy here on earth (468-70).

VIII. (471-510) Accidental joys in heaven.
- a. Here, accidental joys are fleeting (471-96).
- b. Heaven's accidents are eternal and perfect (487-96).
- c. Elizabeth has gone to heaven and her reward, where we may rejoin her (497-510).

IX. (511-528) Conclusion.

If the preceding outline is acceptable, the poem cannot be read as the narrative of the soul's journey to heaven. Sections II, III, and IV could be loosely construed as a journey if their sub-divisions were ignored; but only Section IV actually describes an ascent. Moreover, it is not at all clear that Section IV is intended to be a continuation of the earlier sections. Chronologically, it follows them, since transfiguration follows death. On the other hand, a careful examination of Sections II through VIII of the *Progresse* will show that they fall into two parts. Sections II and III deal with the corruption of earthly life in much the same way as the *Anatomy*. The following sections, however, treat a new subject—the state of the soul in heaven in contrast to its state on earth. First, there are the new physical and intellectual powers of the soul (IV and V); second, the new society (VI); third, the release from mutability, for in heaven, Donne tells us, essential and accidental joys are permanent (VII and VIII). As the outline shows, these sections differ from the preceding ones by having four rather than three sub-divisions. The reason is instructive. Sections IV through VIII are developed by comparison and contrast: the miseries of earth are contrasted to the joys of heaven. Those matters are independent of Elizabeth. Donne begins with a general contrast between earth and heaven (the *a* and *b* parts of IV-VII). Then, in order to relate the meditation to Elizabeth, he asserts that Elizabeth was a pattern of the virtue of each section while she lived (the *c* part), and by her death encourages us to anticipate the perfection of each virtue in heaven (the *d* part). The plan is simple and unambiguous, and has these advantages over the *Anatomy*. Instead of a metaphorical "old" and "new" world, the *Progresse* deals with a literal earth and heaven.

Donne has carried the method of the *Anatomy* to its logical conclusion. Dante did the same thing when he moved from the *Vita nuova* to the *Paradiso*. In the *Vita nuova* Dante describes the "new life" which he achieved through the memory of Beatrice. In the *Comedy* the fact that the poet has lived a "new life" has made him worthy of heaven, where he is reunited with his lady. The same idea is frequent in the later sonnet cycles, and, in composing Section IV and following, Donne may have been thinking specifically of Petrarch's sonnet cclxii, "Volo con l'ali de' pensieri al cielo. . . ." At any rate, the Italian development of the theme is as follows: the death of the lady creates desire for virtue in the lover, leading to a new life or, as in the *Anatomy*, a "new world." The lover perseveres in the new life and has a vision in which he learns that after death, he will rise to heaven. As part of his reward in heaven, the lover will be reunited with his lady. Donne's relation to Elizabeth is that of Christian to virtuous girl rather than lover to lady, but otherwise, he follows the *stilnovisti*.

In terms of its over-all movement then, the *Progresse* becomes a meditation on the soul's state in heaven rather than the description of a journey. Critics who have avoided the journey idea have occasionally interpreted Donne's "progress" as a metaphor for the Christian *scala perfectionis*.[41]

Thus, the poem becomes a spiritual journey in the tradition of medieval mystic theology. The theory admits a simple test. The two most famous descriptions of the stages by which the soul attains perfection are those of Bernard of Clairvaux and Bonaventura. Bernard taught that there are seven steps in the process of enlightenment. These are:

1. Fear of God (servile humility—we act from fear of punishment).
2. Understanding of God's ways (voluntary obedience—we act out of hope or reward, like merchants).
3. Love of God's way (virtue and good works—we are moved by love of our fellows).
4. Wisdom (we love virtue because we love God—we are like God's sons).
5. Purity of conscience and nobility of mind (we love ourselves only as we love God; we attempt to perfect His image in ourselves. Thereby we become beautiful and attract the heavenly spouse—the Holy Spirit, or grace).
6. Fecundity (because of our proximity to perfection, we teach and benefit others, begetting spiritual children).
7. Union with God (marriage of the soul and the Holy Ghost).[42]

Saint Bonaventura's system has six steps:

1. Knowledge of God through His traces in the visible world.
2. Knowledge of God through His image stamped on the mind.
3. Knowledge of God refined through the gift of grace.
4. Knowledge of God through His primary name, *Being.*
5. Knowledge of God through His name, *Good.*
6. Revelation of God through mystical experience.[43]

Surely even such a compressed summary shows that these two systems differ radically from anything that could possibly be deduced from the *Progresse.* This does not mean that Donne was unfamiliar with the mystics or even that they had no influence on the *Progresse.* It merely shows that Donne did not use the *scala perfectionis* as a structural basis for his poem.

VI. THE MEANING OF THE PROGRESSE

Once again the best means of understanding Donne's intention is the theory of praise. The *Harbinger* remarks,

> Since thine aspiring thoughts themselves so raise
> That more may not beseeme a creatures praise,
> Yet still thou vow'st her more. . . .
> . . . let thy Makers praise
> Honor thy Laura, and adorne thy laies (31-36).

Donne, himself, writes, "my life shall bee/ To be hereafter prais'd, for praysing thee . . ." (31-32); and, "These Hymnes may worke on future wits, and so/ May great Grand children of thy prayses grow" (37-38).[44] These remarks are elaborated in Section II, which begins the main body of the *Progresse.* Its thought may be paraphrased as follows: this world is rubbish when compared to the perfect world. Elizabeth was as near as possible to perfection, but even she preferred heaven. Therefore, we should imitate her:

> Shee, shee is gone; she is gone; when thou knowest this,
> What fragmentary rubbidge this world is
> Thou knowest, and that it is not worth a thought;
> He honors it too much that thinkes it nought (81-84).

The praise of Elizabeth is twofold, as in the *Anatomy.* She is praised as a paragon of earthly perfection, and as an example stimulating her admirers to virtue.

Section III is equally commonplace. Its topic, the *memento mori,* is one which Donne always found attractive and utilized in the *Devotions* and the sermon *Death's Duel.* The first part is an elaborate description of the process of dying. Next, we are told that Elizabeth was as close as mortals come to a perfect harmony of parts (medical jargon for health), yet she died. This teaches us to accept the fact that "Death must usher, and unlocke the doore" (156) to paradise. Again Elizabeth is praised directly as a person and indirectly as an example.

Section IV is somewhat ambiguous—it seems chronologically connected with the preceding sections but logically connected with the following ones. For the sake of simplicity, it will be treated as the first of five sections dealing with the joys of after-life.

In contemplating the state of the soul after death, Donne reverses what would seem the most natural order. Normally, the contemplation would treat (a) the joys of after-life, and (b) the contrasting triviality and falseness of earthly life. However, Donne consistently introduced the major sections of the *Anatomy* and the *Progresse* with lament, and sections IV and following continue this practice, even though the functional reason for beginning with lament is now absent. In earlier sections contemplation of Elizabeth formed a transition or modulation between the despair of the lament and the affirmation of the consolation. But the rewards of heaven do not depend on Elizabeth, and they are in themselves sufficient reason for despising the world. Elizabeth has become superfluous.

Donne's solution to this problem is awkward. In Section IV the incommodities of the soul in the body are contrasted with its freedom after death. Elizabeth is then introduced in a third section as representative of the highest possible harmony of soul and body. The conclusion might be paraphrased, "Elizabeth was as perfect as possible in this respect, yet she traded earth for heaven and (presumably) has greatly increased her powers.

Therefore, consideration of her teaches us, her inferiors, to look forward eagerly to our release":

> To' advance these thoughts, remember then, that she. . . .
> Shee, shee, thus richly and largely hous'd, is gone:
> And chides us slow-pac'd snailes who crawle upon
> Our prisons prison, earth, nor thinke us well,
> Longer, then whil'st wee beare our brittle shell (220; 247-50).

Since the thought of the succeeding sections is parallel to that of section IV, they need not be examined in detail. Sections IV and V treat the physical and mental phases of the contrast between earthly and heavenly life.[45] Section VI treats the difference between earth's hypocritical society and heaven's perfect one. The final two sections are more difficult. Basically, they treat mutability, and in both Donne says that unlike earthly joys, heaven's joys are everlasting. He divides the joys into accidental and essential ones. The essential joy of heaven is the sight of God:

> Only who have enjoy'd
> The sight of God, in fulnesse, can thinke it;
> For it is both the object, and the wit.
> This is essentiall joy, where neither hee
> Can suffer diminution, nor wee;
> 'Tis such a full, and such a filling good . . . (440-45).

In mystic literature the vision of God is the culmination of mystic discipline. In the *Paradiso,* Dante loses Beatrice as he approaches the final blinding revelation of God, and Petrarch ends the *Canzoniere* with the famous hymn to Mary. It is one of the disappointing features of the *Progresse* that Donne does not imitate the *stilnovisti* at the end of part seven. But Donne's poem is first and always an occasional piece, inspired by and dedicated to a particular girl. To end with the vision of God would be to lose Elizabeth. Therefore, Donne reverses the order of the experiences and takes pains to explain this to the reader:

> Shee, shee doth leave it, and by Death, survive
> All this, in Heaven; whither who doth not strive
> The more, because shees there, he doth not know
> That accidentall joyes in Heaven doe grow.
> But pause, my soule; and study, ere thou fall
> On accidentall joyes, th'essentiall.
> Still before Accessories doe abide
> A triall, must the principall be tride (379-86).

Through this device, Donne manages to end on "accidentall" joys and hence Elizabeth. There is only one advantage to Donne's method. Being one of the joys of heaven, Elizabeth can become a special attraction to her mourners. Therefore, in Section VIII Elizabeth once again becomes essential to the thought being developed. She is the subject of the section, as she could not be the subject of the earlier ones. Donne's eulogy reaches its climax when he describes her condition in heaven:

> Shee, who by making full perfection grow,
> Peeces a Circle, and still keepes it so,
> Long'd for, and longing for it, to heaven is gone,
> Where shee receives, and gives addition (507-10).

Donne's *Anniversaries* are complex, daring, subtle, and crudely direct by turns. They place great demands upon the reader, but their rewards are commensurate with their demands. In an age when "rhetoric" and "convention" are terms of rebuke, they are a reminder that a great artist can be both rhetorical and conventional without sacrificing his art. In fact, Donne's achievement is inconceivable without the rhetorical tradition. Epideictic theory defined his purpose, supplied the topics around which the *Anniversaries* are organized, and suggested several image-themes appropriate to the topics. Unlike the romantic poet, Donne did not have to begin *ab ovo*. Since his materials were given, he could devote his full energies to molding them into artistic shape.

Epideictic theory offers a perspective within which the *Anniversaries* can be read without distortion. They are not lyric responses to a contemporary crisis. They are not Donne's equivalent to the religious devotion. Elizabeth Drury is neither Queen Elizabeth nor a surrogate for the Blessed Virgin, Christ, or the divine *logos*. She is a virtuous young woman concerning whom Donne had received "good report" and whom he undertook to celebrate in two elegies based on traditional topics and images. If the tradition of praise illuminates the poems, the poems are a convincing demonstration of the richness and vitality of the tradition.

CHAPTER VIII

A Chapter of Dogma

The theory of praise has now been examined in its most characteristic phases. Its history has been sketched, its place in Renaissance critical theory illustrated, and its effect on the traditional hierarchy of literary genres demonstrated. Its importance and manifold ramifications need not be reiterated. If the preceding discussion has been convincing these will be self-evident.

But accurate description is not in itself the end of literary scholarship, and it would seem appropriate in this concluding chapter to turn from the genesis and influence of the theory of praise to its value. Does it contain significant truths about literature? Does it offer reasonably adequate solutions to the standard problems of literature and aesthetics? Does it in any way illuminate current conceptions and misconceptions about literary art? Our answers to these questions will perforce be brief and to a certain extent dogmatic, but there is comfort in the fact that all answers to these questions are inconclusive and dogmatic. If they were not, the questions would cease to perplex. Literary scholarship cannot expect to answer its basic questions in the scientific manner of demonstrating one hypothesis and then proceeding to the next, for it is concerned with value, which is constantly changing, rather than with an external and stable nature. As values change, the scholar's vocabulary and his touchstones also change, and no single method can possibly become the true and final one. He is the handyman of a disintegrating mansion. As he replaces one board the shingles on the roof begin to shake loose; nailing the shingles back causes the chandelier to fall from the dining-room ceiling. His work is never finished, but if he stops in despair the whole house may tumble down.

It is not unfair to begin our evaluation of the Renaissance theory of praise by asking how important it was to those qualities which we still admire in Renaissance poetry. Admitted that it was frequently referred to by critics; even admitted that it influenced specific literary works—for all that, is it a major factor in the effect of those poems which we still find successful?

The question is a valid one. It is an indirect way of stating the indubitable truth that the effect of a poem is often quite independent of the intentions and literary theories of the author. Suppose Petrarch did think of himself as writing the praises of Laura rather than lyrics in the romantic sense of the term. Does this affect what we, his modern readers, derive from his sonnets? In fact, may it not tend to diminish their interest by emphasizing their mechanical and formal qualities at the expense of what had previously seemed inspiration? Obviously there are dangers involved in either a *yes* or *no* answer, but the dilemma can be resolved by a proper understanding of the ambiguous term *intention*. As long as we speak of "the author's intention," we are taking an indefensible position, as Professors Beardsley and Wimsatt have convincingly demonstrated in their work on the intentional fallacy. On the other hand, if we deny that the work itself represents an intention—that is, an objectively ascertainable and definable unifying element in terms of which the parts of the work are related—we are reduced to critical impressionism and to the repudiation of the idea of artistic form. Without intention, a literary work would mean all things to all men; *Hamlet* would be no better (and no worse) than *Mickey Mouse,* since all would depend on an unpredictable response within the reader. Likewise, whether or not a given scene or speech were revelvant to the composition would be impossible to determine, since there would be nothing for it to be relevant or irrelevant to.

To avoid this dilemma, we must speak of an intention that is embodied in the work itself. Intention in this sense can be a moral assertion (as in the *exemplum*), the exploration of an idea (like mutability), or a mood (like despair or nostalgia). Often assertion, idea, and emotion coalesce, mutually reinforcing each other. The parts of a unified literary work must be directly or indirectly related to the intention. If they are not so related, they are extraneous and hence unexpressive. Conversely, when all elements—plot, character, setting, style, and the rest—are means of revealing the intention, the work becomes wholly expressive, and the effect of aesthetic unity or purity is achieved.

Intention, then, is a useful though necessarily limited means of determining the quality of the unity and expressiveness of a literary work. It need not imply conscious manipulation by the author, for, let it be admitted, many works of art have been produced by a process closer to automatic writing than to conscious craftsmanship, and the fact was recognized as early as Plato's *Ion*.

Our original question about the value of the theory of praise is thus traceable to a misunderstanding of the idea of the intention. This misunderstanding is in turn the result of the bias of romantic and later critics against attempts to interpret art or the creative process logically. Conventionally, the artist is described as a social rebel, a seer, a holy prophet inspired by some special contact with the spirit world. Rules, the devices of rhetoric, and social obligations stifle him. As Emerson insisted, the true poem creates its own form at the moment of creation; preconceptions only get in the way. By the same token, the vocabulary of criticism has become saturated with vague terms significant chiefly as emotional stimuli. In place of such definable terms as imitation, verisimilitude, decorum, and ornament, the nineteenth century critic often appealed to principles like originality, inspiration, or Arnold's "touchstone." It is natural that readers schooled in the romantic tradition should feel something cold-blooded and anti-poetic in the notion of a poet who plans his work according to a series of rhetorical formulae and calculates his effect for a specific audience and occasion. Yet this is what the Renaissance poet evidently did time and time again, and the theory of praise both encouraged and justified the process. Today, the occasional poet is held suspect; he is often accused of selling out the interests of art for a handful of gold. But Chaucer's *Book of the Duchess,* Spenser's *Epithalamion,* Milton's "Lycidas," Marvell's "Horatian Ode," and Dryden's "To the Pious Memory of . . . Mrs. Anne Killigrew" (to name only a few) are testimony to the high regard in which occasional poetry was formerly held.

The problems created by the romantic tradition are illustrated by the difficulties experienced by nineteenth- and twentieth-century critics in evaluating Petrarch's *Canzoniere.* Are the sonnets intensely personal, or are they a tissue of commonplaces? Is Laura a woman of flesh and blood or an abstraction? Is the cycle primarily biography or allegory? Such questions are only important on the assumption that poetry can be *either* rhetoric *or* emotion, but somehow cannot be both. Would it not be much more fruitful to admit that far from being antithetic the two elements are complementary? To "explain" the *Canzoniere* in terms of conventions alone would be a waste of effort. But it is at least possible that Petrarch is a major artist because he could manipulate conventions more skillfully and develop them into richer harmonies than his rivals. If so, the conventions deserve respect, for they are the means which enable the poet to transform personal experience into universal art.

If nineteenth-century poetic theory is contrasted with that of the Renaissance, the directness and simplicity—call it the naïveté—of the earlier systems is immediately apparent. Schelling, Coleridge, Hegel, and Croce all attain a degree of critical sophistication undreamed of in the philosophies of Minturno, Ronsard, or Sidney. Yet we should beware, I think, of a too-facile equating of complexity and excellence. The increased subtlety of nineteenth-century poetic theory is not necessarily an advance. This could be argued only if it could be shown that nineteenth-century poets are somehow more successful than their sixteenth-century counterparts. It is more logical to assume that criticism is always a function of the larger values of an age. As the relationship between the artist and his audience changes, the vocabulary of the critic also changes. When the relationship between the artist and the audience is relatively simple and explicit—as it was during the Renaissance—criticism is also relatively simple and explicit. But during the nineteenth century the role of the artist became increasingly obscure. Isolated from the masses, alienated from the bourgeoisie, challenged on every hand by the anti-poetry of the utilitarian, the empiricist, the apostle of progress, the artist had to search for new criteria on which to base his claim that art is important.

Naturally criticism proliferated; naturally it became more philosophical; naturally it probed ever more deeply into the human mind and the primitive origins of culture for the principles to defend art. Place on the one hand the simple, self-confident logic of Peacock, Macaulay, Huxley, or Comte as they proclaim that the age of imagination is yielding—in fact, has yielded—to the age of practical reason. Place on the other the theories of Coleridge, Baudelaire, or Croce, and the quality of the ninteenth-century defense of art becomes apparent. Aestheticism, from the idea that beauty is its own excuse for being to the assertion that a poem should not mean but be, is a system whose first premise is that art has no practical significance. It exists for its own sake and this is its special excellence.

Aestheticism has been considered a bold exploration of uncharted literary and psychological domains, but there is also a sense in which it is an attempt to define defeat as victory in the manner of propaganda broadcasts celebrating a retreat as a "strategic regrouping." Theoretically, it is a logical corollary of Kantian epistemology; but practically, it becomes a confession of the desperate condition to which the artist has been reduced: he has nearly been defined out of existence. Despite their many inconsistencies it is the opponents of aestheticism like Nietzsche, Tolstoy, Matthew Arnold, or Irving Babbitt who attempt to carry on the traditional concept of art as a social force.

The results of the nineteenth-century attitude toward art are hard to assess. On the other hand—and this is my chief point—it can hardly be doubted that the decline in the social importance of art had an extremely disturbing effect on the artist. It is no accident that the incidence of insanity among poets was especially high in the last quarter of the eighteenth century and that the nineteenth century artist often suffered from a profoundly disturbed personality—consider, for example, Poe, Tennyson, Baudelaire, and Whitman. Furthermore, the lack of ready answers to the question of the social significance of art must be considered a severe drain on the creative energies of the artist. Whereas the Renaissance poet was often content to compose rhetorical variations on the themes of moral philosophy, the nineteenth-century poet had to discover his theme, define his goals, and invent his linguistic techniques. Today, there are such divergencies of opinion that prior to creating, the poet often takes upon himself the Herculean task of rethinking the major problems of literary criticism, and at times he has even felt compelled to recreate the world as a preface to fruitful artistic activity, as witness the example of Yeats' *A Vision*.

The preceding sketch repeats in outline what are commonplaces in the history of post-romantic literature. If it is valid, it contrasts in every important particular with what I imagine to be the situation of the typical Renaissance artist.

First of all, the Renaissance artist needed have no doubt concerning his importance to society. Priest, philosopher, educator, and critic proclaimed that the record of noble deeds preserved in great poetry is of inestimable value in teaching fortitude, liberality, patriotism, and a whole grab-bag of miscellaneous virtues and amenities. By defining the way in which the poet contributed to the health of society, criticism substantiated his claim to a place among the leaders of his age.

Rhetorical criticism must have been especially helpful. The very subtlety of critics like Coleridge or I. A. Richards severely curtails their utility to a poet looking for rules-of-thumb to guide him in a particular composition. Romantic critical slogans are equally unsatisfying. "Create Beauty!" "Live Life" "Burn with a hard, gem-like flame." Such catch-phrases may describe what poets have done in the past, but they offer little more than a vaguely poetic emotion to a man staring uncomfortably at a blank sheet of paper. On the other hand, rhetorical criticism is direct and specific. The Renaissance lyricist, for example, had his work cut out for him before he began to write. If he decided on a love poem, he knew immediately that his job was to utilize the rhetorical topics of praise to blazon his lady's beauty and virtues, or to praise her indirectly by describing his own delicious agonies. To assist his Muse, he naturally turned to the inexhaustible treasure-house of the divine Petrarch and justified his borrowings with the doctrine of imitation. He would, of course, embellish the conventional topics with his own ingenious "inventions," for his readers expected this.

Viewed as a system that justified the artist and encouraged literary craftsmanship, the theory of praise is at least useful. Moreover, it is not nearly so narrow as historians of criticism have sometimes suggested by labeling it "didactic." Let us admit that there is no absolute way of measuring the adequacy of a theory of literature; and, in fact, that *all* theories are inadequate in the sense that none comes close to answering all the questions that can be asked. Even when the point is admitted, there are some topics that no theory can ignore without becoming trivial. Among these are the relationship of the poem to its object, the relationship of the poem to the frame—be it personal, mythic, philosophical, or theological—within which reality is understood, and the relationship of the parts of the poem to the whole composition. Since the romantic period these topics have most frequently been treated in terms of the post-Kantian theory of imagination. Sixteenth-century treatment of them was conditioned by rhetoric, and the topics themselves emerged as formal categories as a result of the rediscovery of Aristotle's *Poetics*. Aristotle deals with the relationship between poem and object through the theory of *mimesis*. The relationship between poem and "frame" is perhaps most explicitly considered in *Poetics* IX, where poetry is contrasted to history and philosophy. Finally, Aristotle's idea of poetic unity is introduced in his discussion plot as the soul of the literary work and later developed in comments on character, thought, selection, and proportion.

The idea of imitation is at least as important to the theory of praise as it was to Aristotle. Generally, however, the theory of praise treats imitation as a rhetorical technique. Imitation of objects becomes description; imitation of men becomes narration, especially the biographical narrative drawing on the topics of encomium and invective. Aristotle's understanding of imitation is considerably richer, but it is worth recalling that his references to the development of literature from encomium and "lampooning verse" show some interest in rhetoric and formed a significant point of contact between the theory of praise and the *Poetics*.

Aristotle also observed that there are three modes of imitation, presenting men "as better than in real life, or as worse, or as they are."[1] As Northrop Frye has brilliantly demonstrated in *The Anatomy of Criticism,* this apparently simple formula has far-reaching implications for serious criticism. The theory of praise vastly reduced the scope of Aristotle's idea. The presentation of men as "better than" they really are was neatly glossed as the technique of praise; the presentation of men as "worse than" they are became *vituperatio;* the "equal to" category was mentioned in passing or simply ignored altogether as pertaining to discursive prose rather than imaginative literature.

Aristotle's concept of poetry as "more universal" than history is another important insight. Coupled with his insistence that plot is the soul of drama, it looks forward to an understanding of the symbolic nature of action in literature. The theory of praise also deals with the relation of poetry to philosophy and history. Characteristically, it loses the Aristotelian vision and substitutes for it a useful but rather pedestrian formula: history is defined as a bare chronicle of events and philosophy as a systematic exposition of abstract theory, particularly ethics. The one tends to become a jumble of isolated facts, the other a dry exposition of dogma. Literature manages to combine the two disciplines in the exemplary narrative that draws on history for subject matter and on philosophy for moral principles. As Sidney says, "The Philosopher therefore and the Historian are they which would win the gole, the one by precept, the other by example. But both not having both, doe both halte. . . . Nowe dooth the peerelesse Poet performe both: for whatsover the Philosopher sayth shoulde be doone, hee giveth a perfect picture of it in some one, by whom hee presupposeth it was doone. So as hee coupleth the generall notion with the particular example." This quite literally makes literature "more philosophical" than history; it also makes literature "less abstract" than philosophy. Whether it is what Aristotle meant (I am sure it is not) is beside the point. It is a possible and self-consistent interpretation of the issues with which Aristotle was dealing and like other aspects of Renaissance theory makes up for its lack of subtlety by its utility. Coupled with rhetorical formulae, it offers a neat rule-of-thumb for the construction of poetic plots from history.

Aristotle's remarks on formal unity—the organizing of plot materials for the sake of effect—suggest that he considered literature a kind of analogy to experience rather than a re-creation of it. The form is not merely the frame but the soul of the work. It not only animates it but is responsible for the unity of effect which is the condition of aesthetic success. Aristotle's concept of form is perhaps his most remarkable achievement in the *Poetics* and would be difficult to improve. Conversely, the notion of the form is, I believe, the weakest aspect of Renaissance theory, and it is significant that one of the most obvious contrasts between classical and Renaissance narratives, whether epic or dramatic, is the superior unity of the classical works. The reasons for this are legion, but certainly an important one is the idea fostered by the theory of praise that literary unity may be achieved by subordination of diverse elements to an abstract theme, that a *laus virtutis* is as satisfactory a literary form as a *laus hominis*. Spenser's letter to Raleigh indicates that he felt that *The Faerie Queene* could be read as a unified composition; and although Shakespeare successfully employs thematic unity in *Hamlet* and *Lear,* surely he comes closest to the intensity of Greek drama in *Macbeth* and *Othello,* where theme and protagonist are one and where there is relatively little emphasis on sub-plot. Renaissance critics realized the importance of formal unity. It is a central question in the sixteenth century debate concerning the validity of such romances as *Orlando Furioso* and *Gerusalemme liberata;* but it is not unfair, I believe, to conclude that the Renaissance artists evolved no really satisfactory solution to the problem of form and that their failure can be attributed in part to a weakness inherent in their critical theory.

Measured against three important ideas treated in the *Poetics,* the theory of praise emerges as a reasonably comprehensive, consistent, and practical system. This does not mean that it is perfect, that we can go back to it, or that it would be desirable to go back to it if we could. It does mean that the theory of praise expresses a measure of truth about literature and that its truth is worth bearing in mind even in the case of literature that is based on contrary principles. A Renaissance critic, for example, might read T. S. Eliot's *Wasteland* as a conscious *vituperatio* of those conditions which produce cultural sterility. He might even point out that one of Eliot's favorite techniques is the invidious comparison, which is a negative form of the "outdoing" conceit of the encomium. Eric Heller, who is not a Renaissance pedant but a sensitive critic of contemporary German literature, has eloquently stated the basic truth embodied in the theory of praise. "What is it then," he asks, "that poetry means? Its meaning is the vindication of the worth and value of the world, of life and of human experience. At heart all poetry is praise and celebration."[3]

At heart all poetry is praise and celebration. This is the truth asserted by the theory of praise. Although we need not subscribe to it, it is neither perverse nor simple-minded. Certainly it must be kept continually in mind by those who would read and understand the literature of the European Renaissance.

Appendix

A. Menander's List of Epideictic Types from *Peri Epideiktikon,* as Summarized in Burgess, *Epideictic Literature,* pp. 110-11, 174:

HYMNS

1) Invocation of the presence of the God (κλητικός)
2) To a departing god (ἀποπεμπτικός)
3) Physical qualities of the god (φυσικός)
4) Myths about the god (μυθικός)
5) Ancestry and Descendents of the god (γενεαλογικός)
6) Fictions based on myths (πεπλασμένος)
7) Precative hymn—a prayer that something will happen (εὐκτικός)
8) Prayer that something will not happen (ἀπευκτικός)
9) Mixture of two or more of the above (μικτός)

OCCASIONAL TYPES

1) Praise of a country by situation, advantages of climate, products, etc. Its founders, festivals, buildings, etc.
2) Praise of city—as above
3) Praise of harbor
4) Praise of bay
5) Praise of acropolis
6) Praise of a city by its people
7) Praise of a city by its pursuits
8) Praise of ruler (βασιλικὸς λόγος)
9) Speech on debarking. Praises ruler and country; expresses joy on return (ἐπιβατήριος λόγος)
10) λαλιά—a free, flowing style rather than a genre. It has two types, of which only one is epideictic. It is especially appropriate for addressing kings or states.

11) Speech to one departing. Addressed to ruler it is like encomium (προπεμπτικὸς λόγος)

12) Marriage hymn (ἐπιθαλάμιον)

13) Another type of marriage hymn (κατευναστικός)

14) Consolation (παραμυθητικὸς λόγος) It begins with lament, then praises deceased, then employs the commonplace consolation motifs. Similar to μονῳδία and ἐπιτάφιος

15) Welcome of a ruler and like encomium (προσφωνητικός)

16) Funeral oration (ἐπιτάφιος λόγος)

17) Encomium at the presenting of a crown or other important occasion (στεφανωτικὸς [στεφανικός] λόγος)

18) Ambassador's speech—much like preceding (πρεσβευτικὸς λόγος)

19) Speech of invitation addressed to a ruler; praises the ruler, his city, and the event to which the ruler is invited (κλητικὸς λόγος)—found in Scaliger as hymn only

20) Farewell speech; laments need to depart, praises the people who are being left and the people to whom the speaker goes (συντακτικὸς λόγος)

21) Plaint. Is brief and emotional. Related to epitaph and consolation (μονῳδία)

22) Hymn in honor of Apollo (Σμινθιακὸς λόγος)

23) Paradoxical Ecomium (παράδοξα ἐγκώμια)

24) Panegyric (πανηγυρικὸς λόγος) (This type is not in Menander but is treated in Dionysius of Halicarnassus [Burgess, p. 111].)

25) Birthday song (γενεθλιακός)

B. Scaliger's List of Epideictic Types (*Poetices,* 1617, Bk. III, Chs. c-cxxii). The alternation of Greek and Latin titles is Scaliger's:

Bk. III, Chap. c. Epithalamium: praise of the marriage day. Exs.: Catullus; Musaeus de Leandro; Ovid in nuptiis Orphei; Statius in nuptiis Stellae; Claudian de Honorio et Maria.

ci. Oaristys: "confabulationes quae inter virum atque uxorem fieri consuere, quas oaristys veteres apellerunt." Exs.: Homer on Hector and Andromache.

Genethaliacum: Birthday song. Ex.: Statius on Lucan.

cii. προσευκτικὸν: prayer for the good success of an event. Ex.: Virgil, "Armipotens belli praeses Tritonia viro. . . ."

ἀπευκτικὸν: prayer that an event will *not* happen.

ciii. Propempticon: Well-wishing at departure. Ex.: Aeschylus on Prometheus "a quo Io vaticinum audit fugae suae."

Apopemticon: "non est nisi nomine diversum: res eadem."

Hodoeporicon: mentioned but not defined.

civ. συμβουλετικὸν: non-epideictic category. (deliberative).

προτρεπτικὸν: non-epideictic and not included in a *sylva*. It is an excited hortatory speech, esp. to troops entering a battle. Ex.: Aeneid: "nunc, nunc, insurgite remis. . . ."

παραμνετικὸν: "praeceptae sapientiae . . ." Non-epideictic.

νυθετικὸν: "admonitiones cuiusquisque . . ." Non-epideictic.

παραμυθητικὸν: consolation; "adhortamur enim ad animi compositionem, et tranquilitatem."

cv. Epibaterion: Song of returning traveler ("de illustribus viris dico") to assembled citizens.

cvi. Aprobaterion: Song by a traveler about to depart. Ex.: "Huius genus est Aeneae oratio ad Helenam atque Andromachem."

cvii. παιδευτήρια: thanks to our teachers (praeceptoribus), especially for helping us to knowledge of the gods.

cviii. Panegyricon: Praise of a great man. Includes a discussion of appropriate topics. E.g., "Coronatum materia varia. E quercu. Eius laus multa. Victus priorus; Olea non minime praedicatione. . . . Quid? Sterilis arbor est, inde corona fiunt, veluti Pices, Apicum, Cypressus. Ex his enim nullus usus ad vescendum nobis. Pro se satis prestare virtutem sibi." Panegyric must be before a crowd. The *Evagoras* is not a panegyric because it is primarily to be read. Pliny on Trajan fails because it was before the senate, not the public.

cix. Laus, laudatio: Laus, as a special type of poem, summarizes briefly the praise worthy qualities of the individual. Laudatio is the Latin for encomium: "quemadmodum vero Latine dicas ἐγκώμιον, haud sane in mentem venit, nisi sit laudatio." ἄτοπα; "id est res damnati argumenti, quaeque nullum artis admitterent locum etiam nefaria quaedam commendarentur: huiusmodi est oratio de Busiride, de febre quartana, de pestelentia . . . etc."

cx. "Quae quisque laudari possit": a summary, rather brief, of the various subjects of praise.

cxi. Hymni (laus Dei): Includes a list similar to Menander, types of hymn, 1-8. "Greacis ὕμνος; a Latinis, celebratio. . . ."

cxii. Evocatorii sive invocatorii.

cxiii. ἀποπεμπτικοί: Hymns at the end of religious festivals.

cxiv. φυσικοί: "Dies, Nox, Tempestas, Iustitia . . . etc. Sic. Marulus Coelum, Elementa Hymnis canit."

μυθικοί: "Sic Apollonem solem dicis: Dianam Lunam . . . Venus calorem genitatem. . . . Officio numque et opera numinibus attributa multa tegunt arcana manifestis invollucris."

γενεαλογικοί: "natalia deorum."

πεπλασμένοι: "gesta deorum." The latter two are sub-divisions relating to the birth, background, and acts of a god.

cxv. Heroici: "In Heroicis hymnis eadem ratio genealogiae qualis in

Theocriti Heraclisio. Frequentior tamen gestorum narratio, ut in Hesiodi aspide, et in Hercule Leonicida."

Paenes: like *heroici*.

Scolia: school-songs; intended to induce piety.

cxvi. Dithyrambi: Poems written under the stimulus of divine furor.

cxvii. Laudationes: see above, *Ch. cix*.

cxviii. Persona: The topics of personal praise.

cxix. Locus: Praise of place.

cxx. Urbs: Praise of city with appropriate sub-divisions.

cxxi. Epitaphium, Epicedium, Monodia, Inferiae, Parentalia, Threni, Neniae: types of funeral songs. The number of types indicates the importance assigned to the genre. "Epicede" is spoken over the unburied body. It follows that an epicede can be spoken only once. "Epitaph" is a funeral oration at the tomb or an inscription on the tomb. Spoken annually, it becomes an "anniversary."

"Inferias" is similar to epitaph but can include the whole funeral ceremony.

"Threnody" is the song of the mourners; it is wholly lament.

Monody: "fuit enim quoties e Choro prodibat unus, qui defunctum memoriam lugubri carmine celebraret."

cxxii. Consolatio: Consolation of survivors. Here the list of strictly occasional pieces (appropriate for the *sylva*) ends. Scaliger continues with a discussion of lyric, elegy, epigram, and "inscriptio."

Notes

Introduction

1. Joel Spingarn, *A History of Literary Criticism in the Renaissance* (N.Y., 1956); Ciro Trabalza, *La critica letteraria nel Rinascimento* (Secoli XV, XVI, XVII) (Milan, 1915); C. S. Baldwin, *Renaissance Literary Theory and Practice,* ed. D. L. Clark (N.Y., 1939); J. W. H. Atkins, *English Literary Criticism: The Renascence* (London, 1951).

2. The debate, which resulted in a setback for the humanists, may be followed in the two volumes by Norman Foerster, ed., *Humanism and America* (N.Y., 1930), and C. H. Grattan, ed., *The Critique of Humanism: A Symposium* (N.Y., 1930).

3. Ingram Bywater, *On the Art of Poetry* (Oxford, 1909), note on $1460^{b}14$: "Readers of the *Nicomachean Ethics* will remember that in the Aristotelian hierarchy of the arts, all the other arts are regarded as subordinate to the supreme art which deals with the whole social and moral order of the state, and that there is no hint of the so-called 'aesthetic' arts being outside its purview and control." See also Hamilton Fyfe, *Aristotle's Art of Poetry* (Oxford, 1940), p. xv; and Gerald Else, *Aristotle's Poetics: The Argument* (Cambridge, 1957), pp. 68-78.

4. H. B. Charlton, *Castelvetro's Theory of Poetry* (Manchester, 1913), p. 17, ". . . this study will show that [Castelvetro's] main contribution to poetic theory, is not to that of tragedy . . . but to the inclusive idea of poetry as a fine art." See Ch. V, "The Function of Poetry," pp. 66-82.

5. G. Gregory Smith, *Elizabethan Critical Essays* (Oxford, 1950), I, xxvii.

6. Atkins, *English Literary Criticism: The Renascence,* p. 27.

7. Vernon Hall, *Renaissance Literary Criticism: A Study of Its Social Content* (N.Y., 1945).

8. Marvin T. Herrick, *The Fusion of Horatian and Aristotelian Criticism* (Urbana, 1946); J. V. Cunningham, *Woe or Wonder* (Denver, 1951); Madeline Doran, *Endeavors of Art* (Madison, 1956).

9. For a bibliography of this field see R. C. Williams, "Italian Critical Treatises of the Sixteenth Century," *MLN,* XXXV (1920), 506-7; the supplement by Walter L. Bullock, "Italian Sixteenth-Century Criticism," *MLN,* XLI (1926), 254-63; and Bernard Weinberg, *A History of Literary Criticism in the Italian Renaissance* (Chicago, 1961), II, 1113-58.

10. For my indebtedness to Professor Weinberg, see above, "Preface."

11. E.g., D. L. Clark, *Rhetoric and Poetic in the Renaissance* (N.Y., 1922); Sister Miriam Joseph, *Shakespeare's Use of the Arts of Language* (N.Y., 1947); Rosamund Tuve, *Elizabethan and Metaphysical Imagery* (Chicago, 1947).

Chapter I

1. M. H. Abrams, *The Mirror and the Lamp* (Ithaca, 1953).

2. Edwin Wallace, *Outlines of the Philosophy of Aristotle* (Cambridge, 1887), p. 23.

3. E.g., Boethius, *In Porphyrium dialogi* (Migne, *Pat. Lat.,* LXIV, 10ff); Cassiodorus, *De*

artibus ac disciplinis liberalium artium (Migne, *Pat. Lat.*, LXX, 1167); Isidore, *Etymologiarum libri XX*, ed. W. M. Lindsay (Oxford, 1911), II, 24. The evolution of the idea is traced by Ludwig Baur, "Die philosophische Einleitungsliteratur bis zum Ende der Scholastik," in *Dominici Gundissalini De divisione philosophiae, Beiträge zur Geschichte der Philosophie des Mittelalters*, IV, Nos. 2-3 (Münster, 1903), 316-97. See also P. O. Kristeller, "The Modern System of the Arts: A Study in the History of Aesthetics," *JHI*, XII (1951), 496-527; and, especially, Richard McKeon, "Rhetoric in the Middle Ages," in *Critics and Criticism* (Chicago, 1952), pp. 260-96.

4. A. E. Taylor, *Aristotle* (London, 1919), p. 19; George Grote, *Aristotle* (London, 1872), I, 76-78; Wallace, *Outlines of the Philosophy of Aristotle*, pp. 21-23. Cf. Gerald Else, *Aristotle's Poetics: The Argument* (Cambridge, 1957), p. 72.

5. Text in *Dominici Gundissalini De divisione philosophiae*, ed. Baur, pp. 1-44.

6. Ibid., p. 71. For Al-farabi see *Catálogo de las ciencias*, ed. and tr. Angel Gonzalez Palencia (Madrid, 1953). This edition reprints the Latin translation by Gerard of Cremona.

7. A simplified version of the scheme proposed by Baur, *Dominici Gundissalini De divisione philosophiae*, p. 193. For early Renaissance versions see Baur, pp. 376-77, 384, 392; and Ida Maier, "Un inédit de Politien: La classification des 'arts,'" *Bibliothèque d'humanisme et Renaissance*, XXII (1960), 338-55. For a somewhat different (though, I believe, not incompatible) classification of sixteenth-century Italian systems, see Chapter I of Bernard Weinberg, *History of Literary Criticism in the Italian Renaissance* (Chicago, 1961), "The Classification of Poetics Among the Sciences"; and for detailed discussions of individual systems, see the later chapters *passim*.

8. A point emphasized by Richard McKeon, "Rhetoric in the Middle Ages," in *Critics and Criticism*, pp. 260-96.

9. Summary treatment in Joel Spingarn, *A History of Literary Criticism in the Renaissance* (N.Y., 1956), pp. 24-26.

10. Girolamo Fracastoro, *Naugerius sive de poetica*, in *Opera* (Venice, 1555), 155v-166r: "Illi historiarum copias, locorum descriptiones, regionum naturas, vitae instituta tradunt, multa de imperatore, de milite, de patre familias, de republica scribunt, de re rustica, de nautica, de artibus . . . de syderibus insuper, ac naturae rebus, plantisque atque animalibus, de Deo, de inferis . . . atque ut summatim dicamus, de iis omnibus doctrinam videntur facere. . . ." Cf. Antonio Minturno, *De poeta* (Venice, 1559), pp. 91-100; Tasso, *Discorsi dell'arte poetica*, in *Prose diverse*, ed. Cesare Guasti (Florence, 1875), 1, 44-45; Giraldi Cinthio, *Discorsi* (Venice, 1554), p. 93. For an absurd extreme, see Benedetto Fioretti, *Progynnasmi poetici* (Florence, 1695), V, liv (pp. 233-37): "All'interprete, all'umanista è necessaria la dottrina moltiplice."

11. Francesco Patrizi, *Della poetica, la deca disputata* (Ferrara, 1586), p. 156: ". . . se Aristotele in quel detto, negò Empedocle essere poeta; cadde egli stesso, nel dannaggio di quella sentenza." For the opposing view, see Fioretti, *Progynnasmi poetici*, V, iii. The very common view of philosophy as a source for poetry may be illustrated by the following quotation from Giraldi Cinthio, *Discorsi*, pp. 147-48 ". . . esser vano communamente è vitio di coloro, che sono essercitati solo nelle parole, et non hanno atteso agli studii, di Philosophia, senza la quale riescono vanni tutti i componimenti. Però che ella è come un fonte, onde si traggono tutti i rivi delle cose, che danno agli scrittori pregiati i soggetti delle lor compositioni . . . il giudico di chi vuol comporre, dee saper far scielta di quel buono, che gli ha dato la Philosophia, et dal tutto levare quello, che porterebbe danno al suo componimento, lasciandovi sol quello, che al piacevole, et al grave conviene. . . ."

12.

Divini per saecula prisca poetae
. . . dici coeperunt nomine vates.
Quisquis erat vates, vas erat ille dei.
Illa igitur nobis stat contemplanda Poesis,
Altera quae quondam Theologia fuit.

Quoted from E. R. Curtius, *European Literature and the Latin Middle Ages*, tr. Williard Trask (London, 1953), p. 216.

13. Petrarch, *Le familiari*, ed. Vittorio Rossi (Florence, 1934), X, 4.

14. Boccaccio, *Genealogy of the Gods*, tr. Charles G. Osgood (N.Y., 1956), p. 121.

15. *Hieronymi Savonarolae . . . Universae philosophiae epitome. Eiusdem de divisione atque usu omnium scientiarum, nec non de poëtices ratione . . . Witebergae excusa typis Simonis Gronenbergii* (1496), p. 813: "Addunt, similiter Prophetas divinas versibus cantasse: Item Sacram Scripturam quemadmodum & poëticen, metaphoris & similitudinibus uti, nihilque aliud esse poeticam, quam Theologiam."

16. Ibid., p. 822: "Nulla ergo scientia praeter sacram scripturam proprie & vere sensum habet spiritualem. . . . Aliud est enim metaphoris uti propter necessitatem & rerum magnitudinem, aliud vero propter delectationem et veritatis debilitatem."

17. J. W. H. Atkins, *Literary Criticism in Antiquity* (Cambridge, 1934), I, 182-83.

18. " . . . recte loquendi scientiam et poetarum enarrationem."

19. Heinrich Keil, ed., *Grammatici Latini* (Leipzig, 1857 et seq.). Bede's *De arte metrica* is in Vol. VII, pp. 227-60.

20. Ibid., I, 473: "Poetica est fictae veraeve narrationis congruenti rhythmo ac pede composita metrica structura. . . ."

21. Ibid., VI, 274: "Poema est narratio numeris versibus conexa."

22. John of Salisbury, *Metalogicon,* ed., C. I. Webb (Oxford, 1929), I, 43: "Profecto aut poeticam grammatica obtinebit, aut poetica e numero liberalium disciplinarum eliminabitur."

23. In Keil ed., *Grammatici Latini,* I, 494-529.

24. Eduard Norden, *Die antike Kunstprosa* (Leipzig, 1909).

25. *De metris,* in Keil, ed., *Grammatici Latini,* VI, 585: "Dubitare neminem arbitror . . . ut ea quae excellentibus sententiis ac verbis dicerentur carminis etiam certa modulatio dulciora auribus redderet. Quod quid in poematis quasi mollius ac blandius, quid asperius ac durius esset, suas ipsi aures consulebant hisque ita obtemperabant ut conformandis suis carminibus artem cum delectione coniungerent."

26. Samuel Daniel, *A Defence of Rime,* in *Elizabethan Critical Essays,* ed. G. Gregory Smith, (Oxford, 1950), II, 359. Hereafter cited as ECE.

27. For comment, see Bernardo Morsolin, *Giangiorgio Trissino* (Florence, 1894).

28. Francesco Patrizi, *Della poetica, la deca disputata* (Ferrara, 1586). The sixty-four types are listed on p. 132. The chapters are "Che empedocle fu poeta minore, o maggior d'Omero," and "Se d'istoria formar si possa un poema."

29. *Discorso di Agostino Michele in cui contra l'opinione di tutti i più illustri scrittori dell'arte poetica chiaramente si dimostra; come si possono scrivere con molta lode le comedie, e le tragedie in prosa* (Venice, 1592), esp. Sections VIII, IX. Compare Paolo Beni, *Disputatio in qua ostenditur praestare comoediam atque tragoediam metrorum vinculis solvere* (Padua, 1600).

30. Gabriello Chiabrera, *Dialoghi,* in *Canzonette, rime varie, dialoghi,* ed. Luigi Negri (Turin, 1952), pp. 517-86.

31. J. P. Thorne, "A Ramistical Commentary on Sidney's *An Apologie for Poetrie,*" *MP,* LIV (1958), 158-64.

32. See Walter J. Ong, S.J., *Ramus* (Cambridge, 1958), p. 281-82, and p. 371 (note 58), where two Ramists define poetry as "facultas bene scribendi versus" and "ars bene versificandi" respectively.

33. *Dominici Gundissalini De divisione philosophiae,* ed. Baur, pp. 201ff., and 349-97.

34. See Etienne Gilson, *A History of Christian Philosophy in the Middle Ages* (N.Y., 1955), pp. 181-225 and 387-402. For more detail, see Fernand van Steenberghen, *Aristotle in the West* (Louvain, 1955). For the Averroist disputes of the thirteenth century, Pierre Mandonnet, *Siger de Brabant et l'Averroisme Latin* (Louvain, 1902). Still a useful survey despite its many inaccuracies is E. Renan, *Averroës et l'Averroisme* (Paris, 1852).

35. Jaraslav Tkač, "Ueber den arabischen Kommentar des Averroes zum *Poetik* des Aristoteles," *Wiener Studien,* XXIV (1902), 76.

36. For the biography of Hermannus see G. H. Luquet, "Hermann l'Allemand," *Revue de l'Histoire des Religions,* XLIV (1901), 407-22. The manuscripts are listed in George Lacombe, *Aristoteles Latinus, pars prior* (Rome, 1939), and *pars posterior* (Oxford, 1955).

37. Al-farabi, *Catálogo de las ciencias,* ed. Palencia, pp. 138-40. Compare the somewhat different approach in *De ortu scientiarum, Alfarabi über den Ursprung der Wissenschaften,* ed. Clemens Baeumker, *Beiträge zur Geschichte der Philosophie des Mittelalters,* XIX, No. 3 (Münster, 1916), 22-23.

38. Quoted in G. Lacombe, *Aristoteles Latinus, pars prior,* 211: "Quod autem hi duo libri logicales sint, nemo dubitat qui libros perspexerit arabum famosorum, Alfarabi videlicet et Avicenne et Avenrosdi [Averroes] et quorundam aliorum. Imo ex ipso textu manifestius hoc patebit. Neque excusabiles sunt, ut fortassis alicui videbitur propter Marci Tullii rethoricam et Oratii poetriam. Tullius namque rethoricam partem civilis scientiae posuit et secundum hanc intuitionem eam potissime tractavit. Oratius vero poetriam prout pertinet ad grammaticam potius expedivit."

39. *Dominici Gundissalini De divisione philosophiae,* ed. Baur, pp. 53-63 ("De poetica"). "Poetica est scientia componendi carmina metrica." (p. 54).

40. Ibid.: "Genus huius artis est, quod ipsa est pars civilis scientiae . . . quod delectat vel edificat in scientia vel in moribus."

41. Ibid., p. 71: "Secundum Alfarabius octo sunt partes logicae: cathegoriae, perihermenias, analetica prior, analetica posteriora, thopica, sophistica, rethorica, poëtica."

42. Al-farabi, *Catálogo de las ciencias,* ed. Palencia, p. 139.

43. *Dominici Gundissalini De divisione philosophiae,* ed. Baur, p. 74: "Istae ergo sunt species sillogismorum et arcium sillogisticarum et species locuciorum, quibus utuntur homines ad verificandum aliquid in omnibus rebus . . . certificativa, putativa, errativa, sufficiens, ymaginativa."

44. Ibid.: "Proprium est poeticae sermonibus suis facere ymaginari aliquid pulchrum vel fedum, quod non est, ita, ut auditor credat et aliquando abhorreat vel appetat; quamvis enim certi sumus, quod non ita est in veritate, tamen eriguntur animi nostri ad abhorrendum vel appetendum quod ymaginatur nobis."

45. *S. Thomae Aquinatis praeclarissima commentaria in libra Aristotelis Peri hermenias & Posteriorem analyticorum* (Venice, 1553), p. 36^{v}: "Quandoque vero sola existimatio declinat in aliquam partem contradictionis propter aliquam repraesentationem, ad modum quo fit homini abhominatio alicuius cibi, si repraesentetur ei sub similitudine alicuius abhominabilis. Et ad hoc ordinatur Poetica. Nam poetae est inducere ad aliquid virtuosum, per aliquam praecedentem repraesentationem. Omnia autem haec ad Rationalem philosophiam pertinent."

46. Ibid.

47. Roger Bacon, *Opus tertium* in *Opera inedita,* ed. J. S. Breuer (London, 1859), pp. 303-8.

48. Vincent of Beauvais, *Speculum doctrinale Vincentii* (Venice, 1494), I, xvii, and III, iii: ("De partibus logicae"): "[Poetae] volunt sermonibus suis facere imaginari aliquid pulchrum vel fedum quod non est ita . . . animi tunc audientum eriguntur ad horrendum vel appetendum quod imaginatur." (35^{v}). Also, III, cix (48^{r}).

49. A good recent survey of Paduan Averroism is that by Saitta, *Il Rinascimento* (Bologna, 1950), II, 249-451.

50. Fra Girolamo Savonarola, *De divisione* (Florence, 1496), p. 809; "Hic ergo modus metricus & harmonicus non est ei essentialis. Potest enim Poeta uti argumento suo, & per decentes similitudines discurre sine versu."

51. Ibid., p. 810: "Sine Logica neminem posse poëtam appellari manifestum est. . . ." And: "Itaque si quis credit, artem poëticam solum docere dactylos & spondaeos, syllabas longas & brevas, ornatum verborum: magno profecto errore detinetur."

52. Ibid., p. 807: ". . . manifestum est syllogismum illum, qui a Philosopho vocatur Exemplum, objectum esse artis Poeticae, quemadmodum Enthymema objectum Rhetoricae, Inductio ac syllogismus probabilis topicae, Demonstratio libri poster. analyticorum. Syllogismus simpliciter libri priorum analyticorum, Syllogismus sophisticus, libri elenchorum, Enuncatio libri peri ermoneiae, & praedicamentum libri praedicamentorum."

53. Ibid., p. 807: ". . . syllogismus, in quo medium extremo inesse ostenditur per id, quod est simile tertio."

54. Ibid., p. 809: "Finis autem Poëtae est inducere homines ad aliquid virtuosum per aliquem decentem repraesentationem. . . . At quoniam Poëtae proprium est ex particularibus procedere . . . exemplum non est sicut pars ad totum, nec sicut totum ad partem, sed sicut pars ad partem. Et quoniam singularia sunt incerta: necesse est, propter debilitatem rationum suarum ipsum inducere aliquas decentes similitudines, & diversis modis, verborumque ornatibus ac lenociniis animos hominum ad se trahere ac delectare."

55. Francesco Robortello, *In librum Aristotelis De arte poetica explicationes* (Florence,

1548), p. 2. For comment, see Bernard Weinberg, "Robortello on the 'Poetics,'" in *Critics and Criticism* (Chicago, 1952), pp. 319-48.

56. Bartolomeo Lombardi, "Preface," in *Vincentii Madii Bruxiani et Bartholomaei Lombardi Veronensis in Aristotelis librum De poetica communes explanationes* (Venice, 1550), p. 8: "Redeo ad perfectam, neque ulla ex parte vitiosam Poeticam nostram: quam ego nunc, ne quod a me praestari possit, quicquam omnino desyderetis, *in artium scientiarumque divisione inter logicas rationalesque Averoe viro philosopho auctore colloco.* Cum enim logicas quinque dixerit, Demonstrativum, Dialecticam, Sophisticam, Rhetoricam, Poeticam indicasse puto. . . . Nunc Poeticam, quam ille nominatim indicat, de qua non dubitatur, logicam pono." (Italics mine.)

57. Ibid., p. 8.

58. Ibid., p. 9: "[Rhetorica est] facultas videndi in quavis re quod sit ad persuadendum accommodatum"; and: ". . . consilium Poeticae ipsius, id videre quod appositum sit ad faciendum uniuscuiusque actionis, affectionis, moris, suavi sermone imitationem, ad vitam corrigendam, & ad bene beateque vivendum. . . ."

59. Ibid., pp. 9-12.

60. Ibid., p. 9, as in note 58, above.

61. Ibid., p. 16: "Poesim vero, Philosophiam quandam moralem esse, iam aperte demonstravimus. Quod si tractationis eius, ubi de partibus orationis, Nomine, Verbo, & aliis: item de Metaphoris, aliisque exornationibus ad sermonem pertinentibus: item de Legibus habenda primum esset ratio; ita quod praesens liber esset de arte Poetica, profecto sub Philosophia rationali hic liber, ut Averroes, Avicenna, & alii censuerunt, reponi deberet."

62. *Lezzioni di M. Benedetto Varchi* (Florence, 1590), "Della Poetica in Generale," p. 572: "essendo la poetica o parte, o spezie della loica, pigliando per loica tutta la sua filosofia razionale, nessuno può essere poeta, il quale non sia loico. Anzi quanto ciascheduno sarà miglior loico, tanto sarà più eccelente poeta."

63. Ibid., p. 573: "è adunque il subietto della poetica il favellare finto, o favoloso, & il suo mezzo, o strumento, l'esempio." Cf. Torquato Tasso, *Discorsi del poema eroico,* in *Prose diverse,* ed. C. Guasti, I, 98-101, 216, and Varchi, *Lezzioni,* pp. 573-74: ". . . si ristringono non dimeno per lo più, & nella maggior parte, alle cose civili. . . . E chi dubita (devendo la poetica imitare . . . l'azzioni, gli effetti, & i costumi humani) che ella non habbia bisogno dell'Etica, & della Politica?"

64. Giovanni Battista Gelli, *Letture edite e inedite sopra la Commedia di Dante,* ed. C. Negroni (Florence, 1887), I, 44: ". . . poesia è strumento e arte, e non scienza . . . e contiensi sotto la Logica."

65. Jacopo Mazzoni, *Della difesa della Comedia di Dante* (Cesena, 1587), *"Introduction,"* p. 53: ". . . la Poesia per far più conto del credibile, che del vero, si deve drittamente collocare sotto quella facoltà rationale, che fu da gli antichi Sophistica nominata."

66. "La poesia non dipende dalla politica ma dalla sofistica e dalla retorica: suo scopo è il dilettare, non l'ammaestrare." See Ciro Trabalza, *La critica letteraria nel Rinascimento* (Milan, 1915), p. 204.

67. Tasso, *Discorsi del poema eroico,* in *Prose diverse,* ed. C. Guasti, I, 98: ". . . la poetica è collocata in ordine sotto la dialettica insieme con la retorica, la qual, come dice Aristotle, è l'altro rampollo della dialettica facultà, a cui s'appartiene di considerare non il falso, ma il probabile."

68. Trabalza, *La critica letteraria nel Rinascimento,* pp. 269-302.

69. In the paraphrase of the *Poetics,* Averroes defined poetic imitation as the use of metaphor because to speak of an object with the right and proper word is not imitation but representation. For example, to call a tree a tree is not imitation; however, it *is* imitation to call it "an arm reaching to heaven." Thus metaphor is the essential poetic "instrument" for Averroes. This is reflected in St. Thomas' reference to "similitude" as the poetic device. The idea apparently lost ground after "example" became accepted as the "poetic syllogism," as in Savonarola's *De divisione* (above, note 52). Among others, Varchi, Segni, and Tasso make example the basic poetic device. However, toward the end of the century and in the seventeenth century the *concettisti* once again made metaphor supreme. For Averroes, see the edition of the paraphrase published by Philippus Venetus (Venice, 1481), p. 50^r-50^v: "Et sermones poetici sermones sunt imaginativi. Modi autem imaginationis & assimilationis tres

sunt: duo simplices & tertius compositus ex illis: unus duorum simplicium est assimilatio rei ad rem. . . . Secundum autem divisio est ut convertatur assimilatio: ut si dicas sol est quasi talis mulier non talis mulier est quasi sol & non talis mulier est sol. Et tertia species est sermonum poeticorum & posita est ex his duobus."

70. Emmanuele Tesauro, *Il cannocchiale aristotelico* (Venice, 1668), p. 216; "Tutta la forza di un Vocabolo significante . . . consiste nel rappresentare alla mente umana la cosa significata. Ma questa Rappresentazione si può fare ò col Vocabolo nudo e proprio . . . ò con alcuna significatione ingegnosa che insieme rappresenti e diletti."

71. Ibid., p. 98: "Chiamo adunque imitazione una sagacità con cui, propostoli una metafora o altro fiore dell'umano ingegno, tu attentamente consideri le sue radici e, traspiantandole in differenti categorie . . . ne propaghi altri fiori della medesima spezie, ma non gli medesimi individui."

72. Ibid., pp. 245ff. Metaphor is "*il più ingegnoso* e acuto: il più *pellegrino* e *mirabile:* il più *gioviale* e *giovevole:* il *più facondo* e *fecondo* parte dell'umano intelletto" (p. 245).

73. Exhaustively treated in Werner Jaeger, *Paideia,* tr. Gilbert Highet (Oxford, 1950), II, *passim;* and III, Chs. 2, 6, 8, and 10.

74. Cicero, *De inventione,* I, 5, places rhetoric emphatically in "civil philosophy": ". . . hanc oratoriam facultatem in eo genere ponemus, ut eam civilis scientiae partem esse dicamus."

75. Cicero, *De oratore,* tr. E. W. Sutton and H. Rackham (Cambridge, 1942), I, 15, 68-9: "Sed si me audierit, quoniam philosophia in tres partes est tributa, in naturae obscuritatem, in disserendi subtilitatem, in vitam atque mores; duo illa relinquamus, idque largiamur inertiae nostrae: tertium vero, quod semper oratoris fuit, nisi tenebimus, nihil oratori, in quo magnus esse possit, relinquemus. Quare his locus de vita et moribus totus est oratori perdiscendus: cetera si non didicerit, tamen poterit, si quando opus erit, ornare dicendo, si modo erunt ad eum delata, et tradita."

76. Bernardino Tomitano, *Ragionamenti della lingua Toscana dove si parla del perfetto oratore, & poeta volgari, dell'eccellente medico & philosopho Bernardin Tomitano* (Venice, 1545): "Nel Primo [libro] si pruova la Philosophia esser necessaria allo acquistamento della Rhetorica & Poetica."

77. Ibid., pp. 4-5: ". . . molti huomini . . . sviati, credere non esser altro la eloquenza che un parlare commune & volgare, senza alcuno gusto et cognitione del philosophia, per se stesso assequibile. . . ." Tomitano, perhaps following Savonarola, believes theology to be almost contrary to eloquence (p. 92). By "theology" he means, of course, the category of "prima philosophia" or metaphysics, in contrast to the disciplines of "practical philosophy."

78. M. Nizolius, *De veris principiis et vera ratione philosophandi contra pseudophilosophos* (Padua, 1553), III, 3 (pp. 211ff.); Marc Antonio Majoragius, *Aristotelia . . . De arte rhetorica* (Venice, 1572), p. 2.

79. Sperone Speroni, *Dialogo della retorica* in *Dialoghi* (Venice, 1596), p. 121r. Compare B. Segni, *Rettorica, et Poetica d'Aristotile tradotte de Greco in lingua vulgare fiorentina* (Florence, 1549), p. 238, where rhetoric is said to be both civil philosophy and dialectic; and p. 282, where poetry is also said to be concerned chiefly with moral philosophy.

80. Quoted in B. Bulgarini, *Risposte . . . a'ragionamenti del Sig. Ieronimo Zoppio* (Siena, 1586), p. 153: ". . . a quello che si dice che la Poetica non è parte della Filosofia Morale; s'oppone de la Rhetorica, la quale ha somiglianza con la poetica, & di essa nel medesimo modo si danno precetti; & nondimanco la rettorica, è chiamata da Arist. nel primo della Rhet. cap. 2 vers. Ex quo efficitur, parte della Civile; & vien confirmato da Cicerone nel primo de Inventione cap. De iuri Civili, & partibus eius."

81. Trabalza, *La critica letteraria nel Rinascimento,* p. 4.

82. Dante, *Epistle to Can Grande della Scala,* in *Literary Criticism: Plato to Dryden,* ed. Allan Gilbert (N.Y., 1940), p. 205.

83. Giraldi Cinthio, *Discorsi* (Venice, 1554), p. 15: "La Poesia et la Philosophia erano differente tra lor dinome, ma in sostanza erano una cosa medisima." Cf. *Maximi Tyrii dissertationes,* ed. Daniel Heinsius (London, 1703), p. 301: ". . . quid enim poetica est, quam philosophia tempore vetustiore. . . ."

84. Mazzoni, *Della difesa,* "Introduction," p. 76: "la facoltà civile, o la Philosophia morale."

85. Ibid., p. 67: ". . . stimo, che la Poetica sia il nono libro della Politica."

Chapter II

1. E.g., Rupert C. Lodge, *Plato's Theory of Art* (London, 1953).

2. Most recent discussion in Gerald Else, *Aristotle's Poetics: The Argument* (Cambridge, 1957), pp. 12-13, 49-53, 93-94, etc. See also Richard McKeon, "Literary Criticism and the Concept of Imitation in Antiquity," in *Critics and Criticism* (Chicago, 1952), 117-45.

3. George Fiske, *Cicero's "De oratore" and Horace's "Ars poetica"* (Madison, 1929).

4. Theodosius Macrobius, *Saturnalia,* V, 1, 1: "Virgilius non minus orator quam poetam habendum, in quo et tanta orandi disciplina et tam diligens observatio rhetoricae artis extenditur." Cf. the *controversia* topic cited in D. L. Clark, *Rhetoric and Poetic in the Renaissance* (N.Y., 1922), p. 42: "Virgilius orator an poeta." Also Ben Jonson, *Timber,* ed. F. Schelling (Boston, 1892), p. 79: "[The poet is] the nearest borderer upon the orator, and expresseth all his virtues."

5. Compare the following scheme and comment in Lodovico Castelvetro, *Poetica d'Aristotele Vulgarizzata* (Basel, 1576), pp. 76, 80:

Severa	*Piacevole*
Loda	Villania
Epopea	Giambici
Tragedia	Comedia

". . . del numero di coloro che sarebbono stati lodatori tutti, se non fosero venuti gli epopei alcuni si davano ad essere epopei, et di questo numero . . . alcuni si davano ad essere tragici. . . . Ma dell'altra parte furono prima i biasmatori di viti senza tirargli a sciocchezza, et a riso. alli quali succedettero i biasmatori di viti che gli tiravano a sciocchezza, et a riso . . . a quali giambici poi succedettero i comici, che parimente tirarono i viti, e l'attioni in riso et in isciocchezza."

6. For a history of the Theophrastian ideas, see A. P. McMahon, *Seven Questions on Aristotelian Definitions of Tragedy and Comedy* ("Harvard Studies in Classical Philology," Vol. XI [Cambridge, 1929]), 99-198. Euanthius' *De comoedia et tragoedia* is included at the beginning of Donatus' commentary on Terence, ed. Paul Wessner (Leipzig, 1902), I, 13-31.

7. The basic treatment of epideictic literature is Theodore Burgess, *Epideictic Literature* ("University of Chicago Studies in Classical Philology," Vol. III [Chicago, 1902]), 89-261. For the late classical, early medieval continuation of the tradition see Carolus Halm, ed., *Rhetores Latini minori* (Leipzig, 1863). On the popularity of epideictic literature during the Middle Ages, see, e.g., J. W. H. Atkins, *English Literary Criticism: The Medieval Phase* (London, 1952), p. 26: ". . . it is significant that in [the Second Sophistic] rhetorical study was confined to occasional (or epideictic) oratory; that is, to displays of rhetorical skills on great occasions when panegyrics were usually called for. Oratory of the forensic and deliberative kinds was thus ignored; and, as a result, attention in matters of composition was directed solely to points of style. . . ." Also, E. R. Curtius, *European Literature and the Latin Middle Ages,* tr. Willard Trask (London, 1953), p. 155: "Of all the oratorical genres, the epideictic oration had by far the strongest influence on medieval style."

8. Actually the full scheme involved three different sets of formulae. First, there were the three kinds of praise—goods of nature, fortune, and character—and their "places." These included the prefatory profession of inadequacy, the *genos* and *genesis* (ancestry and birth), the *anatrophe* (circumstances of youth), *epitedeumata* (deeds implying choice), *praxeis* (deeds in war and peace), and *epilogos* (summing up). For a schematic version of these topics see Burgess, *Epideictic Literature,* pp. 120-26. Second, there were the virtues to be illustrated by the deeds. Writers differed concerning which virtues should be stressed; however, Aristotle's "nine virtues" is a respectable showing. *Philanthropia* was generally considered the most comprehensive virtue. Finally there were the stylistic devices most appropriate to the epideictic oration. Amplification and comparison were most important, and are discussed in the text, p. 31.

9. The *Ad Herennium* summarizes the standard formulae; see III, 6, 10: "Laus igitur potest esse rerum externarum, corporis, et animi. Rerum externarum sunt ea quae casu, aut fortuna secunda, aut adversa accidere possunt; ut genus, educatio, divitiae, potestates, gloriae, civitas, amacitiae, et quae huiusmodi sunt, et ea quae his sunt contraria. Corporis sunt ea quae natura corpori attribuit commoda (aut incommoda); ut velocitas, vires, dignitas, valetudo, et quae

contraria sunt. Animi sunt ea quae consilio et cognitione nostra constant; ut prudentia, justitia, fortitudo, modestia, et quae contraria sunt. . . ." *Ethopoeia* is given its own chapter (XI) in Aphthonius, *Progymnasmata,* tr. R. Agricola (Amsterdam, 1665), pp. 288-315. For English sixteenth-century versions of the topics of praise see Thomas Wilson, *Arte of Rhetorique,* ed. G. H. Mair (London, 1909), pp. 11-12; Richard Rainolde, *Foundacion of Rhetorike,* ed. F. R. Johnson (N.Y., 1945), xxxvii and following.

10. Cicero, *De oratore,* II, 84, 342: "Genus, forma, opes, divitiae, cetera quae fortuna det, aut extrinsicus aut corpori, non habent in se veram laudem, quae deberi virtuti uni putatur. . . ." Cf. *De inventione,* II, 59, 178; *De partitione oratoria,* XXI, 70-72.

11. Quintilian, *Institutio oratoria,* III, 7, 13: "quod his honeste usus" rather than "quod habuerit quis ea."

12. E.g., *Rhetores Latini minores,* ed. Halm, p. 259: "habent [pro fine] judiciales aequitatem; demonstratio honestatem; deliberatio honestem et utilem."

13. Pliny, *Panegyricus, XII panegyrici veteres,* ed. Jacobus de la Baune (Venice, 1728), p. 6: ". . . sed parendum est senatus consulto, quo ex utilitate publica placuit, et consulis voce, ut sub gratiarum agendarum, boni principes quae facerunt recognoscerent; mali quae facere deberent."

14. Julian the Apostate, *Orations,* tr. Wilmer Wright (N.Y., 1913), I, 277.

15. Curtius, *European Literature,* pp. 162-4. Cf. Aphthonius, *Progymnasmata,* tr. R. Agricola, Ch. X ("Comparatio"), pp. 275-88.

16. As follows: repetition, *Ad Herennium,* IV, 28; periphrasis, *Ad Herennium,* IV, 32; comparison, *Ad Herennium,* IV, 45-8; prosopopoeia, *Ad Herennium,* IV, 53; digression, *De inventione,* I, 19 and 51; description, *De inventione,* I, 24-5; *Ad Herennium,* IV, 49-50.

17. Julian, *Orations,* tr. Wright, I, 7. See also II, 277-78.

18. Aphthonius, *Progymnasmata,* tr. R. Agricola, pp. 180 ff.

19. See Curtius, *European Literature,* pp. 183-202. For a full discussion of *ekphrasis* see Aphthonius, *Progymnasmata,* tr. R. Agricola, Ch. XII, pp. 315-39.

20. The *Mosella* of Ausonius illustrates epideictic description and the Renaissance interest in it. According to its first modern editor (1499), "Est de laudibus Mosellae, ex aquae limpitudine, ex navigandi facilitate, ex piscibus, ex villis & atriis quibus utraque ripa decoratur: ex aliis in ipsum decurrentibus fluminibus, ex pratis, & aliis quaecumque in flumine ullo non tam invenies quam comminiscatur ingeniosus poeta." Quoted in M. de la Ville Mirmont, *De Ausonii Mosella* (Paris, 1892), p. 31.

21. For the paradoxical encomium see Arthur S. Pease, "Things Without Honor," *Classical Philology,* XXI (1926), 27-42; H. H. Miller, "The Paradoxical Encomium with Special Reference to its Vogue in England, 1600-1800," *MP,* LII (1956), 145-78.

22. Curtius, *European Literature,* p. 158. Compare Burgess, *Epideictic Literature,* p. 168.

23. In view of the poetic leanings of rhetoric, it is not surprising to find that rhetoricians sometimes thought of poetry as a sub-category of epideictic literature. Hermogenes of Tarsus pronounced poetry "the most panegyrical of all logoi" (*Rhetores Graeci,* ed. Spengel, II, 405, 7; 408, 15ff.). Quintilian is especially instructive. He used the term *ostentatio* to identify the object of epideictic oratory. Its matter is "ad solum ostentationem compositas" and its mode is praise "quae ostentationi componitur" (*Institutio oratoria,* III, 7, 1-4). Exactly the same terminology is used for poetry. Poetry is a "genus ostentationi comparatum, et praeter id, quod solam petit voluptatem" (X, 1, 28). It seems fair to conclude that Quintilian considered poetry epideictic by nature; at the very least his terms show how strong was the tendency for the two categories to merge.

24. *Donati interpretationes Vergilianae,* ed. Henricus Georgius (Leipzig, 1905), p. 2: "Primam igitur et ante omnia sciendum est quod materiae genus Maro noster adgressus sit; hoc enim non nisi laudativum est, quod idcirco incognitus est et latans, quia miro artis genere laudationis ipse, dum gesta Aeneae percurreret, incidentia quoque aliarum materiarum genera complexus ostenditur, nec tamen ipsa aliena a partibus laudis; nam idcirco adsumpta sunt, ut Aeneae laudationi proficerent. Hoc quisquis Vergilii igenium, moralitatem, dicendi naturam, scientiam, mores, peritiamque rhetoricae metiri volet, necessario primum debet advertere quem susceperit carmine suo laudandum. . . ."

25. Ibid., pp. 4-6.

26. Domenico Comparetti, *Virgil in the Middle Ages,* tr. E. F. M. Beneke (N.Y., 1929), pp. 113ff.

27. *Fabii Planciadis Fugentii opera,* ed. Rudolfus Helm (Leipzig, 1898), pp. 67-8: "Et quamvis oportueris secundum dialecticam disciplinam primum personam edicere sicque personae congruentia enarrare, quo prima poneretur substantiae, deinde accidems substantiae, ut primam virum, sic enim arma edicere, virtus enim in subiecto est corpori: sed quia laudis est adsumpta materia, ante meritus viri quam ipsum virum ediximus, quo sic ad personam veniretur iam recognita merita qualitate . . . multi viri sunt, non tamen omnes laudandi; ergo virtutem primum posui. . . ."

28. Roger Bacon refers to "Master Hermann the translator" as well learned in languages (*Opus majus,* tr. R. B. Burke [Philadelphia, 1928], I, 82); and later, p. 119, to Hermannus' "prologue to the commentary of Averroes on that book" [i.e., the *Poetics*]. The MSS of the paraphrase are listed in George Lacombe, *Aristoteles Latinus, pars prior* (Rome, 1939) and *pars posterior* (Oxford, 1955): Nos. 323, 353, 426, 706, 707, 732, 871, 908, 941, 943, 963, 1191, 1196, 1211, 1247, 1466, 1494, 1630, 1661, 1753, 1814, 1821, 1935.

29. For biography see G. H. Luquet, "Hermann l'Allemand," *Revue de l'Histoire des Religions,* XLIV (1901), 407-22.

30. *De arte poetica Guillelmo de Moerbeke interprete,* ed. E. Valgimigli, *Aristoteles Latinus,* XXXIII (Paris, 1953).

31. Major editions listed in L. Cooper and A. Gudeman, *A Bibliography of the Poetics of Aristotle* ("Cornell Studies in English," Vol. XI [New Haven, 1928]).

32. *Aristotelis rhetorica ex arabico latine reddita interprete Alemanno Todesco ecc. excerpta ex Aristotelis poetica per eundem Ermannum de Averrois textu* (Venice, 1481), 90^r: "Dicit [Aristoteles]: Omne itaque poemata & omnis oratio poetica aut est vituperatio aut est laudatio & hoc patet per inductionem poematum ipsorum quae sunt de rebus voluntariis sive honestis et turpibus."

33. Ibid., 90^v-91^r. The full text of the passage is as follows: "Et ex quo representatores et assimilatores per hoc intendunt instigare ad quasdam actiones quae circa voluntaria consistunt et retrahere a quibusdam erunt necessario ea quae intendunt per suas representationes aut virtutes aut vicia. Omnis nam actio et omnis mos non versatur nisi circa alterum istorum videlicet virtutem aut vicium. Necessario ergo oportebitur quod boni et virtuosi non representent nisi virtutes et virtuoses. Mali autem malitias et malorum. Et quandoquidem omnis assimilatio et representatio non fit nisi per ostentationem decentis aut indecentis sive turpis patens est quum con intenditur per hoc nisi assecutio decentis et refutatio turpis. Et oportet cum hoc necessario ut sint representatores virtutum scilicet qui declinant naturaliter ad ea quae representant virtuosiores seu meliores. Et representatores malitiarum defectiores illis et propinquiores malitiis. Et ab his manieribus hominorum prodiit laudatio et vituperatio scilicet laus bonorum et vituperatio malorum. Et propter hoc quidam poetarum bonorum se habent in laudando et non in vituperando. Quidam, autem e contrario scilicet et in vituperando et non in laudando. Opportet denique ut in assimilatione inveniantur istae duae differentiae scilicet approbatio decentis et detestatio turpis. Non inveniuntur autem duae hae differentiae nisi in assimilatione et representatione quae sunt per sermonem non in representatione quae sit per metrum neque in representatione quae sit per consonantiam."

34. Petrarch, "Letter to Horace," *National Edition,* IV, 249: "Seu fides comites sedulus excitas/ Virtutem meritis laudibus efferens;/ Seu dignis vitium morsibus impetis/ Ridens stultitiam dente vafer levi. . . ."

35. E. Renan, *Averroës et l'Averroisme* (Paris, 1852), pp. 352-53.

36. *Benvenuto Rombaldi da Imola illustrata nella vita e nelle opere e di lui commento Latino,* ed. and tr. Giovanni Tamburini (Imola, 1855), I, 10: "Si farà ciò agevolmente manifesto a chiunque contempli le forze poetiche, come fa testimonianza Aristotele, imperciochè ogni discorso, o poema o è lode, oppure vitupero, essendoche ogni nostra azione, e costume non risguardi se non la virtù, o il vizio. . . ."

37. Ibid.: "niun altro poeta seppe mai laudare, o vituperare con più eccellenza ed efficacia maggiore di quella, che adoperò il perfettissimo poeta Dante: ornò di encomi le virtù, ed i virtuosi: saettò di punture i vizi, ed i viziosi."

38. Coluccio Salutati, *De laboribus Herculis,* ed. B. L. Ullman (Zurich, 1951), 2 vols.

39. Ibid., i, 9-10: "Est poetrie . . . initum laudatio divinitatis atque virtutis quam gentiles

habuerunt cum vera religione communem. . . . Inquit [Averroes] in ipsius libelli fonte omne poema esse orationem vituperationis aut laudis." Compare Lactantius, *Divinarum institutionum libri* IV, i, 5: "Poetae igitur, quamvis Deos carminibus celebraverunt . . . ecc." And Salutati, *De laboribus Herculis,* p. 14: "convenienter possumus cum Aristotile deffinire poesim esse potentiam considerantem laudationes et vituperationes."

40. Ibid., p. 15: "Habet enim hoc definitio materiale suum quocum rhetorica consit, potentiam scilicet considerantem vituperationes et laudes, et formales differentias quibus ab omnibus separatur, metra videlicet et imaginarios figuratosque sermones. . . ."

41. Ibid., p. 68: " 'Aut prodesse volunt aut delectare poetae.' Prodest quidem reprehensor vitiis obvians sed non immediate delectat. Delectat vero commendans sed non statim et immediate prodest. Principaliter igitur utilitate vituperatio correspondet, delectationi laus, licit secundario prosit hoc, illa delectat."

42. "Allo illustrissimo Signore Frederigo D'Aragona," in *Prosatori volgari del quattrocento,* ed. Claudio Varese (Milan, n.d.), pp. 985-90. "L'onore è veramente quello che porge a ciascuna arte nutrimento; nè da altra cosa quanto dalla gloria sono gli animi de' mortali alle preclare opere infiammati." (p. 985) Compare Cicero, *Pro Archia poeta,* 26: "Trahimur omnes studio laudis et optimus quisque maxime gloria ducatur."

43. Bernardino Daniello, *La poetica* (Venice, 1536), p. 19: "Hora non altrimenti che canore cigno, altro le lode dell'altrui virtù portando, con soave canto, de terra al cielo si leva. Hora il vitio biasmando, a basso discende."

44. Scaliger, *Poetices libri septem* (5th ed., 1617), I, iii: "Sapientum namque praemium bona fama. Sic Plato in suis Legibus, malam faman pro supplicio statuit multis. Quod antem dicit idem in Ione. Poetae hoc ipsum quod ipsi sunt, alios quoque esse faciunt. Quare quibus artibus esse reddunt immortales, iisdem illos quoque quos celebrant, consecrant immortalitati. Sic gloriatur Pindarus: sic canit Theocritus: sic caeteri sunt secuti."

45. Antonio Minturno, *De poeta* (Venice, 1559), p. 222: "aemulatio probos ad studia virtutis hortatur, ut ad quam laudem gloriamque contendunt, perveniant. . . . Nam quos poetae, aut scriptores historiarum summis laudibus efferunt, iis profecto non desunt aemulatores."

46. Tommaso Campanella, *Poeticorum liber unus,* in *Opere,* ed. Luigi Firpo (Milan, 1954), I, 908: "Si igitur poetica ars est, habet usum in republica: igitur instrumentum est legislatoris, quoniam non circum vera per se, sed circa bonum versatur. Igitur laudabit bonos et virtutes; vitia detestabatur et pravos; hic legem et religionem stabiliet et cum voluptate propinabit praecepta, quibus respublica et amicitiae servantur."

47. Giovanni Pontano, *Actius,* in *Dialoghi,* ed. C. Previtera (Florence, 1943), p. 193: "utraque enim demonstrativo versatur in genere, nec minus enim in deliberativo, quod ipsum conciones indicant ac consilia."

48. Ibid., p. 232: "uterque versatur in dicendo et . . . utrisque communes sunt laudationes, quod demonstrativum genus dicitur, tametsi et deliberationes quoque. . . ."

49. Ibid., p. 193: "utraque etiam gaudet amplificationibus, digressionibus item ac varietate. . . ."

50. See Francesco Robortello, *Explicationes* (Florence, 1548), p. 35; Lodovico Castelvetro, *Poetica d'Aristotele* (Basel, 1576), pp. 76-80.

51. Trissino wrote several tragedies of which *Sofonisba* (1515) is probably best known, and an epic, *Italia liberata dai Goti.* See Bernardo Morsolin, *Giangiorgio Trissino* (Florence, 1894).

52. Giangiorgio Trissino, *Poetica,* in *Tutte le opere* (Verona, 1729), II, 92-93.

53. Ibid., p. 138: ". . . le Canzoni, e i Serventesi, e gli altri, riceve . . . tutte i due generi de la Poesia, cioè quello di laudare, et ammirare le cose migliori, come fa Tragedia, e lo Eroico, e quello di dileggiare, e biasmare le cattive, come fa la Commedia."

54. Ibid., p. 118: "per lasciare uno exemplare, overo una idea eccellente, la quale gli uomini possono imitare."

55. *Annotationi di M. Alessandro Piccolomini nel libro della poetica d'Aristotele* (Venice, 1575), 6^{v}: "L'arte non sarebbe arte, se qualche fine non reguardasse, che servisse, & giovisse alla vita nostra."

56. Ibid., 7^{r}: ". . . sì come diverse son [le spetie di Poesia] fra di loro spetie, così parimente in diversi modi cercan tutte di recar'utile, & giovamento alla vita nostra. posciachè con l'imitation degli huomini virtuosi, & con la spressione delle lodi loro, veniamo ad infiammarci,

& ad escitarci alle virtù, per devenir simili a quelli, che celebrar'udiamo. se i vitii, & le scelleratezze dall'altra banda sentiamo con poetica imitation esprimere, & esprimando vilipendere, & vituperare, subito comminciamo a disporsi alla fuga, & all'odio delle vitiose attioni; molto più incitati a questo da cotai imitationi, che da quanto si voglia efficace, & aperta particolari ammonitione."

57. *Dialogi di Messer Alessandro Lionardi della inventione poetica, et insieme di quanto alla istoria et all'arte oratoria s'appartiene, et del modo di finger la favola* (Venice, 1554).

58. Ibid., p. 24: "Egli è anco necessario poi, che il poeta sappia in che forma & in qual maniera dee parlare. . . . E cotal perfettione prenderà dall'oratore. Percioche se tratterà de persone o di opere virtuose o vitiose, recorrerà al genere oratorio dimostrativo, acquistandosi delle virtù honore, & de'vitii dishonore."

59. Ibid., p. 25.

60. Giraldi Cinthio, *Discorsi* (Venice, 1554), p. 59: "L'ufficio adunque del nostro Poeta, quanto ad indurre il costume, è lodare le attioni virtuose, et biasmare i vitii."

61. Ibid., p. 58.

62. Torquato Tasso, *Discorsi del poema eroico,* in *Prose diverse,* ed. Cesare Guasti (Florence, 1875), I, 165-66: ". . . i più magnifici [poeti] imitarono l'azioni più belle e de' più simili a loro; ma i più dimessi quelle de' più vili, componendo da prima villanie ed ingiurie, come gli altri laudi e celebrazioni . . . errò senza dubbio il Castelvetro quando egli disse, che al poeta eroico non si conveniva il lodare; perciò che se il poeta eroico celebra la virtù eroica, dee inalzarla con le lodi sino al cieclo. Però san Basilio dice, che l'Iliade d'Omero altro non è che una lode della virtù; ed Averroe, sopra il comento della poesia, porta la medesima opinione; e Plutarco. . . . Ultimamente s'a l'istorico è lecito a lodare . . . molto più dovrebbe esser lecito al poeta. Lasciando dunque i seguaci del Castelvetro nella loro opinione, or noi seguiam quella di Polibio, di Damascio, di san Basilio, d'Averroe, di Plutarco e d'Aristotele medesimo."

63. George Puttenham, *The Arte of English Poesie,* in ECE, II, 25. I have used this edition for its convenience. The complete text of the *Arte* is available in the edition by G. D. Willcock and A. Walker (Cambridge, 1936).

64. Ibid., II, 37.

65. Ibid., II, 37.

66. Ibid., II, 45.

67. Milton, *An Apology . . . Against Smectymnuus,* in *Works,* ed. F. A. Patterson, *et al.* (N.Y., 1931-42), III, Pt. i, 302-3.

68. *The English Philosophers from Bacon to Mill,* ed. E. A. Burtt (N.Y., 1946), p. 588.

Chapter III

1. See K. O. Myrick, *Sir Philip Sidney as a Literary Craftsman* (Cambridge, 1935); The divisions of the *Defense* are based on those by Allan Gilbert, ed., in *Literary Criticism: Plato to Dryden* (N.Y., 1940), pp. 406-58.

2. Philip Sidney, *An Apologie for Poetrie,* in ECE, I, 183-84.

3. Ibid., p. 175.

4. Plato, *Republic,* II, 377, c-d.

5. Aristotle *Poetics,* IX, 4; XXIV, 9.

6. Petronius, *Satyricon,* 118; Plutarch, *How a Young Man Should Study Poetry,* in F. M. Padelford, tr., *Essays on the Study and Use of Poetry* (N.Y., 1902), pp. 52-53.

7. Cornelius Agrippa, *The Vanity of Arts and Sciences* (London, 1684), p. 25.

8. Ibid., p. 21. The Latin reads "architetrix mendaciorum" (ed. 1531), xx.

9. From *A second and third blast of retrait from plaies and Theater,* as quoted in John Dover Wilson, *Life in Shakespeare's England* (London, 1949), p. 204. See also Thomas Nash, *A General Censure,* in ECE, I, 327.

10. The debate is traced by Giovanni Giovannini, "Historical Realism and the Tragic Emotions in Renaissance Criticism," *PQ,* XXXII (1953), 304-20.

11. Udeno Nisiely (pseudonym for Benedetto Fioretti), *Progynnasmi poetici* (Florence, 1695), V, 12-14, 244.

12. The Earl of Sterling, *Anacrisis,* in *Critical Essays of the Seventeenth Century,* ed. Joel

Spingarn (Bloomington, 1957), I, 186. Compare Euanthius, *De comoedia,* VII, 16; Isidore, *Etymologiarum libri* XX, ed. W. M. Lindsay (Oxford, 1911), VII, 7, 6; XVIII, 45.

13. George Puttenham, *The Arte of English Poesie,* in ECE, II, 37. Also, Augustine, *De civitate dei,* XVIII, 12ff.; Boccaccio, *On the Art of Poetry,* tr. Charles G. Osgood (N.Y., 1956), xix.

14. Francesco Patrizi, *Della poetica, la deca disputata* (Ferrara, 1586), p. 132.

15. Giovanni Pontanus, *Actius,* in *Dialoghi,* ed. C. Previtera (Florence, 1943), p. 193.

16. Francesco Robortello, *Explicationes* (Florence, 1548), p. 2: "Cum igitur poetice subiectam sibi habeat pro materie orationem fictam, et fabulosam, patet ad poeticen pertinere, ut fabulam, et mendacium apte confingat; nulliusque alterius artis proprium magis esse mendacia comminisci, quam huius." See also pp. 89-90, 94-96. For comment, see Bernard Weinberg, "Robertello on the 'Poetics,' " in *Critics and Criticism* (Chicago, 1952), pp. 319-48.

17. Ibid., p. 93: "Si nos verisimilia movent, multo magis vera movebunt; verisimilia nos movent, quia ut fieri potuisse credimus, ita rem accidisse. Vera nos movent, quia scimus ita accidisse, quicquid igitur vis est in verisimili, id totum arripit a vero." Also p. 89: ". . . quatenus poeta non confingit, sed unam explicat actionem veram. . . ." The solution proposed is the formula, "Proprium Historici est narrare res gestas, ut gestae fuerint. Proprium Poetae est narrare res, ut geri debuerint: si non confingit. . . ." Later (p. 95) another formula is found: "Quando Argumenta tragoediarum sumuntur a rebus, quae acciderunt, constituunturque ex veris actionibus, non est plane existimandum, eas omnibus esse notas, sed paucis." But the inconsistency between the poet as clever liar and the poet as historian is never wholly resolved by these qualifications. See also the remarks on p. 38 concerning the origin of epic and tragedy from historical materials. Indeed, Aristotle, himself, is far from clear on this matter.

18. Lodovico Castelvetro, *Poetica d'Aristotele* (Basel, 1576), p. 5: "Prendendo . . . ogni sua luce dalla luce dell' historia." Cf. Bernard Weinberg, "Castelvetro's Theory of Poetics," in *Critics and Criticism* (Chicago, 1952), 370: "Castelvetro insists on the close relationship between poetry and history, on treating poetic as if it were a branch of the historical art . . . this wedding of poetry to history may constitute one of the most original features of Castelvetro's system." See also H. B. Charlton, *Castelvetro's Theory of Poetry* (Manchester, 1913), pp. 41-65.

19. Castelvetro, *Poetica d'Aristotele,* p. 29: ". . . ragionevolmente Lucano, Silio Italico, & Girolamo Fracastoro nel suo Giosepho sono da rimuovere dalla schiera de' poeti, & da privare del glorioso titolo della poesia; perciochè hanno trattata materia nelle loro scritture trattata prima da gl'historici, & quando non fosse ancora stata prima trattata da gl'historici. basta bene, che fosse prima avenuta, & non imaginata da loro."

20. Scaliger, *Poetices libri septem* (5th ed., 1617), I, ii.

21. Ben Jonson, "What is a Poet," *Timber,* in *Works,* ed. C. H. Herford and P. Simpson (Oxford, 1947), VIII, 635.

22. See A. J. Bryant, "The Significance of Ben Jonson's First Requirement for Poetry: 'Truth of Argument,' " *SP,* XLIX (1952), 195-213.

23. Torquato Tasso, *Prose diverse,* ed. Cesare Guasti (Florence, 1875), I, 11-15.

24. Theodore Burgess, *Epideictic Literature* ("University of Chicago Studies in Classical Philology," Vol. III [Chicago, 1902]), pp. 119-23, summarizes the standard topics.

25. Stephen Gosson, *School of Abuse,* ed. Arbor (London, 1868), p. 15.

26. Francesco Patrizi, *Della poetica, la deca disputata,* p. 169: "Divino è certemente, ed Enteastico il genere de poeti, lodante molte delle cose per verità avvenute, e con certe grazie, e Muse spessamente le va toccando." And, "La terza occupazione, e furore delle Muse, prendendo tenera, e non profonda anima, e incitandola, e infuriandola, con ode, e con altra poesia, ornando le migliaia de'fatti degli antichi, ammaestra quei c'hanno a venire."

27. Ibid., p. 229. Homer is mentioned as an author of "Eroiche" and the first sentence in the next chapter, "Lodare Prodi," is: "Fu per antico in molto pregio l'Iliada di Omero, come quella che cantava i fatti egrigi degli Eroi" (p. 230).

28. Quoted in Benedetto Fioretti, *Progynnasmi poetici* (Florence, 1695), V, ii (p. 19): ". . . poesis illa, qua vetustissimi homines ad superum aras utebantur, cum laudes eorum canarent. Omino dubitari non debet, quin et antiquissima, et nobilissima omnino sit haec poesis: cuius proculdubio exemplum caeteris mortalibus dederunt, qui et vetustate, et pietate

omnes populos vincebant, Hebraei . . . contendat aliquis solam hance esse veram, et legitimam poesim, quae vel DEUM canit, vel ad DEUM homines ducit: quod et Plato tandem videtur intellexisse: cum pulsis de Repub. sua poetis, solos hymnographos retinuit. . . ."

29. Sidney, *Apologie,* in ECE, I, 178.

30. For the history of this distinction, see G. Carducci, "Dello svolgimento dell'ode in Italia," *Opere* (Bologna, n.d.), XVI, 363-452.

31. Giordano Bruno, *De gli heroici furori,* in *Opere di Bruno e Campanella,* eds. A. Guzzo and R. Amerio (Milan, n.d.), p. 572: "Si vantano et possono vantarsi di mirto quei che cantano d'amore. . . . Possono vantarsi d'allori quei che degnamente cantano cose eroiche. . . ."

32. G. G. Vossius, *De artis poeticae natura* (Amsterdam, 1647), p. 12: "Siquidem primitus *carmine* tractarunt partim amores non fictos, sed veros; unde et *poesis* videtur initium sumsisse partim laudes numinis . . . partim virorum praestantium gesta."

33. Gabriello Chiabrera, *Dialoghi,* in *Canzonette, rime varie, dialoghi,* ed. Luigi Negri (Turin, 1952), p. 570: ". . . possiamo affermare per cosa vera. Che la maniera del poetare la quale si chiama lirica è tutta d'amori e di conviti e sua materia è ciò che ha forza di dare diletto a'sentimenti. . . . Non niego pertanto che si lodino dal poeta lirico cavalieri ed alti personaggi, non per tutto questo si fatta lode è da porsi fuori del confine del verseggiare liricamente con alquanto più dignità, è vero, ma non già con l'altezza del verseggiare eroicamente. . . ."

34. William Webbe, *A Discourse of Englishe Poetrie,* in ECE, I, 231.

35. Puttenham, *The Arte of English Poetrie,* in ECE, II, 25; also, II, 209, 309.

36. The image of the bee making honey from weeds (from Plutarch's essay on "How a Young Man Should Study Poetry") was often used to define the way in which the proper reader would extract profit from off-color comic or lyric poetry. E.g., ECE, I, 59, 79; II, 309. See also I, 186-87, 322-23.

37. For the "panegyrical biography" in antiquity, see Duane Stuart, *Epochs of Greek and Roman Biography* (Berkeley, 1924), pp. 68ff.

38. Cornelius Agrippa, *The Vanity of Arts and Sciences* (London, 1684), p. 26.

39. For history as an epideictic type, see Cicero, *Orator,* 37, 65, 207; Quintilian, *Institutio oratoria,* X, 1, 28, 31, 33. For the later opinion, note Pontanus, *Actius,* in *Dialoghi,* ed. Previtera (Florence, 1943), p. 209: "Atque in historia, cuius prima cum sit lex neque in gratiam loqui neque opticere odio vera aut ea dissimulare, efficitur ut laudentur quae sint commendatione digna, suo quidem et loco et tempore utque improbentur turpiter atque imprudenter facta; alterum sine spe, sine pretio, alterum sine simultate et metu; ita uti et tuae pariter et illius de quo suscepta est laudatio famae honorique pudenter ac modeste consulas. . . . Ac mihi quidem in laudando aut improbando videtur rerum gestarum scriptor iudicies quasi cuiusdam personam debere induere, ne ab aequo et iusto illo recedat, quod est inter praemium ac poenam medium." See also Henry Immerwahr, "*Ergon:* History as a Monument in Herodotus and Thucydides," *AJP,* LXXXI (1960), 261-90.

40. Scaliger, *Poetics libri septem* (5th ed., 1617), I. ii: "Laudat orator quempiam: non potest sine enarratione vitae, familiae, nationis. Hoc cum Historico. is saepenumero addit elogia: qualia legimus de Camillo, Scipione, Hannibale, Iugurtha, Cicerone: atque interponit quasi decreta sua."

41. Plato, *Protagoras,* 325-26.

42. E.g., *De oratore,* II, 84, 342; *De partitione oratoria,* XXIf., 71-82; Pliny, in *XII panegyrici veteres,* ed. Jacobus de la Baune (Venice, 1728), 6; Julian, *Orations,* tr. Wright (N.Y., 1914), I, 247, 49. The source is Isocrates. See, e.g., *Evagoras,* 6-8. For a typical Renaissance explanation, Campanella, *Rhetorica,* in *Opere,* ed. Luigi Firpo (Milan, 1954), I, 740: "Neque enim, cum laudamus aut vituperamus hominem, laus et vituperamen est finis actionis, sed suasio et hortatio ad bonum et dehortatio a malo. Sic enim virtus laudata servatur et crescit in laudato, et alii eum imitari student." Discussion in Burgess, *Epideictic Literature,* pp. 122-25, 136-38.

43. Treated concisely in E. R. Curtius, *European Literature and the Latin Middle Ages,* tr. Willard Trask (London, 1953), pp. 174-76.

44. Torquato Tasso, *Discorsi dell'arte poetica,* in *Prose diverse,* ed. C. Guasti, I, 54: "La composizione, che è la terza parte dello stile, avrà del magnifico se saranno lunghi i periodi, e lunghi i membri, de'quali il periodo è composto. E per questo la stanza è più capace di questo

eroico, che'l terzetto." And ibid., I, 52: "Può nascere la magnificenza da' concetti, da le parole, e da le composizioni delle parole; e da queste tre parti risulta lo stile, e quelle tre forme le quali dicemmo. . . . Per isprimere questa grandezza accommodate saranno quelle figure di sentenze, le quali o fanno parer grandi le cose con le circostanze; come l'ampliazone o le iperboli, che alzano la cosa sopra il vero; o la reticenza, che accennando la cosa, e poi tacendola, maggiore la lascia a l'imaginazione. . . . Perciò che così proprio del magnifico dicitore è il commover e il rapire gli animi. . . ."

45. Joel Spingarn remarks in *A History of Literary Criticism in the Renaissance* (N.Y., 1956), p. 53: "The poet must incite in the reader an admiration of the example, or the ethical aim of poetry will not be accomplished. Poetry . . . becomes like Oratory, an active exhortation to virtue, by attempting to create in the reader's mind a strong desire to be like the heroes he is reading about." The term apparently originates in Aristotle's *Poetics* in connection with the use of the marvelous in poetry [cf. Marvin Herrick, "Some Neglected Sources of *Admiratio*," *MLN*, LXII (1947), 222-6]. It is frequently used in rhetoric as a stylistic quality which the orator must strive to gain, as in *De oratore*, I, 33, 152; *Brutus*, 53, 198; *Orator*, 57, 192. Significantly, it is associated specifically with epideictic oratory, as in *De partione oratoria*, XVII, 58: "In illis enim causis quae ad delectationem exornantur [i.e., epideictic speeches] ei loci tractandi sunt qui movere possunt exspectationem, *admirationem*, voluptatem. . . ." (italics mine); also ibid., 73. The term obviously survives during the Middle Ages, for Pontanus says in his *Actius*, in *Dialoghi*, ed. Previtera, p. 146; ". . . poetae sive officium sive finem esse dicere apposite ad admirationem. . . ." See also 232f. It is used in Latin translations of the *Poetics* and the *Rhetoric*; and Robortello frequently uses the term in his *Explicationes* on the *Poetics*. It occurs *passim* in the later critics. See, for example, Tasso, *Discorsi del poema eroico*, in *Prose diverse*, ed. Guasti, I, 83 (where *maraviglia* and *ammirazione* are closely connected), Scaliger, *Poetices*, III, xcvi; Sidney, *Apologie*, in ECE, I, 177, and Smith's note on Sidney, which cites examples from the seventeenth century; also *Essays of John Dryden*, ed. W. P. Ker (Oxford, 1900), II, 159.

46. Cf. Antonio Minturno, *De Poeta* (Venice, 1559), p. 222: ". . . aemulatio probos ad studia virtutis hortatur, ut ad quam laudem gloriamque contendunt, perveniant. . . . Quam ob rem cum ea nos in primis aemulari oporteat, quae maxime appetenda ducantur, haec vero sint, quae inter bona longe praestant, necesse est, ut aemulatio sit praecipue rerum earum, et quae amplitudinem gloriamque afferant his, qui potiuntur permagnam, caeteris opem et utilitatem. . . . Nam quos poetae, aut scriptores historiarum summis laudibus efferunt, iis profecto non desunt aemulatores." The term *aemulatio* is also used by Renaissance critics to describe the emotion stimulated in the audience of an epideictic composition. Scaliger, for example (*Poetices libri septem*, III, cix): "Veteres Graecos tenuit consuetudo, certis ut celebrationibus unum in locum universi convenierent: ut eorum animi vel praeceptionibus sapientium, vel fortium *aemulatione*, componerentur, atque colerentur. . . ." (italics mine).

47. See above, pp. 34-35.

48. The tradition is traced in A. P. McMahon, *Seven Questions on Aristotelian Definitions of Tragedy and Comedy* ("Harvard Studies in Classical Philology," Vol. XL [Cambridge, 1929]), 99-178.

49. Sidney, *Apologie*, in ECE, I, 177.

50. E.g., Torquato Tasso, *Discorsi del poema eroico*, in *Prose diverse*, ed. C. Guasti, I, 114. Compare Heywood, *An Apology for Actors*, ed. R. H. Perkinson (N.Y. 1941), F3^v: "If we present a Tragedy we include the fatall and abortive ends of such as commit notorious murders, which is aggravated and acted with all the art that may be, to terrifie men from the like abhorred vices." This theory, which emphasizes the tragic flaw, is opposed to the widespread theory, derived in part from the *Poetics* and in part from the Averroes tradition, that tragedy is a form of praise and the tragic hero a figure who arouses *admiratio*. The term *admiratio* and its cognates, such as *wonder* or *awe*, are discussed in J. V. Cunningham, *Woe or Wonder* (Denver, 1951); Clarence Green, *The Neo-Classic Theory of Tragedy* (Cambridge, 1934), pp. 27-33; Bernard Weinberg, "The Poetic Theories of Minturno," *Studies in Honor of Frederick W. Shipley* (St. Louis, 1942), p. 109; and above, note 45.

51. E.g., Giraldi Cinthio, *Discorsi* (Venice, 1554), p. 58; ". . . scrive il poeta accompagnando convenevolmente le cose, che portano con esso loro il vitio, con l'horribile, et col

miserabile . . . purga gli animi nostri da simili passioni, et ci desta alla vertu, come si vede nella definitione, che da Aristotile della Tragedia."

52. See below, Ch. IV, pp. 102-5.

53. This can best be illustrated by quotations from Elizabethan translators of historical works. North remarks in his preface to Plutarch's *Lives,* ed. W. E. Henley ("Tudor Translations," 1892-1903), p. 4: ". . . among all the profane books, that are in reputacion at this day, there is none more . . . that teacheth so much honor, love, obedience, reverence, zeale, and devocion to Princes as these lives of Plutarke doe. Howe many examples shall your subjects read here of severall persons, and whole armyes, noble and base, of younge and olde, that both by sea and lande, at home and abroad, have strayned their wits, not regarded their states, ventured their persons, cast away their lives, not only for the safetie, but also for the pleasure of their princes. . . ." The translation of *Jugurtha* by Barclay (c. 1520) claims that the "gentlemen readers" will find it "a ryght fruytful hystorie: bothe pleasaunt / profitable / & ryght necessary unto every degre: but specially to gentlymen which coveyt to attayne to clere fame and honour." Quoted in H. B. Lathrop, *Translations from the Classics into English from Caxton to Chapman* (Madison, 1933), p. 81. *Jugurtha* was later translated for Prince Henry by Thomas Heywood, its introduction being Heywood's rendition of Chapter IV of Jean Bodin's *Methodus ad facilem historiarum delectum.* John Brende, in his translation of Quintus Curtius, *History of the Acts of Alexander* (1553), advises reading, ". . . specially the histories of antiquitye, whych both for the greatnes of the actes done in those daies, and for the excellencie of the writers have much majestie and many ensamples of vertue. . . ." Quoted Lathrop, *Translations,* p. 87. Thomas Stocker, in his translation of Diodorus Siculus (1564), claims that in his work, ". . . is shewed the uncerteintie of fortune . . . and chiefley that whiche is moste meete and becomming a noble personage, whereof he is called *magnanimous.*" Quoted Lathrop, *Translations,* p. 192. Machiavelli, *The Prince,* tr. Allan Gilbert (Chicago, 1941), XIV, 5, is apparently thinking of example when he advises the Prince, ". . . to read history, and give attention to the actions of great men related in it . . . and to examine the causes of their victories and defeats, in order to imitate the first and avoid the second; above all, he should learn to do as some great men have done in the past, for they have taken for imitation some earlier character *who has been praised and lauded,* and have always kept his deeds and actions before them" (italics mine). The criterion of example sometimes made the history of one period better than that of another. Tasso, *Prose diverse,* ed. Guasti, I, 14-17 and 110-11, urges Christian history for the epic because it is more adaptable to the purposes of the poet; but James Colyn, in a preface to Thomas Nichols' *Thucydides* (1550), preferred the example of the noble ancient heroes: ". . . in steede of Tristrams, Girons and Lancelotes and other, which do fylle bookes wyth dreames, and wherin many have evill bestowed theyr good houres, ye have, by the benefyt of the Kynge, no lesse frutefull than pleasante passetyme, for to knowe what people were Pericles, Nycias, Antigonus, Lysimachus, Eumenes, Hanibal, Scipion, and many other sage and valyant Capitaynes" (Lathrop, *Translations,* p. 86).

54. Fra Girolamo Saronavola, *De divisione . . . scientiarum* (Florence, 1496), p. 807.

55. Antonio Minturno, *De poeta,* I, 38: "Sed tamen docendus erat populus, et ad virtutem informandus, non praeceptis philosophorum, sed exemplis, quae non historici, sed poetae protulissent." Segrais prefaced his *Aeneid* translation with the comment that epic ". . . est d'instruire par de beaux esemples; & comme un ancien l'a si ben dit, d'exciter les Princes & les hommes de courage à entreprendre de grandes choses." Ben Jonson ends *Sejanus* with the following verse: "Let this example move th' insolent man/ Not to grow proud and careless of the gods. . . ."

56. Benedetto Varchi, *Lezzioni* (Florence, 1590), p. 573: "il suo mezzo, o strumento è l'esempio."

57. Torquato Tasso, *Prose diverse,* ed. Guasti, I, 77: "l'ottimo fine è quello di giovare a gli uomini con l'esempio dell'azioni umane. . . ."

58. Giordano Bruno, *De gli heroici furori,* eds., Guzzo and Amerio, p. 572: "Celebrandoli et mettendoli per specchio exemplare a gli gesti politici et civili."

59. Sidney, *Apologie,* in ECE, I, 164.

60. *The Reason of Church Government Urged Against Prelaty,* in *Works,* ed. F. A. Patterson *et al.* (N.Y., 1931-42), III, Pt. i, 239.

61. E. R. Curtius, *European Literature and the Latin Middle Ages,* tr. Willard Trask (London, 1953), p. 60, uses the term "exemplary figures" and equates it with *ikon* and *imago.* Other treatments of the same problem can be found in D. S. Brewer, "The Ideal of Feminine Beauty in Medieval Literature," *MLR,* L (1955), 257-69; and E. H. Gombrich, "Icones Symbolicae: The Visual Image in Neo-Platonic Thought," *Journal of the Warburg and Courtauld Institutes,* XI (1948), 163-92.

62. Bernardino Daniello, *La poetica* (Venice, 1536), pp. 24-25: ". . . [era] stata essa Poetica da gli antichi et sapientissimi huomini alla pittura assomigliata; et detto essa pittura altro non esser che un tacito et muto Poema. Et allo'ncontro pittura parlante la Poesia. Perciochè come l'imitatione del dipintore si fa con stili, con penelli, et con diversità di colori . . . così quella del Poeta si fa con la lingua, et con la penna, con numeri, et harmonie."

63. Antonio Minturno, *De poeta,* p. 145: "Postremo imitandi sunt optimi pictores, ut quemadmodum illi pulchriores dipingunt, *imaginem* propriam veraeque simillimam expressuri, ita magnanimos, timidos, industrios, ignavos, mites, iracundos, ac cetera morum genera descripturus poeta, quod saepe admonuimus, de sua quidque *exemplum* specie sibi petit. Nam in Achille vim bellicam et ferociam Homerus, in Aenea pietatem et fortitudinem Virgilius effinxit." Also Patrizi, *Della poetica, la deca disputata,* pp. 77-78: "Il quale [the painter], si come co'colori esprimea, cose e figure varie di tante guise, quante quivi Platone annovera, cosi il poeta, con le sue parole, verbi e nomi, che a lui sono in vece di colori, tutte le cose che in mente gli venieno, esprimea." Also, Tasso, *Discorsi dell'arte poetica,* in *Prose diverse,* ed. Guasti, I, 31, 40; and Sidney, *Apologie,* in ECE, I, 158: "Poesie therefore is an arte of imitation . . . that is to say, a representing, counterfetting, or figuring foorth: to speake metaphorically, a speaking picture: with this end, to teach and delight." And North says in the introduction to Plutarch's *Lives,* 10: "[History] is a picture, which (as it were in a table) setteth before our eies things worthy of remembrance. . . ."

64. Euanthius, *De comoedia,* 8, 7: ". . . comoediam esse Cicero ait imitationem vitae, speculum consuetudinis, imaginem veritatis . . . aitque esse comoediam cotidianae vitae speculum, nec iniuria. nam ut intenti speculo veritatis lineamenta facile per imaginem colligimus, ita lectione comoediae imitationem vitae consuetudinisque non aegerrime animadvertimus." Although Cicero did not write the words ascribed to him by Evanthius, he did use the mirror image in *Republic,* II, 64, where he urges of the good man, ". . . ut sese splendore animi et vitae suae sicut speculum praebeat civibus." In *Piso,* 71, we learn, ". . . in quibus versibus possit istius tamquam in speculo vitam intueri."

65. Antonio Minturno, *De poeta,* p. 31: "Hunc vocat imitatorem . . . qui quaecumque natura in ortum ciet, quaecumque cavernis terrae clauduntur . . . mirifice possit aemulare . . . rem omnem tibi *speculo* repraesentat. . . . Nam ut illo eodem *speculo* rerum *imagines,* non res ipsae ad vivendum praebentur, sic imitatione ipsa non ut quidquid est sed uti videtur expressum appare." Italics mine.

66. L. B. Campbell, ed., *The Mirror for Magistrates* (Cambridge, 1938), p. 49: ". . . every apology for history in the period affirmed that history was a glass wherein the present might see and learn the patterns of conduct which had brought happiness or unhappiness to nations or men in the past. . . ." Miss Campbell's later claim that Sidney effected the transfer begun in *The Mirror for Magistrates* from history to poetry should be modified. The date of the "transfer" seems several centuries before Christ, and the probable direction is from poetry to history rather than the reverse.

67. Giraldi Cinthio, *Discorsi,* pp. 32-33: "mi pare che Virgilio in ciò imitasse gli eccelenti dipintori, i quali volendo formare una imagine singolare, che rappresenti la donnesca bellezza, mirano tutte le belle donne, che mirar ponno; et da ciascuno togliono le parti migliori . . . tante, quante lor paiono bastare a compire la Idea c'hanno nell'animo. . . ."

68. See below, note 74.

69. Francesco Patrizi, in *Della poetica, la deca disputata,* p. 161; asks whether Homer "formò Agamennone, e gli altri Rè, e Capitani del campo Greco, alla Idea de' buon Rè, e di buoni Pastor di popoli . . .?" Cf. also Sidney, *Apologie,* in ECE, I, 157; Giraldi Cinthio, *Discorsi,* p. 193; Fracastoro, *Naugerius,* p. 158r, 164r; Minturno, *De poeta,* p. 31.

70. Jacopo Mazzoni, *Della difesa della comedia* (Cesena, 1587), "Introduction," 8-12, 62-64.

71. Torquato Tasso, *Discorsi del poema eroico* in *Prose diverse,* ed. C. Guasti, I, 98-103. Sidney follows Tasso in ECE, I, 186-87.

72. G. G. Vossius, *De artis poeticae natura*, p. 49: "Nullum, inquiunt [the enemies of poetry] hominum genus magis est pestilens adulatoribus: nulli autem exquisitius adulantur poetis. . . . Verum non omnes laudationes pro adulationibus sunt habendae. Saepe promeritae sunt, et dignae . . . ut alii ad simile excitentur exemplum."

73. Antoni Minturno, *De poeta*, p. 25: ". . . tales ne fuerint, quales describuntur, ignoramus. Sed eos ita tamen credimus esse descriptos, cuiusmodi illi existere debuissent. Qui scribunt dialogos . . . illorum non quae fuissent virtutes, exponere conantur, sed quas esse decuisset."

74. Giangiorgio Trissino, *Poetica*, II, 118: ". . . per lasciare uno esemplare, overo una idea eccellente, la quale gli uomini possono imitare, chè sempre lo esemplare dee essere molto [più] eccellente di ciò, che comunemente è."

75. Lodovico Castelvetro, *Poetica d'Aristotele*, p. 669: "Alcuni vogliono, che questa sia la ragione, perche i poeti, e i dipintori rassomiglino le cose, come deono essere, & le facciono più eccellenti, che in verità non sono, o non possono essere, ciò è, che essi le rassomiglino tali, perchè sieno essempio, nel quale gli huomini riguardando, & proponendoselo nella mente, debbano, operando secondo quello, dirizzare le loro attioni. . . ." Compare Robortello, *Explicationes*, p. 89: "Proprium poetae est narrare res, ut geri debuerint; si non confingit. . . ."

76. Tommaso Campanella, *Opere*, ed. Firpo, I, 318-19: ". . . fu bisogno quelli dipingere non come erano, ma come dovevano essere. Quindi ebbe luogo la favola, con la quale, imitando il vero, si accresce la virtù d'alcuno, e il male quando s'odia, come fece Virgilio in Enea e Didone. Di più, non potendosi alla scoperta riprendere i vizi de'tirranni, fu mestiere per via di favole da'dotti solamente intese andarli descrivendo."

77. Sidney, *Apologie*, in ECE, I, 169.

78. Puttenham, *The Arte of English Poesie*, in ECE, II, 41-42.

79. Sidney, *Apologie*, in ECE, I, 169-70. Cf. Daniello, *Poetica*, p. 47; Minturno, *De poeta*, pp. 37-38; Sir John Harington, *A Preface, or rather a Brief Apologie of Poetrie*, in ECE, II, 201.

80. *The Poems of George Chapman*, ed. Phyllis Bartlett (N.Y., 1941), p. 407.

81. Aristotle, *Poetics*, IX and XXIV, 10.

82. For a discussion of this important rhetorical idea, see Bromley Smith, "Corax and Probability," *QJS*, VII (1921), 38.

83. *Reason of Church Government*, in *Works*, ed. Patterson *et al.*, III, Pt. i, 237.

84. Bernardino Daniello, *La poetica*, p. 19: ". . . il Poeta sotto varie fittioni et favolosi velami utile ammaestramento ricoprendo, gli animi per gli orecchi alletta et a se trahe degli ascoltanti, o de leggente. . . ."

85. Andrea Alciati, *Emblemata* (Lyons, 1621), pp. 26-32.

86. Ibid., p. 27, col. I: "Eodem plane modo veteres illi poetae sub aliquo quasi velo, certe obscuro, fabulosisque ornamentis res suas occultarunt, ut imperitam plebeculam a mysteriis sapentiae reconditioris arcerent."

87. *De civitate Dei*, VI, 5. Augustine attributes the scheme to Varro. Cf. also Boccaccio, *De genealogiis deorum gentilium*, XV, 8.

88. Thomas Nash, *A General Censure*, in ECE, I, 328; see also Harington, *A Preface*, in ECE, II, 203.

89. See Plato, *Cratylus*, 394ff., and Xenophon, *Memorabilia*, II, 1, 21-33.

90. C. S. Lewis, *The Allegory of Love* (Oxford, 1951).

91. Tasso, *Prose diverse*, ed. Guasti, I, 301: "L'eroica poesia, quasi animale in cui due nature si congiungono, d'imitazione, e d'allegoria è composta."

92. For the supplanting of allegory by example, see D. L. Clark, *Rhetoric and Poetic in the Renaissance* (N.Y., 1922), pp. 154-61, and W. Woodward, *Vittorino da Feltre and other Humanist Educators* (Cambridge, 1897).

93. Thomas Wilson, *Arte of Rhetorique*, ed. G. H. Mair (London, 1909), p. 195.

94. These are among the figures exemplifying justice in the *Divine Comedy, Paradiso*, XX. Exactly the same technique is suggested by Sidney, *Apologie*, in ECE, I, 165: "Anger, the *Stoicks* say, was a short madnes: let but *Sophocles* bring you *Ajax* on a stage, killing and whipping Sheepe and Oxen, thinking them the Army of Greeks, with theyr Chiefetaines *Agamemnon* and *Menelaus*, and tell mee if you have not a more familiar insight into anger then finding in the Schoolemen his *Genus* and difference. See whether wisdome and temperance in *Ulisses* and *Diomedes*, valure in Achilles, friendship in *Nisus* and *Eurialus*, even

to an ignoraunt man carry not an apparent shyning. . . ." Basically the same approach seems behind such exemplary stories as Chaucer's *Clerk's Tale,* where a single personified virtue (patience, equals Griselda) is illustrated in a lengthy but repetitive series of episodes whose only progression is the fact that each one is a more severe test than the one before. This is not allegory because the "tests" are essentially the same; they could not be analyzed as embodying different facets of a "philosophy of endurance."

95. H. S. V. Jones, *A Spenser Handbook* (N.Y., 1940), pp. 249-77, notes the heavy reliance on *Nicomachean Ethics V.* See also F. M. Padelford, "Talus: The Law," *SP,* XV (1918), 97-104.

96. Torquato Tasso, *Prose diverse,* ed. Guasti, I, 303-4.

97. Ibid., I, 301-2: "E sì come l'epica imitazione altro già mai non è che somiglianza ed imagine d'azione umana; così suole l'allegoria degli Epici, dell'umana vita esserci figura. . . . Or della vita dell'uomo contemplante è figura la Comedia di Dante, e l'Odissea . . . ma la vita civile in tutta l'Iliade si vede adombrata; e nell' Eneide ancora. . . ." Cf. Minturno, *L'arte poetica* (Venice, 1563), p. 28; Campanella, *Opere,* ed. Firpo, p. 361; Thomas Lodge, *Defence,* in ECE, I, 65, 68; Sidney, *Apologie,* in ECE, I, 165-66, 179-80; Webbe, *A Discourse,* in ECE, I, 234-5, 237; etc. Often this interpretation is attributed to Maximus Tirius or Plutarch; it is elaborately developed in Fulgentius' reading of the *Aeneid.*

98. Francis Bacon, *Advancement of Learning,* in *Critical Essays of the Seventeenth Century,* ed. Joel Spingarn (Bloomington, 1957), I, 8.

99. Wilson, *Arte of Rhetorique,* ed. Mair, p. 198.

100. Sidney, *Apologie,* in ECE, I, 164. Also, Fracastoro, *Naugerius,* pp. 163r-v; Minturno, *De poeta,* pp. 33-48; Giraldi Cinthio, *Discorsi,* pp. 147-48; Alciati, *Emblemata,* pp. 21-8.

101. See, for example, Giraldi Cinthio, *Discorsi,* pp. 80-82; Tasso, *Prose diverse,* ed. Guasti, I, 40-41; 79-81; Fracastoro, *Naugerius,* pp. 161r-v.

102. Tasso, *Discorsi dell'arte poetica,* in *Prose diverse,* ed. C. Guasti, I, 43: "Concedo io quel che vero stimo, e che molti negarebbono; cioè, che'l diletto sia il fine della poesia."

103. "Le Considerazione Sopra Tre Canzoni di M. Gio. Battista Pigma." ibid., II, 77: "ciò ch' è buono è bello; e volgendo l'ordine ciò ch' è bello è buono. . . ."

104. S. H. Butcher, *Aristotle's Theory of Poetry and Fine Art* (London, 1911), p. 150.

105. Bernard Bosanquet, *A History of Aesthetic* (London, 1910), p. 113. See also, G. Martano, *L'Uomo e Dio in Procolo* (Naples, 1952), pp. 102-9.

106. P. O. Kristeller, *Il pensiero filosofico di Marsilio Ficino* (Florence, 1953), p. 257. Ficino distinguished between the "formula" that exists in the mind and the "idea" that exists in the mind of God. By seeking the *formula,* we move one step toward highest reality. By moving from *formula* to *idea,* we ascend the highest rung of the Platonic ladder.

107. Giraldi Cinthio, *Discorsi,* p. 193: "L'Idea e'hanno nell'animo."

108. Antonio Minturno, *De poeta,* p. 24: "videtur mihi quidem nihil exprimi posse dilligenter, cuius non haereat vera species in animo imitatoris." The equation of *idea* and *species,* and also the definition of the three types of imitation, is given on page 31: ". . . tria in quaque re docet esse consideranda, speciem, quam Ideam appellat, rem ipsam, et simulacrum. Speciem unam esse, uniusque modi, et sempiternam. Res plures unius generis una eademque specie constare, simulacra posse vel rei cuiusque plurima constari. Quemadmodum enim uno annulo multa sigilla imprimuntur, ita quam plurimas una specie res informari, unius eiusdemque rei figura complures imagines effingi. . . ."

109. Sidney, *Apologie,* in ECE, I, 157.

110. Girolamo Fracastoro, *Naugerius sive de poetica,* in *Opera* (Venice, 1555), 158r: "Poeta vero illi assimiletur qui non hunc, non illum vult imitari, non uti forte sunt, et defectus multos sustinent, sed universalem, et pulcherrimam ideam artificis sui contemplatus res facit, quales esse deceret. . . ." Cf. Tasso's comment on this in *Discorsi del poema eroico, Prose diverse,* ed. C. Guasti, I, 80.

111. Compare Sidney, *Apologie,* in ECE, I, 157: "Neyther let it be deemed too sawcie a comparison to ballance the highest poynt of mans wit with the efficacie of Nature: but rather give right honor to the heavenly Maker of that maker, who, having made man to his owne likenes, set him beyond and over all the workes of that second nature, which in nothing hee sheweth so much as in Poetrie, when with the force of a divine breath he bringeth things forth for surpassing her dooings, with no small argument . . . of that first accursed fall of

Adam: sith our erected wit maketh us know what perfection is, and yet our infected will keepeth us from reaching unto it." In the *Discorsi del poema eroico,* in *Prose diverse* ed. Guasti, I, 101, Tasso makes his point extremely clear: ". . . il conducere a la contemplazione delle cose divine, e il destare in questa guisa con l'imagini, come fa il teologo mistico ed il poeta, è molto più nobile operazione, che l'ammaestrar con le demonstrazioni, com' è officio del teologo scolastico."

112. Girolamo Fracastoro, *Naugerius,* pp. 158r, 160r, 164r: "[Poeta] verum ideam sibi aliam faciens liberam et in universum pulchram, dicendi omnes ornatus, omnes pulchritudines quaeret, quae illi rei attribui possunt. . . . Poeta certe hic est, cuius officium erit ac finis nulla eorum praetermittere, quae simpliciter pulchrum ac perfectum sermonem faciant . . . finem poetae esse delectare et prodesse imitando in uno quoque maxima et pulcherrima per genus dicendi simpliciter pulchrum ex convenientibus." Compare Ficino, quoted Kristeller, *Il Pensiero Filosofico,* p. 286: "Bonum quidem ipsa supereminens Dei existentia dicitur, pulchritudo actus quidam sive radius inde per omnia penetrans, primo in angelicam mentem, secundo in animam totius et reliquos animos, tertio in naturam, quarto in materiam corporum. Mentem idearum ordine decorate, animam rationum serie complete, naturam fulcit seminibus, materiam formis exornat." Also Giraldi Cinthio, *Discorsi,* p. 84: ". . . dee il Poeta porre molto ingegnio, et molto studio in questa parte, che alle voci appartiene: che essendo eglino quelle, che vestono i nostri concetti, et gli portano agli occhi dell'intelletto, debbono esser ornate di tutta quella bellezza, che loro può dare la industria di chi compone." Also, Tasso, *Discorsi del poema eroico,* in *Prose diverse,* ed. C. Guasti, I, 77, 84; II, 120ff.; George Puttenham, *Arte,* in ECE, II, 142-43.

113. Cinthio, *Discorsi,* p. 25: ". . . [porta] questa diversità delle attioni con esso lei la varietà, la quale è il condimento del diletto, et si da largo campo allo Scrittore, di fare Episodii, ciò è digressioni grati, et introdurvi avenimenti, che non possono mai avenire . . . nelle Poesie, che sono di una sola attione. . . ."

114. Quoted in Benedetto Fioretti, *Progynnasmi poetici* (Florence, 1695), I, 516f.: "Epopeia pluribus episodiis *amplificanda* est, ne si nullis digressionibus dilatetur, sterilis, & inornata sit, omnis leporis, & venustatis expers." And p. 53: "Excidium Ilii in secundo Aeneidos, & Aeneae errores in tertio, ad haec Didonis interitus in quarto, & ludorum pompa in quinto, & inferorum descriptio in sexto admirabili ornatu fabulam *amplificant.* Omitto multas & illustres locorum, temporum, rerum, & personarum descriptiones, quibus incredibiliter augetur, & ornatur poesis. . . . Est autem digressione opus, cum ea vel a fabulae necessitate requiritur non *amplificationis* modo, verum etiam connexionis, & dissolutionis gratia, vel ornandi causa accersitur. . . . Italics mine.

115. Fioretti, *Progynnasmi poetici,* IV, 51: "Voco autem digressiones cum a re proprosita in aliam declinamus; sicuti Livius in transitum Alexandri in Italiam, & Sallustius in mores Caesaris, & Catonis digressus est. Et apud Oratores, praesertim in genere demonstrativo, & apud Poetas qui se totos ad delectandum compararunt, frequentiores sunt & longiores digressiones. . . ." Also, p. 52: "Digressio, quae excursus, & egressio vocatur, est, qua delectationis, ornatus, & *amplificationis* gratia in aliquem communem locum ad utilitatem causae pertinentem excurrimus" (italics mine). Emphasis on the need for variety occurs in many of the discussions of romance, as well as generally in discussions of epic. It seems at times to be related to the idea of plenitude—if the poet is a kind of minor god, creating his own world, as he is depicted by Tasso, Scaliger, Sidney, and others, he will imitate the fullness of God's world in his art. Cf., for example, Tasso, *Discorsi dell'arte poetica,* in *Prose diverse,* ed. C. Guasti, I, 44-5; and *Discorsi del poema eroico,* ibid., I, 155.

116. E.g. the instructions for epideictic works in Cicero's *De partitione oratoria,* XXX, 73, advise: "Adhibendaque frequentius etiam illa ornamenta rerum sunt, sive quae admirabilia et nec opinata, sive significata monstris, prodigiis, oraculis, sive quae videbuntur ei de quo agimus accidisse divina atque fatalia."

Chapter IV

1. Joel Spingarn, *A History of Literary Criticism in the Renaissance* (N.Y., 1956), p. 165, calls Patrizi the founder of modern literary history. J. W. H. Atkins, *English Literary Criticism: The Renascence* (London, 1951), p. 30, gives the honor to Politian.

2. ". . . a questo fine imprendiamo a fare, perchè in su la storia fondandoci, e gli argomenti, e gli usi, dell'antica poesia si verrem discoprendo, e da gli usi raccogliendo i veri fini, e da fini le proprie forme, e da queste la varietà, e le materie; e dalle materie i trovati . . . e gli ornamenti tutti. Le quali cose, le poesie de'valenti informarono a que'tempi, e possonle per l'avenir formare, e sopra le quali noi, arte poetica verrem formando, a fine ch'altri intenderne bene a dentro, e nuove poesie possa formar con lode." Francesco Patrizi, *Della poetica, la deca istoriale* (Ferrara, 1586), pp. 2-3.

3. Gerald Else, *Aristotle's Poetics: The Argument* (Cambridge, 1957), pp. 31-33, 66-67.

4. "Quoniam Respublica habet pro fine Deum, et pro conservatore et creatore, primum poema erit nobis sacrum, quemadmodum psalmodia et hymnodia. Non modo David, sed Orpheus, et Homerus laudes (Dei ille, deorum isti) cecinerunt." Tommaso Campanella, in *Opere,* ed. Firpo (Milan, 1954), I, 1054. Cf. George Puttenham, *The Arte of English Poesie,* in ECE, II, 31: "These hymnes to the gods was the first forme of Poesie and the highest the statliest, they were song by the Poets as priests, and by the people or whole congregation, as we sing in our Churches the Psalmes of David. . . ."

5. Puttenham, *The Arte of English Poesie,* in ECE, II, 158.

6. Vernon Hall, *Renaissance Literary Criticism: A Study of Its Social Content* (N.Y., 1945), esp. pp. 37ff. Lodovico Castelvetro, *Poetica d'Aristotele* (Basel, 1576), p. 79, wrote: "Et forse quindi si divise la poesia in due parti, cio è secondo le conditione delle persone . . . cio è o secondo la dispositione dello stato divino, o reale, o dello stato privato, o servile. . . ." And Antonio Minturno, *L'arte poetica* (Venice, 1563), p. 5, asserted, ". . . propriamente l'Epica e la Tragica imitatione sia delle migliori, e delle grandi persone; la Comica e le Satyrica delle peggiori, e delle minori; la Melica di quelle che son degne di laude. . . ."

7. "Non lecito parmi che in essa [tragedy] si debbiano introdurre huomini giusti, e virtuosi, in vitiosi et in inguiusti per adversità della fortuna cangiati, cosa piùtosto scelerata che misera et spaventevole." Bernardino Daniello, *La poetica* (Venice, 1536), p. 38.

8. ". . . rechiede la tragedia persone nè buone nà cattive, ma d'una condizione di mezzo . . . l'epico, a l'incontro, vuole nelle persone il sommo delle virtù. . . ." Torquato Tasso, *Discorsi dell'arte poetica,* in *Prose diverse,* ed. C. Guasti (Florence, 1875), I, 19.

9. ". . . un mer, une forme et image de l'univers," from Jacques Peletier du Mans, *Art poétique* (1555), quoted, E. M. W. Tillyard, *English Epic and its Backgrounds* (London, 1954), p. 235.

10. Tasso, *Prose diverse,* ed. C. Guasti, I, 44-5; Dryden insisted that "A heroic poem, truly such, is undoubtedly the greatest work which the soul of man is capable to perform," in *Essays of John Dryden,* ed. W. P. Ker (Oxford, 1900), II, 154. Concerning Aristotle's preference for tragedy he says, "It is one reason of Aristotle's to prove that Tragedy is the more noble because it turns in a shorter compass. . . . He might prove as well that a mushroom is to be preferred before a peach . . ." (ibid., p. 158).

11. ". . . theologorum ille omnium fortasse et gravissimus, et certe (ut mihi videtur) eloquentissimus Basilius . . . fateretur: totam Homeri poesin laudem esse virtutis." Angelo Politian, *Praefatio in Homerum,* in *Opera* (Lyons, 1546), III, 95.

12. He asserts, "duplex extitisse genus poematis; alterum convitiosum et humile; alterum laudativum, et grave. Et quoniam de laudative, et grave satis constabat, omnes enim norant Odysseam, et Iliada . . ." Francesco Robortello, *Explicationes* (Florence, 1548), p. 36.

13. Castelvetro, *Poetica d'Aristotele,* p. 80.

14. ". . . gravi, e laudatrici de le opere grandi, e de i gloriosi fatti. . . ." Giangiorgio Trissino, *Opere* (Verona, 1729), II, 93.

15. ". . . in laude d'Achille Homero l'Iliada compose: et in laudare Ulysse l'Odyssea . . ." Minturno, *L'arte poetica,* p. 28.

16. ". . . raccontando i fatti da diversi Eroi adoperati. & ciò con proponimento non solo di lodare, et esaltare chi meritato se l'havea, ma anche per muovere altri, con l'altrui esempio . . ." Francesco Patrizi, *Della poetica, la deca istoriale,* p. 229.

17. ". . . poema heroicum, in quo . . . heroum laudes canuntur et omnis hominum exempla contexuntur." Tommaso Campanella, in *Opere,* ed. Firpo, I, 1058.

18. William Camden, *Britannia* (London, 1789), I, 59.

19. Puttenham, *The Arte of English Poesie,* in ECE, II, 43.

20. The first French translation was made in 1370 by Vasque de Luceine. Two Latin

translations were popular, that by Filelfo (pr. 1476) and that by Reuchlin (1495). The Greek text was published by Giunta (Florence, 1516). An English translation was made by John Free (Phrea) in the late fifteenth century. For later translations see H. B. Lathrop, *Translations into English from the Classics* (Madison, 1933), pp. 211, 247.

21. Lathrop, *Translations* p. 247.

22. *Il Libro del Cortegiano,* in *Opere di Castiglione,* eds. Giovanni and Antonio Volpi (Padua, 1733), p. 10. Cicero had called Cyrus an "effigiem iusti imperii" in *Ad Quintum fratrem,* I, i, 8.

23. *The Prince,* tr. Allan Gilbert (Chicago, 1941), XIV, 5. Cf. Francesco Robortello, *Explicationes,* p. 87.

24. Puttenham, *The Arte of English Poesie,* in ECE, II, 43; for the Earl of Sterling, see *Anacrisis,* in *Critical Essays of the Seventeenth Century,* ed. Joel Spingarn (Bloomington, 1957), I, 186-87.

25. Sidney, *Apologie,* in ECE, I, 160, 166, 169, 172, 178, 179, 186.

26. Ibid., 160. The *Cyropaedia* is discussed by Marvin T. Herrick, *The Fusion of Horatian and Aristotelian Criticism* (Urbana, 1946), p. 36.

27. Cf. Scaliger, *Poetices libri septem* (5th ed., 1617), III, xvc: "Hanc disponendi rationem splendidissimam habes in Aethiopica historia Heliodori. Quem librum epico Poetae accuratissime legendum ac quasi pro optimo sibi proponendum." The idea goes back at least to the late classical period when rhetoric permitted parallel verse and prose versions of each poetic type; e.g., the *Opus Paschale* and *Carmen Paschale* of Sedulius. The Earl of Sterling (in *Critical Essays of the Seventeenth Century,* ed. Spingarn, I, 186-88) wrote: "I like not the *Alexander* of *Curtius* so well as the *Cyrus* of *Xenophon,* who made it first appear unto the World with what Grace and Spirit a Poem might be delivered in prose. The *Aethiopian* History of *Heliodorus,* though far inferiour to that for the Weight and State of the Matter . . . yet above it for the Delicacy of the Invention . . . *S.P. Sidney,* as in an Epick Poem, did express such things as both in War and in Peace were fit to be practised by Princes."

28. *Dialogi di Messer Alessandro Lionardi della inventione poetica* . . . (Venice, 1554), p. 25.

29. Cornelius Agrippa, *The Vanity of Arts and Sciences* (London, 1684), p. 31.

30. Tillyard, *English Epic,* p. 51, makes this charge: ". . . in the *Cyropaedia* the hero achieves a monotonous success, there is no hazard because he is too virtuous for the gods to allow him to fail, and he advances in glory with an even and predictable rhythm." On this basis Professor Tillyard dismisses the *Cyropaedia* from the ranks of the epic. This is valid only if one is indifferent to Renaissance theories of epic. Louis Ball, "Minor English Renaissance Epics," *ELH,* I (1934), 76, asserts that Renaissance admiration for the *Cyropaedia* shows "impressive lack of literary theory." In fact, it shows excessive "literary theory."

31. *Fabii Planciadis Fulgentii Opera,* ed. Rudolfus Helm (Leipzig, 1898), p. 87. See above, pp. 33-34.

32. "Magnanimity" is Aristotle's term for the sum of virtue; "justice, courage, temperance, magnificence, magnanimity, liberality, gentleness, prudence, wisdom" are the specific virtues for which a man is to be praised according to the *Rhetoric* (I, 9). Late classical criticism reduced the epic virtues to *sapientia* and *fortitudo,* as in Isidore, *Etymologiarum libri XX,* ed. W. M. Lindsay (Oxford, 1911), I, 39, 9: ". . . heroes appellantur viri quasi aerii et caelo digni propter sapientiam et fortitudinem." Achilles was conventionally interpreted as an example of valor and Ulysses of wisdom, while Aeneas combined the two virtues. Christian authorities often added *pietas* to the list of virtues; e.g., Tasso, *Prose diverse,* ed. Guasti, I, 19: "Si ritrova in Enea l'eccellenza della pietà; della fortezza militare in Achille; della prudenza in Ulisse. . . ." William Webbe, *A Discourse of English Poesie,* in ECE, I, 237, wrote, "Under the person of *Aeneas* he [Virgil] expresseth the valoure of a worthy Captaine and valiaunt Governour. . . ." According to the Earl of Sterling, in *Crital Essays of the Seventeenth Century,* ed. Joel Spingarn, I, 187, the characters of Sidney's *Arcadia* show "the Author, as he was indeed, alike well versed both in Learning and in Arms." John Dryden, *Essays,* ed. W. P. Ker (Oxford, 1900), II, 177-8, remarked, "Of [Aeneas'] character, as a king or as a general, I need say nothing; the whole *Aeneas* is one continued instance of some one or the other of them . . ."; and observed (ibid., p. 179) that Tasso "has split his hero in two: he gave Godfrey piety, and Rinaldo fortitude."

33. In the preface to *Ab urbe condita* and the preface to the *Life of Theseus.*

34. Sir John Harington, *A Preface, or rather a Briefe Apologie of Poetrie,* in ECE, II, 211, observes, "*Virgill* extolled *Aeneas* to please *Augustus,* of whose race he was thought to come; *Ariosto* prayeth *Rogero* to the honours of the house of *Este. . . .*" The point is, of course, commonplace.

35. See esp., M. Y. Hughes, *Virgil and Spenser* ("University of California Publications in English," II [1929]), 365-404, and W. Webb, "Virgil in Spenser's Epic Theory," *ELH,* IV (1937), 62-84.

36. Spenser, *The Poetical Works,* ed. J. C. Smith and E. de Selincourt (Oxford, 1935), p. 458.

37. Ibid. See the following prefatory poems: ii, 5; iv, 8; vi, 16-18; xi, 7-8, 10-11; xii, 6; xiii, 10; xv, 12-14; xix, 14; xx, 1-4, 14 (pp. 409-413).

38. Ibid., p. 3.

39. For discussion of the problem of the letter's relevance, see Josephine Bennett, *The Evolution of the "Faerie Queene"* (Chicago, 1942), and, more recently, A. Hamilton, "Spenser's *Letter to Ralegh,*" *MLN,* LXXIII (1958), 481-85, where the letter's relevance is defended. Also, the reply to Hamilton by W. Owen, "Spenser's *Letter to Ralegh*—a Reply," *MLN,* LXXV (1960), 195-97. The quotations from the letter which follow are from Spenser, *The Poetical Works,* ed. J. C. Smith and E. de Selincourt, pp. 407-8.

40. Their virtues are examined by Viola Hulbert, "Spenser's Twelve Moral Virtues 'According to Aristotle and the Rest,'" *University of Chicago Abstracts, Humanities Series,* III (1926), 479-85; J. J. Jusserand, "Spenser's Twelve Moral Virtues," *MP,* III (1906), 373-83; and F. W. de Moss, "Spenser's Twelve Moral Virtues 'According to Aristotle,'" *MP,* XIV (1918), 23-38.

41. ". . . di formar con parole un perfetto Cortegiano, esplicando tutte le condizioni e particolar qualità che si richieggono a chi merita questo nome." *Cortegiano,* in *Opere,* p. 23.

42. Ibid., p. 10. Like Spenser, Castiglione relied on Aristotle. See Albert Menut, "Castiglione and the *Nicomachean Ethics,*" *PMLA,* LVIII (1943), 309-21.

43. Arthur's sixteenth-century vicissitudes are examined in Chapter IV of Bennett, *Evolution of the "Faerie Queene,"* and Edwin Greenlaw, *Studies in Spenser's Historical Allegory* (Baltimore, 1932).

44. The superiority of Christian to pagan poetry is a platitude of Renaissance criticism. Tasso, *Discorsi dell'arte poetica,* in *Prose diverse,* ed. C. Guasti, I, 14ff., argues that Christian epic is superior because the audience will believe in its miracles. Abraham Cowley, *Poetry and Prose,* ed. L. C. Martin (Oxford, 1949), pp. 71-72, wrote, ". . . those mad stories of the *Gods* and *Heroes,* seem in themselves so ridiculous; yet they were then the *whole body* (or rather *Chaos*) of the theology of those times. . . . There was no other *Religion,* and therefore *that* was better than *none at all.* But to us who have no need of them, to us who deride their *folly,* and are wearied with their *impertinencies. . . .* What can we imagine more proper for the ornaments of *Wit* or *Learning* in the story of *Deucalion,* then in that of Noah. . . ." Although Boileau opposed Christian epic in *L'art poétique,* III, 193ff. Dryden defended it strongly in *Essays,* ed. W. P. Ker, II, 34: "Christian poets have not hitherto been acquainted with their own strength. If they had searched the Old Testament as they ought, they might have found the machines which are proper for their work; and those more certain in their effect, than it may be the New Testament is, in the rules sufficient for salvation."

45. For the problem of topical allusions and their significance (or lack of significance) in *The Faerie Queene,* see Greenlaw, *Studies in Spenser's Historical Allegory.*

46. Spenser says in the *Letter to Raleigh,* "In the end the Lady told him that unless that armour which she brought would serve him (that is the armour of a Christian man specified by Saint Paul v. Ephes.) that he could not succeed in that enterprise. . . ."

47. For *in medias res* during the Renaissance, see John W. Draper, "The Narrative Technique of the *Faerie Queene,*" *PMLA,* XXXIX (1924), 310-24.

48. M. Y. Hughes, "The Christ of *Paradise Regained* and the Renaissance Heroic Tradition," *SP,* XXXV (1938), 254-77, discusses the parallels between the Red Cross Knight and Christ.

49. Cf. Harington, *A Preface,* in ECE, II, 216. Giraldi Cinthio's *Discorsi . . . intorno al comporre dei romanzi . . .* (Venice, 1554) contain a representative treatment of the problem of epic unity. See also W. L. Renwick, *Edmund Spenser* (London, 1925), p. 51.

50. Torquato Tasso, *Discorsi dell'arte poetica,* in *Prose diverse,* ed. C. Guasti, I, 54: "La composizione, che è la terza parte dello stile, avrà del magnifico, se saranno lunghi i periodi,

e lunghi i membri, de'quali il periodo è composto. E per questo la stanza è più capace di questo eroico che il terzette. . . ."

51. ". . . convenit heroicum carmen his, nec de est unitas, cum ad unam finem et consimilia exemplariter conglobentur, nec magnitudo. . . . Nam et qui unius generis sunt et ad unae reipublicae conditionem fortunamque dicendam spectant, faciunt unitatem: similiter et qui tamquam exemplaria unius, quamvis et diversis nationibus accersuntur, faciunt unitatem, ut in *Triumpho Pudicitiae* omnes pudici. . . ." Tommaso Campanella, *Opere,* ed. Luigi Firpo, I, 1092.

52. Webbe, *A Discourse of English Poetrie,* in ECE, I, 239; Puttenham, *The Arte of English Poesie,* in ECE, II, 64; Francis Meres, *A Comparison of English Poets,* in ECE, II, 319.

53. David Masson, *Drummond of Hawthorndon* (London, 1873), p. 84.

54. "Si cantarono poi le cose animate come effetti del gran Iddio, le quali sono mezzi a conoscerlo e lodarlo, non potendosi far più gusto ad un artefice, che guardare le sue opere con ammirazione e dichiarare agli altri con che virtù e magistero sono fatte. . . ." Campanella, *Opere,* ed. Firpo, I, 318.

55. E.g., Gabriello Chiabrera, in *Canzonetti, rime varie, dialoghi,* ed Luigi Negri (Turin, 1952), p. 522: "Virgilio compose la Georgica col verso esametro, onde possiamo affermare che al la *Coltivazione* si voglia dare quel verso il quale egli diede all'*Avarchide,* si come Virgilio le diede quel dell'*Eneide.*"

56. For the *laus quattuor temporum* and other topics of natural description see E. R. Curtius, *European Literature and the Latin Middle Ages,* tr. W. Trask (London, 1953), pp. 183-202. See also A. D. McKillop, *The Background of Thompson's Seasons* (Minneapolis, 1942); and Robert Aubin, *Topographical Poetry in the XVIII Century* (N.Y., 1934).

57. ". . . scrive il Poeta . . . accompagnando convenevolmente le cose, che portano con esso loro il vitio, con l'horribile, et col miserabile . . . purga gli animi nostri da simili passioni, et ci desta alla vertù, come si vede nella definitione, che da Aristotele della Tragedia. . . ." Giraldi Cinthio, *Discorsi,* p. 58. He adds (p. 59), ". . . l'officio adunque del nostro Poeta, quanto ad indurre il costume, è lodare le attioni virtuose, et biasmare i vitii et col terribile et miserabile porgli in odio a chi lui legge."

58. The *Margites* and the *Iliad* are the standard Renaissance examples of admonitory epic. The lack of an established label for the form is illustrated by Tasso's reference to ". . . una specie di poesia narrativa, la quale in comparazione della comedia è come l'Iliada parogonata a la tragedia, perchè in lei s'imitano le cose brutte, come fece Omero nel Margite . . ." (*Discorsi del poema eroico,* in *Prose diverse,* ed. C. Guasti, I, 82). For the parallels and contrasts between tragedy and comedy, see below, p. 104. For the *Iliad* as admonitory epic, compare Dryden's comment in *Essays,* ed. W. P. Ker, II, 159: "If the hero's chief quality be vicious, as, for example, the choler and obstinate desire of venegeance in Achilles, yet the moral is instructive; and besides, we are informed in the very proposition of the *Iliad,* that this anger was pernicious; that it brought a thousand ills on the Grecian camp. . . . We abhor those actions while we read them; and what we abhor, we never imitate. The poet only shows them as rocks or quicksands, to be shunned." (Note the parallel between Dryden's "abhor" and Cinthio's theories in note 57.) Other epics considered admonitory are Lucan's *Pharsalia,* depicting the tragic ruin of *Respublica;* and Daniel's *Civil Wars,* which did for England what Lucan did for Rome. See Tillyard, *English Epic,* p. 324. Occasionally it was suggested that the ancients usually presented vice allegorically in the form of monsters whose exterior deformity was emblematic of their depravity. Thomas Hobbes ("Answer to Davenant," in *Critical Essays of the Seventeenth Century,* II, 64) remarked on "the uncomliness of representing in great persons the inhumane vice of Cruelty or the sordid vice of Lust and Drunkenness. To such parts as those the Ancient approved Poets thought it fit to suborn, not the persons of men, but of monsters and beastly Giants, such as *Polyphemus, Cacus,* and the *Centaures.*" In the light of the obvious kinship of admonitory epic and tragedy it is noteworthy that Hobbes goes on to say that when the poet desired to describe depraved *men,* the Muse "should maidenly advise the Poet to set such persons to sing their own vices upon the Stage, for it is not so unseemly in a *Tragedy.*" The idea of admonitory epic was sufficiently commonplace in the eighteenth century to form the basis of the ironic "Author's Preface" of Fielding's *Joseph Andrews.*

59. Jessie Crossland, "Lucan in the Middle Ages," *MLR,* XXV (1930), 32-35.

60. *Essays of John Dryden,* ed. W. P. Ker, I ("Of Heroic Plays").

61. In *Critical Essays of the Seventeenth Century,* ed. Spingarn, II, 17. For discussion, see H. H. Perkinson, "The Epic in Five Acts," *SP,* XLIII (1946), 465-81.

62. *De comoedia,* in *Donatus,* ed. Paul Wessner (Leipzig, 1902), i, V, 7.

63. ". . . riprendere i vizi de'tiranni," Tommaso Campanella, in *Opere,* ed. Firpo, I, 319.

64. Puttenham, *The Arte of English Poesie,* in ECE, II, 34.

65. Philip Sidney, *An Apologie for Poetrie,* in ECE, I, 177; also Webbe, *A Discourse,* in ECE, I, 249; and Harington, *A Preface,* in ECE, II, 210.

66. Sidney, *Apologie,* in ECE, I, 170; also Puttenham, *The Arte of English Poesie,* in ECE, II, 34-35.

67. *Essays of John Dryden,* ed. W. P. Ker, I, 150. Compare Corneille, *Oeuvres* (Paris, 1854), XII, 261: "La succès heureux de la vertu, en dépit des traverses et des périls, nous excite à l'embrasser; et le succès funeste du crime ou de l'injustice est capable de nous en augmenter l'horreur naturelle, par l'appréhension d'un pareil malheur." Tasso, *Discorsi del poema eroico* in *Prose diverse,* ed. C. Guasti, I, 115, observed that when the epic and tragic poet treat the same figure "è da loro considerata diversamente e con vari rispetti. Considera l'epico in Ercole, in Teseo, in Agamennone, in Aiace, in Pirro, il valore e l'eccellenza dell'armi; gli risguarda il tragico come caduti per qualche errore nell'infelicita."

68. The manuscript is conveniently summarized by J. H. Hanford, in *A Milton Handbook* (N.Y., 1932), pp. 164-68. Allan Gilbert, "The Cambridge Manuscript and Milton's Plans for an Epic," *SP,* XVI (1919), 172-76, argues against undue emphasis on the manuscript.

69. Arthur Barker, "Structural Pattern in *Paradise Lost,*" PQ, XXVIII (1949), 17-30.

70. "Original and Progress of Satire," *Essays of John Dryden,* ed. W. P. Ker, II, 89.

71. *Spectator,* No. 267.

72. The analogues to *Paradise Lost* are listed in Watson Kirkconnell, *The Celestial Cycle* (Toronto, 1952).

73. Juvencus, *Evangeliorum libri VI* (Migne, *Pat. Lat.,* XIX, 58-59); Sedulius, *Carmen paschale* (Migne, *Pat. Lat.,* XIX, 553-55); Aldhelm, *Opera, MHG* (Berlin, 1919), XV, 97.

74. Harvey's note is reprinted in ECE, I, 359 (note for page 48, line 17).

75. A. O. Lovejoy, "Milton and the Paradox of the Fortunate Fall," *ELH,* IV (1937), 161-79. The parallels noted in the text between *Paradise Lost* and Book I of *The Faerie Queene* were first observed by Edwin Greenlaw in "A Better Teacher than Aquinas," *SP,* XIV (1917), 214-17, where they are adduced as proof of Spenser's influence on Milton. Direct influence can certainly not be discounted, but I believe that the pressure of similar critical theories is a more important factor, especially in view of the differences between the narrative materials used by the two poets.

76. Milton, *Reason of Church Government,* in *Works,* ed. F. A. Patterson *et al.* (N.Y., 1931-42), III, Pt. i, 238.

77. William Farnham, *The Medieval Heritage of Elizabethan Tragedy* (Berkeley, 1936); introduction to the *Mirror for Magistrates,* ed. L. B. Campbell (Cambridge, 1938); and L. B. Campbell, *Tudor Conceptions of History and Tragedy in "A Mirror for Magistrates"* (Berkeley, 1936). For a moral tradition, see esp. J. V. Cunningham, *Woe or Wonder* (Denver, 1951); and for the psychological explanation of the tragic flaw, L. B. Campbell, *Shakespeare's Tragic Heroes, Slaves of Passion* (Cambridge, 1930).

78. Thomas Heygood, *An Apology for Actors,* ed. R. H. Perkinson (N.Y., 1941), $F3^v$.

79. Puttenham, *Arte of English Poesie,* in ECE, II, 36.

80. T. W. Baldwin, *Shakespeare's Five Act Structure* (Urbana, 1947), demonstrates conclusively the influence of Terentian structure on Shakespeare, especially in regard to the use of protasis, epitasis, catastasis (Scaliger's addition to classical terminology), and catastrophe. The epideictic structure stressed in the text is not, I feel, in any way inconsistent with Baldwin's findings. In fact, the two are supplementary. Terentian conventions helped the Elizabethan dramatist to time the events of the play. Epideictic conventions helped him to select his materials and shape them for maximum emphasis on a unifying theme The essay by Euanthius on tragedy and comedy, a source for the idea that these forms are "reprehension," was commonly printed with the commentaries of Donatus and often in editions of Terence. Book III of Thomas Heywood's *Apology for Actors* clearly illustrates the fusion by its direct borrowings from Euanthius.

81. "Laudare et pregare," Minturno, *L'arte poetica,* p. 171. Lyric is defined (ibid., p. 5) as imitation of "quelle che sono degne di laude."

82. "Quoniam laude digni alii insignites ob beneficia populo praestita et virtutis ostensionem in morte, vel actione praeclare, sicuti sancti et heroes, proptereaque inventi sunt hymni, et odi, et quae lyra canimus carmina." Campanella, *Opere,* ed. Firpo, I, 1054.

83. "Materia carminis lirici primo fuit in argumento gravi. Ut sunt laudes deorum, vel heroum," G. G. Vossius, *De artis poeticae natura* (Amsterdam, 1647), p. 65.

84. Sidney, *Apologie,* in ECE, I, 178.

85. Ibid., 179.

86. ". . . mihi videtur hoc tam iucundo carmine, vel in convivio, vel in ludis, qui quidem laudatur, inflammari ad id gerendum, quo magis laudari possit. Qui vero audit, excitari, ut eum se praestet, qui tantundem mereat laudationes, cum plane uterque arbitretur in laude summum esse positum praemium virtutis . . . ad res honestas, atque praeclaras hominem [lyricus] impellat," *De poeta,* p. 381.

87. Thomas Lodge, *Defence of Poetry,* in ECE, I, 71.

88. Milton, *Paradise Regained,* IV, 335ff. Cf. George Sandys, *Works,* ed. Richard Harper (London, 1872), I, ixxi: "Sion transcends Parnassus, and the stone / Moses cleft flows more than Helicon. . . . All poetry had but one Sacred Spring / A quire of angels. . . ." Moses was often called the Christian *ur*-poet because of the poems in *Exodus* 15: 1-21, and *Deuteronomy* 32 and 33.

89. Jerome, in *A Select Library of the Nicene and Post-Nicene Fathers 2nd Series,* ed. Philip Schaff (N.Y., 1905), VI, 484.

90. Ibid., p. 101. Cf. Petrarch, *Le familiari,* ed. Vittorio Rossi (Florence, 1934), X, 4

91. Milton, *Reason of Church Government,* in *Works,* ed. F. A. Patterson *et al.,* III, Pt. i, 238.

92. Israel Baroway, "The Lyre of David," *ELH,* XIII (1946), 119-42, discusses efforts to reduce the psalms to metrical regularity.

93. The influence of the psalms on lyric poetry is traced by Samuel Singer, *Die Religiöse Lyrick des Mittelalters: das Nachleben der Psalmen* (Bern, 1933).

94. Still a good treatment of English psalm-writing is Thomas Warton, *History of English Poetry* (London, 1840), III, 143ff. For more recent discussion, see John Gillinan, *The Evolution of the English Hymn* (N.Y., 1927), 141ff., and the discussion s.v. *psalters, English* in Julian, *Dictionary of Hymnology* (London, 1892). L. B. Campbell devotes two chapters of *Divine Poetry in Sixteenth-Century England* (Berkeley, 1959), pp. 34-54, to the subject.

95. *Expositions on the Book of Psalms* in *A Select Library of the Nicene and Post-Nicene Fathers,* VIII, 665 (comment on Psalm 147). The habit of etymology is responsible for the critical theory. *Psalm* is from Hebrew *hallel*—"song of praise." The Heberw title was, however, usually restricted to Psalms 143 to 148. In another medieval definition we learn, "Psalmus autem est . . . quo divina praeconia canebantur; canticum quod supernas laudes humanis vocibus personabat." Quoted in R. L. Ramsey and James Bright, "Notes on the Introductions of the West Saxon Psalms," *Journal of Theological Studies,* XIII (1912), 532.

96. Vulgate, II, Par. vii, 6.

97. Comment on Psalm 149 in *A Select Library of the Nicene and Post-Nicene Fathers,* VIII, 677.

98. E.g., "Hymus est canticum laudantium quod de Graece in Latinum laus interpretatur, pro se quod sit carmen laetitiae et laus." Isidore, *Etymologiarum libri XX,* ed. W. M. Lindsay (Oxford, 1911), VI, xix, 17. Julian's *Dictionary of Hymnology,* s.v. *Latin Hymnology* quotes the definition of Gregory of Nazianus: "Modulata laus est hymnus"; and the comment in the *Anglo-Latin Hymnary:* "It is clear that David the prophet first composed and sang hymns, then the other prophets; afterwards, the three youths when cast into the furnace. . . . Whatever poems, then, are sung in praise of God, are called hymns. A hymn, moreover, is of those who sing and praise, which from the Greek into Latin is interpreted *laus,* because it is a song of joy and praise; but properly hymns are those containing praise of God." Concerning later forms: "In the XI, XII centuries hymns were no longer confined to direct worship and praise of the Creator, of Christ, of the Holy Ghost; to the honours of the Blessed Virgin, and of the Apostles and certain principal saints . . . they became amplified and refined into eulogies, descriptions of, and meditations upon, the Passion and Wonds of Christ, on His sacred coun-

tenance, on His cross, on the vanity of life, on the joys of Paradise, on the Terrors of judgment . . . most especially into the praises of the Blessed Virgin, on her dignity, on her Joys, and Dolours. . . ." The hymns of Wither's period are examined in F. J. Gillinan, *Evolution of the English Hymn*, 160ff. In the preface to his hymns Masson says, "If I were a Nightingale I would sing like a Nightingale, but now that I am a Man, I will sing the praises of God as long as I live . . ." (ibid., p. 171).

99. E.g., J. H. Chaytor, *The Troubadours* (Cambridge, 1912), p. 17: "The troubadour who knew his business would begin with the praises of his beloved; she is physically and morally perfect, her beauty illuminates the night. . . . The effects of this love are obvious on his person. His voice quavers with supreme delight or breaks in dark despair; he sighs and weeps and wakes at night to think of this one object of contemplation." So Alfred Jeanroy, *La poésie lyrique des Troubadours* (Paris, 1934), II, 94-115; esp. 106-7; so also John Rutherford, *The Troubadours* (London, 1873), pp. 34-39.

100. Karl Vossler, *Die Gottliche Komodie: Entwicklungsgeschichte und Erklarung* (Heidelberg, 1908), II, i, 719-20.

101. The *laudesi* are discussed in G. Bertoni, *Il duecento* (Milan, 1951), pp. 213-34. The most important of the *laudesi* is Jacopone da Todi; his *Laude* are available in the edition of G. Ferri (Bari, 1930). Curiously, during the revival of the *stil novo* in the late fifteenth century, the *lauda* also briefly regained popularity. Lorenzo de'Medici composed *laude* in which Florentine Neoplatonism mixes exotically with traditional devotional motifs. Thes are available in the second volume of his *Opere*, ed. Attilio Simioni (Bari, 1913).

102. Cino da Pistoia, *I rimatori del dolce stil novo*, ed. G. Ceriello (Milan, 1950), p. 223; G. Volpi, *Il trecento* (Milan, 1912), p. 31.

103. Charles Singleton, *An Essay on the Vita Nuova* (Cambridge, 1949), pp. 20-23.

104. Petrarch, *Canzoniere*, ed. Michele Scherillo (Milan, 1918), p. 111 (Sonnet iv).

105. ". . . propuosi di prendere per materea de lo mio parlare sempre mai quello che fosse loda di questa gentilissima . . ." Dante, *Vita Nuova*, ed. Magugliani (Milan, 1952), p. 40 (Section XVIII).

106.

"Quando io movo i sospiri a chiamar voi
E'l nome che nel cor mi scrisse Amore,
Laudando s'incommincia udir di fore
Il suon de'primi dolci accenti suoi. . . ."

(Petrarch, *Canzoniere*, ed. M. Scherillo, Sonnet v).

Compare cclxv, 11, 84-5: L'angelica sembianza umile e piana/ Ch'or quinci or quidi udia tanto lodarsi . . ."; clxxxiii: "Etella diforme, e fato sol qui reo,/ Commise [Laura] a tal, che'l suo bel nome adora./ Ma forse sceme sue lode parlando"; and ccliv: "Dammi signor, ch'l mio dir giunga la segno/ De le sue lode, ove per se non sale. . . ."

107. "Cantuncules inanes, falsis et obscoenis mulercularum laudibus refertae," Petrarch, *Le familiari*, ed. Vittorio Rossi, X, 5.

108. "Loda il Petrarcha la sua donna per tutto il canzoniere dalla nobilità del sangue, dall'ingegno, dall'animo . . . che la maggior parte delle sue rime sono ordite all subbio di questo genere dimonstrativo . . . le parole, le lettere, le sillabe, i semplici articoli non che gli interi versi o compositioni del poeta, [sono] pieni delle lodi di Laura," *Ragionamenti della lingua Toscana* (Venice, 1545), pp. 168-69. For Petrarch's influence see Antèro Meozzi, *Il Petrarchismo Europeo*, Parte Prima: Secolo XVI (Pisa, 1934).

109. Vossler, *Die Gottliche Komodie*, II, i, 692, ascribes the abstracting tendency to Guittone d'Arezzo: "Guittone aber lasst auch die letzten Reste der Körperlichkeit verschwinden. Nur diejenigen Teile, die mit der Theorie der Minne verknupft sind, halt er fest: das Herz, welches als Wohnung, und die Augen, welches als Fenster oder auch Schlupfloch des Liebesgottes nicht wohl zu entbehren waren. So hat er wenigstens negativ, durch Enthebung der Lame, die symbolische und mystische Auffassung des Minnedienstes, den *dolce stil nuovo* und die Apotheose Beatricens vorbereitet."

110. "Il morire della donna amata nei canti di questi poeti corrisponde, nella mistica del medio evo, al morire della ragione umana nel rapimento e nell'estasi della mente, al morire, insomma . . . di Rachele, la quale muore misticamente per levarsi alla somma contemplazione," Bertoni, *Il duecento*, p. 290.

111. ". . . se lo amore ha in se quella perfezione che già habbiamo detto, è impossible venir a tale perfezione se prima non si muore," Lorenzo de'Medici, in *Opere,* ed, Simioni, I, 24. Cf. Singleton, *An Essay on the Vita Nuova,* p. 96: "In the *Vita Nuova* . . . we must see the death of Beatrice, the last of the three subject matters, as the cause of the other two. That is, the new life has commenced before the composition of the poem from Dante's 'libro della memoria,' and part of that new life will consist in writing about the old one." A study of this pattern in Lorenzo de'Medici is offered by Angelo Lipari, *The Dolce Stil Nuovo According to Lorenzo de'Medici* (New Haven, 1936). For further discussion, see the section on the *Canzoniere,* below, Chapter VI.

112. Bernardino Daniello, *La poetica,* pp. 27-28. Although Renaissance authors like Cinthio, Tasso, Bacon, and Hobbes occasionally complained against excessive allegory, none was consistent, and it appears that all retained a fondness for it.

113. George Gascoigne, *Certayne Notes of Instruction,* in ECE, I, 48.

114. Gabriel Harvey, *Against Thomas Nash,* in ECE, II, 259.

115. "Dolci durezze," *Canzoniere,* ed. Scherillo, lxi, lxxii, cccli, etc.

116. Lorenzo de'Medici, in *Opere,* ed. Simioni, I, 51f.

117. "Hymne to Heavenly Beautie," ll. 295-98. Cf. Sidney on lyric, *Apologie,* in ECE, I, 201.

118. There are three useful discussions of the history of the ode: G. Carducci, "Dello Svolgimento dell'Ode in Italia," in *Opere* (Bologna, n.d.), XVI, 363-452; George Shuster, *The English Ode from Milton to Keats* (N.Y., 1940), esp. pp. 1-109; and Carol Maddison, *Apollo and the Nine* (Baltimore, 1960). I do not wish to imply that the Pindaric was the *only* alternative to Petrarchan lyric. Horatian, elegiac, and Anacreontic lyrics, as well as native vernacular forms, abound in Renaissance poetry. The point is that critics usually distinguished between the "noble" lyric, of which the Pindaric is the supreme example, the "love lyric" on the Petrarchan model, and various lower forms which are, in Puttenham's words, "not alwayes of the gravest or of any great commoditie or profit, but rather in some sort vaine, dissolute, or wanton, so be it not very scandalous & of evill example" (*The Arte of English Poesie,* in ECE, II, 25).

119. Gilbert Highet, *The Classical Tradition* (N.Y., 1957), p. 242.

120. Comment in Shuster, *The English Ode,* p. 137.

121. E.g., Lorenzo de'Medici, *Opere,* ed. Simioni, I, 22: "È sentenza di Platone che il narrare brevemente e dilucidamente molte cose non solo pare mirabile tra gli uomini, ma quasi cosa divina. La brevità del sonneto non comporta che una sola parola sia vana; ed il vero subietto e materia de'sonetti per questa ragione debbe essere qualche acuta o gentile sentenzia narrata attamente ed in pochi versi ristretta, fuggendo la oscurità e durezza. Ha grande similitudine e conformità questo modo di stile, con l'epigramma, quanto all'acumo della materia e alla destrezza dello stile, ma è degno e capace il sonetto di sentenzie più gravi, e però diventa tanto più difficile."

122. "Lo stile del lirico poi, se bene non così magnifico come l'eroico, molto più deve essere fornito ed ornato: la qual forma di dire fiorita (come i retorici affermano) è propria della mediocrità. Fiorito deve essere lo stile del lirico; e perchè più spesso appare la persona del poeta, e perchè le materie che si pigliano a trattare per lo più sono, le quali inornate di fiore e di scherzi, vili ed abietti si rimarrebbono," Tasso, *Discorsi dell'arte poetica, Prose diverse* ed. C. Guasti, I, 51. In the "Considerazioni sopra Tre Canzoni di M. Gio. Battista Pigna," ibid., II, 81, Tasso discusses the "noble" lyric which aspires to heroic status because of its "magnificence" of style and subject matter. Compare also Gabriello Chiabrera's fourth dialogue on poetry in *Canzonetti, rime varie, dialoghi,* ed. Luigi Negri (Turin, 1952), pp. 570-74.

123. Puttenham, *The Arte of English Poesie,* in ECE, II, 158.

124. A standard treatment of the subject is that by Euanthius, *De comoedia,* in *Donatus,* ed. Paul Wessner, I, 13-31. For discussion, A. P. McMahon, *Seven Questions on Aristotelian Definitions of Tragedy and Comedy* ("Harvard Studies in Classical Philology," XL [Cambridge, 1929]), 99-198.

125. Puttenham, *The Arte of English Poesie,* in ECE, II, 33.

126. ". . . cum vellent male viventes notare, in vicos et compita ex omnibus locis laeti alacresque veniebant ibique cum nominibus singulorum vitia publicabant, unde nomen compositum, ut comoedia vocaretur." Euanthius, *De comoedia,* V, 6.

127. ". . . universorum delicta corripiunt; nec vetabatur eis pessimum quumque describere, nec cuiuslibet peccata moresque reprehendere." Isidore, *Etymologiarum libri XX,* ed. Lindsay, VIII, vii, 7.

128. "I comici . . . parimente tirarono i vitii, et l'attioni in rise, et in isciocchezza," Lodovico Castelvetro, *Poetica d'Aristotele,* p. 80.

129. Lodge, *Defence of Poetry,* in ECE, I, 81.

130. Sidney, *Apologie,* in ECE, I, 177.

131. Ben Jonson, in *Critical Essays of the Seventeenth Century,* ed. Joel Spingarn, I, 58.

132. "Induction," ll. 115-20. The whole passage suggests the tone of the *comoedia vetus* rather than the *comoedia nova.*

133. "Biasmatori di vitii senza tirargli a sciocchezza," Castelvetro, *Poetica d'Aristotele,* p. 80.

134. The full passage reads: "Quoniam scelerosi insignes aliquando sunt in mundo, quorum vituperatio reipublicae prodest valde, propterea satira inventum est, vitiorum execrativa," Tommaso Campanella, *Opere,* ed. Firpo, I, 1056.

135. Puttenham, *The Arte of English Poesie,* in ECE, II, 32.

Chapter V

1. George Puttenham, *The Arte of English Poesie,* in ECE, II, 28-55.

2. The moral is that the life of rural retirement is best. Compare Statius, "Villa Surrentina Pollii Felicis,"' *Silvae,* II, ii. For a discussion of the possibilities of the genre see Ruth Wallerstein's discussion of Marvell's "Upon Appleton House" and "The Garden" in *Seventeenth Century Poetic* (Madison, 1950), pp. 295ff. Jonson's attitudes are different from Marvell's, but there is an important continuity observable.

3. Donne, *Poetical Works,* ed. Sir Herbert Grierson (Oxford, 1953), I, 179-80.

4. Cf. F. W. Weitzmann, "A Note on the Elizabethan 'Elegie,'" *PMLA,* L (1935), 435-43; A. L. Bennett, "The Principal Rhetorical Conventions of the Renaissance Personal Elegy," *SP,* LI (1954), 107-25.

5. Theodore Burgess, *Epideictic Literature* ("University of Chicago Studies in Classical Philology," Vol. III [Chicago, 1902]), p. 148. The principal source for the tradition of verse epitaph, or funeral elegy, is Latin, and as follows: Catullus, No. 101 (on the death of his brother; cf. also 65 and 68, where the theme is also treated)—Virgil, *Eclogues,* V, 20-44 (lament for the death of Daphnis—probably Julius Caesar—in the normal pastoral elegy manner); V, 56-80 (also on Daphnis, discussing his deification); *Aeneid,* VI, 867-85 (lament for Marcellus, son of Octavia); *Virgilian Appendix,* "Maecenas" (generally considered two poems rather than one after Scaliger's original emendation; only very doubtfully Virgilian on the basis of their poor quality)—Horace, *Odes,* I, 24 (on the death of Quintilius; quite pessimistic); Propertius, III, 7 (lament for the death at sea of Paetus, a friend of the poet, and a possible influence on *Lycidas*); III, 18 (lament for the death of Marcellus, son of Octavia, at Baiae); IV, 11 (a consolation spoken to Pantus by his dead wife's spirit)—Ovid, *Amores,* III, 9 (a lament for the death of Tibullus; markedly pessimistic); *Ex Ponto,* I, 9 (on the death of his friend, Celsus; very poor in quality); *Consolatio ad Liviam* and *Epicedion Drusi* (repr. in Loeb, *Heroides;* probably humanistic forgeries); Martial, V, 34, 37; VI, 85 (brief epitaphs influenced by the *Greek Anthology*)—Statius, *Silvae,* II 1 (see text, pp. 119-20); II, 6; III, 3; V, 1, 2, 5 (the last of these is incomplete). Of these sources, the dominant one was Statius, who developed the form to its fullest classical elaboration and exerted much influence on later Christian Latin writers, as well as having great prestige in the Renaissance after Politian's "Oratio super Quintiliano, et Statii Sylvis," and his edition.

6. Thomas Wilson, for example, treats consolation as a separate, demonstrative form: *Arte of Rhetorique,* ed. G. H. Mair (London, 1909), pp. 65-84.

7. Scaliger, *Poetices libri septem* (5th ed., 1617), III, cxxi: "Est igitur, Epitaphum aut recens aut anniversarium. In recenti partes hae: Laudes, iacturae, demonstratio, luctus, consolatio, exhortatio. In anniversario haec eadem omnia, praeter luctum. Nemo enim iam annum bienniumve defunctum deflet. . . . Laudes non solum mortui, sed etiam mortis. quemadmodum fecimus nos in eorum Epitaphio qui ad Viennam bello Turcico occumbere. Iactura demonstratur suave primum, mox incitatiore narratione, in qua immortatio et amplificatio auget amissae rei desiderium. a qua parte statim luctus . . . amisso namque tam

gloriae claro pignore, nihil aliud quam lugendum. Post hoc est consolatio aggredienda. Tam grave dammum sarciri posse, puta amisso Rege, successoris virtutibus. Cuius laudes accerima, sed brevi explicatione exitabis . . . Claudendum Poema exhortationibus: tantum abesse, ut illi sint lugendi, ut eorum praesens felicitas, quae superstitibus obtegit, non contemnenda: illorum virtus, animus, exitus sit exoptandus."

8. Antonio Minturno, *De poeta* (Venice, 1559), pp. 407f., distinguishes three types of elegy on the basis of the speaker of the poem: ". . . sive se ipsum poeta, sive alterum fingit, qui queratur, et quod triste, luctuosumve est, exprimat. . . . Mixtum autem hoc dicendi genus cum sit, poeta runc suum tenet, nunc alienam summit personam. . . . Quod vero plerumque fit, est ubi nemo alius, quam poeta ipse loquatur."

9. Puttenham, *The Arte of English Poetie,* in ECE, II, 50, compares the poet to a "Paracelsian" who cures *"similia similibus,"* i.e., "one short sorrowing [becomes] the remedie of a long and grievous sorrow."

10. For a true Renaissance lament see Politian's "Monodia in Laurentium Medicem, Intonata per Arrighum Isac," *Opere* (Lyons, 1546), III, 319-20.

11. Cf. for example, Thomas Wilson, *Arte of Rhetorique,* ed. G. H. Mair (Oxford, 1909), p. 66: "Those harmes should be moderately borne, which must neede happen to every one, that have chaunced to any one. As Death, which spareth non, either King nor Keisar, neither poore nor riche. Therefore, to be inpacient for the losse of our frends, is to fall out with God, because he made us men and not Angels. But the Godly (I trust) will alwaies remit the order of things, to the will of God, and force their passions to obeie necessitie."

12. Wilson, *Arte of Rhetorique,* ed. Mair, pp. 11-12. For classical sources, see Aristotle, *Rhetoric,* I, 9: Aphthonius, *Progymnasmata,* tr. R. Agricola (Amsterdam, 1665), pp. 180ff.; Quintilian, *Institutio Oratoria,* III, 7.

13. Wilson, *Arte of Rhetorique,* ed. Mair, p. 13.

14. Thus Statius, *Silvae,* V, 3, claims that he can never properly celebrate his father. He solves the problem only by the conceit of having his dead father speak through his mouth. The topic goes back to the Greek rhetoricians. Cf. E. R. Curtius, *European Literature and the Latin Middle Ages,* tr. W. Trask (London, 1953), pp. 159ff.

15. Cf. Curtius, *European Literature,* pp. 162-65. (Curtius calls this "outdoing.")

16. Although it is not true lament, Horace's comment on death is anything but Christian affirmation, and to modern ears, at least, extremely gloomy: ". . . levius fit patientia / Quidquid corrigere est nefas" is his answer to the problem of death (*Odes,* I, 24, ll. 19-20).

17. A penetrating analysis of pastoral elegy is given by Ruth Wallerstein, *Seventeenth Century Poetic* (Madison, 1950), pp. 63ff. The studies of themes, conventions, and patterns are innumerable if articles on *Lycidas* be included. A good collection of pastoral elegies, with a general essay, is T. P. Harrison, *The Pastoral Elegy: An Anthology* (Austin, 1939).

18. The chief classical examples of *consolatio* are by Cicero and Seneca. For Cicero, *Brutus,* I, 9; *Tusculans,* I and III; *Familiares,* IV, 5; V, 16. For Seneca, *Dialogues,* VI (*Ad Marciam*); XI (*Ad Polybium*). Cf. also the pseudo-Ovidian *Consolatio ad Liviam.*

19. Wilson, *Arte of Rhetorique,* ed. Mair, p. 65.

20. Summarized from *Arte of Rhetorique,* ed. Mair, pp. 116-23. Cf. Bennett, "Principal Rhetorical Conventions," pp. 116-23.

21. Virgil, *Ecologue* V, ll. 56-80. For a beautiful expression of Virgil's mature ideas, *Aeneid,* VI, 719-51.

22. Bishop Jewel, *Works,* ed. Ayre (Cambridge, 1847), II, 865-66.

23. F. J. Raby, *Christian Latin Poetry* (Oxford, 1953), p. 105. For more on Paulinus, see T. R. Glover, *Life and Letters in the Fourth Century* (N.Y., 1924), 121-24; and P.C. de Labriolle, *Latin Christianity,* tr. H. Wilson (N.Y., 1925), pp. 329-32.

24. Statius, *Silvae,* ed. Henri Clouard (Paris, n.d.), pp. 66-79.

25. Ibid., II, i, ll. 218-19; "Quidquid init ortus, finem timet: ibimus omnes,/ Ibimus: immensis urnam quatit Aeacus ulnis."

26. The lines follow: "Sed tamen et nobis superest operam dare qua te/ possimus simili simplicitate sequi./ Tum nostro socio poterimus vivere Celso/ dulce et aeternum pignore esse pars" (Migne, *Pat. Lat.,* LXI, 676ff., ll. 627-30).

27. Statius, *Silvae,* II, i, ll. 203-5: ". . . quae munera mollis / Elysii, steriles ramos, mutasque volucres / Porgit, et obtuso pallentes germine flores."

28. Paulinus, *Panegyricus,* 585-88: ". . . cum Bethlaeis infantibus in paradiso/ quos malus Herodes percutit invidia,/ Inter odoratum ludit nemus atque coronas / texit honorandis praemia martyribus."

29. Statius, *Silvae,* II, i, ll. 87-95.

30. The following lines are based on this device: 80-95, 96-100, 111-20, 124-25, 141-46, 180-84. A similar, or perhaps still more pronounced dependence on this technique is found in II, vi.

31. Martial, *Epigrams,* V, 37, ll. 1-17: "Puella senibus dulcior mihi cygnis/ agna Galaesi mollior Phalantini,/ concha Lucrini delicatior stagni/ cui nec lapillos praeferas Erythraeos/ nec modo politum pecudis Indicae dentem/ nivesque primas liliumque non tactum;/ Quae crine vicit Baetici gregis vellus/ Rhenique nodos aureamque nitellam;/ fragravit ore quod rosarium Paesti,/ quod Atticarum prima mella cerarum,/ quod sucinorum rapta de manu gleba;/ cui comparatus indecens erat pavo,/ inamabillis sciurus et frequens phoenix/ adhuc recenti tepet Erotion busto,/ quam pessimorum lex amara fatorum/ sexta peregit hieme, nec tamen tota,/ nostros amores gaudiumque lususque." This epitaph was especially popular for obvious reasons. Politian uses its technique in his lyric piece, "D. Anli. Puella," *Opera,* III, 306-9, where the devices of Martial are rather strangely mixed with the diminutives of Hadrian's "Animula vagula blandula." Later, Jonson uses the epitaph's imagery in his "Celebration of Charis" ("Her Triumph," ll. 21-31). See Skuli Johnson, "The Obituary Epigrams in Martial," *The Classical Journal,* XLIX (1949), 265-72, for Martial's themes and techniques in his other epitaphs.

32. Virgil, in *Maecenas,* ll. 141-44: ". . . nunc ego quod possum: 'Tellus, levus ossa teneto/ pendula librato pondus et ipsa tuom./ semper serta tibi dabimus, tibi semper odores./ non umquam sitiens, florida semper eris.' " The 'sit tibi terra levis' theme strikes the true epitaph note. It is very common. See, for example, Martial, *Epigrams,* V, 34, ll. 4-10; Jonson, "On My First Daughter"; Herrick, "Upon a Child that Died."

33. Virgil, *Eclogues,* V, 34-39: ". . . postquam te Fata tulerunt/ ipsa Pales agros atque ipse reliquit Apollo./ grandia saepe quibus mandavimus hordea sulcis,/ infelix lolium et steriles nascunter avenae;/ pro molli viola, pro purpureo narcisso/ carduus et spinis surgit paliurus acutis."

Chapter VI

1. The history of the *Greek Anthology* in the Renaissance is discussed by Sir John Sandys, *A History of Classical Scholarship* (Cambridge, 1908), II, 74f. Pontamus' epigrams are in *Carmina,* ed. I. Oeschger (Bari, 1948), pp. 248-70.

2. *Michaelis Marulli Carmina,* ed. A. Perosa (Zurich, n.d.), pp. 1-102.

3. More's epitaphs are reprinted with discussion in Leicester Bradner and Charles Lynch, eds., *The Latin Epigrams of Sir Thomas More* (Chicago, 1953). More's chief source was the *Planudean Anthology,* from which he derived "at least 102 epigrams" (p. xix). Martial was known to More, but More did not borrow directly from him except in once case (Martial, VI, 78). In the preface to the Basel edition of the *Utopia* (1518), which included eighteen epigrams by More and William Lily, Beatus Rhenanus speaks of Pontanus and Marullus as the most admired contemporary writers of epigram but notes that Marullus is excessively enigmatic and Pontanus often is in questionable taste. (Preface quoted in *Latin Epigrams of Sir Thomas More,* p. 5.) For additional comment on More and discussion of the later history of the epigram see Hoyt Hudson, *The Epigram in the English Renaissance* (Princeton, 1947).

4. Ben Jonson, *Works,* ed. C. H. Herford and P. Simpson (Oxford, 1947), VIII, 79.

5. A curious aspect of rhetorical theory is the fact that just as length could add stature to a composition, so could brevity. This idea is found in classical rhetorics such as the *Ad Herennium,* I, 15; *Brutus,* 50; and *Institutio oratoria,* IV, 2-32; 40ff. It is picked up again in the *Poetria* of John of Garland, where we learn that the figures of brevity are emphasis, disjunction *(asyndeton), verbum conversum in participium, ablativus absolute positus, dictiomum materiam exprimentium electio,* exclusion of repetition and *occupatio*—refusal to describe an object (while describing it). Later in Torquato Tasso, *Prose diverse,* ed. Cesare Guasti (Florence, 1875), I, 52, we find that "reticenza" is one of the devices whereby a poet can achieve "magnificenza": "la reticenza, che accennando la cosa, e poi tacendola, maggiore la

lascia a l'imaginazione. . . ." This figure should not be confused with what Thomas Wilson calls diminution (*Arte of Rhetorique,* ed. Mair [Oxford, 1909], p. 121) and which is the opposite of amplification. The present topic is literally the use of brevity to achieve great effects, and although the suggestion has not been made, it might well explain some of the interest of Renaissance authors in epigrams and epitaphs. Cf. also E. R. Curtius, *European Literature and the Latin Middle Ages,* tr. W. Trask (London, 1953), pp. 487-94 ("Brevity as an Ideal of Style").

6. *Carmina poetarum nobilium* (Milan, 1563), 30r-32v. "Bernardini Buccarini in Obitu Luciae Faustinae Mancinae Romanae").

7. This quotation is taken from 31r; the following, from 32r.

8. See Margaret de Schweinitz, *Les épitaphes de Ronsard* (Paris, n.d.) for Ronsard's main themes and conventions.

9. Miss de Schweinitz asserts (p. 77) that Ronsard popularized the "biographical" elegy.

10. *Oeuvres completes de P. de Ronsard,* ed. Paul Laumonier (Paris, 1914-19), V, 297.

11. Ibid., pp. 299, 301.

12. Ibid., p. 299.

13. Ibid., p. 298.

14. Ibid., pp. 298, 301-2.

15. Ibid., pp. 299, 300-1.

16. Chapman's poem is his "Epicede or Funerall Song," *Poems,* ed. Phyllis Bartlett (N.Y., 1941), pp. 253ff. The borrowing was first noted by F. L. Schoell, "George Chapman and the Italian Neo-Latinists of the Quattrocento," *MP,* XIII (1916), 23-46. See also Alessandro Perosa, "Febris: a Poet Myth Created by Poliziano," *Journal of the Warburg and Courtauld Institutes,* IX (1946), 74-95.

17. According to Perosa, "Febris," pp. 78ff., Ovid is the main influence, Statius and Claudian also being important. Statius should, perhaps, receive greater credit in view of the fact that Politian edited the newly-recovered *Silvae* in which several funeral elegies are included. Claudian is important for his examples of the way to mix myth and history in epideictic poetry.

18. E.g., Angelo Politian, *Opera* (Lyons, 1546), III, 261: "Occidis Albiera prima fraudata iuventa,/ Exigeres vitae cum tria lustra tuae."

19. All quotations come from the edition previously cited. To facilitate reading, page numbers are cited in the text rather than in the footnotes.

20. Politian's archeological discoveries about the temple of the goddess Fever in ancient Rome should be mentioned. This information (given in the poem, p. 263, bottom) lends an air of scholarship to the work and was probably intended to give it verisimilitude as well.

21. P. de Ronsard, *Oeuvres,* ed. Laumonier, V, 269.

22. This ode is reprinted in the great collection of neo-Latin poetry by Jan Gruter, under the name of Ramutius Gherus, *Delitiae CC Italorum poetarum huius superiorisque aevi . . . in officina Ionae Rosae,* 1608, I, 1333ff. The achievement of Lampridius as a writer of odes is examined by Carol Maddison, *Appollo and the Nine* (Baltimore, 1960), pp. 205-9.

23. For comparison, note the natural upheavals accompanying the death of Macina (*Carmina Nobilium . . .* , 31r): ". . . igne coruscat/ Aether; & irriguis Diva madet lacrymia . . . Quin tumidus Tiberis testatur. iam ipsius undae/ Ah Roman rapidis vorticibus superant. . . ."

24. This might be called the topic of "religion reversed."

25. Jakob Burckhardt, *Civilization of the Renaissance in Italy,* tr. S. G. C. Middlemore (London, 1945), p. 93, notes that "In more than one remarkable and dreadful undertaking the motive assigned by serious writers is the burning desire to achieve something great and memorable." The idea seems to have been current that infamy was, as a last resort, better than obscurity.

26. Ben Jonson, *Works,* ed. C. H. Herford and P. Simpson, VIII, 268-72.

27. Compare "To the Memory of . . . Shakespeare," ll. 2-16.

28. Ronsard uses a similar conceit in his epitaph on Aubespine, *Oeuvres,* ed. Laumonier, V, 300.

29. For a parallel, see Statius, *Silvae,* II, i, ll. 209-26. The *consolatio* of Marullus to Andrea Aquavita (*Carmina,* ed. Perosa, 22, ll. 51ff.) is similar in tone. Of course, the idea is not unique with Statius.

30. Itrat-Husain, *The Mystical Element in Metaphysical Poetry of the Seventeenth Century* (London, 1948), pp. 43-44. For a criticism of the Petrarchan view of the metaphysicals, see J. A. Mazzeo, "A Critique of Some Modern Theories of Metaphysical Poetry," *MP,* L (1952), 88-96.

31. The edition used is that by Michele Scherillo, *Canzoniere* (Milan, 1918). Except in the case of the longer canzoni, I have felt it unnecessary to refer to line numbers. Roman numerals refer to the number of the poem in the Scherillo edition.

32. Discussed by Angelo Lipari, *The Dolce Stil Nuovo According to Lorenzo de'Medici* (New Haven, 1936), pp. 64ff.

33. Cf. also cccii, cclxix, etc.

34. Apparently, De Sanctis and others have regarded the poem as inferior, because otherwise they feel forced to interpret Petrarch's final statement as a rejection of Laura—a courtly palinode. By asserting that the poem is inferior, they can maintain that it shows insincerity and is Petrarch's unwilling observance of a convention. However, the poem implies neither rejection of Laura, nor an identification of Laura and the Blessed Virgin; both extremes are repugnant and unnecessary. How much simpler to accept Petrarch's statements in the *Canzoniere* and in the *Trionfi* that he seeks to rejoin Laura in heaven. To achieve this he must recognize the source of love—God—and offer proper allegiance. While Laura was alive he was in the service of the false god Amor.

35. See Charles Singleton, *An Essay on the Vita Nuova* (Cambridge, 1949), pp. 25-54.

36. ccix; *Vita nuova,* xxix. For comment, Singleton, *Essay on the Vita Nuova,* pp. 20-37.

37. Singleton, *Essay on the Vita Nuova,* pp.4 ff. discusses both the censored versions of the *Vita nuova* and the justification for Dante's language. I am strongly indebted to this discussion for my own conclusions in regard to Petrarch.

38. For the image of the sun extinguished, see cclxviii, ccclxiii, etc. The apotheosis of this image occurs in the final canzone, where the Virgin is addressed as "Vergine bella, che di sol vestita,/ Coronata di stelle, al sommo Sole/ Piacesti sí che 'n te sua luce ascose. . . ." Surely this must be a conscious device in view of the prominence of the image elsewhere in the *Canzoniere.* For the wasteland image, see cccvi, cclx, ll. 41-60.

39. E.g., cclxx, 31-45; ccxcii; ccxciii; ccciv; cccviii; cccxxix, etc.

40. We are not surprised to find that this sort of style pleased Leo X, Clement VII, and Bembo so highly that they wrote testimonials for Sannazaro; the praise that came from Erasmus is more surprising. However, Sannazaro's neo-Latin fame came principally from his piscatory eclogues and his brief epic *De partu virginis,* and even in the latter, the classical paraphernalia is not as obtrusive as in the *Lamentatio.* Cf. for the opinions mentioned, *Actii synceri Sannazarii . . . poemata* (Venice, 1752), l-lxxxviiii. A recent and sympathetic treatment of the *Lamentatio* is found in Vittoria Borghini, *Il più nobile umanista* (Società Editrice Internazionale), pp. 397-401.

41. All references are to the edition cited in the preceding note, pp. 43-46.

42. Of great interest in connection with Sannazaro's treatment is the idea that God is inexpressible. Normally a man is praised by beginning with his birth and ending with his death. God, however, is timeless and cannot be so praised. Puttenham, *The Arte of English Poesia,* in ECE, II, 28, remarks that the gentiles debased their gods by treating them according to the normal topics of praise and giving them "fathers and mothers, and kinred and allies, and wives and concubines. . . ." Milton's solution, and the common one, was to hold that the Bible exhibited God, "not as he really is, but in such a manner as may be within the scope of our comprehension. . . ." (*De doctrina Christiana,* II). Critics turned the idea to remarkable use. In Boileau, it becomes an argument against the epic based on scripture. Cf. *L'Art poétique,* III, 160ff.

43. Neoclassic critics often had a stricter view of decorum, as is illustrated by Boileau's strictures on Christian epic and Dr. Jonson's famous attack on *Lycidas.*

44. Sannazaro's descriptions of hell and heaven are visual and detailed. In the *Canzoniere,* Petrarch fights against the "cosa mortale" or the worldly love which distracts him from true love. Oviously, the fear of this "cosa mortale" is a fear of damnation by the "mortal thing." Sannazaro expresses this fear directly—in a picture of a gaping hell mouth and angels blandly watching the merited tortures of the damned (97-102). It is implied that all good Christians will escape this horrible fate through Christ's intercession.

45. *Poems of George Chapman*, ed. Phyllis Bartlett (N.Y. 1941), pp. 220-27.

46. Chapman's emphasis on man's capacity for growth is treated by Ennis Rees, *The Tragedies of George Chapman* (Cambridge, 1954), Ch. I, *passim*.

47. F. L. Schoell, "George Chapman and the Italian Neo-Latinists," 23-46.

Chapter VII

1. Scaliger, *Poetices libri septem* (5th ed., 1617), III, cxxi.

2. Ibid.: "Nemo enim iam annum bienniumve defunctum deflet."

3. E.g., Edmund Gosse, *The Life and Letters of John Donne* (N.Y., 1899), I, 275; Sir Herbert Grierson, *Donne's Poetical Works* (Oxford, 1953), II, 187-88; Hugh I'Anson Fausset, *John Donne: A Study in Discord* (London, n.d.), p. 181; Marius Bewley, "Religious Cynicism in Donne's Poetry," *Kenyon Review*, XIV (1952), 619ff.

4. *Donne's Poetical Works*, ed. H. Grierson, II, 178, 186; also, Marjorie Hope Nicolson, *The Breaking of the Circle* (Lake Forest, 1950), pp. 70-74. The letters, of course, specifically state that the publication was with Donne's knowledge. See John Donne, *Letters to Severall Persons of Honour*, ed. Edmund Merrill, Jr. (N.Y., 1910), pp. 65, 206.

5. The other two poems were the brief prefatory poem to *Coryat's Crudities* (1611), and elegy to Prince Henry, first printed in Sylvester's *Lachrymae lachrymarum*, third edition (1613).

6. A recent re-examination by R. C. Bald, *Donne and the Drurys* (Chicago, 1959), pp. 69-70, suggests that the *Anniversaries* may have been the result of the relationship, not its cause. However, if Donne's work had been considered rank flattery, it would surely have alienated the Drurys, whereas just the opposite is the case, as Bald's study makes clear.

7. *Donne's Poetical Works*, ed. H. Grierson, I, 389.

8. Ibid., I, 382-83.

9. In the *Literary History of England* (N.Y., 1948), p. 635, Tucker Brooke speaks of the "enormous influence" of the *Anniversaries*, and one would be glad to know his reasons for using this phrase, especially since few other critics have stressed this aspect of the *Anniversaries*.

10. John Donne, *Essays in Divinity*, ed. E. M. Simpson (Oxford, 1952), xiii ff.

11. *Poems of George Chapman*, ed. Phyllis Bartlett (N.Y., 1941), p. 271. Chapman never composed a sequel to *Eugenia*.

12. Ibid., p. 277.

13. Ben Jonson, *Works*, ed. C. H. Herford and P. Simpson (Oxford, 1947), VIII. 269. The elegy was composed in 1631.

14. Ibid., p. 271.

15. John Donne, *Letters to Severall Persons of Honour*, p. 65.

16. Ibid., p. 206. The second letter to Gerrard is probably an alternate version of this one.

17. Ibid.

18. Above, note 1.

19. Louis I. Martz, "John Donne in Meditation," *The Poetry of Meditation* (New Haven, 1954), pp. 211-48.

20. Ben Jonson, *Conversations with Drummond*, in *Selected Works*, ed. H. Levin, p. 990.

21. For a concise definition of these terms, see William Elton, *A Guide to the New Criticism* (rev. ed.; Chicago, 1953), *s.v.*, tenor.

22. E.g., William Empson, *English Pastoral Poetry* (London, 1935), p. 84; Martz, "John Donne in Meditation," and Nicolson, *Breaking of the Circle*. Miss Nicolson also considers Elizabeth in relation to Queen Elizabeth.

23. Quintilian, *Institutio Oratoria*, III, 7: "Animi semper vera laus, sed non una per hoc opus via ducitus. Namque alias aetatis gradus gestarumque rerum ordinem sequi speciosius fuit, ut in primis annis laudaretur indoles, tum disciplina, post hoc operum id est factorum dictorumque contextus; alias in species virtutum dividere laudem, fortitudinis, iustitate, continentiae, ceterarumque, ac singulis assignare, quae secundum quamque earum gesta erunt." The passage is paraphrased by Leonard Cox, *The Arte or Crafte of Rhethoryke*, ed. F. I. Carpenter (Chicago, 1899), p. 57, and repeated as a summary scheme of virtues to be praised (prudence, justice, fortitude, temperance) by Thomas Wilson, *The Arte of Rhetorique*, ed. G. H. Mair (Oxford, 1909), p. 31.

24. Two especially useful analyses of the poem are Louis Martz, "John Donne in Meditation," and Sam L. Hynes, "A Note on Donne and Aquinas," *MLR,* XLVIII (1953), 179-81.

25. John Donne, *Devotions upon Emergent Occasions,* ed. John Sparrow (Cambridge, 1923), p. 97.

26. E.g., *Donne's Poetical Works,* ed. H. Grierson, II, xxv, xxvi, 202; Don Cameron Allen, "The Double Journey of John Donne," *A Tribute to George Coffin Taylor* (Chapel Hill, 1952), pp. 94-95; Martz, "John Donne in Meditation."

27. See J. A. Mazzeo, "A Critique of Some Modern Theories of Metaphysical Poetry," *MP,* L (1952), 86-96.

28. Reprinted in E. M. Simpson's *Study of the Prose Works of John Donne* (Oxford, 1948).

29. E.g., Don Cameron Allen, "The Double Journey of John Donne," pp. 314-15.

30. In *A Garland for John Donne,* ed. T. Spencer (Cambridge, 1931), pp. 60-61.

31. Lorenzo de'Medici, *Opere,* ed. A. Simioni (Bari, 1913), I, 24.

32. Ibid., pp. 24-25: ". . . questo novello Clizia [the poet-lover] non può avere maggior refrigerio che tenere la mente e il pensiero volto alle ultime impressioni e più care cose del suo sole, che sono a similitudine dell' orizzonte occidentale, che lo hanno privato della sua amata visione." This metaphor is clarified by the philosophers, for, according to Lorenzo, "È sentenza de' buoni filosofi la corruzione d'una cosa essere creazione d'un 'altra . . ." (p. 24); and "se lo amore ha in sè quella perfezione che già habbiamo detto, è impossible venire a tale perfezione se prima non si muore, quanto alle cose più imperfette." In sum (p. 25), "il principio della vera vita è la morte della vita non vera."

33. John Donne, *Anatomy,* ll. 455-68. Memory is, of course, the instrument whereby the epideictic *pictura* is kept alive and capable of attracting to virtue. For Singleton's extremely stimulating comments on memory in the *Vita nuova,* see *An Essay on the Vita Nuova* (Cambridge, 1949), pp. 25-54.

34. John Donne, *Progresse,* ll. 214-18: "For when our Soule enjoyes this her third birth,/ (Creation gave her one, a second, grace,)/ Heaven is as neare, and present to her face,/ As colours are, and objects, in a roome/ Where darknesse was before, when Tapers come."

35. The letter is translated by the editor in *Early Christian Fathers,* ed. Cyril C. Richardson (London, 1953), pp. 205-24. In addition to the references to the Christian's relation to the world, the letter parallels Donne's poem in its reference to paradise, to the soul as imprisoned in the body, to the soul as a temporary visitor, to Christ as *Logos* (which roughly parallels the "name" image in the *Anatomy*), etc.

36. *Claritas* is the term suggested by Hynes, "A Note on Donne . . . ," pp. 179-81. In view of the rich implications which Ruth Wallerstein has found in the term "various light" (*Seventeenth Century Poetic* [Madison, 1950], pp. 329-31), this term seems appropriate. Note especially the following passage: "When nature was most busie, the first weeke,/ Swadling the new borne earth, God seem'd to like/ That she should sport her selfe sometimes, and play,/ To mingle, and vary colours every day:/ And then, as though shee could not make inow,/ Himselfe his various Rainbow did allow./ Sight is the noblest sense of any one,/ Yet sight hath only colour to feed on,/ And colour is decai'd . . . (*Anatomy,* ll. 347-55). For a gloss on this passage, see *Works,* ed. H. Alford (London, 1839), I, 411-12.

37. The source is Platonic, *via* the elaboration by Dionysius the Areopagite. For the Renaissance development of the idea, see Erwin Panofsky, *Studies in Iconology* (N.Y., 1939), pp. 129ff.

38. *Donne's Poetical Works,* ed. H. Grierson, II, 188.

39. Ibid., II, 219.

40. Jonson, *Selected Works,* ed. Levin, p. 992.

41. Allen, "The Double Journey of John Donne," pp. 94-96.

42. Bernard of Clairvaux, *The Steps of Humility,* tr. George Burch (Cambridge, 1942), pp. 101-7, 109-10.

43. St. Bonaventura, *The Mind's Road to God,* tr. George Boas (N.Y., 1953).

44. The use of the word, *hymn,* should be noted. The epideictic type, *hymn,* could be used for gods and demi-gods, according to classical rhetoric. Donne's use of the term, together with his later reference to the possibility of worshiping Elizabeth as a saint (ll. 511ff.), suggests that he considered the saint as a kind of Christian demi-god and felt that this concept removed the dangers of Catholic "misdevotion." Elizabeth Drury thus becomes a kind of

Christian heroine, and one is tempted to conclude that Donne felt he was making of her the same kind of epideictic type-figure that Homer made of Ulysses, or Virgil of Aeneas, although his job is greatly complicated by the fact that Elizabeth died without overt acts such as can furnish epic material. Cf. especially ll. 67ff.

45. It is here that reference to scientific doctrines enters the *Progresse*. The fact that the soul is explicitly made to ignore the complications raised by the new science is no grounds for using these references to prove Donne's disillusionment because of the new science. The soul now knows via the *mens* or intuitive faculty, and hence knows all the truth without the laborious and only approximate methods of the reasoning soul. Donne is simply showing how much the soul grows in knowledge after death. Compare the following passage from the sermons: "How imperfect is all our knowledge! What one thing do we know perfectly? Whether we consider Arts or Sciences, the sergeant knows but according to the proportion of his Master's knowledge in that Science; young men mend not their sight by using old men's Spectacles; and yet we look upon Nature, but with Aristotle's spectacles; and upon the body of man, but with Galen's, and upon the frame of the world, but with Ptolemy's Spectacles. Almost all knowledge is rather like a child that is embalmed to make Mummy, than that is nursed to make a Man; rather conserved in the stature of the first age, than grow to be greater; And if there be any addition to knowledge, it is rather a new knowledge, than a greater knowledge; rather a singularity in a desire of proposing something that was not known at all before, than an improving, an advancing, a multiplying of former inceptions; and by that means, no knowledge comes to be perfect . . ." *Works*, ed. H. Alford, III, 472.

Chapter VIII

1. Aristotle, *Poetics*, II, 1.
2. Philip Sidney, *An Apologie for Poetrie*, in *ECE*, I, 164.
3. E. Heller, *The Disinherited Mind* (N.Y., 1957), 268.

Index